3/12

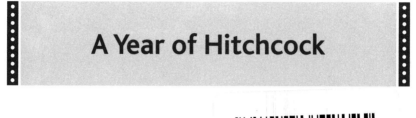

A Year of Hitchcock

A Year of Hitchcock

52 Weeks with the Master of Suspense

JIM McDEVITT

ERIC SAN JUAN

The Scarecrow Press, Inc.
Lanham, Maryland • Toronto • Plymouth, UK

Published by Scarecrow Press, Inc.
A wholly owned subsidary of The Rowman & Littlefield Publishing Group, Inc.
4501 Forbes Boulevard, Suite 200, Lanham, Maryland 20706
www.scarecrowpress.com

Estover Road, Plymouth PL6 7PY, United Kingdom

Distributed by National Book Network

British Library Cataloguing in Publication Information Available

Library of Congress Cataloging-in-Publication Data
The hardback edition of this book was previously cataloged by the Library of
Congress as follows:

McDevitt, Jim, 1974–
    A year of Hitchcock : 52 weeks with the master of suspense / Jim McDevitt,
Eric San Juan.
        p. cm.
    Includes bibliographical references and index.
    1. Hitchcock, Alfred, 1899–1980—Criticism and interpretation. I. San Juan,
Eric, 1973– II. Title.
PN1998.3.H58M36 2009
791.4302'33092—dc22   2008044923

    ISBN: 978-0-8108-8139-6 (pbk. : alk. paper)
    ISBN: 978-0-8108-6389-7 (ebook)

Contents

Acknowledgments

We would be remiss if we did not offer a few brief thanks. First, we are in debt to Tim Granda and the readership of dvdinmypants.com, which played a vital role in this project's first steps. We worked out kinks in our embryonic text in front of a "live audience," soliciting feedback from the site's community of film enthusiasts. Their response told us we were on the right track, and the staff's generosity in allowing us to utilize the site's resources and readership helped us hone our craft. They deserve our thanks. But those early drafts would never have been molded into the book you hold in your hands without the input of our editor at Scarecrow Press, Stephen Ryan, whose suggestions, direction, and advice helped transform this book at every stage of its development, always for the better. This project would have been nothing more than a grand idea without his careful guidance and support. Our gratitude also extends to Linda Siemon, whose detailed reading and generous commentary helped us polish our first draft, and Dave Traupman, Natalie-Erin San Juan, and Eric Ceresa, whose input was of great assistance in fine-tuning the finished product. A thank you is also warranted to our family and friends, who weathered a year of nonstop Hitchcock talk and nonstop Hitchcock films right alongside us. If ever they grew weary of how this project consumed our lives—and consume our lives it did—we never heard a word of complaint. Thank you.

Finally, and most importantly, our thanks go out to Alfred Hitchcock himself. After all, this project would not have been possible without his immense talents and endlessly entertaining films. His work proved to be the ultimate source for everything you are about to read.

Introduction

O ne year of Alfred Hitchcock films, viewed in order. That is the journey we chose to undertake, and the journey we now invite you to take
along with us.

It began with a casual discussion of our mutual love for the cinema of
Alfred Hitchcock—a talk about his artistic technique and how it grew over
the years. From there, the seeds of this project were planted. What if we
watched every readily available Alfred Hitchcock film? How would we view
his motion pictures if we watched them in the order in which they were
released? Would we see them differently? Would we come to better appreciate his work? What would such a viewing reveal about the way in which
his tremendous talents developed?

The thought of not only revisiting the films we loved so much, but of
doing so in such a unique way, was thrilling. It proved an idea impossible to
resist. The book you now hold in your hands is the result.

When we first set out to watch, in chronological order, almost the
entirety of Alfred Hitchcock's body of work in a single year—and spend the
year examining the ever-evolving cinematic themes and techniques of the
Master of Suspense—the magnitude of the task before us was not immediately clear. What we saw was an opportunity to revisit some beloved film
favorites, and to do so in a way that forced us to see them in a new light.
What resulted from this opportunity—and what we hope our readers will
benefit from—was an eye-opening journey through the career of the twen-
tieth century's greatest director.

Our plan was simple enough. Each week we would watch an Alfred
Hitchcock film. We would start at the beginning of his career and would
end at, well, the end. We would watch. Contemplate. Discuss. Examine. See
if such a viewing offered us new insights into the body of work that has
entertained countless viewers over the years.

It did. To say we see the work of Alfred Hitchcock in a new light would
be an understatement. As you will see in the fifty-two chapters (covering
sixty-eight pieces of work) that follow, we watched as each aspect of his sig-

nature style first appeared, noticed when he tried a new storytelling approach, and marveled at how tirelessly inventive he was throughout a career spanning more than fifty years.

Our journey was, admittedly, just short of complete. We limited ourselves to Hitchcock films legally available for home viewing in North America. That means Hitchcock's first film, the 1925 silent *The Pleasure Garden*, did not mark the starting point of our year of Hitchcock, as the film is legally available only in select European countries, and most commonly available in the United States as an illegal bootleg culled from a German TV broadcast. So, too, did we skip his second film, *The Mountain Eagle*, though that one by necessity. The film is long since lost, and no prints are known to exist. So it was that we began with *The Lodger*. A more appropriate start we could not have had. Murder? Suspense? A man on the run? That's the Alfred Hitchcock we know and love, as this book's first chapter clearly outlines.

Three other films did not make the cut for similar reasons. *Waltzes from Vienna*, his 1934 "musical," was also a casualty of unavailability in North America. That film, described by Hitchcock as "the lowest ebb of my career," is available only as a French-dubbed bootleg of poor quality. *Mary*—the little-known German-language version of *Murder!*—is not only unavailable, only one print is said to still exist. Finally, Hitchcock's 1927 film *Downhill* is available only in a German boxed set, and thus was excluded from our trip through his filmography.

Yet despite those easily overlooked holes, we covered territory most guides to the work of Alfred Hitchcock tend to gloss over—if they cover it at all. All seventeen episodes of *Alfred Hitchcock Presents* directed by the titular director are examined over the course of our dissection of his work. In addition, his comedic 1928 silent film *Champagne*, only recently made available in North America, was a stop on our journey (and a surprisingly enjoyable one at that). So, too, do we cover *Aventure malgache* and *Bon Voyage*, the two French-language short films he made for the Allies during World War II. All are available for North American audiences and, as we argue within, are worthwhile viewing for any fan of Alfred Hitchcock's work. And naturally, we devote extensive space to examining career landmarks like *The 39 Steps*, *Rebecca*, *Shadow of a Doubt*, *Notorious*, *Rear Window*, *Vertigo*, *Psycho*, and other enduring classics.

Why limit ourselves only to those films available to the average consumer? Why not seek out whatever bootlegs we could get our hands on, so as to provide a complete assessment of Alfred Hitchcock's work? The reason is simple. We want you, the reader, to be able to take this journey with us. We want you to study the films of Alfred Hitchcock along with us. Our hope is that this book inspires you to do as we did and dive headlong into the career of this great master of cinema. Consider this not just a chronological examination of Hitchcock's work, but a guidebook to his films.

For your convenience, each chapter includes notes on DVD availability, the quality of the most common releases, and, where applicable, our recommendations on which release to purchase. We have rated each DVD on a five-star scale, denoting both our opinion of the film and of the DVD release. We not only hope to inspire others to take a similar journey, we hope to help you along in the process, too. You will also find that each chapter is amended with notes on the film's production, trivia and points of interest, details on each and every Hitchcock cameo appearance, and a list of common themes and techniques, which we discuss in further detail in appendix A.

All in all, we feel that *A Year of Hitchcock* is more than an examination of his work; it is a guidebook to his films that will hopefully be an entertaining and informative tool for your own forays into his work.

As we made our way through the films of the Master of Suspense, several works of Hitchcock scholarship proved invaluable. Patrick McGilligan's *Alfred Hitchcock: A Life in Darkness and Light* offered us an unparalleled look into the life and times of Sir Alfred, while Donald Spoto's *The Art of Alfred Hitchcock: Fifty Years of his Motion Pictures* and *The Dark Side of Genius: The Life of Alfred Hitchcock* provided an examination of his art and the author's theories on his state of mind, respectively. The work of an acclaimed director in his own right, François Truffaut's simply titled *Hitchcock* was a fabulous resource, offering us the best glimpse possible into Sir Alfred's mind—Hitchcock's own words. Additionally, the excellent documentaries accompanying most North American releases of these films not only entertained, they informed. These resources, along with other articles, reviews, and interviews, were of great assistance in compiling this text. We urge all fans of Hitchcock work to seek out these works.

We hope you enjoy venturing with us on our year of Alfred Hitchcock as much as we did. Now pull up a chair—and get ready for some suspense.

The Lodger
(1927)

FILM FACTS

PRODUCTION YEAR: 1926
RELEASE DATES: February 14, 1927 (UK); June 10, 1928 (U.S.)
STUDIO: Gainsborough Studios
FILMING LOCATION: Gainsborough Studios, Islington, London, England
PRESENTATION/ASPECT RATIO: Black & White/1.37:1

SYNOPSIS

A serial killer known as "The Avenger" is terrorizing London. Each Tuesday, the mysterious killer murders a young blonde woman, plunging the city into a state of fear and panic. It is in this atmosphere of terror that a lodger (Ivor Novello) comes to stay at the home of Mr. and Mrs. Bunting (Arthur Chesney and Marie Ault), whose daughter, Daisy (June), just so happens to be a young, attractive blonde. To make matters worse, the lodger is a reclusive man, prompting suspicion from Daisy's boyfriend, Joe (Malcolm Keen). Joe is a detective investigating the Avenger case, and he thinks the lodger may be the killer. But not Daisy. She grows closer to the lodger, even as Joe's suspicion mounts. Has she met a new love interest . . . or is her life in grave danger?

IMPRESSIONS

To say Alfred Hitchcock is not typically associated with silent cinema would be something of an understatement. While film scholars are well aware of his work during the silent era, Hitchcock's most lauded and studied work came decades later. Hitch was a highly visual filmmaker, but sound and dialogue played a vital part in all of his best work. Because of this, his silent period is largely overlooked. Yet it is in Hitchcock's least-known period that any foray into his career must begin. ·

Watching *The Lodger*, one thing is abundantly clear: From the very start of his career, Hitchcock was a filmmaker with a unique vision. More Hitchcockian than his other early work, the film represents the Alfred Hitchcock we know and love, but in embryonic form. Many of the elements that come into play throughout his career—a man wrongly accused, mounting tension, murder, a chase, love blossoming under dire circumstances, dramatic theatrical flourishes—are present and accounted for, but in an unpolished state.

That's what makes this a delight to watch. Though made years before he would be dubbed the Master of Suspense, *The Lodger* is all Hitchcock. Sir Alfred himself recognized this, telling François Truffaut that his first English-language picture, "was the first true 'Hitchcock Movie.'"[1]

Even in this, just his third film and the earliest readily available for home viewing (his first, *The Pleasure Garden*, is unavailable in most parts of the world, and his second, *The Mountain Eagle*, is long since lost), Hitch's flair for using evocative, memorable techniques to set mood or comment on a situation is evident. At the outset, Hitchcock does a beautiful job in exposing the Avenger backstory, and, more importantly, of the menace he brings to the city. The opening scene, where we see the terror-stricken face of a woman screaming directly at the camera, is shocking for its time, but fitting for what the viewer is about to discover. On the heels of that image is a flashing shot of the word "MUR-DER," further drawing the viewer into the world Hitchcock is creating. He establishes a sinister mood, introducing elements that begin to build tension (in this case, the titular lodger taking a room in the Bunting household), and then the story explodes in a chaotic, plot-twisting climax. Overcoming the sketchy quality of the available prints, the on-screen tension here works well with or without sound.

What makes this motion picture exciting is seeing how even in 1927 Hitch had an eye for evoking mood and offering commentary through eye-catching directorial flourishes. At one juncture, the Bunting family, having just taken in their mysterious lodger, hears the news that another Avenger murder has taken place. As they tremble with the news in the kitchen, the lodger paces in his room above them. Growing ever more suspicious, the thought arises that the man they have taken in may be the murderer plaguing London's foggy city streets. The family gazes to the ceiling, tense with doubt. Before our eyes the ceiling fades, and the lodger is now visible, pacing above us as if on a glass floor, looming like a malevolent spirit. As he will do often in the years to come, Hitch manages to impress with his technical abilities while injecting a sense of dread and suspense into the proceedings.

An equally evocative shot comes when we are first introduced to the lodger. Mrs. Bunting opens her front door to find a tall, cryptic figure standing in the shadowy doorway, the London fog swirling around him, his face obscured by a flowing scarf and wide hat. All we can see clearly are Ivor Novello's cold eyes and the fog behind him. Those strong eyes create a foreboding

> **WHERE'S HITCH?**
>
> Hitchcock, in the first of his many cameos, can be seen sitting at a desk in the pressroom about five minutes into the film.

sense that everything isn't quite right with this guy—which, of course, we eventually learn is true. It is a scene that conjures images of F. W. Murnau's *Nosferatu* (1922)—not surprising, because during this period Hitchcock was heavily influenced by German cinema.

Another sequence worth noting is the scene during which the handcuffed lodger, whom the audience now knows is innocent, is chased by a crowd intent on killing him. The pursuit ends with the lodger hanging helplessly from the top of a fence, the crowd trying to get at him from both above and below. The imagery here is terrific. We see the lodger's face; all hope appears to be lost. Just as quickly as the chase began, he is spared as word gets out that the real Avenger has been arrested. The pacing of this action is outstanding.

Hitchcock makes appropriate choices with regard to symbolism and thematic commentary, too. For instance, Daisy and the lodger play chess, which is an interesting method of developing the relationship between these characters. The chess games serves as a metaphor for the games they play with each other.

And take note of Hitchcock's sparse use of title cards. It is apparent that Hitch preferred to tell this story with images instead of words, a trait he would take with him well after the silent era ended. This is ironic when one considers Hitch got his start in the film business as a title card designer.

However, early Hitchcock is still a work in progress. At times, his storytelling is choppy (though footage cut from the film long ago may account for that), and the editing during the climactic mob scene is jumpy and

Ivor Novello in *The Lodger*. (Artlee Picures/Photofest © Artlee Picures)

unfocused, yet Hitch's sense for building tension comes through all the same. Again, it's embryonic Hitchcock, but Hitchcock all the same.

The Lodger could not be a more ideal starting point for a yearlong journey through the films of Alfred Hitchcock. His next few films were assignments and are not truly reflective of the tone and style that would make him famous. Starting here, with an unquestionably Hitchcockian film, makes for a natural jump into the cinematic world of the Master of Suspense.

CONCLUSION

Modern-day viewers might find themselves surprised at *The Lodger*, a 1927 film that, despite its silence, feels exactly like an Alfred Hitchcock picture. It is an excellent early example of what makes his work special, featuring elements used in many of his later, more prominent pictures. Dark, tense, and entertaining, *The Lodger* is a wonderful way to begin exploring the films of Alfred Hitchcock.

HITCHCOCKIAN THEMES

Blonde Leading Lady • Handcuffed Man and Woman • Ineffectual Authority Figures • Love Triangle • Man (or Woman) on the Run • Murder • Woman Screaming Directly at Camera • Woman with Cop Boyfriend • Wrongly Accused

THINGS TO LOOK FOR

- Clever use of flashing graphic images.
- Silent shrieks so well photographed the viewer can almost feel the sound.
- The use of triangles as imagery throughout the film. It's the Avenger's calling card, and the story centers on the love triangle of Daisy, Joe, and the lodger.
- Hitchcock's focus on the eyes as a means of revealing character and motivation. In later films, he frequently allows an actor's eyes to tell the story, forgoing the use of dialogue.

TRIVIA/FUN STUFF

- ✦ Hitchcock originally planned for an uncertain ending, but the studio, Gainsborough Pictures, would not allow it to be construed that the lodger was really the murderer.
- ✦ *The Lodger* is based on a novel of the same name by Marie Belloc Lowndes. The novel was purportedly based on a story told by a landlady to the painter Walter Sickert. The landlady claimed the previous renter was none other than Jack the Ripper.
- ✦ The film is subtitled *A Story of the London Fog*.
- ✦ This is the first film in which Hitch makes one of his famous cameos.

DVD RELEASES

RELEASE: MGM (2008)
(1.33:1 Black & White)
RATING: ✳✳✳✳

EXTRAS: Commentary with film historian Patrick McGilligan; featurette "The Sound of Silence: The Making of *The Lodger*"; Hitchcock 101; 1940 radio play directed by Alfred Hitchcock; Peter Bogdanovich interviews Hitchcock; François Truffaut interviews Hitchcock; restoration comparison; trailers; still gallery.

NOTES: Available as a stand-alone disc or as part of a set with seven other Hitchcock films, *Alfred Hitchcock: Premiere Collection*.

RELEASE: Cobra Entertainment LLC (2011)
(Dolby Digital 2.0 Mono, 1.33:1 Black & White)
RATING: ***
NOTES: Packaged along with *Sabotage*.

RELEASE: Synergy Ent (2009)
(Dolby Digital 2.0 Mono, 1.33:1 Black & White)
RATING: **1/2

RELEASE: BCI/Sunset Home Visual Entertainment (SHE; 2005)
(Dolby Digital 2.0 Mono, 1.33:1 Black & White)
RATING: **1/2

NOTES: Part of a set with nine other Hitchcock films, *Alfred Hitchcock: Master of Suspense*.

RELEASE: Delta (2001)
(Dolby Digital 2.0 Mono, 1.33:1 Black & White)
RATING: **1/2

NOTES: Part of the *Alfred Hitchcock: The Early Years* boxed set.

RELEASE: Laserlight (1999)
(Dolby Digital 2.0 Mono, 1.33:1 Black & White)
RATING: **1/2

EXTRAS: Packaged with *Sabotage*.
NOTES: Available with *Sabotage* or as part of *The Collection* boxed set.

RELEASE: Whirlwind Media (2001)
(Dolby Digital 2.0 Mono, 1.33:1 Black & White)
RATING: **

NOTES: Packaged with *Murder!*

RELEASE: Rph Productions (2002)
RATING: *

NOTES: Packaged with *The Lost World* and *The Eagle*. Avoid.

The Ring
(1927)

FILM FACTS

PRODUCTION YEAR: 1927
RELEASE DATE: October 1, 1927 (UK)
STUDIO: British International Pictures
FILMING LOCATION: Elstree Studios, Borehamwood, Hertfordshire, England
PRESENTATION/ASPECT RATIO: Black & White/1.37:1

SYNOPSIS

"One Round" Jack Sander (Carl Brisson), a carnival boxer who challenges all comers, wants to impress his young wife, The Girl (Lillian Hall-Davis), with his athletic prowess. But when Bob Corby (Ian Hunter) defeats Jack in the ring and then begins to woo The Girl, Jack finds he has to fight his way through the ranks to defeat Corby—secretly a boxing champion all along—in order to win back the love of his wife.

IMPRESSIONS

When one thinks of Alfred Hitchcock, boxing is likely among the last things to spring to mind. And yet that is exactly what is at the root of his fourth film, *The Ring*. Boxing. Surprisingly enough, not only did Hitch direct this boxing film, he wrote it as well.

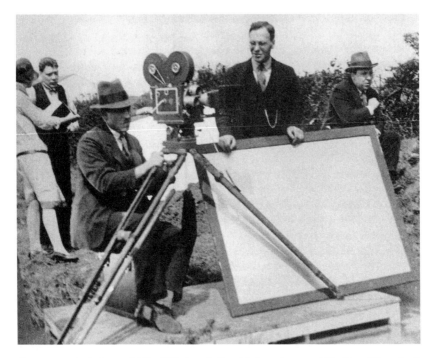

Cameraman Jack Cox and Alfred Hitchcock (far right) on the set of *The Ring*. (Photofest)

To be fair, *The Ring* is not a boxing film per se as much as it is a story about two men fighting over the same woman. In that respect, boxing could have been replaced with almost any other competitive endeavor and the story would remain largely intact.

The Ring represents a dramatic shift in style, story, and mood from Hitchcock's preceding film, *The Lodger*. While *The Lodger* is dark, chilling, and mysterious, *The Ring* is bright, spirited, and comedic, but at the same time serious. Despite not being a Hitchcockian story, it possesses elements that mark it as a Hitchcock film. His complete control over the motion picture is evident.

Throughout *The Ring*, Hitchcock uses circular objects as symbols. The drum and the carousel swing at the outset, the rolls of tickets, the bracelet Bob gives to The Girl, and the boxing ring are all symbolic of the love triangle that develops between Jack, The Girl, and Bob. Hitch was notorious for his use of symbols to punctuate the meaning of a story. We see an early example of this on display in *The Ring*.

As was also seen in *The Lodger*, during his silent era Hitchcock preferred to tell stories with moving images and minimal use of title cards. This is never more evident than in *The Ring*. Amazingly, *The Ring* has fewer title cards than the film it followed, yet it tells an even more detailed narrative with a wide range of characters and emotions. His ability to convey a story using image alone improves from what is seen in *The Lodger*. Hitch deftly uses on-screen action to convey narrative and evokes wonderful facial expressions from his actors. Here we see particularly enjoyable work by the actors, both leading and supporting. These performers were veterans of silent film and thus were used to the expressive acting inherent in such work, and it's apparent Hitchcock used their abilities to great advantage. The film could easily be watched sans title cards and the viewer would never feel lost—quite an achievement for a silent film.

Also impressive is the way in which Hitchcock illustrates the progression of Jack's boxing career; he does this by showing advertisements for his bouts. At first, Jack's name is seen at the bottom of these announcements, the lettering as unremarkable as his status. As he wins bouts and his career evolves, we see his name higher and higher on the page, in larger and larger print each time. Showing "One Round" Jack's name slowly creep up the boards was a simple way to chronicle his rise through the ranks of boxing without resorting to a montage of random fight footage, as most directors would have done. This is an effective visual touch.

> **WHERE'S HITCH?**
>
> Hitchcock does not make one of his famous cameos in *The Ring*.

Hitch's editing early in the film, when he is still establishing relationships between characters, is deft and effective. And very nice indeed is the fight footage near the end of the film; Hitchcock fools the audience into thinking our protagonist and antagonist are fighting in a packed arena through subtle camera trickery.

Without question, the story here is quaint and would not fly in this century—the notion of having to become a boxing champion in order to win your wife back from the current champion is antiquated—but the storytelling certainly would. In crisp, clean strokes Hitchcock lays out the characters and situations that drive the narrative forward. Even more impressive, he does it with few words, relying instead on the camera as a storytelling device. This is a technique he would hone and refine throughout his career.

And really, that's what is impressive about *The Ring*: Hitch's ability to tell a story economically, through image alone; his ability to convey emotion and motivation, and to sketch out events, through the camera's eye. It's still unrefined at this point—still a work in progress—but the early signs of his later brilliance are clear.

Because of the context of the time in which *The Ring* was made, it is interesting to note the appearance of several black characters and the portrayal of said characters. One of the bazaar montage sequences features children throwing eggs at a black man in an organized game. There is also a reference on one of the title cards that indicates if Jack wins his next fight "with the nigger," he will fight for the championship. These now unacceptable depictions, however, are in stark contrast to the depiction of another black man as a member of Jack's fight team, clearly indicating that this is a man the audience should side with. This black character is never seen in a disparaging light.

While *The Ring* rates far below Hitchcock's best films, his visual style, story and character development, and flair for doing things just a little bit differently are all present.

CONCLUSION

The bottom line is simple: With *The Ring*, it is clear at this point in his career Hitchcock could tell a story and could do so effectively. But this also isn't the kind of story he was born to tell. *The Ring* offers a fine look at Hitchcock's developing cinematic style and storytelling abilities, though the subject matter may not thrill fans looking for crime, intrigue, and suspense.

HITCHCOCKIAN THEMES

Love Triangle

THINGS TO LOOK FOR

- The repeated use of round or ring-shaped imagery throughout the film.
- The sparse use of title cards.
- The special effects used to create the look of a packed arena.

TRIVIA/FUN STUFF

✦ This is the only entry in Hitchcock's filmography to receive a full "Written by Alfred Hitchcock" credit.
✦ Carl Brisson, who played "One Round" Jack, was a real boxer.

DVD RELEASES

RELEASE: Cobra Entertainment LLC (2011)
(Dolby Digital 2.0 Mono, 1.33:1 Black & White)
RATING: ***
NOTES: Packaged along with *Number 17*.

RELEASE: Synergy Ent (2009)
(Dolby Digital 2.0 Mono, 1.33:1 Black & White)
RATING: **1/2

RELEASE: BCI/Sunset Home Visual Entertainment (SHE; 2005)
(Dolby Digital 2.0 Mono, 1.33:1 Black & White)
RATING: **1/2

NOTES: Part of a set with nine other Hitchcock films, *Alfred Hitchcock: Master of Suspense*.

RELEASE: Lionsgate (2002)
(Dolby Digital 2.0 Mono, 1.33:1 Black & White)
RATING: **1/2

NOTES: Part of *The Alfred Hitchcock Box Set* with *The Manxman, Murder!, The Skin Game*, and *Rich and Strange*.

RELEASE: Delta (2001)
(Dolby Digital 2.0 Mono, 1.33:1 Black & White)
RATING: **1/2

NOTES: Part of the *Alfred Hitchcock: The Early Years* boxed set.

RELEASE: Laserlight (1999)
(Dolby Digital 2.0 Mono, 1.33:1 Black & White)
RATING: **1/2

EXTRAS: Packaged with *Number Seventeen*.

Easy Virtue
(1928)

FILM FACTS

PRODUCTION YEAR: 1927
RELEASE DATE: March 5, 1928 (UK)
STUDIO: Gainsborough Studios
FILMING LOCATION: Islington, London, England
PRESENTATION/ASPECT RATIO: Black & White/1.37:1

SYNOPSIS

Larita Filton (Isabel Jeans) is wrongly accused of adultery in a scandalous divorce trial. Her life destroyed, she flees to France, where she meets and marries John Whitaker (Robin Irvine), a man from a well-to-do family. John's mother (Violet Farebrother) is immediately suspicious of Larita, certain something isn't right about her. She thinks she's seen Larita before. Eventually, John's mother discovers Larita's past and reveals the truth to John, leading to an unhappy outcome for all.

IMPRESSIONS

In *Easy Virtue*, Alfred Hitchcock deals with romance and mistrust, someone with dark secrets trying to start a new life, and oppressive mothers and loose-living women. It's compelling subject matter, but as a narrative the film leaves one cold. Thankfully, Hitchcock's technical prowess and dramatic flair makes *Easy Virtue* worthwhile, even if the story does not.

Where did this film—an assignment rather than a script chosen by Hitchcock—go wrong? Maybe it is simply a sign of the times, but the notion that a woman would have to hide her involvement in an ugly divorce hardly strikes one as the sort of sinister secret this plot suggests. While appropriate for the 1920s, for a modern viewer the hook is quaint at best. Compounding the issue are flowery, overwritten title cards, characters with unclear motivations, and a story with a lackluster dramatic arc that fails to sustain interest despite a relatively brief eighty-nine-minute running time. There is little sense of urgency and no suspense.

Worse yet, the characters do little to pull the viewer into the story. If we are supposed to sympathize with the female lead, Larita Filton, it's difficult to muster up sympathy because she offers little for the audience to love. Hitchcock portrays her as a dour, downcast chain-smoker content to dwell in half-truths—that is, when she's not pouting or moping. John Whitaker, the male lead, is equally unsympathetic. Actor Robin Irvine fails to convey

Isabel Jeans as Larita in *Easy Virtue*. (Photofest)

romantic urgency, making his courtship with Isabel Jeans's character unconvincing. In addition, as the film progresses, Whitaker allows his mother to bully him, until his mother's mistrust of Larita finally becomes his own. Hitchcock frequently dealt with people who were not all they seemed to be and who were hiding dark secrets, but his success here is fleeting.

The Mrs. Whitaker character is worth discussing. Here is the (allegedly) typical Hitchcock mother: overbearing, dark, mistrusting, and manipulative. It's a charge that is somewhat off base—see *Shadow of a Doubt* and *North by Northwest* for two endearing mother figures—but one can't help but point out what a dreadful woman the mother in *Easy Virtue* is. She spies and pushes and prods. She tries to separate her son and his wife. She turns her entire family against Larita. In short, she encapsulates everything some critics have said makes up the prototypical Hitchcock mother, and he does it much earlier than some critics have noted.

In *The Dark Side of Genius*, Donald Spoto wrote of *Notorious*, "The role of the mother is at last fully introduced and examined. No longer relegated to mere conversation, she appears here as a major character for the first time in an Alfred Hitchcock picture, and all at once . . . Hitchcock began to make the mother figure a repository of his anger, guilt, resentment, and a sad yearning."[2]

> **WHERE'S HITCH?**
>
> Hitchcock appears about twenty-one minutes into the film as a man at a tennis court carrying a walking stick.

Clearly, however, the theme of a dark and manipulative mother came much earlier, rearing its ugly head for the first time right here.

There are also parallels between *Easy Virtue* and one of Hitchcock's far more visible films, *Rebecca*. Both films center on a young woman who marries a well-to-do man only to find she is unwelcome in her husband's home. Most notably, there are striking similarities between *Easy Virtue*'s Mrs. Whitaker and *Rebecca*'s Mrs. Danvers. Both of these women are cold and suspicious. Obviously, there are also differences—the former is the mother-in-law and the latter is a servant—but the similarities in tone and feeling are inarguable.

Though the conceit upon which this story is built may seem quaint by modern standards, the story is an interesting reflection of the time in which it is set, specifically the stigma associated with a nasty divorce. Society has changed, but there is value in the story told in *Easy Virtue*. The ostracizing of someone who has broken society's conventions is a timeless theme.

It's fascinating that the film ultimately ends on an unhappy note. Who made the decision—Hitchcock, the writer, the producer—is hard to say for sure, but, in a way, it makes for a more satisfying close. Because the story is not particularly engaging, the ending breaks the melodrama mold. Still, when all is said and done, this is a less than compelling narrative.

If it fails in story and character, *Easy Virtue* succeeds in showing off Hitchcock's developing technical skills. The entire opening sequence is simply brimming with interesting touches, creative shots, and effective use of the language of cinema. As an early courtroom scene opens, the judge dramatically lifts his head into the shot, his gaze penetrating the camera. It feels like a shot from Carl Theodor Dreyer's 1928 masterpiece, *The Passion of Joan of Arc*. In another impressive use of the camera, Hitchcock allows us to see through the judge's eyes as he surveys his courtroom through an eyeglass. The "picture-in-picture" effect here just jumps off the screen. Even the narrative structure in these courtroom scenes is interesting, jumping backward in time as details of the Filtons' marriage come forward. This fractured, scattered narrative is handled well and is engaging throughout.

In the early courtroom scene, note the use of a juror's notes to illustrate to the film audience what is happening in the trial. It's a brilliant move, eliminating the need for potentially distracting title cards.

In the most interesting sequence in the film, Hitchcock tells the story of the engagement of Larita Filton and John Whitaker not by depicting a man asking a woman's hand in marriage, but instead focusing on the facial reactions of a telephone operator listening in on the conversation between Larita and John. The actress, an uncredited Benita Hume, does a marvelous job conveying the emotion of the engagement with her expressions. Without the use of a single title card, Hume is able to portray John's proposal, Larita's uncertainty, and, finally, her acceptance. This is a truly innovative method to further the story and is far more interesting than what could have been a paradigmatic marriage proposal scene.

But on the technical level, what jumps out in *Easy Virtue* is that the camera begins to *move*. Whereas his previous films were made up of static shot after static shot, here Hitchcock begins to play with the idea of the camera as a roving eye, moving to watch the action, peering in on scenes like a voyeur. This is a technique he would go on to develop and refine in ways few other directors would match. Here is where it first begins to blossom. It is unfortunate it could not come in a better film.

Given the interesting and tense intracharacter struggles, this could have been a compelling film in the hands of a more mature Hitchcock. As it stands, however, *Easy Virtue* is technically impressive but ultimately uninteresting.

CONCLUSION

There really is no other way to put it: *Easy Virtue* is not one of Hitchcock's better films. But even with that in mind, it is worth seeing for its highly creative storytelling techniques. Anyone wanting to chart Hitch's development as an artist would be making a mistake to pass over *Easy Virtue*.

HITCHCOCKIAN THEMES

Dark Secret · Handcuffed Man and Woman · Manipulative Mother · Unwelcome New Woman

THINGS TO LOOK FOR

- The riveting scene of engagement told strictly through the reactions of the phone operator.
- The use of a juror's notes to further the story during the opening trial.

TRIVIA/FUN STUFF

✦ *Easy Virtue* is based on a play by Noël Coward. Eliot Stannard is given scenario credit. The play was first performed in both New York and London in 1925.

✦ The title phrase, *Easy Virtue*, is a reference to "society's reward for a slandered reputation."

DVD RELEASES

RELEASE: AFA Entertainment (2011)
(Dolby Digital 2.0 Mono, 1.33:1 Black & White)
RATING: ***

RELEASE: Cobra Entertainment LLC (2011)
(Dolby Digital 2.0 Mono, 1.33:1 Black & White)
RATING: **1/2

NOTES: Packaged along with *Blackmail*.

RELEASE: Synergy Ent (2009)
(Dolby Digital 2.0 Mono, 1.33:1 Black & White)
RATING: **1/2

RELEASE: BCI/Sunset Home Visual Entertainment (SHE; 2005)
(Dolby Digital 2.0 Mono, 1.33:1 Black & White)
RATING: **

NOTES: Part of a set with eight other Hitchcock films, *The Essential Alfred Hitchcock Collection*.

RELEASE: Westlake Budget (2004)
(Dolby Digital 2.0 Mono, 1.33:1 Black & White)
RATING: **

RELEASE: Delta (2001)
(Dolby Digital 2.0 Mono, 1.33:1 Black & White)
RATING: **

NOTES: Part of the *Alfred Hitchcock: The Early Years* boxed set.

RELEASE: Laserlight (1999)
(Dolby Digital 2.0 Mono, 1.33:1 Black & White)
RATING: **

EXTRAS: Packaged with *Blackmail*.
NOTES: Available with *Blackmail* or as part of *The Collection* boxed set.

RELEASE: Digiview Entertainment (2006)
(Dolby Digital 2.0 Mono, 1.33:1 Black & White)
RATING: *

NOTES: Packaged with *Jamaica Inn*, *Sabotage*, and *The 39 Steps* on the same disc. Avoid.

RELEASE: Miracle Pictures (2003, 2005)
(Dolby Digital 2.0 Mono, 1.33:1 Black & White)
RATING: *

NOTES: Available as a stand-alone or 2005 version packaged with *Jamaica Inn*.

Champagne
(1928)

FILM FACTS

PRODUCTION YEAR: 1928
RELEASE DATE: August 1928 (UK)
STUDIO: British International Pictures
FILMING LOCATION: Elstree Studios, Borehamwood, Hertfordshire, England
PRESENTATION/ASPECT RATIO: Black & White/1.37:1

SYNOPSIS

Champagne tells the story of Betty (Betty Balfour), a young woman whose rich father (Gordon Harker) does not approve of her fiancé (Jean Bradin). This prompts her to run off to France and live the good life on her father's money. To teach Betty a lesson, the father tells her the family fortune, made in the champagne business, has been lost. Betty must make a living on her own. She finds a job working in a club serving the very same champagne her family once sold. Her father eventually comes to his senses, tells Betty the truth—their fortune is not lost—and allows her to marry the man she loves.

IMPRESSIONS

With *Champagne*, Alfred Hitchcock dabbles in what would today be called a romantic comedy . . . and it works. This is surprising, given his body of work, but *Champagne* is a playful romp that manages to entertain. Stylistically, it makes no great strides forward. The craftsmanship is solid, and there are a few scattered shots that will draw your attention, but *Champagne* is notable only for its light tone, softly comedic story, and whimsical leading lady.

About that leading lady. Without a strong lead to hold things together, there is always a danger that a film like this will fall apart. Leading lady Betty Balfour, however, a silent film veteran, not only manages to keep things afloat, she positively shines. She carries this film and is the first of many blonde lead actresses Hitchcock filmed with affection. His camera is in love with her, and for good reason. Her warm smile, bright eyes, and ability to change expression in the blink of an eye add depth to a lightweight character—were she a young lady today, she'd be a party girl, famous simply for being famous. If her turn here is any indication, Balfour was called Britain's Queen of Happiness for a reason. Balfour evokes such a fresh personality, one can't help but be enamored with her.

There are a few large set pieces in *Champagne* that are an indication of the early success Hitchcock was enjoying at this point, affording him a bigger budget. Multiple scenes aboard a cruise ship and dozens of lavish costumes are a step up from the relatively low-budget look of *The Lodger* and *The Ring*. They also offer the first glimpse at two elements—ships (cruise or otherwise) and lavish costumes—that we will see again in this exploration of Hitchcock's filmography. While *The Lodger* is all dark alleys and claustrophobic rooms, *Champagne* is

> **WHERE'S HITCH?**
>
> Hitchcock does not make a cameo in *Champagne.*

expansive parties and grand ballrooms. Late in the film, when Betty gets a job in the club, the cast of extras explodes larger than any seen thus far—dozens of men and women dancing, drinking, talking, and carousing.

Champagne is smattered with amusing sight gags, the funniest involving a drunkard who has trouble walking straight when the ship is steady, but walks perfectly when the ship is unsteady, even as passengers are falling all over each other. Also enjoyable is the gag when Betty's father, who is a powerful businessman, is angered and smashes his desk call buttons. His aides march into the office, unaware that he is simply throwing a fit and not summoning their services. This is funny stuff.

While *Champagne* is a fun film, there are hints of the classic Hitchcock sensibility. Betty, a young blonde woman, is forced into an unpleasant situation, much of which is built on a lie. We see two men vying for the same woman, one of them with unclear motives. We see Hitchcock's deft use of the camera to lead the audience, such as when he pulls in close to Ferdinand von Alten's (credited as The Man) eyes in order to make the audience suspicious of his character, who was hired by Betty's father to keep an eye on her. And we see a revelation late in the film in which the audience is given knowledge the main character does not have. All will arise again in later Hitchcock films (though almost always in darker circumstances).

Like all Hitchcock films, *Champagne* is worth watching for its filmmaking qualities in addition to its story. This isn't one of his technical masterpieces, but it does have its share of slick camera tricks and innovative techniques. As seen earlier in *Easy Virtue*, Hitch uses a creative early establishing shot unlike anything else in his filmography. In this case, we view a dancing crowd through a tilting champagne glass—not two minutes into the film and the audience is treated to a truly imaginative piece of camerawork. This is part of what makes Hitchcock an intriguing director to study. Lesser directors would not make the effort to pull off such tricks in an otherwise unremarkable film. The shot is not essential, but certainly worth noting.

Champagne may not be a vital film in Hitch's development from a technical standpoint, but it shows his ability to work with more costuming and larger sets, and one can almost imagine his eyes being opened to the storytelling potential he held in his hands. For that alone, *Champagne* is worth watching. Consider the fact that it's a fun, delightful little film an added bonus.

Yet Hitchcock was not particularly fond of *Champagne*, telling the great French filmmaker François Truffaut in his marvelous study, *Hitchcock*, "That was probably the lowest ebb of my output."[3] (This would not be the last time he shared such a sentiment.) *Champagne* is no masterpiece, but to hold it in such low regard is a disservice to what is a genuinely fine film. Perhaps this is simply a case where an artist is his own worst critic.

CONCLUSION

Champagne is a worthy entry in the Hitchcock catalog. The story is not typically Hitchcockian, but its humorous moments, fun camera tricks, and truly enjoyable leading lady make it an entertaining film. Though the subject matter may not thrill fans looking for crime, intrigue, and suspense, it is well worth watching to track the progress of Hitchcock's eye for film.

HITCHCOCKIAN THEMES

Blonde Leading Lady • Love Triangle

THINGS TO LOOK FOR

- The truly inventive shot in which the action is seen through a tilting champagne glass.
- Elaborate sets and busy casts. Hitchcock had obviously been allowed resources that were not present in his earlier films.

TRIVIA/FUN STUFF

✦ Hitchcock adapted *Champagne* from a story by Walter C. Mycroft. Eliot Stannard is given scenario credit.

✦ Along with *Mr. & Mrs. Smith* and *The Farmer's Wife*, *Champagne* is one of just three straight comedies directed by Hitchcock. Other films contain many comedic elements, but were primarily dramas, mysteries, and thrillers.

DVD RELEASES

RELEASE: BCI/Sunset Home Visual Entertainment (SHE; 2005)
(Dolby Digital 2.0 Mono, 1.33:1 Black & White)
RATING: ***

NOTES: Part of a set with eight other Hitchcock films, *The Essential Alfred Hitchcock Collection*.

RELEASE: AFA Entertainment (2010)
(Dolby Digital 2.0 Mono, 1.33:1 Black & White)
RATING: **1/2

WEEK

5

The Farmer's Wife
(1928)

FILM FACTS

PRODUCTION YEAR: 1927
RELEASE DATES: March 1928 (UK); January 4, 1930 (U.S.)
STUDIO: British International Pictures
FILMING LOCATION: Elstree Studios, Borehamwood, Hertfordshire, England
PRESENTATION/ASPECT RATIO: Black & White/1.37:1

SYNOPSIS

Desperate to marry again, widowed farmer Samuel Sweetland (Jameson Thomas) sits down with his housekeeper, Minta (Lillian Hall-Davis), and crafts a list of prospective brides. The next step? To convince one of these women to marry him. Samuel, in increasingly absurd comedic situations, is rejected again and again, until finally realizing the perfect woman was right in front of him the whole time.

IMPRESSIONS

The Farmer's Wife is the funniest of the Hitchcock silent pictures. It's also smart, endearing, and completely different from his other work. The worst cricitism one can offer of this warm, humorous, and accessible film is that the dialogue is so funny it's a shame you cannot hear it spoken.

The writing in *The Farmer's Wife* stands out as among the best of Hitch's early films. There's a real sense of humor in the narrative and title cards, and we also see a fair amount of slapstick comedy, something not seen in other Hitchcock films. Eliot Stannard, who received scenario credit for both *Champagne* and *Easy Virtue* and is credited for the adaptation here, does a beautiful job in creating charming situations for lead character Samuel Sweetland.

The story told in *The Farmer's Wife* is simple, with a predictable ending, yet it's fun to watch. It's endearing seeing Samuel work his way through a list of women, proposing to each and failing each time, always in hilarious fashion. The reason this is not a sad story is because we know how it will end before Samuel does. Lillian Hall-Davis, who also played the female lead in *The Ring*, shines in *The Farmer's Wife* as Samuel's housekeeper, Araminta, or Minta. She's sweet, loving, and wonderful to Samuel. Why Samuel doesn't pick up on this until the end is a mystery—hence the humor—but in the end, Samuel doesn't let us down. He comes to his senses and realizes Minta is a special lady, everything he could want, and a far better catch than the women he was chasing.

> **WHERE'S HITCH?**
>
> *The Farmer's Wife* is a rare film in which Hitchcock does not make a cameo.

No, the story won't set the world on fire with cleverness. In fact, it's predictable. Maybe even pedestrian. But the characters are so well realized and the dialogue so witty, you don't mind that *The Farmer's Wife* breaks little new ground. The highlights come in the performances. Jameson Thomas's turn as Samuel Sweetland, the titular farmer, is excellent. Samuel is a modest man attempting to put on an air of sophistication and irresistibility, an air repeatedly shattered when his advances are rebuffed, much to his chagrin. In contrast, Maud Gill's eccentrically wonderful Thirza Tapper steals every scene she's in with a bouncing, writhing, gut-busting comedy performance. And one would be remiss not to mention Gordon Harker as Churdles Ash, Samuel's handyman, who turns in a delightful performance. Harker, who also played Jack's trainer in *The Ring* and Betty's father in *Champagne*, is brilliant, providing one laugh after another with his rubber face and slacking demeanor. The moments when he is alone on screen are some of the best in the film. And while extremely funny, Churdles also displays warmth that shows he cares a great deal for Samuel.

From a presentation standpoint, *The Farmer's Wife* doesn't have the kind of technique that grabs your attention with innovation. There is the occasional composition that strikes one as appealing to the eye, but by and large this film is a showcase for Hitchcock's workmanlike ability to tell a story effectively. That said, *The Farmer's Wife* does have some things to watch out for, notably the use of imagery and symbolism in a key sequence. A set of chairs Samuel and his deceased wife used to sit in help the viewer (and Samuel) visualize the potential future he might have with the ladies he pursues. He desperately wants another woman to fill that seat, and we see these chairs come up throughout the film to symbolize the future Samuel sees.

We first saw Hitchcock put the camera in motion during *Easy Virtue*, and this technique is again utilized in *The Farmer's Wife*. It feels more natural here, but that may simply be due to improving technology. Hitchcock shows a developing sense of how to further his storytelling with effective camera movement. Simple character actions were not all Hitch was interested in filming. He realized that by using the camera to follow his actors, he could better draw the viewer into the drama. Such camera movements are common and expected in today's films, but such was not the case in 1928. Hitchcock would continue to develop his skills with the moving camera throughout his career.

With a running time of 129 minutes, *The Farmer's Wife* is by far the longest of the Hitchcock films to this point in his filmography, and will remain among his longest. The pacing is slow, but it works well for this story. From shot to shot and scene to scene, the narrative is never less than crisp, clean, and easy to follow. While it wouldn't have been hurt by tighter editing, *The Farmer's Wife* doesn't feel overly long. A 97-minute cut of the film exists, but it remains unavailable on North American home video. And that's fine, because to cut 32 minutes from this comedy would do more harm than good.

So, if Hitchcock doesn't really develop his ability to tell a story with *The Farmer's Wife*, if we see none of the themes developed that would come to define his most famous work, and if he makes no great technical strides, is this essential viewing for those exploring Hitch's development as an artist? It is. Hitch developed a feel for comedy with these early features, a comfort with the lighter aspects of storytelling and character that would later serve his thrillers well. Comedic touches are a hallmark of the Hitchcock suspense film; it was here, with films like *Champagne* and *The Farmer's Wife*, that the Master of Suspense was able to refine his ability to use whimsy to lighten otherwise dark films. *The Farmer's Wife* is an excellent entry in the Hitch library. Both casual film fans and those who want to deeply explore Hitchcock's work are likely to enjoy this overlooked silent gem.

CONCLUSION

The Farmer's Wife is thematically and stylistically unlike the typical Alfred Hitchcock film, but that doesn't mean it isn't worth watching. While not vital to his development as the future Master of Suspense, it is an endearing, entertaining film—a great look at a rarely seen side of Hitchcock's filmmaking.

HITCHCOCKIAN THEMES

The Farmer's Wife is an atypical Hitchcock film, a straight romantic comedy with none of the thematic overtones we see in his other works.

THINGS TO LOOK FOR

- Hitch's use of slapstick comedy; you'll rarely see it in a Hitchcock film.
- The witty, often racy dialogue used on the title cards.
- Hitchcock's increasing comfort with moving the camera rather than framing static shots.

TRIVIA/FUN STUFF

✦ Gordon Harker (Churdles Ash) is one of Hitchcock's first repeating actors, previously enjoying roles in *The Ring* and *Champagne*.

DVD RELEASES

RELEASE: Cobra Entertainment LLC (2011)
(Dolby Digital 2.0 Mono, 1.33:1 Black & White)
RATING: ***

RELEASE: PR Studios (2010)
(Dolby Digital 2.0 Mono, 1.33:1 Black & White)
RATING: ***

RELEASE: BCI/Sunset Home Visual Entertainment (SHE; 2005)
(Dolby Digital 2.0 Mono, 1.33:1 Black & White)
RATING: ***

NOTES: Part of a set with eight other Hitchcock films, *The Essential Alfred Hitchcock Collection*.

RELEASE: Delta (2001)
(Dolby Digital 2.0 Mono, 1.33:1 Black & White)
RATING: ***

NOTES: Part of the *Alfred Hitchcock: The Early Years* boxed set.

RELEASE: Laserlight (1999)
(Dolby Digital 2.0 Mono, 1.33:1 Black & White)
RATING: ***

NOTES: Part of *The Collection* boxed set.

RELEASE: Synergy Ent (2009)
(Dolby Digital 2.0 Mono, 1.33:1 Black & White)
RATING: **

The Manxman
(1929)

FILM FACTS

PRODUCTION YEAR: 1928
RELEASE DATES: December 6, 1929 (UK); December 16, 1929 (U.S.)
STUDIO: British International Pictures
FILMING LOCATIONS: Elstree Studios, Borehamwood,
Hertfordshire, England; Isle of Man; Polperro, Cornwall, England
PRESENTATION/ASPECT RATIO: Black & White/1.37:1

SYNOPSIS

Two old friends—Pete (Carl Brisson), a fisherman, and Philip (Malcolm Keen), a lawyer—have remained close despite leading wildly different lives. Pete is in love with Kate (Anny Ondra), the daughter of the local innkeeper. When he leaves on a lengthy fishing trip to earn money enough to marry Kate, he asks his friend Philip to watch over her. Things don't work out as planned, however, when Kate and Philip grow close and fall in love.

IMPRESSIONS

Developing a strong sense of composition, becoming comfortable with a moving camera, and honing his ability to tell a story with efficiency: This is what Alfred Hitchcock learned in creating his earliest work. His silent film efforts culminate in . . . *The Manxman*?

Over the course of his long and varied career, Hitch developed a reputation for sometimes going on autopilot, sleepwalking through films he had no interest in, content to simply get it done so he could move on to his next project. No one can claim to know what was going through his head during the filming of *The Manxman*, his last fully silent feature (*Blackmail* would be released as both a silent film and as a "talkie"), but were critics to claim Sir Alfred did not throw his heart and soul into the film, few would argue. This is a seriously flawed picture, not at all indicative of the craftsman Alfred Hitchcock was.

At its core, *The Manxman* has all the makings of a compelling drama. We have a sailor, Pete, who falls in love with a beautiful young woman, Kate. Kate promises she will wait for him until he returns from a long sailing expedition, but during his absence she falls in love with Pete's best friend, Philip, an attorney and aspiring judge. When Pete returns, the secret relationship is broken off, and Kate must live with a man she does not love, pining all the while for Philip. Things are further complicated when, in a twist shocking considering the era in which this film was produced, it is revealed that she is pregnant with Philip's child.

> **WHERE'S HITCH?**
>
> *The Manxman* is another early film with no cameo.

All this puts into place an interesting drama built upon the interwoven threads of friendships and relationships, themes the legendary director would explore throughout his career. The friendship between Pete and Philip is established early, as is Pete's love for Kate. The dynamic between the three is never less than clear. But maybe it's made *too* clear. For the first and only time in the Hitchcock silents, we encounter the kind of showy, overly expressive acting common in the silent era. The main culprit is Carl Brisson as Pete, who tries so hard to be the incredibly caring friend and lover that it comes across almost as parody. He is expressive to a fault. It's so over the top, one almost gets the feeling the director is playing it for laughs—but he isn't. Hitch doesn't help by letting the camera linger on him, for long stretches, again and again and again. Subtle this isn't. It becomes very hard to let yourself believe in the plot, because Pete is so oblivious to what's going on around him. After Pete and Kate wed, Kate is obviously miserable, but Pete never notices or questions why. This rings false. How could a man as obviously devoted as Pete is to Kate be so blind to her pain? You want to laugh at, not sympathize with, his inability to see that Kate does not love him.

While one can imagine Hitchcock was limited by the story's source material (based on a novel by Hall Caine), the bottom line is that this story was poorly adapted for the screen. Eliot Stannard, who receives scenario credit on *The Manxman* and worked with Hitchcock on many of his early films, should have found a way to address these issues, because they detract from the film.

Of course, this could have been tempered with some eye-catching direction by a man with a propensity to insert creative, bold moments into even his minor films, but alas, it was not to be. A nice jump cut and a well-handled attempted suicide aside, *The Manxman* is largely pedestrian. Because this was a studio assignment, a story based on a popular book of the time and handed to him for a quick adaptation, the end result shouldn't be surprising. It's not a failure by any means; it simply does little to rise above the pack.

Another problem with *The Manxman* is in its use of title cards. As seen in his previous silent work, it is apparent Hitch preferred to tell a story using as few title cards as possible. This is generally worthy of praise, but it doesn't work in this film. Was Hitchcock overconfident in his ability to convey the story sans title cards? Arguably so. Too often we see characters engaging in lengthy conversations, with no indication given as to what is being discussed. In a crucial scene where Kate reveals to Pete that she's having a baby, there is a bit of back and forth dialogue during which the viewer can only guess what's going on before it's finally revealed that she's pregnant. A plethora of title cards are not needed, but one or two would have made a world of difference.

There are a few high points, however, most notably in the director's choice of location. Hitchcock effectively uses the Isle of Man setting to his advantage. The island setting fits well with the story surrounding Pete and Philip's friendship. The story has merit, too. It's an intriguing, if typical, tale of two men who fall for the same woman. Throw in a (largely) charismatic cast, beautiful cinematography, and the addition of betrayal to the typical love triangle, and the film is not a total failure.

No, Alfred Hitchcock's *The Manxman* isn't a bad film, but it's probably the least essential of the early Hitchcocks. Little in the way of technical audacity, too much in the way of campy melodrama, and a nagging sense that even Hitchcock wasn't interested in anything other than getting this film done and over with makes this film a destination only for those studying the work of the Master of Suspense.

CONCLUSION

The Manxman is, at its core, a solid drama with a decent third act, but the flaws make this one of Hitchcock's least essential silent films—worthwhile for the Hitch enthusiast, but something to be skipped by the casual fan.

HITCHCOCKIAN THEMES

Love Triangle • Suicide/Attempted Suicide

THINGS TO LOOK FOR

- Beautiful photography from the Isle of Man.
- The return of Carl Brisson and Malcolm Keen to roles in a Hitchcock film.

TRIVIA/FUN STUFF

✦ *The Manxman* was Alfred Hitchcock's last fully silent feature. *Blackmail* was released in versions both with and without sound.
✦ In 1917 a film based on the same story was released in the United States. It was also called *The Manxman*.

DVD RELEASES

RELEASE: Cobra Entertainment LLC (2011)
(Dolby Digital 2.0 Mono, 1.33:1 Black & White)
RATING: ***

RELEASE: Synergy Ent (2009)
(Dolby Digital 2.0 Mono, 1.33:1 Black & White)
RATING: **1/2

RELEASE: BCI/Sunset Home Visual Entertainment (SHE; 2005)
(Dolby Digital 2.0 Mono, 1.33:1 Black & White)
RATING: **

NOTES: Part of a set with eight other Hitchcock films, *The Essential Alfred Hitchcock Collection*.

RELEASE: Lionsgate (2002)
(Dolby Digital 2.0 Mono, 1.33:1 Black & White)
RATING: **

NOTES: Part of *The Alfred Hitchcock Box Set* with *The Ring*, *Murder!*, *The Skin Game*, and *Rich and Strange*.

RELEASE: Delta (2001)
(Dolby Digital 2.0 Mono, 1.33:1 Black & White)
RATING: **

NOTES: Part of the *Alfred Hitchcock: The Early Years* boxed set.

RELEASE: Laserlight (1999)
(Dolby Digital 2.0 Mono, 1.33:1 Black & White)
RATING: **

NOTES: Part of *The Collection* boxed set.

Blackmail
(1929)

FILM FACTS

PRODUCTION YEAR: 1929
RELEASE DATES: June 30, 1929 (UK); October 6, 1929 (U.S.)
STUDIO: British International Pictures
FILMING LOCATIONS: Elstree Studios, Borehamwood,
Hertfordshire, England; London, England
PRESENTATION/ASPECT RATIO: Black & White/1.37:1

SYNOPSIS

Alice White (Anny Ondra), the daughter of a London shopkeeper, and her boyfriend, Scotland Yard detective Frank Webber (John Longden), argue while out at a restaurant. Alice leaves with another man, The Artist (Cyril Ritchard), who invites her to visit his studio. While in the studio, The Artist attempts to rape Alice, but she is able to grab a knife and kills him in self defense. She leaves the studio and returns home—but the body of The Artist is found. Frank is assigned to the case and quickly comes to the conclusion that Alice is responsible for the killing. Tracy (Donald Calthrop) is a criminal who witnessed Alice entering the studio building. He attempts to blackmail Alice, but Webber implicates Tracy, which leads to a chase through London.

IMPRESSIONS

When working your way through the cinema of Alfred Hitchcock, there are milestones that signal the ending of one era and the dawning of a new. His last British picture. His first American film. His first color movie. All important moments. The first major milestone comes right here.

There is no question that *Blackmail* is a landmark work. It was the first sound film not only for Alfred Hitchcock, but for England. That alone makes it noteworthy—but does it hold up as entertainment? As a groundbreaking film filled with technical achievements, there is a lot to admire about *Blackmail*, but as a suspense film it is a mild disappointment when viewed against Hitchcock's other work. Despite this, the technical aspects of the film are remarkable enough that, in the end, it stands out as an essential film.

One has to admire Hitchcock's willingness to turn this into a talkie in the first place. Production was already well under way when studio bosses, hoping to capitalize on the success of *The Jazz Singer* (1927), decided to add sound, so it was no small matter to switch gears in mid-production. It would have been easier to wait until the next film to make the

> **WHERE'S HITCH?**
>
> Hitchcock appears a little more than ten minutes into the film in a very amusing sequence on a train.

move, but Hitch recognized the benefits of sound and knew the hassle was worth the reward. The desire to take advantage of improving technologies in filmmaking is something that long marked Hitchcock as an innovator.

The most striking aspect about the switch to sound is not so much that it was made mid-production, but that Hitchcock did it with an off-screen actress supplying the voice for lead actress Anny Ondra's Alice White. Ondra's thick German accent would not have worked well for the character, but with production already under way, how could Hitch address this issue? With a bit of innovation. Because dubbing capabilities did not yet exist, he had British actress Joan Barry stand off-screen and read the dialogue into a microphone as the scenes were filmed. That he tried something like this for his first film with sound is remarkable; that it worked is even more impressive.

That's what may stand out most about *Blackmail*: Hitch's ability to utilize new technology to its fullest. Though he was working with something entirely new—not just to him but to the world—he utilized sound in an effective way right from the start. The ambient sounds of the streets of London or the clatter of a busy restaurant feel natural and unforced, as if

Anny Ondra in *Blackmail*. (Sono Art–World Wide Pictures/Photofest © Sono Art–World Wide Pictures)

Hitch had been dabbling in sound design for years. He didn't lean on audio as a gimmick, as many early talkies did. Yes, there is a song thrown in—common in early sound pictures—but it doesn't feel out of place. Notably, Hitchcock used sound to comment on the state of the main character and to set mood. In *Blackmail*, this happens most famously in a sequence in which the main character, terrified she will be arrested for killing a man who tried to rape her, blocks out everything being said but the word "knife," a chilling reference to the weapon she used to slay her attacker. The repetition of the word to the exclusion of all else brings us into the character's head without heavy-handed exposition. Alfred Hitchcock was a technical visionary, and, great movie or not, *Blackmail* demonstrates this. His ability to think outside the box—to look at not just the current state of film, but where it could be in a few years—is obvious even in a mediocre film like *Blackmail*.

The most noteworthy Hitchcockian technique comes during the rape scene. Remember, this film was made in 1929. Showing a violent rape attempt on screen was out of the question. But Hitchcock brilliantly overcame this hurdle by setting the incident behind a curtain, depicting the action with shadows. This is an intense scene.

It is also pleasing to see the captivating visual effects used to illustrate Alice's fear shortly after the killing. We see Alice looking at a sign for Gordon's London Gin, which features an animated cocktail shaker. Both Alice and the viewer see this image evolve into an animated hand holding a knife. This shot is effective in depicting our leading lady's mental state.

Another impressive sequence is when the landlady discovers the body of the villain. First we see Alice walking down a sidewalk, where she comes across a homeless man. The focus is placed on the man's outstretched arm. Alice is startled. We immediately hear a scream. But this scream is not from Alice. It is from the landlady. Before the scream is over, the scene cuts to the landlady discovering the corpse of The Artist, his outstretched arm poking from beyond a curtain. It is a startling bit of editing, and this touch of flare adds to the impact of the moment.

Yet *Blackmail* ultimately fails because it does not deliver suspense. For a movie that has just about every essential Hitchcock element—beautiful compositions, a blonde lead, a dead body, a link between sex and death, a chase at a famous landmark, dark conversations over dinner, the police as a figure of menace—it manages to lack suspense or drama. No doubt the production's moving from silent to sound partway through played a role in softening what could have been a tense thriller, but regardless, apart from some fantastic camera tricks, *Blackmail* is a bland experience. Despite these flaws, there are moments of storytelling genius and a pervading sense of fear that make it a film worth seeing.

CONCLUSION

Blackmail is notable as Alfred Hitchcock's first film with sound, but it is more than that. It lacks the suspense one would expect from a Hitchcock murder drama—a considerable detriment to the film, to be sure—but *Blackmail* is important in studying Hitch's development as a filmmaker because there are some remarkable technical achievements on display. It never quite lives up to the promise of its Hitchcockian subject matter, yet remains an impressive jump into a new era.

HITCHCOCKIAN THEMES

Blackmail • Blonde Leading Lady • Climactic Showdown at an Iconic Location • Dark Secret • Discussion of Murder at Dinner • Man (or Woman) on the Run • Woman with Cop Boyfriend

THINGS TO LOOK FOR

- Hitchcock's masterful job of depicting the action of the attempted rape in a manner that conveys terror without on-screen violence.
- The shot in which Alice visualizes the advertisement for gin as a hand with a stabbing knife.
- The first Hitchcock chase against the backdrop of a well-known landmark, the British Museum.
- The film's obvious roots as a silent film, both technically and stylistically.

TRIVIA/FUN STUFF

- ✦ *Blackmail* was originally conceived—and production began—as a silent film. Before filming completed, sound technology became available to British International Pictures, and Hitchcock jumped at the opportunity to add sound to the film. Several scenes were reshot to facilitate the addition of sound.
- ✦ Anny Ondra spoke with a thick German accent and was therefore unfit for Alice's speaking parts. Her lines were read into a microphone by British actress Joan Barry as the scenes were filmed.

DVD RELEASES

RELEASE: British International Pictures (2011)
(Dolby Digital 2.0 Mono, 1.33:1 Black & White)
RATING: ***1/2

RELEASE: Desert Island Films (2011)
(Dolby Digital 2.0 Mono, 1.33:1 Black & White)
RATING: ***

RELEASE: BCI/Sunset Home Visual Entertainment (SHE; 2005)
(Dolby Digital 2.0 Mono, 1.33:1 Black & White)
RATING: ***

NOTES: Part of a set with nine other Hitchcock films, *Alfred Hitchcock: Master of Suspense*.

RELEASE: Delta (2001)
(Dolby Digital 2.0 Mono, 1.33:1 Black & White)
RATING: ***

NOTES: Part of the *Alfred Hitchcock: The Early Years* boxed set.

RELEASE: Laserlight (1999)
(Dolby Digital 2.0 Mono, 1.33:1 Black & White)
RATING: ***

NOTES: Available as a stand-alone or as part of *The Collection* boxed set.

RELEASE: Cobra Entertainment LLC (2011)
(Dolby Digital 2.0 Mono, 1.33:1 Black & White)
RATING: **1/2

NOTES: Packaged along with *Easy Virtue*.

RELEASE: Synergy Ent (2009)
(Dolby Digital 2.0 Mono, 1.33:1 Black & White)
RATING: **1/2

RELEASE: Whirlwind Media (2001)
(Dolby Digital 2.0 Mono, 1.33:1 Black & White)
RATING: **

EXTRAS: Packaged with *Juno and the Paycock*.

WEEK

8

Juno and the Paycock
(1930)

FILM FACTS

PRODUCTION YEAR: 1930
RELEASE DATE: June 29, 1930 (U.S.)
STUDIO: British International Pictures
FILMING LOCATION: Elstree Studios, Borehamwood, Hertfordshire, England
PRESENTATION/ASPECT RATIO: Black & White/1.37:1

SYNOPSIS

Set during the Irish Revolution, *Juno and the Paycock* follows the Boyle family, who learn they are set to receive a large inheritance. The Boyles—Juno, Captain, Johnny, and Mary (Edward Chapman, Sara Allgood, John Laurie, and Kathleen O'Regan)—take to living the good life, all the while forgetting what had always been important to them. Eventually, the Boyles find they will not be receiving the inheritance and are forced to sell their home and live as vagrants.

IMPRESSIONS

Even the greatest of artists are prone to producing a work they'd rather forget. *Juno and the Paycock* is such a film. A talky stage play put to film, the only reason it can't be called "forgettable" is that it's difficult to forget being so bored by a Hitchcock film.

Sir Alfred built his career on tight plots and sharply honed drama, the kind of films that, even when you see their inner workings, rarely fail to play the viewer like a violin. In this case, however, the plot meanders, never quite finding its focus. Had Hitch been given greater control over the writing, perhaps some drama could have been salvaged from this melodramatic mess, but that was unlikely to happen; *Juno and the Paycock* was—and remains— a hugely popular stage play in Ireland. Yet that's the problem. This film was a studio assignment, and it shows. Hitchcock wasn't afforded a lot of room to play with the script, written by acclaimed writer Sean O'Casey.

Hitchcock told François Truffaut, "I must say that I didn't feel like making the picture because, although I read the play over and over again, I could see no way of narrating it in cinematic form. It's an excellent play, though, and I liked the story, the mood, the characters, and the blend of humor and tragedy very much."[4] Had the project come later in Hitchcock's career, he could have simply turned it down. This was not an opportunity he was afforded in 1930.

WHERE'S HITCH?

Hitchcock does not make one of his famous cameos in this film.

A further frustration is that watching the film demands slow, patient attention—not because it is filled with subtle and intelligent moments, but because it's painfully difficult to understand a word being said. This isn't because the sound quality is poor (it is), but because the Irish accents are thick and the banter is rambling.

Talk, talk, talk, most of it difficult to understand. That's *Juno and the Paycock* in a nutshell.

It's no surprise that top directors were assigned dialogue-heavy dramas with the emergence of sound. The idea of people talking and singing on screen was a novelty, something the public hadn't seen before. That meant moviegoers were going to get a lot of talking and singing, whether the story demanded it or not. This isn't necessarily a bad thing—some of the greatest films of all time are talkative—but talking alone does not a good film make, especially when the dialogue is neither interesting nor intelligible. We need more than the novelty of speech, but *Juno and the Paycock* fails to deliver.

It also fails as a film adaptation because it's too static. There is little character movement and almost none by the camera. It feels like someone simply set a camera in front of a stage and filmed the actors. As even Hitchcock said, this film is not cinematic in any way. Throughout his career, he managed to insert interesting moments into even his most mundane films. *Juno and the Paycock*, however, boasts few cinematic touches of note, and, when placed in the context of his career, even these are minor at best.

First, several times Hitchcock uses the sound of gunfire over a static shot of an open window to illustrate the violence of this time in Irish history. These scenes are well executed and show that despite his disinterest in the project, he couldn't let the entire production get by without some cinematic flair. In a better film it would have offered real dramatic punch and a commentary on how continuing violence invades the lives of families in ways great and small, but sadly, the technique is wasted here. Rather than offer the atmosphere intended, it only serves to fracture what little narrative there is.

Second, at one point Hitchcock pulls the camera close on a character's face, focusing on his reactions while two other off-camera characters discuss matters of importance. Despite the novelty of sound to cinema, Hitchcock recognized this new technology could be used to comment on characters and their situations—in this case, getting the audience inside a character's head without his having to say a word. This is an effective and clear indication that Hitch was always eager to see what technological innovations could do for his storytelling.

Finally, the film closes with a dramatic pullback that would be unnoticed in most Hitchcock films but stands out here because it's the only creative use of camera movement seen in these ninety-six minutes. Mary Boyle, distraught over what her family has done to itself, sorrowfully wails to the Lord as the camera pulls away, showing her alone and broken.

Juno and the Paycock is a film that offers no forward progress for Hitchcock's art. Not only is it not essential viewing, it's a downright chore to get through. At best, it is worth watching only to see that even a master can fail at his craft.

CONCLUSION

Juno and the Paycock is a challenging film to watch—and for all the wrong reasons. It's overly talkative, it lacks cinematic qualities, and it fails to sustain any level of interest. Only those interested in seeing everything Hitchcock directed should consider seeing this film.

HITCHCOCKIAN THEMES

Along with *The Farmer's Wife, Juno and the Paycock* is highly unusual in that it does not contain any of the prevalent themes seen in Hitchcock's other films.

THINGS TO LOOK FOR

- The use of sound rather than moving images to illustrate multiple occurrences of gunfire.

TRIVIA/FUN STUFF

- ✦ *Juno and the Paycock* was based on a popular stage play of the time by Sean O'Casey.
- ✦ Another version was filmed in 1960. Directed for television by Paul Shyre, it starred Hitchcock collaborator Hume Cronyn.

DVD RELEASES

RELEASE: Desert Island Films (2011)
(Dolby Digital 2.0 Mono, 1.33:1 Black & White)
RATING: **1/2

RELEASE: Synergy Ent (2009)
(Dolby Digital 2.0 Mono, 1.33:1 Black & White)
RATING: **1/2

RELEASE: AFA Entertainment (2010)
(Dolby Digital 2.0 Mono, 16:9 Black & White)
RATING: *
NOTES: Not in original aspect ratio. Avoid.

RELEASE: BCI/Sunset Home Visual Entertainment (SHE; 2005)
(Dolby Digital 2.0 Mono, 1.33:1 Black & White)
RATING: *

NOTES: Part of a set with nine other Hitchcock films, *Alfred Hitchcock: Master of Suspense.*

RELEASE: Whirlwind Media (2001)
(Dolby Digital 2.0 Mono, 1.33:1 Black & White)
RATING: *

Murder!

(1930)

FILM FACTS

PRODUCTION YEAR: 1930
RELEASE DATES: July 31, 1930 (UK); November 24, 1930 (U.S.)
STUDIO: British International Pictures
FILMING LOCATION: Elstree Studios, Borehamwood, Hertfordshire, England
PRESENTATION/ASPECT RATIO: Black & White/1.37:1

SYNOPSIS

When an actress is found murdered, the identity of the killer seems obvious to all—a colleague found at the scene, murder weapon next to the body. The evidence in hand, the accused, Diana Baring (Norah Baring), is quickly found guilty by a jury. But one of the jurors, Sir John Menier (Herbert Marshall), has second thoughts after the trial is over. He believes the young actress has been wrongly accused, and so goes on a quest to find the real murderer. What follows is a mystery in the classic Hitchcock style.

IMPRESSIONS

Hitchcock ventures back into familiar territory with *Murder!* It's not a perfect motion picture by any means, but coming on the heels of *Juno and the*

Paycock, it's practically a revelation. The film is also a big indication that Hitchcock would easily make the transition from silent to sound. *Blackmail* was a noteworthy but flawed effort, *Juno* was pure drudgery, but *Murder!* is an artistic success.

The story is simple enough: An actress in a theater group is murdered, and the murderer is obviously a colleague. In a brief segment that looks forward to Sidney Lumet's *12 Angry Men* (1957), a jury vigorously debates the case behind closed doors before offering (unlike Lumet's film) a guilty verdict.

But maybe the actual murderer isn't so obvious after all. One juror, Sir John Menier, also an actor, suspects there is more to the story and vows to find the real killer. He looks for clues and finds them, and by the end of the film the real killer is revealed. The story is a cliché, to be sure, but thanks to Hitch's

> **WHERE'S HITCH?**
>
> About an hour into the film, Sir Alfred walks past the house in which the murder occurred.

growing confidence and his ceaseless quest to find new and inventive ways to present clichéd events—or, as we see in the climax, to create unique situations—*Murder!* is a study in early Hitchcock technique.

Murder! brings to the table many of the elements that make a great Hitchcock film. We have a dead body, mounting suspense, clever cinematic flourishes, and a charismatic lead to guide us through the action. It's more a straightforward mystery than a Hitchcockian meditation on suspense, but when coupled with *Blackmail*, *Murder!* offers an early glimpse at what the future would hold for the Master of Suspense.

In something we'll see in later films, the cinematic flourishes start right from the opening. Sir Alfred pans the camera down a city block and across a series of windows, each framing a tiny glimpse of story. (The shot calls to mind a film Hitch would make nearly twenty-five years later: *Rear Window*.) We see a crowd gathered at the site of the titular murder, and once inside the apartment in which the killing took place, we are given the information we need not with words, but with a flawless four-point move of the camera. Focus on a constable looking down, a concerned look on his face; pan left to a woman crouching next to him, shocked at what she is seeing; pan to a woman who looks as if she is in shock, wide-eyed and dazed; and finally draw the camera right for one last image, focusing on a corpse, the murder weapon laying next to the body. After the static camera work of *Juno and the Paycock*, Hitchcock's bold, focused eye jumps off the screen. He knows just what he wants to show and how he wants to show it.

He also knows when to use playful banter to lighten the mood—and, more importantly, how to use that same banter as a means to provide exposition. In a great sequence that immediately follows the scene described above, two women are making tea and chattering about the details of the murder. The women walk back and forth between rooms, the camera sliding along with them. It's wonderfully realized. One wonders if the experience Hitchcock had filming this sequence would later serve as the seed for his bold camera experimentation in *Rope*. And in what may be one of the funniest bits seen from Hitch thus far, one of the victim's neighbors speaks incoherently for a short while, only to be understood when he puts his dentures in his mouth. This amusing moment comes during what is an otherwise serious sequence of events. Hitchcock often used such techniques to great effect. Rarely is it done better than it is in this sequence.

Murder! is the first Hitchcock film that completely takes advantage of the new technology in sound production. Hitch knew sound was yet another way to convey feeling and emotion. The use of audio and editing to set the tone during the opening sequence is pitch-perfect. One would not guess that sound was a new tool to the future Master of Suspense. In what is arguably the most creative piece of filmmaking seen thus far from Hitchcock, there's a wonderful scene in which Sir John, the juror who has second thoughts, is thinking to himself while looking into his bathroom mirror. We don't see him talking, but we hear his thoughts as a voiceover. In this day and age, it's common for a character's thoughts to be made audible, but this was certainly not the case in 1930. The technology to dub audio onto film had not yet been invented; this required creativity on Hitchcock's part. He was able to accomplish this bit of audio trickery by playing a recording of the dialogue along with a live orchestra hidden behind the set. It looks and sounds so natural that the viewer would never guess how it was accomplished.

Another technique worth noting in *Murder!* is Hitchcock's use of shadows to convey action. Though not particularly inventive, it demonstrates that he didn't want to simply point a camera at actors and let them do their thing. The status quo was never enough for him. He thrived on the challenge of discovering ways to improve his work. While a lot of these early films are a far cry from the masterpieces that made him a household name, they clearly illustrate that Hitchcock was an artist, not just a filmmaker.

By 1930 it had become clear that there was a type of story Alfred Hitchcock was born to tell. With the exception of *The Farmer's Wife*, his most enter-

Norah Baring and Herbert Marshall face each other in *Murder!* (British International Pictures [America] Inc./Photofest © British International Pictures [America] Inc.)

taining films up to this point included murder, people under suspicion, and clashes with authority—all frequent Hitchcock themes. *Murder!* is, to this point, the most well-realized example of this: a film that tells a simple story, but tells it well—a film brimming with the kind of touches that scream Hitchcock. In just the third sound film of his career, he was already making bold technical leaps and innovating with new technology in order to tell his story in the most compellingly stylistic way possible—and all without losing his grasp on accessibility. That's important to note. Above all else, no matter how artistic he got, Hitchcock was always accessible to the average viewer. This film may be laden with the stuff of cinema, from the brilliant stage curtain–to–jail cell cut (especially apropos considering the victim and the accused) to the dramatic silhouette of the rising hangman's rope to the dizzying madness of the climactic suicide, but it never fails to work as direct and easy-to-digest storytelling. This was the tightrope Hitch would walk throughout his career.

There's a feeling one gets when viewing a good Hitchcock film. This is apparent while watching *Murder!* more than any of the films seen to this point. In many ways, *Murder!* feels like *The Wrong Man*, a film Hitch would make twenty-five years later. In the latter picture, the innocent victim

(Henry Fonda) attempts to prove his innocence, while in *Murder!* a juror does the work. The process is comparable and the resulting tone is almost identical. It's interesting, then, that while so many of Hitchcock's films have similar themes and dramatic devices, they are quite different in overall feel. These differences, slight as they sometimes are, make each of Hitchcock's films a unique experience.

Murder! has its share of flaws. The story is predictable and the performance from the actors is less than stellar, but that's not the point. What we should appreciate about *Murder!* is that Hitchcock gets back to being Hitchcock. That's a good thing.

CONCLUSION

If this analysis makes it appear that *Murder!* is a classic Alfred Hitchcock film, that's largely because the context in which it appeared makes it stand out as one of his most Hitchcockian films thus far. Make no mistake: *Murder!* is a flawed experience, but because it is the most notable step to date toward the kind of film upon which his legacy would be built, it is also essential viewing for the Hitchcock student. The early look at his developing feel for suspense is enlightening, while the numerous cinematic flourishes make for good entertainment.

HITCHCOCKIAN THEMES

Bathroom Scene/B.M. • Chaos in an Unexpected Location • Ineffectual Authority Figures • Man (or Woman) on the Run • Murder • Suicide • Wrongly Accused

THINGS TO LOOK FOR

- An opening pan that looks ahead in time to *Rear Window.*
- The bold, confident movements of the camera, signaling Hitch's further storytelling development.
- A scene during which Sir John Menier's thoughts can be heard as he gazes into a bathroom mirror, a creative use of sound technology used at the dawn of the sound era.
- Creative editing and use of audio during the dramatic jury deliberations.
- Cross-dressing and suicide in a film from 1930.

TRIVIA/FUN STUFF

✦ A German version of *Murder!* exists, called *Mary*. It was filmed using the same script and on the same sets, but featured a German cast.

✦ When Sir John's thoughts are audible to the audience during the bathroom sequence, the technology available did not allow the audio to be dubbed in later, so it had to be created "live" for the camera. In order to create the scene, Hitchcock had a real orchestra playing off-camera, with a recording of Sir John's thoughts being played just off set.

✦ The UK version of the film is approximately twelve minutes longer, featuring an extended jury deliberation, further scenes of Sir John's quest for the killer, and even a landlady, whose role was cut entirely from the U.S. release.

✦ This was Hitchcock's third sound film, and his third film featuring a murder.

DVD RELEASES

RELEASE: Cobra Entertainment LLC (2011)
(Dolby Digital 2.0 Mono, 1.33:1 Black & White)
RATING: ***1/2

RELEASE: Osiris Entertainment (2011)
(Dolby Digital 2.0 Mono, 1.33:1 Black & White)
RATING: ***

RELEASE: BCI/Sunset Home Visual Entertainment (SHE; 2005)
(Dolby Digital 2.0 Mono, 1.33:1 Black & White)
RATING: **1/2

NOTES: Part of a set with eight other Hitchcock films, *The Essential Alfred Hitchcock Collection*.

RELEASE: Lionsgate (2002)
(Dolby Digital 2.0 Mono, 1.33:1 Black & White)
RATING: **1/2

NOTES: Part of *The Alfred Hitchcock Box Set* with *The Ring*, *The Manxman*, *The Skin Game*, and *Rich and Strange*.

RELEASE: Delta (2001)
(Dolby Digital 2.0 Mono, 1.33:1 Black & White)
RATING: **1/2

NOTES: Packaged with *Jamaica Inn* or as part of the *Alfred Hitchcock: The Early Years* boxed set.

RELEASE: Laserlight (1999)
(Dolby Digital 2.0 Mono, 1.33:1 Black & White)
RATING: **1/2

NOTES: Part of *The Collection* boxed set.

RELEASE: Madacy Entertainment (1998)
(Dolby Digital 2.0 Mono, 1.33:1 Black & White)
RATING: **1/2

NOTES: Available as a stand-alone or as part of *The Alfred Hitchcock Collection*.

RELEASE: Whirlwind Media (2001)
(Dolby Digital 2.0 Mono, 1.33:1 Black & White)
RATING: **

RELEASE: Unicorn Video (2001)
(Dolby Digital 2.0 Mono, Dolby Digital 5.1 Surround, 1.33:1 Black & White)
RATING: **

The Skin Game
(1931)

FILM FACTS

PRODUCTION YEARS: 1930–1931
RELEASE DATES: February 26, 1931 (UK); June 20, 1931 (U.S.)
STUDIO: British International Pictures
FILMING LOCATION: Elstree Studios, Borehamwood, Hertfordshire, England
PRESENTATION/ASPECT RATIO: Black & White/1.37:1

SYNOPSIS

The Skin Game tells the story of the Hillcrists (C. V. France and Helen Hay), a rich family fighting for the rights of poor farmers in danger of losing their homes to Mr. Hornblower (Edmund Gwenn), a real estate speculator. Hornblower is interested in acquiring the farmers' homes so he can use the land to build factories. A financial battle ensues, with Mr. Hornblower outbidding the Hillcrists at auction for the land, much to their dismay. But when Mrs. Hillcrist learns that Mr. Hornblower's daughter, Chloe (Phyllis Konstam), was once a prostitute, she uses this information to blackmail the Hornblowers.

IMPRESSIONS

In 1931 Alfred Hitchcock adapted John Galsworthy's *The Skin Game*, which was, like *Juno and the Paycock*, a popular play of the era. Focusing on two families playing tug-of-war over the fate of a plot of land, it's a talky, dialogue-driven film that feels longer than its seventy-seven minutes. But unlike in the burdensome *Juno and the Paycock*, Hitch's vision shines through the dense layers of dialogue and makes for a more cinematic—and more enjoyable—experience. *The Skin Game* isn't a particularly thrilling film, and its strict adherence to the source material keeps it too closely confined to stagey dramatics, but there are enough indications of Sir Alfred's artistic hand at work to make *The Skin Game* a strong step forward for his art.

After the initial experiment with sound in *Blackmail*—and then the impressive use of full (yet embryonic) sound in *Murder!*—what stands out here is how much the sound *doesn't* stand out. When seeing these films in sequence, the speed at which using audio became second nature to Alfred Hitchcock is remarkable. For the first time, the sound is truly seamless. It is a full-blown sound film rather than an "early" sound film. You'd never know that his (and England's) first talkie was released a mere eighteen months before.

The Skin Game really needs that sound, because the plot is pushed forward not through action, but through talk. Lots of talk. Unlike *Juno and the Paycock*, however, *The Skin Game*'s dense dialogue is more effective in driving the plot and certainly more enjoyable overall. "I could never hate properly. It's a confounded nuisance," Mr. Hillcrist says late in the film, just one example of this film's crisp, clever dialogue.

Still, once again we're seeing a filmed version of a stage production, and once again it shows. Thankfully, this time around Hitch takes full advantage of his growing arsenal of cinematic tricks to make *The Skin Game* an engaging experience. Several times he uses 180-degree cuts, later popularized by legendary Japanese director Akira Kurosawa. Each time the technique jumps off the screen. He pushes and pulls the camera into and out of scenery and characters, dramatically highlighting key parts of the story. The most notable example comes near the end, when Mr. Hornblower and his daughter are left alone in a room, her status as a former prostitute just revealed. Their shame and isolation is powerfully punctuated when the camera pulls back, revealing the extravagant emptiness around them. They may be wealthy, but their lives are empty. Orson Welles would take this bit of camera-based commentary into the stratosphere a decade later with *Citizen Kane*.

His most eye-catching trick is typical of Alfred Hitchcock in that it was done simply because he could. A pastoral expanse of countryside real estate is the focal point for the conflict in *The Skin Game*. Early in the film, the

Hillcrists, who do not want to see Mr. Hornblower purchase and develop the land, are gazing out over the tranquil scenery at issue. As they talk, the camera cuts to a shot of the rolling hills and trees they are discussing, back to the Hillcrists for some more dialogue, and back again to the hills and trees. This time, though, the camera draws back to reveal that the hills and trees we are seeing are not the real thing, but are instead a poster at an auction for the land. Inventive and eye-catching, the transition also serves to punctuate an important story point.

And it is much more than just a simple close-up pulled back to reveal a larger picture. After the pullback, the shot continues, uncut, moving back to reveal action on the street. It is not unlike the long steadicam shots we see in modern films. This lengthy shot would have required a tremendous amount of planning on Hitch's part. For this trickery alone, it's amazing Hitchcock did not more fondly recall *The Skin Game*.

Also enjoyable is the camerawork during the auction sequence. In any other film, this would likely be a static scene, yet is anything but in *The Skin Game*. While there is almost no character movement, the camera itself is constantly moving, panning, zooming, and cutting. The editing is wonderful and helps to create tension. It's a notable example of how Hitchcock was able to take a scene obviously written for the stage and give it cinematic flair without appearing gimmicky.

WHERE'S HITCH?

Hitchcock does not make one of his famous cameos in *The Skin Game*.

The theme of blackmail is prominent in *The Skin Game*. In fact, it is executed more effectively here than in *Blackmail* itself. While the blackmail in the aforementioned film is crucial to the plot, it never feels urgent. One does not get the sense that the characters being blackmailed are really in danger of having their secrets revealed. Such is not the case in *The Skin Game*, and it's much more believable as a result.

The film is not all perfection, of course. Two of the three leading ladies are so similar in appearance—slender, pretty brunettes with a similar style of dress and nearly identical haircuts—that it becomes far too easy to lose track of who is who, and hence lose focus on the plot. And speaking of the plot, real estate dramas, no matter how much back-stabbing and blackmailing they feature, are not likely to arouse the interest of those looking for a suspense film. Ultimately, *The Skin Game*'s roots as a play cannot be overcome; for long stretches the talk does little but wear you down.

Yet even when the dialogue begins to grate, there is the performance of Edmund Gwenn as Mr. Hornblower to focus on. In his book *Alfred Hitchcock: A Life in Darkness and Light,* author Patrick McGilligan calls Gwenn's performance "ferocious" and "arresting."[5] Strong words, but entirely true. Hitch must have liked him, too, because Gwenn appears in several later Hitchcock productions, including *Foreign Correspondent, The Trouble with Harry,* and an episode of *Alfred Hitchcock Presents.*

It's worth noting that Hitchcock's *The Skin Game* is itself a remake of a 1921 film of the same name directed by B. E. Doxat-Pratt. Interestingly, Gwenn also played Mr. Hornblower in the earlier version. Malcolm Keen, who was seen in Hitchcock's *The Lodger* and *The Manxman,* also appears in the 1921 version.

The Skin Game is not held in high regard by the majority of film critics, or even by Alfred Hitchcock himself. Donald Spoto, in what is reputed to be a definitive study of all of Hitchcock's films, wrote just *one paragraph* about *The Skin Game.* "Hitchcock rightly called this the low point in his career," argued Spoto.[6] Hitch himself told François Truffaut, "I didn't make it by choice, and there isn't much to be said about it."[7] Yet the film in question is filled with more creativity than one would expect in a story about a struggle over land ownership. Despite the limitations imposed on it by its stage play source, this film is rife with clever cinematic choices. The filmmaking prowess on display is some of the best Hitchcock had offered viewers up to this point in his career. No, *The Skin Game* is not a classic, and it does not fit the mold of later Hitchcock films, but there are enough interesting things happening on the screen and enough fascinating directorial choices on display to make this motion picture a clear indication that Alfred Hitchcock could inject life into even the most ordinary of plots.

Taken in the chronological context of his other films, *The Skin Game* is a logical step forward in the progression of his development as an artist. This is an example of a film that does not impress as much by itself as when placed in the context of Hitchcock's filmography.

CONCLUSION

One would not expect a talky real estate drama to have much to offer a Hitchcock fan, yet such is not the case. *The Skin Game* is an admirable step forward for the art of Alfred Hitchcock. Here Hitchcock can be seen using creative touches to make what might have been a bland film something well worth seeing. It's a shame that both Hitchcock and others do not fondly recall *The Skin Game*, because there is much to see and clear evidence of continued artistic growth.

HITCHCOCKIAN THEMES

Blackmail • Dark Secret • Suicide/Attempted Suicide

THINGS TO LOOK FOR

- A mesmerizing pullback shot from a still image of land, to an auction, and finally to action on the street.
- Terrific use of camera work and editing in the auction scene, creating tension in what is an otherwise static scene with little character movement.

TRIVIA/FUN STUFF

+ *The Skin Game* was adapted from a popular stage play by John Galsworthy. Hitchcock adapted it himself for the screen, but kept most of the dialogue from the play.
+ Hitchcock's *The Skin Game* was actually a remake of a 1921 silent film by B. E. Doxat-Pratt, a film that also starred Edmond Gwenn as Mr. Hornblower, the same role he played in Hitchcock's adaptation. This earlier film also featured Malcolm Keen, who we saw in Hitchcock's *The Lodger* and *The Manxman*.

DVD RELEASES

RELEASE: BCI/Sunset Home Visual Entertainment (SHE; 2005)
(Dolby Digital 2.0 Mono, 1.33:1 Black & White)
RATING: ***

NOTES: Part of a set with eight other Hitchcock films, *The Essential Alfred Hitchcock Collection*.

Release: Lionsgate (2002)
(Dolby Digital 2.0 Mono, 1.33:1 Black & White)
Rating: ***

Notes: Part of *The Alfred Hitchcock Box Set* with *The Ring, The Manxman, Murder!,* and *Rich and Strange.*

Release: Delta (2001)
(Dolby Digital 2.0 Mono, 1.33:1 Black & White)
Rating: ***

Notes: Part of the *Alfred Hitchcock: The Early Years* boxed set.

Release: Laserlight (1999)
(Dolby Digital 2.0 Mono, 1.33:1 Black & White)
Rating: ***

Notes: Available as a stand-alone or as part of *The Collection* boxed set.

Release: Cobra Entertainment LLC (2011)
(Dolby Digital 2.0 Mono, 1.33:1 Black & White)
Rating: **

Rich and Strange
(1931)

FILM FACTS

PRODUCTION YEAR: 1931
RELEASE DATE: December 10, 1931 (UK)
STUDIO: British International Pictures
FILM LOCATIONS: Elstree Studios, Borehamwood, Hertfordshire, England;
Marseille, Bouches-du-Rhône, France; and Port Said, Egypt
PRESENTATION/ASPECT RATIO: Black & White/1.37:1

SYNOPSIS

In *Rich and Strange*, a work-weary married couple, Fred and Emily Hill (Henry Kendall and Joan Barry), come into an unexpected inheritance. The newfound wealth gives them the opportunity to travel the world, but they learn that money doesn't buy happiness when Fred falls for a phony princess (Betty Amann) and Emily is courted by a ship's captain, Commander Gordon (Percy Marmont). The Hills suffer a brief estrangement before coming together again and learning their love is more important than a jet-setting lifestyle.

IMPRESSIONS

Rich and Strange is certainly an appropriate title for this, one of Hitchcock's most scattered and chaotic early films. Its myriad sights and sounds are unfocused and seemingly random, yet richly interesting and strangely compelling. A masterpiece? Maybe not, but a far better whole than the sum of its parts would suggest. It features no murder, no dead body, no blackmail, no wrongfully accused man, and no man on the run. It is largely a romantic comedy/drama with a focus on themes Hitch rarely explored in his long and varied career. Still, it's a highly inventive work with terrific sound, music, editing, camera work, and even some amusing dialogue.

As we have seen in films like *Blackmail* and *The Skin Game*, Sir Alfred had recently become adept at using the camera in creative ways to tell a story. He continued to develop this skill in *Rich and Strange*. In the opening shot the camera is zoomed tight on a book-keeper's ledger before pulling back to reveal a room full of people hard at work. But the shot does not end there. The camera continues to pan around the room, revealing a mass of people

WHERE'S HITCH?
Rich and Strange does not feature an Alfred Hitch-cock cameo.

leaving the workplace. The swirling, panning, roving camera that opens *Rich and Strange* hearkens to a similar shot in Terry Gilliam's *Brazil* (1985), in which the sprawling, hectic offices of a dystopian future are unveiled in all their frantic glory. Hitchcock manages to capture the claustrophobic professional life that prompts Fred and Emily to get away when money comes their way. From there, the film is off and running, pausing only to take a breath before rushing headlong into another disjointed, often out-of-place sequence.

The camera work is not the only beautifully executed aspect of this early sequence. For the first time in a Hitchcock film, we see music set in perfect tune with the on-screen action. And this music is an ideal match with what we're seeing. Hitchcock famously used musical scores to enhance the action in his later work, most famously in his collaboration with the great film composer Bernard Herrmann, but it's evident with *Rich and Strange* that Hitch was already aware of the power of music to embellish what we see on screen.

In addition to the opening camera work, we see that Hitchcock has continued to develop his skills in moving the camera, through both zooming in on characters as well as in the development of his point-of-view shots. We have seen Hitch experiment with camera movement in several of his early films; it's obvious he recognized the benefits of constant experimentation here.

And of course we combine that wonderful camera work with some excellent work in the editing room. Even more so than in *The Skin Game*, Hitchcock uses a series of short cuts back-to-back-to-back in *Rich and Strange* to establish a brisk pace. As a director who at this point was now well-established in England, it's apparent Hitchcock had become confident in his ability to conceive how his shots would come together in editing even before he shot them, a crucial element to his later great successes.

Pinpointing noteworthy aspects of the plot is difficult because, to be frank, the plot is both literally and figuratively all over the map. It surges forward in fits and starts, sometimes sprinting along at a rapid pace, sometimes slowing to a crawl. At times it wants to be lightly comedic, at other times heavily dramatic. The tone hops from richly celebratory to strangely meditative, and then back again. *Rich and Strange* doesn't know what it wants to be, and sometimes suffers for it. Yet despite this everything-but-the-kitchen-sink approach, Hitchcock managed to hold things together just enough to make the experience an enjoyable stop on his career path.

Maybe things held together because *Rich and Strange* serves as a depository for all the cinematic tricks he had accumulated up to this point, a closet stuffed with the odds and ends of his life both on and off the screen. *Rich and Strange* is not so much a push forward for Hitchcock's art as much as it is an excuse to show off what he had learned to this point, wrapped up in a narrative that is largely an excuse to photograph whatever tickled his fancy at the time. It makes for a cluttered film—sometimes it's damn near a mess—but one loaded with things to see.

An exhaustive list of "interesting sights" in *Rich and Strange* would be long indeed. From the start Sir Alfred piles on the imagery, and he doesn't quit until the film is over. From the swirling camera of the opening shots we jump to ships, harbors, ports, travel, dining, French shows, glistening waterways, Chinese junks, newborn babies, seafaring vessels, beautiful people, and exotic lands—all shown through some of Hitchcock's most stylistic lens work to date.

Though *Rich and Strange* is a sound picture, Hitchcock recalls his silent film days with frequent use of title cards. In this case, it works pretty well, as they are never distracting and are always pertinent to the on-screen action. Perhaps these title cards were made necessary by limitations in the screenplay, but they never feel out of place.

While thematically *Rich and Strange* is not a typical Hitchcock film, there are a few thematic ties to some of the films seen thus far. First, there are elements of love triangles, involving both Fred and Emily Hill, similar to those seen in *The Ring* and *Champagne*. In addition, the theme of ordinary people living the good life after an inheritance is repeated from *Juno and the Paycock*, this time with much more success.

One particularly notices that Hitchcock's emphasis on witty dialogue is coming to the forefront as he becomes more comfortable with the use of sound. *Rich and Strange* contains both dramatic and funny dialogue. Lines like Fred saying to the princess, "Having developed a taste for champagne, what's the use in sticking to water?" are terrific in helping to keep the mood light.

Not all is perfect, however. There are some distracting continuity errors, first regarding the Hills' inheritance letter—the text changes between scenes—and then again with a doodle drawn by Emily that changes between scenes. These are minor quibbles, to be sure, but surprising given Hitchcock's notorious attention to detail.

If all this sounds scattered, that's because it is. This doesn't mean the film doesn't work—it does—but it is an atypical Hitchcock film. Rather than exploring the limits of visualization via the camera for the purpose of accenting the story, the opposite is true here: *Rich and Strange*'s story seems to exist almost solely for the purpose of toying with the camera. The story is window dressing, in place only to serve the next shot. It's a bit clumsy, and the scattershot approach results in a few previously noted continuity flaws, but it's hard to fault Hitchcock for trying to cram so many ideas into one film.

To digress for just a moment (appropriate, considering the film), *Rich and Strange* boasts one of the most unusual moments of Hitchcock's career when, late in the film, we witness the almost surreal, strangely compelling birth of a baby aboard a rickety old Asian boat. Why is this scene in the film? It doesn't fit anything that comes before or any of what will come after. It does nothing to serve the narrative. It just *is*. But somehow, it works. Couple this with an out-of-the-blue (and entirely pointless) drowning a few minutes before, and you begin to understand what an alien, haphazard film *Rich and Strange* is. The tight plotting you expect from an Alfred Hitchcock film is nowhere to be found.

Alien and haphazard, but, for reasons difficult to put in words, oddly right.

No, *Rich and Strange* isn't an Alfred Hitchcock classic, but it's a good summation of where his art had reached, as well as a funhouse mirror look into where it would stylistically go.

CONCLUSION

Essential Hitchcock? Not quite. But this step in his development as a great artist offers a pleasant diversion before plunging headlong into Hitch's upcoming series of British thrillers, while also offering some nice cinematic moments.

HITCHCOCKIAN THEMES

Chaos in an Unexpected Location · Exotic Location · Love Triangle

THINGS TO LOOK FOR

- Hitchcock's rapid-fire editing, prevalent throughout the rest of his British period.
- A glaring continuity error with a drawing by Emily; each time the drawing is shown, it is slightly different.

TRIVIA/FUN STUFF

✦ The title is a quote taken from William Shakespeare's *The Tempest*, upon which the 1956 cult science-fiction classic *Forbidden Planet* was loosely based

✦ Joan Barry, who plays Emily Hill, also provided the voice of Alice White in Alfred Hitchcock's first talkie, *Blackmail*.

DVD RELEASES

RELEASE: British International Pictures (2010)
(Dolby Digital 2.0 Mono, 1.33:1 Black & White)
RATING: ***1/2

RELEASE: Cobra Entertainment LLC (2011)
(Dolby Digital 2.0 Mono, 1.33:1 Black & White)
RATING: ***

RELEASE: Synergy Ent (2009)
(Dolby Digital 2.0 Mono, 1.33:1 Black & White)
RATING: ***

RELEASE: BCI/Sunset Home Visual Entertainment (SHE; 2005)
(Dolby Digital 2.0 Mono, 1.33:1 Black & White)
RATING: **1/2

NOTES: Part of a set with nine other Hitchcock films, *Alfred Hitchcock: Master of Suspense.*

RELEASE: Lionsgate (2002)
(Dolby Digital 2.0 Mono, 1.33:1 Black & White)
RATING: **1/2

NOTES: Part of *The Alfred Hitchcock Box Set* with *The Ring, The Manxman, Murder!,* and *The Skin Game.*

RELEASE: Delta (2001)
(Dolby Digital 2.0 Mono, 1.33:1 Black & White)
RATING: **1/2

NOTES: Part of the *Alfred Hitchcock: The Early Years* boxed set.

RELEASE: Laserlight (1999)
(Dolby Digital 2.0 Mono, 1.33:1 Black & White)
RATING: **1/2

NOTES: Part of *The Collection* boxed set.

Number Seventeen
(1932)

FILM FACTS

PRODUCTION YEAR: 1931
RELEASE DATE: 1932
STUDIO: British International Pictures
FILMING LOCATION: Elstree Studios, Borehamwood, Hertfordshire, England
PRESENTATION/ASPECT RATIO: Black & White/1.37:1

SYNOPSIS

A group of thieves gather in a London safe house. Hot on their trail is a detective trying to track down a missing necklace. Inside the seemingly abandoned house, they clash, struggling over the stolen goods. A long chase sequence ensues, culminating in a raucous confrontation on a train.

IMPRESSIONS

Number Seventeen is a quiet caper flick hinging on a climactic chase sequence. But the caper isn't terribly interesting, and the climactic chase, while rendered with dazzlingly quick editing, fails to bring any real excitement to the screen.

No, *Number Seventeen* is not a winner.

Where Alfred Hitchcock went wrong with *Number Seventeen* is unclear, but go wrong he did. Quite unexpected when one considers that a number of his immediately forthcoming films would, in fact, be adventurous romps built upon extended chases. One could argue that this film afforded him the opportunity to try out some chase-related cinematic techniques before applying them to films with more rewarding stories, but it is hardly a compelling reason to recommend this to any save those who want to see every film Hitchcock made, because what little story there is in *Number Seventeen* is anything but rewarding.

Worse still, finding the story beneath the murky dialogue, vague setting, and overall lack of clarity is nothing short of a chore. That's ultimately this film's fatal flaw. At sixty-three minutes, the pace is brisk—but *too* brisk. We're never granted time to figure out where we are, who's around, and what they're doing. The film opens with an establishing shot of a darkened, forbidden-looking tenement. A man goes inside. He finds a dead body. He confronts another man he doesn't know. Then other people they don't know. The cast begins their sinister machinations . . . whatever they might be. And we're left wondering what the heck is going on.

> **WHERE'S HITCH?**
>
> Hitchcock does not make one of his famous cameos in *Number Seventeen.*

What was Hitchcock doing here? Was he bored? Did he want to get this job over with as soon as possible? Maybe. *Number Seventeen* is yet another in a string of films based on plays, this one on a surprise hit from 1925. If that wasn't enough to sour his disposition, it was a project forced on him. Between assignments and seeking clout enough to make a more personal movie (*Rich and Strange*, filmed after *Number Seventeen* but released before it), Hitchcock was handed this project by studio boss Walter Mycroft in spite of his preference for the John Van Druten play *After Office Hours*. That project was given to director Thomas Bentley, though, and Hitch was stuck with an assignment he didn't want. For the notoriously stubborn Alfred Hitchcock, that was never a good thing.

According to Hitchcock biographer Patrick McGilligan, Hitch himself admitted that *Number Seventeen* was "little better than a quota quickie." McGilligan notes most critics today consider the film, his last for British International Pictures, "a sour shrug of the shoulders from the director, and one huge practical joke on management."[8] Hitchcock described it as "[a] disaster!"[9] to the great French filmmaker François Truffaut. And Hitchcock was right. For a film purporting to be a crime thriller, it displays a glaring lack of intrigue and suspense. As with *Easy Virtue, The Manxman,* and *Juno and the Paycock*, one wonders what a more mature Hitchcock might have done with this film.

Something must have clicked for Hitch here, though, because many of the elements that make up *Number Seventeen* would inform his upcoming films. Criminal cartels, light comedy, secret agents, and rousing chases will come to define the rest of Hitchcock's British period. Everything done here would later be done to greater effect, most notably the climactic chase

Barry Jones, Leon M. Lion, Donald Calthrop, and John Stuart in *Number Seventeen*. (British International Pictures/Photofest © British International Pictures)

(simply laughable in this film) and the male and female leads being caught in an awkward and dangerous situation together (played to perfection two films later in *The 39 Steps*), but for the student of Hitchcock they're here on display in all their half-hearted glory.

In that respect, all is not lost when considering *Number Seventeen* and where it fits in Hitchcock's growth as an artist. It's not a powerhouse of Hitchcockian flair, but it's not without its excellent artistic choices.

As seen so many times already, *Number Seventeen* opens with a beautiful and creative shot. This time, it's a heavy wind blowing the branches of a tree, followed by leaves blowing down a street, until we come upon the house in which the first act takes place. This would have been a wonderful tone-setter in a film with more suspense and intrigue, but, unfortunately, the shot is wasted in *Number Seventeen*. Still, it's a noteworthy continuation of a trend seen throughout Hitch's career: wonderfully realized opening shots.

Of particular artistic note in *Number Seventeen* is the repeated use of shadows. Throughout the film, shadows are used rather than direct images of the items we're seeing. The technique is not especially thrilling or even well executed, but it does at the very least offer something interesting to see.

Hitchcock continued to develop his use of humor to lighten tense moments, something seen time and again in his career. There is a funny bit early in the film where a character empties his pockets, revealing a long piece of string, a sausage, and half a cigarette. Including a sausage was absurd, and surely that was the point. Hitchcock loved to inject levity into otherwise tense moments.

It is also pleasing to see the continued use of music appropriate to the situation, another hallmark of Hitchcock's greatest works. Though still relatively early in the development of sound and music technique in motion pictures, it's obvious Hitchcock was already aware of the potential impact of music on a scene. Many early sound films had musical scores simply because they could. Hitchcock helped refine that concept by integrating the score into the on-screen action. Again, *Number Seventeen* isn't the best example of this technique, but we do see evidence that musical cues were drawn specifically for the action seen on screen.

Saying that *Number Seventeen* is a dismal failure may be overstating the case—with a short running time and a few Hitchcockian touches, it's not entirely a waste of time—yet it can't be denied that Hitch clearly cobbled this film together in a rush to get it done. The notable use of strong shadows in the film and rapid-fire editing do little to inject excitement into this muddy entry into the Hitchcock filmography.

CONCLUSION

Number Seventeen is one of the least enjoyable films in the Alfred Hitchcock film library. It lacks suspense, is not very interesting, and is difficult to understand. It's not entirely a waste of time. To its credit, it offers a few Hitchcockian touches, but these would likely be of interest only to those devoted to watching every Hitchcock film. Its short running time makes it easier to digest. And that is indeed damning with faint praise.

HITCHCOCKIAN THEMES

Handcuffed Man and Woman • Murder • Trains

THINGS TO LOOK FOR

- The highly creative opening shots, something we'll see with increasing frequency in the films to come.
- The near constant use of shadows throughout the film, particularly inside the safe house.

TRIVIA/FUN STUFF

✦ *Number Seventeen* is based on a play by British playwright Joseph Jefferson Farjeon. The play was first adapted for the screen in the 1928 German film *Haus Nummer 17* (*House Number 17*).

DVD RELEASES

RELEASE: AFA Entertainment (2010)
(Dolby Digital 2.0 Mono, 1.33:1 Black & White)
RATING: ***

RELEASE: BCI/Sunset Home Visual Entertainment (SHE; 2005)
(Dolby Digital 2.0 Mono, 1.33:1 Black & White)
RATING: **

NOTES: Part of a set with eight other Hitchcock films, *The Essential Alfred Hitchcock Collection*.

RELEASE: Delta (2001)
(Dolby Digital 2.0 Mono, 1.33:1 Black & White)
RATING: **

NOTES: Part of the *Alfred Hitchcock: The Early Years* boxed set.

RELEASE: Madacy Entertainment (1998)
(Dolby Digital 2.0 Mono, 1.33:1 Black & White)
RATING: **

NOTES: Available as a stand-alone or as part of *The Alfred Hitchcock Collection*.

The Man Who Knew Too Much
(1934)

FILM FACTS

PRODUCTION YEAR: 1934
RELEASE DATES: December 1934 (UK); March 22, 1935 (U.S.)
STUDIO: Gaumont British Picture Corporation
FILMING LOCATION: Lime Grove Studios, Lime Grove,
Shepherd's Bush, London, England
PRESENTATION/ASPECT RATIO: Black & White/1.37:1

SYNOPSIS

The Lawrence family—Bob (Leslie Banks), Jill (Edna Best), and Betty (Nova Pilbeam)—are on holiday when a friend of the family is mysteriously shot and killed, passing along a vague snippet of information just before dying. The murder and the information they now hold plunge the Lawrences into a plot of international espionage when the culprits kidnap Betty in an effort to keep the family quiet about what they've learned. The chase is on as Bob and Jill try to track down the spy syndicate and save their daughter. Their efforts lead to a climactic assassination attempt at England's Royal Albert Hall.

IMPRESSIONS

After the relative disappointment of *Number Seventeen*, Alfred Hitchcock rebounded strongly with his 1934 version of *The Man Who Knew Too Much*. This is a film loaded with suspense, intrigue, drama, humor, and artistic choices that mark it as undeniably Hitchcockian. He would remake this film with an American cast in 1956, and in many ways the latter is a superior film, but the original British version is nothing to sneeze at. It's not the monumental turning point his next film would be, but it's an open doorway into the world of fully Hitchcockian cinema.

Because of this, those engaging in a casual, less complete trek through Hitch's catalog of films will find *The Man Who Knew Too Much* an obvious point to jump on board. While his next film, *The 39 Steps*, is credited as his best-known British work, it's fair to argue that *The Man Who Knew Too Much* is equally well known. It's not as seemingly effortless as his later work—the nuts and bolts are too often visible—but the original *The Man Who Knew Too Much* hits all the right notes, offering an introduction of sorts to the stretch of thrillers that would cap off Hitchcock's British period.

> **WHERE'S HITCH?**
>
> This version of *The Man Who Knew Too Much* does not feature a Hitchcock cameo.

In stark contrast to *Number Seventeen*, *The Man Who Knew Too Much* succeeds in its quest to deliver real intrigue and suspense. Where the earlier film is something of a jumbled mess, awkward and disorganized, this film is more clearly defined and understandable, and succeeds in keeping the viewer on the edge of his seat. *The Man Who Knew Too Much* is not without faults—the plot has its share of holes and the climax feels overdone—but these flaws are relatively minor.

As in his best thrillers, Hitchcock wastes no time diving right into things. When operating in peak form, he wrapped up vital character backstory and information in seemingly innocuous introductory scenes, planting the seeds of what will come later in short, nimble strokes. Such is the case here, where in mere minutes we're introduced to the main players and thrust headlong into the plot. He would mine techniques like this throughout his career, and here we see them from the moment we're introduced to the Lawrence family. We quickly learn they have a daughter, Betty, whom they love very much; that Bob Lawrence is an unflappable sort when his wife playfully flirts with another man, a trait that will serve him well in the

Frank Vosper points a gun at Leslie Banks under the "watchful" eye of Peter Lorre. (Gaumont British Picture Corporation of America/Photofest © Gaumont British Picture Corporation of America)

events to come; and, in the most Hitchcockian of touches for reasons that won't be revealed until later, that Jill Lawrence is a fantastic shot with a rifle. It's an efficient setup indicative of the economical storytelling we'll increasingly see later on. In fact, it is often in the opening moments of a film that Hitch is at his best.

The Hitchcock setup. Few of his tools are more powerful, and, often, more subtle. He knew and embraced the old rule that if you show the audience a gun in the first act, it had better be used in the third. He not only followed this rule here, he exploited it. Who could guess that when we're shown Jill Lawrence taking part in a shooting contest, what we're really seeing is the figurative first-act gun. It's not the obvious, "Look at this important plot point!" you encounter in most mainstream thrillers, but a subtler, and therefore more effective, bit of foreshadowing. This is one of the best early examples of Hitch's teasing the audience, a purposeful effort to make them say, "Oh!" when they reach the climax.

About that climax: We saw in *The Lodger* a slow-burning suspense film explode into a frantic chase. We saw it again in *Blackmail*. *Number Seventeen* culminated in an extended action-oriented climax, too. Hitchcock knew the power of launching into a frenzy of panic at the end of his films, frequently using the technique to great effect. From this point forward, Hitchcock's cinematic finishes would become increasingly stylistic and increasingly iconic. Most important, they would be memorable. It's true that the final showdown in *The Man Who Knew Too Much* is probably drawn out far longer than it should be, but it's an exercise in tension building from which he likely learned some lessons. And who could forget the superb buildup to that showdown? The assassin's gun slowly creeping out from behind a curtain is one of cinema's high points, made all the more memorable by its perfect merging of music and image. Hitch would never forget how such marriages of sight and sound make for more powerful film, culminating in a certain shower scene twenty-six years later that is now hailed as one of the greatest moments in cinematic history.

What makes *The Man Who Knew Too Much* by-the-book Hitchcock is the way it relies on previous scenes to build the tension of the next, a house of cards that could topple in the hands of a lesser director but one that he managed to erect, successfully, time and again. It comes close to toppling here more than once, ensuring it falls just short of being ranked among his best films, but Hitch never quite lets the movie get away from him.

This film was Hitchcock's first after leaving British International Pictures. He purchased the rights from BIP and sold them to producer Michael Balcon, who produced some of Hitchcock's earliest films and later worked with him at the Gaumont British Picture Corporation. Here he was afforded greater film budgets. It shows in *The Man Who Knew Too Much*. We have lavish sets and a larger cast, not to mention the exotic Swiss resort location in St. Moritz. Hitchcock used these greater resources to his advantage; a strong film results.

Hitch often made great use of what he would famously refer to as a "MacGuffin," a nonsense word referring to a story element of the utmost importance to the participants, but completely unimportant to the viewer. In the case of *The Man Who Knew Too Much*, the MacGuffin is the reason the assassins wanted to kill the foreign statesman they've targeted. It's irrelevant to us, the viewer, but serves as the sole motivation for the film's antagonists. This is the first of many uses of the MacGuffin device for Hitchcock.

Hitchcock once again uses humor adroitly to lighten the mood during otherwise heavy dramatic moments. An excellent example of this comes right before the opening assassination. The end of a knitted scarf is tied to a man dancing on a crowded dance floor. As he continues to dance, the scarf unravels, entangling the other dancers. It's not very realistic, but realism is not the point. The brief comedic moment lightens the tone just before the shooting. It is a springboard to the film's first instance of serious drama. Another is a scene at a dentist's office, where Bob Lawrence is trying to track down the location of his daughter. In this scene, we dance back and forth between oppressive darkness and black humor, a tightrope walk played well both as a bleak way to lighten the tone and as a means to push the plot forward.

Another thematic element present is Hitchcock's fondness for setting scenes of chaos in places where they'd be least expected. Here we see murder and attempts at murder in places like ritzy ski resorts and the Royal Albert Hall. The introduction of chaos in such locations drives up the level of intrigue and suspense through the stark contrast it offers. Again, this is a common theme, seen already in films like *The Manxman* and *Blackmail*, that will reappear continuously throughout the rest of Hitchcock's career.

The editing in *The Man Who Knew Too Much* is particularly strong. Jump cuts such as when a Scotland Yard detective tells Bob Lawrence his daughter has been kidnapped, shifting to a new scene immediately after the word "kidnapped," stand out. Here Hitchcock quickly cuts to Jill and another relative playing with a toy train set, emphasizing the family's love for Betty by playing up the family dynamic. It's a deftly executed moment.

As noted above, the ending is overdone and drawn out, but that flaw is not enough to seriously diminish the quality of this film. It is said this ending is based on a 1911 incident called the Sidney Street Siege, but being loosely based on real events does not excuse the tedium of the scene. Similar complaints can be aired about an earlier sequence featuring characters who are fighting by throwing chairs at one another. This sequence goes on a bit too long, but, at the same time, the absurdity of it all is amusing. It's an atypical way to have a major confrontation with the film's villains, a strange choice that somehow works. Though this is one of those scenes that threaten to knock down the cards Hitch has stacked, the twist on the traditional fight with the antagonists works well.

In Hitchcock films, the world is not a safe place. Average people quickly find themselves thrust into situations bigger than they are, roped into plots they know nothing about, and confronted with dangers heretofore impossible to imagine in their quiet, ordinary lives. If anything, this is what makes

The Man Who Knew Too Much special. Every move the characters make are an effort to avoid meeting a bad end. It becomes, from this point forward, *the* Hitchcock theme.

The Man Who Knew Too Much is a wonderful gateway from Hitchcock's early sound period into an excellent stretch of pre-America thrillers. It's not without faults, but those faults are relatively minor and easily redeemed by an exciting story, great suspense, a plethora of intrigue, and moments of real humor. This is a major step forward for Hitchcock's artistic development.

CONCLUSION

The original version of *The Man Who Knew Too Much* may suffer from flaws that ensure it falls short of masterpiece status, but it remains one of the best films of Alfred Hitchcock's British period, displaying the kind of adventure, humor, and intrigue that would transform Hitch from a good director to a legend.

HITCHCOCKIAN THEMES

Blackmail • Chaos in an Unexpected Location • Climactic Showdown at Iconic Location • Ineffectual Authority Figures • Man (or Woman) on the Run • Murder • Music Plays a Role in Plot • Spy Syndicate

THINGS TO LOOK FOR

- The dramatic and memorable shot of the assassin's pistol slowly emerging from behind a curtain.

TRIVIA/FUN STUFF

✦ Hitchcock remade the film in 1956, this time with the leads played by James Stewart and Doris Day.

✦ Peter Lorre, who plays the head villain, spoke only limited English during the filming. He learned and performed most of his lines phonetically.

✦ The film's title, but not the story, was snatched from a book of the same name by author G. K. Chesterton.

✦ The concerto played during the climactic assassination attempt appears in both versions of the film, and was written specifically for the movie by composer Arthur Benjamin.

✦ Early on, Hitch hoped to make the film part of the then-popular *Bulldog Drummond* series, but failed to get the rights to the Drummond name.

✦ A real-life gun battle known as the Sidney Street Siege was the inspiration behind the film's climactic shootout. The sequence was dropped in the 1956 remake.

✦ Joan Harrison, who plays a secretary in an uncredited role, later went on to become a key Hitchcock collaborator (screenplay credits on *Rebecca*, *Foreign Correspondent*, and *Suspicion*, among others) and a producer of *Alfred Hitchcock Presents*.

DVD RELEASES

RELEASE: PD Productions (2011)
(Dolby Digital 2.0 Mono, 1.33:1 Black & White)
RATING: ****

RELEASE: Synergy Ent (2009)
(Dolby Digital 2.0 Mono, 1.33:1 Black & White)
RATING: ***1/2

RELEASE: Cobra Entertainment LLC (2011)
(Dolby Digital 2.0 Mono, 1.33:1 Black & White)
RATING: ***

RELEASE: AFA Entertainment (2010)
(Dolby Digital 2.0 Mono, 1.33:1 Black & White)
RATING: ***

RELEASE: BCI/Sunset Home Visual Entertainment (SHE; 2005)
(Dolby Digital 2.0 Mono, 1.33:1 Black & White)
RATING: ***

EXTRAS: Episode of *Alfred Hitchcock Presents*, "The Cheney Vase"
NOTES: Part of a set with nine other Hitchcock films, *Alfred Hitchcock: Master of Suspense*.

RELEASE: Delta (2001)
(Dolby Digital 2.0 Mono, 1.33:1 Black & White)
RATING: ***

NOTES: Part of the *Alfred Hitchcock: The Early Years* boxed set.

RELEASE: Whirlwind Media (2001)
(Dolby Digital 2.0 Mono, 1.33:1 Black & White)
RATING: ***

NOTES: Packaged with *Young and Innocent*.

RELEASE: Laserlight (1999)
(Dolby Digital 2.0 Mono, 1.33:1 Black & White)
RATING: ***

NOTES: Available as a stand-alone or as part of *The Collection* boxed set.

RELEASE: Madacy Entertainment (1998)
(Dolby Digital 2.0 Mono, 1.33:1 Black & White)
RATING: ***

NOTES: Available as a stand-alone or as part of *The Alfred Hitchcock Collection*.

RELEASE: Vintage Home Entertainment (2004)
(Dolby Digital 2.0 Mono, 1.33:1 Black & White)
RATING: *

NOTES: Packaged with *Secret Agent* and *The Lady Vanishes* on the same disc. Avoid.

The 39 Steps
(1935)

FILM FACTS

PRODUCTION YEAR: 1935
RELEASE DATES: June 1935 (UK); August 1935 (U.S.)
STUDIO: Gaumont British Picture Corporation
FILMING LOCATIONS: Dumfries and Galloway, Scotland; Edinburgh, Scotland;
Highlands, Scotland; London, England
PRESENTATION/ASPECT RATIO: Black & White/1.37:1

SYNOPSIS

Richard Hannay (Robert Donat), a Canadian visiting London, meets
Annabella Smith (Lucie Mannheim) amidst the turmoil of gunfire after a
show by Mr. Memory, a man with an incomparable capacity to recall facts
and figures. Annabella, who is being chased by foreign agents, asks to spend
the night in Richard's flat. Richard agrees, but finds Annabella murdered
the next morning. Knowing his life is in danger and he will be accused of
the crime, Richard makes a run for it. Now fleeing the authorities, he
attempts to both prove his innocence and prevent the loss of a state secret
to the foreign agents.

IMPRESSIONS

Watching a film a week, it takes thirteen films over the course of just about three months to come to *The 39 Steps*. For both Alfred Hitchcock and a journey through his career, arriving at this point is a landmark moment.

It might be overstating the case to suggest that for Alfred Hitchcock, a decade of filmmaking led to this point. After all, such a statement to some extent implies that his previous films were somehow unworthy of artistic praise, that they were spiritual test runs for this film, or that they were the work of an amateur not yet ready to craft a film this good. Such suggestions are, of course, ridiculous. Anyone taking a journey through the film career of Alfred Hitchcock can see clearly that Hitch's cinematic eye was present almost from the start. He was a bold storyteller from frame one of *The Lodger*. Young, yes; not quite polished, arguably; but unquestionably a director with a vision. Make no mistake, in the first ten years of his career Hitchcock made some fine films worth watching both for enjoyment and for their artistic merits. So no, one would be hard-pressed to argue that all previous roads led to this, at least in absolute terms. But it is fair to argue that *The 39 Steps* represents the first true Alfred Hitchcock masterpiece, a masterpiece created with skills honed over the course of more than a dozen previous motion pictures. They were all worthy in their own right, but here everything comes together as never before.

Taken in the context of this point of his career, *The 39 Steps* is nothing short of a remarkable high point; maybe even a quantum leap forward. This may be the first Hitchcock film one can argue is near flawless, a seamless merging of humor, direction, writing, acting, action, and that most Hitchcockian of ingredients, suspense. It is a harnessing of all the technical skills that came before, and, more importantly, it is in many ways a unique entry at this point in Hitchcock's career. (It wouldn't be for long, as he would return to this formula several more times with great success.) *The 39 Steps*, more than any other film he directed to this point, signals a paradigm shift in what it means to be called a Hitchcock film. *The Lodger* was a forward-looking glimpse into the future; *Blackmail* was a hint at what was to come; *The Man Who Knew Too Much* was the introduction to peak Hitchcockian craft. With *The 39 Steps*, we've now fully entered the world of Alfred Hitchcock. That this film was made by a man of thirty-five is impressive. That this man later went on to make at least a half dozen better films is unequivocally astonishing.

Maybe the first and most notable shift is in the sheer scope of the film. We've traveled before in Hitchcock's work, most recently in *Rich and Strange* and *The Man Who Knew Too Much*, but no previous film offers the sense of journey present here. From the start we're on the move, in constant motion, no longer confined to a few glorified set pieces. *The 39 Steps* has a sense of urgency completely new to the Hitchcock arsenal: a sense that if the movement ever stopped, like a shark, it would die. This pressing urgency is stronger here than we've previously

WHERE'S HITCH?

Hitchcock appears about seven minutes into the film as he walks in front of the bus Richard Hannay and Annabella Smith board.

seen, and will go on to become one of his most powerful weapons.

From the first frame of the opening credits, you get the idea that this is a forward step for Hitchcock. The three-dimensional artwork is different and attractive, and calls to mind similar-looking titles seen in films of the 1940s and 1950s.

And then, as the film opens, we see Richard Hannay purchase a ticket to a show, give the ticket to a ticket taker, and find a seat in a crowded hall. All this takes place before we get a glimpse of his face. This technique tells us that even Richard, while the central character in the story, is not as important as the plot. Hitch understood the value of a strong opening sequence; this is a wonderful way to draw the viewer into the story. The editing here hearkens back to the auction scene in *The Skin Game*. And of course, Mr. Memory commands this sequence as a genuinely unique character. That he later comes back in an unexpected turn of events is creative and fascinating.

As we've already seen several times, Hitchcock makes great use of unleashing chaos in an unexpected location, in this case, the hall within which Mr. Memory performs. We hear gunshots; panic breaks out; Richard meets up with the mysterious Miss Annabella Smith; the plot begins.

And then she's dead, barely fifteen minutes into the film, a stabbing victim in Richard's apartment. Viewers might have assumed Annabella would be the leading female character. But she's not, setting up the wonderful double chase that will occupy the rest of the film: the police chasing after Richard, thinking he's Annabella's killer, and Richard's own chase of the truth he believes is the only way he will retain his freedom.

The editing in *The 39 Steps* is the best we have seen thus far, enhancing the quick pace of the film. Several edits add real punch to the action on the screen. There are many examples of creative editing, for instance, a great bit where we see Richard and Annabella get onto an elevator; after the doors close, there is a wipe cut to simulate the movement of the elevator. Also striking is the choice to cut from the screaming of a charwoman (the building's housekeeper) who had just discovered Annabella's body to the whistle of a train. It's crisply executed and puts an exclamation point on the murder.

The scene where Richard finds himself speaking in front of a large group at a political meeting is both funny and suspenseful. That Richard does well for himself and is able to come through unscathed allows us to respect his wits; we root for his eventual discovery of the truth.

Of course, we would not root for our heroes if they were unlikable; that is not an issue here. Both of the leads are excellent. Robert Donat (probably best known for his role as the titular character in the excellent 1939 film *Goodbye, Mr. Chips*) and Madeleine Carroll, who plays Pamela, the young lady who gets caught up in Richard's flight, are engaging, funny, and believable, and they have terrific chemistry. The famous scene where Richard and Pamela are handcuffed together works wonderfully thanks to this chemistry. It's funny, especially when Richard plays up the idea he actually *is* a murderer.

Hitchcock again made use of a MacGuffin in *The 39 Steps*. Hitchcock loved the MacGuffin, an unseen driver of action completely superfluous to the viewer but vitally important to the characters. This time it's the secret the foreign agents are after. We learn what the secret is at the end, but the contents of said secret are never of concern to the viewer. All we care about is Richard's proving his innocence.

Also new to the Hitchcock repertoire is the idea of escape being the focal point of a film. We've had chases and we've had escapes, but they were always high points, climaxes to a building plot. Here the chase *is* the film. Richard Hannay is on the run almost from the start, evading law enforcement officers and suspicious civilians and shadowy spies. The plot is revealed through the danger Richard faces or while our hero is running for his life. It's a theme that would from this point forward appear again and again in Hitchcock's films: Flight, evasion, fear of capture, being on the run. The climactic chase that finished off *Blackmail* was an impressive early foray into ground he would cover many times in years to come, but never before had he devoted an entire film simply to getting away. Here, he does. And it works in spades. This is important not simply because it makes for exciting cinema, but because it helped him craft the most powerful tool in his arsenal: suspense. This makes *The 39 Steps* truly special.

Hitch tapped into something here, a sense of foreboding and of teetering on the brink of disaster he would find worked not just for his "chase" pictures, but for film after film after film. That heart-stopping sense of being on the edge of capture would later become an absolutely essential part of his work. Whether or not his pictures involve literal chases, Hitch's films from this point forward have an urgent sense of pursuit. Wrapped up in *The 39 Steps'* film-long on-the-run sequence is a new level of suspense and a new dynamic of tension building we simply haven't seen from Hitchcock before. There were previous hints of it, to be sure, but here it all comes into focus for the first time. Suddenly he could not only make us hold our breath, he could make us hold our breath for the entire length of a film. Our respites are brief and fleeting, with only an incredibly humorous (and rather racy for its time) scene in a hotel to let us catch our breath.

About that scene in the hotel. That classic scene. That wonderful scene. Richard Hannay and Pamela are handcuffed together, hiding in a room they have just rented after having fled from apparent spies. Though they pretend they are newlyweds, the fact is, they hate one another. She thinks he's a criminal. He just wants to clear his name. Cold, wet, tired, and in desperate need of sleep, it's all they can do to not strangle one another. This awkward situation is mined for movie magic. The first bits of comedy since the opening scenes reach the screen—just in time, after the nonstop action that came before—and it's played to perfection by Donat and Carroll. Lots of innuendo, some playful physical humor, and dialogue witty enough to be

Robert Donat silences Madeleine Carroll in *The 39 Steps*. (Gaumont Pictures/Photofest © Gaumont Pictures)

funny and straight enough to be taken seriously. The scene gives the film a much-needed chance to settle down and breathe, injecting a quick dose of humor at just the right time. And it is humor with a purpose, because here is where the two leads finally come together and join forces to bring the central conflict of the film to a close.

For all *The 39 Steps* does that is new and fresh in the world of Hitchcock films, it brings to the table even more that is familiar in a form more refined and polished than we've seen thus far. From a technical standpoint, this film is a British standout. The rear projection work is impeccable, the cinematography is excellent, and Hitch's distinctive touches are all over. Witness the fabulous opening scene. We're in a music hall, with a rowdy and raucous crowd on hand to enjoy the entertainment. When Mr. Memory, the man around which the whole film turns, comes on-stage to give his performance of dazzling feats of the mind, we haven't yet been introduced to our leading man. The camera cuts and pans its way around the audience as Memory works with the crowd. Shouts, catcalls, and one-liners are cackled from the drunken crowd. We're introduced to one, two, three, four characters. More. And then, Hitch artfully brings both Richard, who the audience will follow for the rest of film, and Memory, who will ultimately (and unexpectedly) bring the proceedings to a close, together on the screen in a small moment of cinematic synchronicity that reveals itself to be a tease only upon second viewing. A wonderful piece of work . . . and it's only the opening scene.

There is a lot to recommend when it comes to the masterful way the drama unfolds and the suspenseful way the action builds. Each sequence efficiently leads us to the next. Each is laced with an important dynamic for the film. Whether suspense, drama, thrills, or mystery, Hitch finds a way to get it into the story in the most effective way possible. Never awkward, never forced. Quick. Tidy. Without a wasted frame. A near flawless thriller.

After ten years and some very strong films, suddenly Alfred Hitchcock found his stride in *The 39 Steps*. He found a place where his unique cinematic language could thrive.

Now the ride truly begins.

CONCLUSION

The 39 Steps is nothing short of a masterpiece. It offers all of the traditional Hitchcockian themes in a tight, tense, and thrilling package filled with great humor. This is a must-see film, and it's easy to see why. Here marks Hitchcock's real start as a master of the directorial craft. And he is only just beginning.

HITCHCOCKIAN THEMES

Blonde Leading Lady · Chaos in an Unexpected Location · Handcuffed Man and Woman · MacGuffin · Man (or Woman) on the Run · Murder · Music Plays a Role in Plot · Spy Syndicate · Trains · Wrongly Accused

THINGS TO LOOK FOR

- The editing, particularly in the Mr. Memory scene.
- Strong use of rear projection techniques.

TRIVIA/FUN STUFF

✦ Sixty-two sheep were brought to a sound stage to film the sheep sequence. The sheep ate the bushes and plants that had also been brought to the stage. This necessitated additional plants to be brought in from a local nursery.

DVD RELEASES

RELEASE: Criterion Collection (1999)
RATING: *****

EXTRAS: Commentary by Hitchcock scholar Marian Keane; complete 1937 *Lux Radio Theatre* adaptation; *The Art of Film: Vintage Hitchcock* documentary; 1935 press book excerpts; production drawings.

NOTES: Priced much higher than most British-period releases. Also available as part of the out-of-print boxed set *Wrong Men & Notorious Women*.

RELEASE: Criterion (2009)
(Dolby Digital 2.0 Mono, 1.33:1 Black & White)
RATING: ****

RELEASE: Cobra Entertainment LLC (2011)
(Dolby Digital 2.0 Mono, 1.33:1 Black & White)
RATING: ***1/2

RELEASE: Desert Island Films (2011)
(Dolby Digital 2.0 Mono, 1.33:1 Black & White)
RATING: ***

RELEASE: Osiris Entertainment (2011)
(Dolby Digital 2.0 Mono, 1.33:1 Black & White)
RATING: ***

RELEASE: Big D Films (2009)
(Dolby Digital 2.0 Mono, 1.33:1 Black & White)
RATING: ***

RELEASE: Synergy Ent (2009)
(Dolby Digital 2.0 Mono, 1.33:1 Black & White)
RATING: ***

RELEASE: BCI/Sunset Home Visual Entertainment (SHE; 2005)
(Dolby Digital 2.0 Mono, 1.33:1 Black & White)
RATING: ***

NOTES: Part of a set with eight other Hitchcock films, *The Essential Alfred Hitchcock Collection.*

RELEASE: Delta (2001)
(Dolby Digital 2.0 Mono, 1.33:1 Black & White)
RATING: ***

NOTES: Part of the *Alfred Hitchcock: The Early Years* boxed set.

RELEASE: Laserlight (1999)
(Dolby Digital 2.0 Mono, 1.33:1 Black & White)
RATING: ***

NOTES: Available as a stand-alone or as part of *The Collection* boxed set.

RELEASE: RCF (2008)
(Dolby Digital 2.0 Mono, 1.33:1 Black & White)
RATING: **1/2

RELEASE: Diamond Entertainment Corp. (2001)
(Dolby Digital 2.0 Mono, 1.33:1 Black & White)
RATING: **1/2

RELEASE: Whirlwind Media (2001)
(Dolby Digital 2.0 Mono, 1.33:1 Black & White)
RATING: **

NOTES: Packaged with *The Lady Vanishes.* Avoid.

Secret Agent
(1936)

FILM FACTS

PRODUCTION YEAR: 1935
RELEASE DATES: May 1936 (UK); June 15, 1936 (U.S.)
STUDIO: Gaumont British Picture Corporation
FILMING LOCATIONS: Frutigen, Switzerland; London, England
PRESENTATION/ASPECT RATIO: Black & White/1.37:1

SYNOPSIS

When novelist Edgar Brodie (John Gielgud) returns home to Britain after
World War I, the last thing he expects is to find that the British government has falsely reported him dead. But so it has. Brodie is asked by the
government to change his name and go to Switzerland to track down a German agent. Traveling as Richard Ashenden, he meets up with Elsa Carring-
ton (Madeleine Carroll), and then is caught up in a whirlwind of intrigue,
drama, and endlessly shifting sides in a clash of spies.

IMPRESSIONS

Secret Agent is an excellent follow-up to *The 39 Steps* for Alfred Hitchcock.
The earlier film is likely the highest achievement of his British career, but

Secret Agent is not far behind. It again contains innumerable Hitchcockian elements, and is conceived and executed in such a way that the viewer is treated to a great combination of drama, suspense, intrigue, adventure, mystery, and comedy.

It is easy to see why this story, based on the novel *Ashenden* by W. Somerset Maugham, appealed to Hitchcock. Throughout his career, but particularly during this period, he was fascinated by stories of spies, counterspies, double agents, and secret agents. In this film, virtually every character is something of a secret agent. Nobody is quite what he seems. Ashenden is actually the novelist Edgar Brodie; The General, who claims to be Mexican, is neither a general nor Mexican; Elsa is not really Ashenden's wife; and Robert Marvin isn't really the innocent American he would have everyone believe. The juxtaposition of all these characters makes the film. What are their motives? What are they striving for? What drives them?

WHERE'S HITCH?
Yet another early Hitchcock film that does not feature a cameo.

To play these great characters, Hitchcock assembled a terrific cast, perhaps the best of all his British films. The legendary John Gielgud, the never less than amazing Peter Lorre (*The Man Who Knew Too Much*), Madeleine Carroll (*The 39 Steps*), and Robert Young (who would later become famous for his roles in *Father Knows Best* and *Marcus Welby, M.D.*). Each of these accomplished actors brought something unique to the table and they all made these parts their own.

At this point in his career, Alfred Hitchcock began to hit his stride, finding the realm of film in which he was most comfortable. Put someone in danger or give someone a task riddled with questions, moral or otherwise; set in motion events that force your protagonist to keep one step ahead of said events (or, in many cases, to be swallowed up by them); tease the audience for ninety minutes or so with plot twists and suspense; and pay it off with a grand conclusion. Sounds like formula. Maybe it is formula. But Alfred Hitchcock rarely made it anything less than entertaining. Of course, he had not yet perfected the technique, even during this excellent stretch of his career. His British budgets paled in comparison to what he would later enjoy in America, he had not yet developed the level of script control he would enjoy later in his career, and he was still obliged to churn out two (and sometimes more) films a year, all factors that limited his ability to fully realize his talents.

Percy Marmont, Peter Lorre, and John Gielgud in *Secret Agent*. (Gaumont/Photofest © Gaumont)

At a mere eighty-eight minutes, *Secret Agent* doesn't waste much time pushing its story forward. This is hardly unusual for this period; Hitchcock's running times routinely came in under ninety minutes, and rare was the atmosphere building that later became common in his best work. This is hardly a bad thing. Despite being more cerebral than the action-oriented *The 39 Steps*, *Secret Agent* rips along at a steady, quick pace, helped along by the superb ensemble cast.

The dialogue in *Secret Agent* is particularly noteworthy, not because it is brimming with memorable lines, but because it is essential in illustrating the world these people occupy. The language used is intentionally difficult to understand, reflecting the agents' need to speak in code. It is not so much that the dialogue is difficult for the *viewer* to understand, but that it's troublesome for the *characters*. Language barriers ensure that character interactions are laced with confusion and awkwardness. This also allows for moments of humor, such as when Marvin is talking to Elsa in front of the Swiss coachman, who obviously cannot understand when he says, "Look at that nose. I bet you could squeeze it and get a whole quart of whiskey out of it." *Secret Agent* has the elegant charm and playful humor of later films like *To Catch a Thief*, with attractive people delivering clever dialogue while dressed to impress. They masterfully turn phrases and slip innuendo into seemingly innocuous talk.

There are several likeable story elements portrayed in *Secret Agent*. The hero of the story, Ashenden, is given an unsavory task to complete—killing a man—but, out of loyalty to his country, he follows through. But the wrong man is killed, and we learn that the person they really should have been after was Marvin. This twist adds punch to the conclusion of the film.

While *Secret Agent* is satisfying, it's not entirely perfect. The one great loss is—ironically enough, given Hitchcock's unofficial title in the world of film—the lack of deep suspense. The characters are enjoyable and intriguing, the story largely interesting, and the set pieces outstanding, but it lacks that edge-of-your-seat feeling that makes the best Hitchcock films so special. This is a relatively minor complaint, but just a few adjustments could have elevated *Secret Agent* to among Hitch's best.

CONCLUSION

Secret Agent lacks the sense of urgent suspense present in films like *The 39 Steps* and *The Man Who Knew Too Much*, but the witty banter and excellent cast help it overcome these shortcomings to become one of the better films in Hitchcock's British period. Well worth watching, especially for an early glimpse of how Hitch enjoyed casting his dashing heroes in roles that let them live the high life.

HITCHCOCKIAN THEMES

Discussion of Murder at Dinner · Exotic Location · MacGuffin · Murder · Spy Syndicate

THINGS TO LOOK FOR

- The dramatic way the killing of a wrong man is handled—viewed through a telescope, at a distance, with the sad whimpering of a dog setting the tone.

TRIVIA/FUN STUFF

+ The text of Ashenden's resignation letter changes each time it is shown on screen.

DVD RELEASES

RELEASE: Desert Island Films (2011)
(Dolby Digital 2.0 Mono, 1.33:1 Black & White)
RATING: **1/2

RELEASE: Cobra Entertainment (2011)
(Dolby Digital 2.0 Mono, 1.33:1 Black & White)
RATING: **1/2

RELEASE: Synergy Ent (2009)
(Dolby Digital 2.0 Mono, 1.33:1 Black & White)
RATING: **1/2

RELEASE: BCI/Sunset Home Visual Entertainment (SHE; 2005)
(Dolby Digital 2.0 Mono, 1.33:1 Black & White)
RATING: **1/2

NOTES: Part of a set with nine other Hitchcock films, *Alfred Hitchcock: Master of Suspense*.

RELEASE: Delta (2001)
(Dolby Digital 2.0 Mono, 1.33:1 Black & White)
RATING: **1/2

NOTES: Available as a stand-alone or as part of the *Alfred Hitchcock: The Early Years* boxed set.

RELEASE: Whirlwind Media (2001)
(Dolby Digital 2.0 Mono, 1.33:1 Black & White)
RATING: **1/2

NOTES: Packaged with *Sabotage*.

RELEASE: Laserlight (1999)
(Dolby Digital 2.0 Mono, 1.33:1 Black & White)
RATING: **1/2

NOTES: Available as a stand-alone or as part of *The Collection* boxed set.

RELEASE: Madacy Entertainment (1998)
(Dolby Digital 2.0 Mono, 1.33:1 Black & White)
RATING: **1/2

NOTES: Available as a stand-alone or as part of *The Alfred Hitchcock Collection*.

RELEASE: Gaumont-British Productions (2010)
(Dolby Digital 2.0 Mono, 1.33:1 Black & White)
RATING: **

RELEASE: Vintage Home Entertainment (2004)
(Dolby Digital 2.0 Mono, 1.33:1 Black & White)
RATING: *

NOTES: Packaged with *The Man Who Knew Too Much* (1934) and *The Lady Vanishes* on the same disc. Avoid.

Sabotage
(1936)

FILM FACTS

PRODUCTION YEAR: 1936
RELEASE DATES: December 1936 (UK); January 11, 1937 (U.S.)
STUDIO: Gaumont British Picture Corporation
FILMING LOCATION: Shepherd's Bush, London, England
PRESENTATION/ASPECT RATIO: Black & White/1.37:1

SYNOPSIS

Karl Anton Verloc (Oskar Homolka), a foreign saboteur intent on bringing terror to London, operates a cinema with his wife (Sylvia Sidney) and her young brother, Steve (Desmond Tester). Neither know of his secret life. Detective Ted Spencer (John Loder) is assigned to observe Verloc's gang from a neighboring shop. The action grows tense when Verloc is assigned by the gang's leader to bomb the metro train.

IMPRESSIONS

Alfred Hitchcock had a way with villains. As his career reached its peak in the 1940s, 1950s, and 1960s, he would give audiences some of the most memorably charming villains ever to grace the screen in films like *Shadow of a Doubt, Strangers on a Train, Psycho,* and *Notorious.* In 1936 Hitch took his fascination with villains—a fascination not yet fully explored at this point in his career—and ran with it, placing the antagonist front and center as *Sabotage*'s male lead. Charming but slithery, stocky but handsome, manipulative but somewhat inept, Karl Anton Verloc is the man of foul deeds around whom the film's plot revolves, the man audiences are asked to both love and hate.

Yes, Hitchcock liked his villains.

Unfortunately, Oskar Homolka isn't exactly given the most compelling narrative in which to shine. The hook—a movie theater operator secretly leading a double life as a foreign saboteur—is thoroughly Hitchcockian, but the execution ultimately falls flat. But the film is far from a failure. In fact, there is a lot to recommend, but that "edge of your seat" feeling is noticeably lacking. Save for an infamous bombing scene (which we will discuss below), there is little tension in a film that should be rife with it. Had that bombing set into motion a thrilling climax, maybe the tone of the whole work would have changed for the better. Instead it serves only to render the ending anticlimactic, an abrupt end to a story that never feels as if it's going somewhere.

> **WHERE'S HITCH?**
>
> Yet another early Hitchcock that does not feature a cameo. Starting with his next film, *Young and Innocent*, Hitchcock appeared in almost all the rest of his films.

Where *Sabotage* triumphs is in Hitchcock's stylistic decisions. Early in the story, London is plunged into darkness thanks to the actions of the foreign saboteurs with whom Verloc works. Here Hitch takes the German-influenced editing of *The Lodger*'s early scenes and takes it to the next level. With well-chosen rapid-fire images we see a bustling city, a massive power outage, the panic of the populace, and the confusion of authority figures. The masterstroke in this editing is how Hitchcock naturally uses focused clips not just to show us the anger and confusion of London's people, but to smoothly bring the audience to the movie theater from which the plot unfolds. We see scenes of how the outage impacts London, scenes during which Sir Alfred sets the tone for the city. From there we move to the street outside a movie theater, where patrons are demanding refunds. At first glance, we're still being shown the chaos caused by the blackout, but what's really happening is that we're meeting the main characters and exploring the film's key location. Effortlessly, Hitchcock puts all the building blocks

The doomed Desmond Tester is given instructions by Oskar Homolka. (Gaumont British/Photofest © Gaumont Pictures)

of the plot in place: a bombing, uneasy authority figures looking for the culprit, and, long before we realize just how important the location is, the place from which the next terrible bombing will originate.

Even more notable is that the strong, effective editing techniques in these opening scenes are not even the best examples of wonderfully executed editing in the film. That honor goes to one of the most controversial sequences in Alfred Hitchcock's career: the accidental killing of a teenage boy by a bomb. In this notorious sequence, Verloc's young brother-in-law, Steve, is asked to deliver a package containing a bomb. The audience knows this; Steve does not. The bomb is set to go off at a specific time, so he must be punctual with his delivery . . . but as teenage boys are prone to do, he is drawn in by distraction after distraction, from sidewalk salesmen to parades and more. With an achingly deliberate, teasing style, Hitch heightens the tension, dragging the sequence out until finally, as Steve sits on a bus with the package, clocks ticking, ticking, ticking around him—boom! The bomb explodes. The bus is destroyed. And the boy is killed.

The stunning death—this was 1936, remember—may have played a big part in the failure of British audiences to fully embrace this film. The scene is frequently cited as having been somewhat controversial in its day.

Many have questioned the reason for killing the boy. After all, he's made to be a sympathetic character. The audience likes this kid and doesn't want to see him killed. Hitchcock himself agreed this story choice was a mistake when he told François Truffaut, "The boy was involved in a situation that got him too much sympathy, so that when the bomb exploded and he was killed, the public was resentful." Hitch went on to say, "The way to handle it would have been for Homolka to kill the boy deliberately, but without showing that on the screen, and then for the wife to avenge her young brother by killing Homolka."[10] This would have been more effective because it would have made Verloc less likeable.

However, all the blame for the film's failure to light a box office fire cannot be laid solely at this scene's feet. While biographer Patrick McGilligan called *Sabotage* a "near masterwork," Hitch himself was closer to the mark when he called his film "a little messy."[11] Despite the strong editing, the film never finds the kind of focus it needs to keep the audience anticipating the next scene. Genuine moments of tension are often bookended by dull stretches. The sum of all these parts is uneven, as if the director wasn't always sure how he wanted to tell his story.

Hitchcock and screenwriter Charles Bennett made several changes to the story, which was adapted from a Joseph Conrad novel called *The Secret Agent* (not to be confused with Hitchcock's previous film, *Secret Agent*). The most important change from Conrad's novel is the setting. In the novel, Verloc's business was as a tobacconist; here he's the operator of a movie theater. This decision offers more storytelling choices for Hitchcock, and he uses this to his advantage. For example, the use of the Disney cartoon *Who Killed Cock Robin?* is an inspired choice, the murder of the cartoon bird reflecting the murder in *Sabotage*.

At this point it became a trend for Hitchcock to use what he referred to as a MacGuffin, a plot point important only because of its importance to the characters. As also seen in *The Man Who Knew Too Much*, *The 39 Steps*, and *Secret Agent*, all of which had plots centered on the actions of spies and secret agents, the viewer is not privy to the motivations of Verloc and his associates. It is enough to simply know they want to inflict chaos on the residents of London. The viewer is left in the dark about what is driving the villains, discovering only at the end that *why* these people are doing things is far less interesting than *what* they are doing. It's a critical element in so much of Hitchcock's art, and also goes a long way toward helping us understand Hitch as a man. He was always more interested in the strange things people did than in why they did what they did. One sees examples of this behavior in almost all of Hitchcock's films from this point forward.

Could Hitchcock's well-documented troubles with actress Sylvia Sidney (credited here as Sylvia Sydney) have contributed to the seeming lack of focus here? After all, she vociferously fought many of Hitch's directorial demands. Neither had flattering things to say about the other, with Sidney even decades later more than happy to tell interviewers about her dire experience working with Hitchcock. But such troubles were far from unusual for Hitch, who had a reputation among some as being difficult to work with. (Just as many, including notable superstars like James Stewart and Ingrid Bergman, had nothing but praise for Hitchcock's work style.)

It certainly does not help the film's cause that the villain is a more sympathetic character than the protagonist. Despite being responsible for a young boy's death, Verloc is likeable. He's an engaging character, much more so than the detective. It's not so much a problem that he's an intriguing and likeable character; what film viewer doesn't love a charismatic criminal? The problem is that the detective is positioned to make a play for Mrs. Verloc, a storytelling decision that doesn't work because the audience grows to like Verloc more than the detective.

In the end, *Sabotage* is a fine thriller that shows flashes of sheer brilliance but pales when set next to the remarkable British work he did immediately before and after. Of course, even the best thriller would look pretty tame when surrounded by films like *The 39 Steps*, *The Man Who Knew Too Much*, and the forthcoming *Young and Innocent* and *The Lady Vanishes*.

Yet let none of this discourage a viewing, because while the sum of the parts doesn't quite add up, those parts are well worth watching as a study in how Hitchcock used dynamic editing to create mood, set tone, and build tension.

CONCLUSION

Sabotage is at times an enjoyable film with a few strong artistic decisions, but is ultimately a disappointing experience thanks to some flaws that are difficult to ignore. It lacks suspense and suffers from some questionable story choices. While worth seeing, *Sabotage* is not a must-see Hitchcock film.

HITCHCOCKIAN THEMES

Chaos in an Unexpected Location · Dark Secret · Murder · Spy Syndicate

THINGS TO LOOK FOR

- The terrific manner in which Hitchcock slowly increases tension before the bus bombing.
- The clever use of the Disney cartoon *Who Killed Cock Robin?* as a symbol for murder.

TRIVIA/FUN STUFF

- ✦ *Sabotage* is based on a Joseph Conrad novel called The *Secret Agent*. Verloc is a tobacconist in the novel, but operates a cinema in the film. Hitchcock directed an unrelated film called *Secret Agent*, which was released earlier in 1936.
- ✦ Robert Donat, who played the lead in *The 39 Steps*, was the original choice to play the detective, but Donat was unable to secure release from his contract to another studio.

DVD RELEASES

RELEASE: MGM (2008)
(1.33:1 Black & White)
RATING: ****

EXTRAS: Commentary with film historian Leonard Leff; Peter Bogdanovich interviews Hitchcock; restoration comparison; still gallery; trailer farm.
NOTES: Part of a set with seven other Hitchcock films, *Alfred Hitchcock: Premiere Collection*.

RELEASE: Cobra Entertainment LLC (2011)
(Dolby Digital 2.0 Mono, 1.33:1 Black & White)
RATING: ***
NOTES: Packaged along with *The Lodger*.

Release: Gaumont British Picture Corporation (2011)
(Dolby Digital 2.0 Mono, 1.33:1 Black & White)
Rating: **1/2

Release: Synergy Ent (2009)
(Dolby Digital 2.0 Mono, 1.33:1 Black & White)
Rating: **1/2

Release: BCI/Sunset Home Visual Entertainment (SHE; 2005)
(Dolby Digital 2.0 Mono, 1.33:1 Black & White)
Rating: **1/2

Notes: Part of a set with nine other Hitchcock films, *Alfred Hitchcock: Master of Suspense.*

Release: Delta (2001)
(Dolby Digital 2.0 Mono, 1.33:1 Black & White)
Rating: **1/2

Notes: Part of the *Alfred Hitchcock: The Early Years* boxed set.

Release: Whirlwind Media (2001)
(Dolby Digital 2.0 Mono, 1.33:1 Black & White)
Rating: **1/2

Notes: Packaged with *Secret Agent.* Avoid.

Release: Laserlight (1999)
(Dolby Digital 2.0 Mono, 1.33:1 Black & White)
Rating: **1/2

Extras: Packaged with *The Lodger.*
Notes: Available with *The Lodger* or as part of *The Collection* boxed set.

Release: Madacy Entertainment (1998)
(Dolby Digital 2.0 Mono, 1.33:1 Black & White)
Rating: **

Notes: Available as a stand-alone disc or as part of a set with seven other Hitchcock films, *Alfred Hitchcock: Premiere Collection.*

Young and Innocent
(1937)

FILM FACTS

PRODUCTION YEAR: 1937
RELEASE DATES: November 1937 (UK); February 10, 1938 (U.S.)
STUDIO: Gaumont British Picture Corporation
FILMING LOCATIONS: Lime Grove Studios, Lime Grove, Shepherd's Bush,
London, England; London, England; Pinewood Studios,
Iver Heath, Buckinghamshire, England
PRESENTATION/ASPECT RATIO: Black & White/1.37:1

SYNOPSIS

When a young actress is murdered, Robert Tisdall (Derrick De Marney) finds her body washed up on the shore. Witnesses who saw him near the corpse mistake him as the culprit. The situation already looks suspicious, and only gets worse. It turns out he knew the victim, and so is charged with the murder. In true Hitchcockian fashion, Robert goes on the run, looking for the vital piece of evidence that will clear his name with the help of the police chief's daughter, Erica Burgoyne (Nova Pilbeam).

IMPRESSIONS

It would be impossible to deny that *Young and Innocent* screams "boilerplate Hitchcock." Witness the setup: A young actress is murdered. Her body washes up on the beach, where it is found by Robert Tisdall, a young man who (we later discover) knew the victim. The situation looks suspicious, he is charged with the murder, and before you can say, "We have seen this before," Tisdall is on the run, looking for the vital piece of evidence that will clear his name.

But don't yawn too soon. While it's true that thematically *Young and Innocent* offers nothing new to Hitchcock's repertoire, and in fact the film is thematically stale when stacked up next to the other "wrong man" films in his career, the movie manages to be the kind of lighthearted romp Hitch did like few other directors. Upbeat, always on the move, by the book but not suffering for it, *Young and Innocent* is a highly underappreciated entry in the Hitchcock canon. It came during a period when Hitchcock's creativity was firing on all cylinders—the first of several such stretches in his career—and has a playful energy that makes it a fun, if not particularly artful, piece of film.

It's only natural to compare *Young and Innocent* with *The 39 Steps*, as so many of the crucial story elements are virtually the same: A smart, resourceful man is wrongfully accused of murder and hits the road to prove his innocence with the help of an initially unwilling young lady. The execution is similar, and the two films evoke the same general feeling of fun and adventure along a tension-filled road to the truth. It's a great formula. No wonder Hitchcock chose such a similar project.

What stand out as the greatest strength of *Young and Innocent* are its two leads. Nova Pilbeam's Erica Burgoyne and Derrick De Marney's Robert Tisdall are beautiful together, creating a likeable team the viewer cannot help but root for. Nothing else about the movie would work if not for these two.

> **WHERE'S HITCH?**
>
> One of his most memorable cameos: As Robert Tisdall is being taken from the police station, Hitchcock appears just outside the station door as a hapless photographer with a terribly small camera.

Robert is charming, witty, and innocent. Erica is beautiful, intelligent, and capable. What's not to like? That there is never a question of Derrick's innocence is superfluous, because the viewer is squarely on Derrick's side from the beginning.

In something of a break from the last few Hitchcock films, *Young and Innocent* features no spies, spy rings, or secret agents. However, it does contain another, older Hitchcock standard: murder. We don't actually see the

Nova Pilbeam sleeps as danger lurks. (Gaumont British Picture Corporation of America/Photofest © Gaumont British Picture Corporation of America)

murder that sets the film's events in motion, but the discovery of a body washing up on the beach was certainly a striking image for a film released in 1937. Hitch was always one to push the boundaries of what was socially acceptable, constantly seeking new ways to illustrate the distasteful.

As was the case with *The 39 Steps*, almost the entire story of *Young and Innocent* is a lengthy chase sequence. We take a jaunt through the English countryside (this time in an automobile rather than on foot), peer in on a frantic fight in a dingy café that trumps the chair-throwing scuffle of *The Man Who Knew Too Much*, watch as a car narrowly avoids being smashed to pieces by a speeding train, and stand by as that same car plunges into the collapsing floor of an abandoned mine. But the execution isn't nearly as tight in this film. Where *The 39 Steps* featured one tense moment after another, *Young and Innocent* isn't as consistent, bogged down in several places by slow segments during which little is done to advance the plot. There are some exciting and tense moments, yes, but the pacing simply isn't on the same level as the earlier classic.

Young and Innocent is at times uneven. Unsteady. While Hitch repeated the formula of *The 39 Steps*, he was unable to recapture the tempo. On more than one occasion the plot's forward motion inexplicably grinds to a halt—and not the kind of quiet reprise that allows the audience to catch its breath, as we see in the earlier film. This is most evident in the later portions of the story. Just as the climax should be kicking into gear, we experience a lengthy slowdown. Robert has turned himself in to the police, while his female cohort, Erica, mopes about with a vagrant, Old Will. They want desperately to find the man who holds this film's MacGuffin—a jacket and belt that would prove Robert's innocence—but there isn't much they can do other than sit around. Which is just what they do.

That said, *Young and Innocent* redeems itself with one of the most ostentatious shots not just of this period, but of Hitch's entire career. It's a flexing of the camera's muscle unfortunately overlooked because it comes not at the end of a thrilling carnival ride of suspense, but at the end of an anticlimactic, low-key third act during which much of the suspense of the previous two acts evaporates. Too bad, because this shot is as bold and daring in its execution as any other in Hitchcock's entire catalog. And that's no exaggeration.

We begin with Erica and Old Will entering a luxurious hotel, searching for the man who could vindicate Robert. The camera sweeps right, out of the lobby, "through" a wall and into a crowded ballroom, to the wide shot of the partygoers within. Dozens of extras. Many costumes. A grand presentation. But the sweeping look at the gathered revelers is not enough. Now the camera pushes into the crowd, gliding over their heads, deeper into the ballroom. We coast in, focusing now on the band at the rear of the festivities. They come into frame, beginning to fill up the screen: a classic swing band jamming out a tune. But the camera doesn't stop moving. It keeps pushing forward, past the band members, until we're standing among them. Now it focuses on the drummer. And once on the drummer, it continues, getting closer. Closer. Onto his face. And then zooming into his eyes. Closer and closer. So close, even Sergio Leone would feel claustrophobic. And finally, Hitch reveals what we've been waiting for, the hint he dropped in the film's very first scene.

We have found the real killer.

Even now, a shot like this would be an eye-opener. That Hitchcock did it in 1937 in a seemingly throwaway thriller speaks volumes about his boldness and is a testament to his creative vision.

It's interesting to note that *Young and Innocent*, like so many other Hitchcock films, features police and authority figures that are, to put it kindly, bumbling. The police are rarely portrayed in a thoroughly positive light in

Hitch's work. He famously told a story about an incident during which his father, after Hitch had done something wrong, allegedly left him in a jail overnight. He used this story to explain his fear of the police. Whether this was a true story, a complete fabrication, or something in between, nobody can say, but it seems in place with the depiction of police in his films. As Sir Alfred himself said, "I'm not against the police; I'm just afraid of them."[12]

A full dozen years into his directorial career, it is obvious the Master of Suspense was enjoying supreme confidence in his abilities. Everything about the last four or five films moved toward a fully realized Alfred Hitchcock. Here was a man with a unique vision and the ability to bring that vision to the screen. It's no wonder that near the end of his British period, Hollywood producers were stumbling over one another to import the Hitchcock talent.

CONCLUSION

Underappreciated? Maybe. By the book? Unquestionably. Flawed? Undoubtedly. But there remains a lot to recommend about *Young and Innocent*. It is in many ways strikingly similar to Hitch's earlier *The 39 Steps*, but while there are shared thematic elements between the two, it would be unfair to say the latter is simply a retread of the former. This is a playful, fun adventure that came during the height of Hitchcock's British period.

HITCHCOCKIAN THEMES

Blonde Leading Lady • Chaos in an Unexpected Location • Handcuffed Man and Woman • Ineffectual Authority Figures • MacGuffin • Man (or Woman) on the Run • Murder • Music Plays a Role in Plot • Trains • Woman Screaming Directly at Camera • Wrongly Accused

THINGS TO LOOK FOR

- The surprisingly grim scene during which a body washes up on the beach. During this same scene, we see bird imagery Hitchcock would revisit decades later.
- Hitch's bold, long-take push-in shot near the end of the film that takes the viewer from outside a ballroom into a deep close-up of a drummer's eyes.

- Nova Pilbeam having "grown up" since *The Man Who Knew Too Much* (1934). Here she plays a woman, not a child.
- Hitchcock's almost Keystone Kops–like treatment of police officers

---

TRIVIA/FUN STUFF

✦ The film received a dire assessment by some studio bosses, who thought it was a low point in Hitchcock's career. Yet other studio previews resulted in great praise and helped to draw increasing attention from American studios.

DVD RELEASES

RELEASE: MGM (2008)
(1.33:1 Black & White)
RATING: ****

EXTRAS: Commentary with film historians Stephen Rebello and Bill Krohn; isolated music and effects track; Peter Bogdanovich interviews Hitchcock; François Truffaut interviews Hitchcock; restoration comparison; trailers; still galleries.
NOTES: Part of a set with seven other Hitchcock films, *Alfred Hitchcock: Premiere Collection*.

RELEASE: Desert Island Films (2011)
(Dolby Digital 2.0 Mono, 1.33:1 Black & White)
RATING: **1/2

RELEASE: BCI/Sunset Home Visual Entertainment (SHE; 2005)
(Dolby Digital 2.0 Mono, 1.33:1 Black & White)
RATING: **1/2

EXTRAS: Episode of *Alfred Hitchcock Presents*, "The Sorcerer's Apprentice."
NOTES: Part of a set with nine other Hitchcock films, *Alfred Hitchcock: Master of Suspense*.

RELEASE: Alpha Video (2002)
(Dolby Digital 2.0 Mono, 1.33:1 Black & White)
RATING: **1/2

RELEASE: Delta (2001)
(Dolby Digital 2.0 Mono, 1.33:1 Black & White)
RATING: **1/2

NOTES: Available as a stand-alone disc or as part of a set with seven other Hitchcock films, *Alfred Hitchcock: Premiere Collection.*

RELEASE: Whirlwind Media (2001)
(Dolby Digital 2.0 Mono, 1.33:1 Black & White)
RATING: **1/2

NOTES: Packaged with *The Man Who Knew Too Much* (1934). Avoid.

RELEASE: Laserlight (1999)
(Dolby Digital 2.0 Mono, 1.33:1 Black & White)
RATING: **1/2

EXTRAS: Episode of *Alfred Hitchcock Presents*, "The Cheney Vase."
NOTES: Available as a stand-alone or as part of *The Collection* boxed set.

RELEASE: Synergy Ent (2009)
(Dolby Digital 2.0 Mono, 1.33:1 Black & White)
RATING: **

The Lady Vanishes
(1938)

FILM FACTS

PRODUCTION YEAR: 1937
RELEASE DATES: December 25, 1938 (UK); November 1, 1938 (U.S.)
STUDIO: Gainsborough Pictures
FILMING LOCATION: London, England
PRESENTATION/ASPECT RATIO: Black & White/1.37:1

SYNOPSIS

When severe weather delays their trip, passengers on a trans-European train are forced to spend the night in a small village hotel. There, Iris Henderson (Margaret Lockwood) meets a kindly governess named Miss Froy (Dame May Whitty). Shortly after their travel resumes, Miss Froy disappears from the train. With the help of musician Gilbert (Michael Redgrave), Iris attempts to find her new friend, only to find that the other passengers claim Miss Froy was never on the train at all—and, in fact, that she never existed in the first place.

IMPRESSIONS

It would not be entirely unfair to suggest that his British period was essentially a testing ground for Hitchcock's genius, a time during which he tried new ideas to see how well they worked on screen, developed techniques that would become mainstays in his filmmaking arsenal, and worked out the philosophies that would serve as building blocks for the superior filmmaking to come. It also would not be unfair to argue that *The Lady Vanishes*, among his best British films, encapsulates all of these things in one neat, clean, and highly entertaining package.

From playful humor to witty banter to mounting suspense to thrilling action, *The Lady Vanishes* is in many ways a showcase of all Hitchcock's British period has to offer. Very few, if any, are better examples of Hitch's broad directorial range than *The Lady Vanishes*.

What we have here is really pretty simple: Iris Henderson's search for her new friend, who seemingly disappears without a trace from the train they are traveling on, uncovers a conspiracy by—you guessed it—spies and foreign agents. But this simple setup is far from simple in execution.

One reads a lot about classic three-act structure and what it means in storytelling. In *The Lady Vanishes*, the three-act structure cannot be more obvious, with the distinctions between each almost serving to divide the movie into three separate (and unique) films. The feel of the first act is very much at odds with the second, which itself feels remarkably dissimilar from the third. It

> **WHERE'S HITCH?**
>
> Near the end of the film, Hitchcock appears smoking a cigarette while walking across the screen at the train station.

works, despite the seeming lack of continuity, largely because Hitch knows exactly which elements to carry over from the previous act.

In act one, Hitchcock's playful side is on display. The humor is abundant, both in the kind of witty wordplay we saw in *Secret Agent* and in the slapstick physical humor of his silent film *The Farmer's Wife*. Hitch uses that humor to ease the audience into a sense of comfort. All is well with the world. It's a zany place with strange happenings and people, but the heart of things is light and cheerful. Secondly, and, in the long run, more importantly, he uses the first act to set up the key characters of the suspense drama that will follow.

And what an ensemble it is. This is a terrific cast featuring a wide array of quirky characters, many of them playing an important role in the story. Iris and Gilbert are obviously the central characters, but this is very much an ensemble piece. Hitchcock was not known for sprawling ensembles, but it is evident here that he was thoroughly comfortable; he effortlessly cut from one

Michael Redgrave and Margaret Lockwood encounter Dame May Whitty. (Gaumont British Picture Corporation of America/Photofest © Gaumont British Picture Corporation of America)

character moment to another with nary a stumble. It reminds one of the great ensemble director Robert Altman. This is a testament to the great adaptive nature of Hitch's directorial skills. Yet despite all these introductions, in this first act it's not even clear who the main characters are intended to be.

During this portion of Hitch's career, it had become almost standard practice to introduce the protagonist in an elusive fashion. Such is the case here. Among the first people we see is the lady who will vanish, but she doesn't say a word, walking off the set just seconds after her entrance. The audience is then treated to a frantic and scattered barrage of character introductions: the couple on holiday with something to hide, the two cricket-obsessed friends, the young girl on her way to her wedding, the cheerful cad of a musician, and more. We do not focus on any one group for a lengthy period. Instead, we're given small glimpses of who they are and what they're about. All of this information, in one way or another, will become important in the second and third acts.

Hitchcock is giving us the first-act gun.

This lengthy series of introductions is treated with light humor, some of it slapstick, most of it of the dry British variety. It's not belly-laugh material, but it certainly is fun. Watching Hitchcock let his characters bump their heads on low ceilings and engage in clever pokes and prods is a delight. And coming off a string of spy thrillers, it's downright unexpected.

But at the end of the first act, we are reminded that we're dwelling in Hitchcock's world when, with no warning, a street singer is mysteriously strangled.

It's a curious shift in tone as the film moves into the second act, all the more dramatic and effective because of the predominance of humor in the first. The viewer has settled in comfortably at this point. We appear to be enjoying a delightful little romp, one funny moment after another, when the mood is shaken by this scene of violence. Hitch was becoming a master at contrasting scenes of suspense and tension with moments of humor. At this point in his career, *The Lady Vanishes* is the best example of this.

Act two is where the true suspense comes into play. It is also a brilliant stretch of filmmaking, among the best of Hitchcock's career. Very quickly the myriad threads he tossed out in the first act are drawn together. After boarding the train, the audience gets to know a few characters a bit better with further glimpses into their lives; come to understand that Iris Henderson, the young woman on her way to her wedding, will be our lead; are treated to a series of subtle, well-placed clues that will later become keys to the mystery at the center of the film; and settle into the story. Iris and her new friend, Miss Froy, enjoy a pleasant chat over tea. But things won't be pleasant for long. When Iris falls asleep, the world the audience knew is turned upside down. Iris loses track of Miss Froy—and so do we. The lady, it seems, has vanished. Now we have a mystery on our hands, because none of the other passengers seem to remember Miss Froy existed—or so it seems. A frantic search begins, but no trace of Miss Froy remains save Iris's foggy memory. Finally, even she begins to doubt her own story. How could this be?

How could it be, indeed. The Master of Suspense teases the audience with this over and over, and to great effect. Act two is nothing short of brilliant, one of the best sustained stretches of suspense in Hitch's career. It's a real treat watching as, one after another, he trots out the clues he so carefully planted earlier in the film. A stumble into a cabin on the train. Miss Froy asking for sugar. A packet of tea. A name written on a window.

All seemed so innocent a short while ago. Now they are nothing short of vital.

The way in which Iris's self-doubt is portrayed is so well executed that the viewer, at least on first viewing, is left to wonder if Miss Froy was real or if she really was a figment of Iris's imagination. The effect is not lost in subsequent viewings, either, because we are then better able to appreciate her frustration. This is a crucial sequence. The audience must believe the confusion Iris experiences is real or else the impact of the mystery and its eventual conclusion is lost.

The lady, of course, truly did vanish—but not into thin air. And so enters that key element of 1930s and 1940s Hitchcock: spies.

During act three, action-film Hitch comes out to play. All hell breaks loose. The two leads (the playful musician Gilbert, in a charismatic performance by Michael Redgrave, has by this time joined forces with Iris) find Miss Froy, but also find themselves in a desperate plight as they try to slip her away to safety without being caught by the spies who want her. This, of course, is simply not going to happen—not with Hitchcock as the director. The protagonists are caught, the spies are on to them, and now it's confrontation time.

Here is where all the character building devoted to the supporting cast truly comes to fruition. The characters we met in the previous hour are now holed up in a stopped train, locked down in a shootout with agents from a fictional foreign country. Here, the character traits and quirks we've come to know play out for the climax. A bit of humor. A bit of sacrifice. A stubborn decision that leads to death. All the loose ends are tied together in a train chase and shootout, two of the hallmarks of Hitch's British action. Good fun all around.

Worth noting is how adroitly Hitchcock maneuvers the camera throughout the story. Cinematographer Jack Cox, who previously worked with Hitch on *Number Seventeen*, *Rich and Strange*, *The Skin Game*, *Murder!*, *Juno and the Paycock*, *The Manxman*, *Blackmail*, *The Farmer's Wife*, *Champagne*, and *The Ring*, moves the camera in and out and around the many key characters, helping the narrative meander to its conclusion. It's as if the camera is a character unto itself, and a most voyeuristic character at that.

Throughout *The Lady Vanishes*, Sir Alfred displays a flawless sense of pacing, juggling a huge supporting cast and a mystery set largely on a train with the kind of ease only a master could muster. The film may lack the kind of iconic moments most great Hitchcock's are known for—there may not be a single "wow!" shot with the camera here—but the sum total is pure suspense.

CONCLUSION

The Lady Vanishes is one of Alfred Hitchcock's best British films. A true highlight of the British period that goes a long way to show off the flexibility of Hitch's directorial skills, it is without a doubt a must-see.

HITCHCOCKIAN THEMES

Handcuffed Man and Woman • MacGuffin • Murder • Spy Syndicate • Trains

THINGS TO LOOK FOR

- A wonderfully executed opening sequence, done with miniatures, that efficiently introduces the story as well as the many key characters.
- The famous shot of the nun's full habit and high heels.

TRIVIA/FUN STUFF

✦ The film was shot on a set that measured just ninety feet in length.
✦ The characters of Charters (Basil Radford) and Caldicott (Naunton Wayne) proved so popular they were teamed together on a radio show and in several other films, including *Night Train to Munich* (1940), *Crook's Tour* (1941), and *Millions Like Us* (1943). Directed by Carol Reed, *Night Train to Munich* (available on VHS) also stars Margaret Lockwood. Frank Launder and Sidney Gilliat, screenwriters of *The Lady Vanishes*, also wrote the screenplays for *Night Train to Munich* and *Millions Like Us*.

AWARDS

- New York Film Critics Circle Win: Best Director

DVD RELEASES

RELEASE: Criterion Collection (2-disc set; 2007)
(Dolby Digital 1.0 Mono, 1.33:1 Black & White)
RATING: *****

EXTRAS: New, restored high-definition digital transfer; *Crook's Tour*, a 1941 feature-length film starring Basil Radford and Naunton Wayne, reprising their Charters and Caldicott roles from *The Lady Vanishes*; excerpts from François Truffaut's 1962 audio interview with Alfred Hitchcock; "Mystery Train," a new video essay about Hitchcock and *The Lady Vanishes* by Hitchcock scholar Leonard Leff; stills gallery of behind-the-scenes photos and promotional art; new essays by critic Geoffrey O'Brien and Hitchcock scholar Charles Barr; audio commentary by film historian Bruce Eder (also found on 1998 version).

RELEASE: Criterion Collection (single disc; 1998)
(Dolby Digital 2.0 Mono, 1.33:1 Black & White)
RATING: *****

EXTRAS: Commentary by Hitchcock scholar Bruce Eder.
NOTES: Out of print, replaced by the 2-disc 2007 edition. Also available as part of the out-of-print boxed set *Wrong Men & Notorious Women*.

RELEASE: Desert Island Films (2011)
(Dolby Digital 2.0 Mono, 1.33:1 Black & White)
RATING: ***

RELEASE: Osiris Entertainment (2011)
(Dolby Digital 2.0 Mono, 1.33:1 Black & White)
RATING: ***

RELEASE: Public Domain Films (2008)
(Dolby Digital 2.0 Mono, 1.33:1 Black & White)
RATING: **1/2

RELEASE: BCI/Sunset Home Visual Entertainment (SHE; 2005)
(Dolby Digital 2.0 Mono, 1.33:1 Black & White)
RATING: **1/2

NOTES: Part of a set with nine other Hitchcock films, *Alfred Hitchcock: Master of Suspense*.

RELEASE: Delta (2001)
(Dolby Digital 2.0 Mono, 1.33:1 Black & White)
RATING: **1/2

NOTES: Available with *The 39 Steps* or as part of the *Alfred Hitchcock: The Early Years* boxed set.

RELEASE: Laserlight (1999)
(Dolby Digital 2.0 Mono, 1.33:1 Black & White)
RATING: **1/2

NOTES: Available as a stand-alone or as part of *The Collection* boxed set.

RELEASE: Whirlwind Media (2001)
(Dolby Digital 2.0 Mono, 1.33:1 Black & White)
RATING: **

RELEASE: Vintage Home Entertainment (2004)
(Dolby Digital 2.0 Mono, 1.33:1 Black & White)
RATING: *1/2

NOTES: Packaged with *The Man Who Knew Too Much* (1934) and *Secret Agent* on the same disc. Avoid.

RELEASE: Diamond Entertainment Corp. (2003)
(Dolby Digital 2.0 Mono, 1.33:1 Black & White)
RATING: *1/2

Jamaica Inn
(1939)

FILM FACTS

PRODUCTION YEAR: 1938
RELEASE DATES: May 15, 1939 (UK); October 11, 1939 (U.S.)
STUDIO: Mayflower Pictures Corporation, Ltd.
FILMING LOCATIONS: Elstree Studios, Borehamwood, Hertfordshire, England;
Cornwall, England; Jamaica Inn, Bolventor, Bodmin Moor, Cornwall, England
PRESENTATION/ASPECT RATIO: Black & White/1.37:1

SYNOPSIS

A band of local thugs, holed up in a shadowy place called Jamaica Inn, are causing ships to run ashore so they can be plundered—and the local justice of the peace (Charles Laughton) is secretly behind it all. When a relative (Maureen O'Hara) of the inn's owners comes to visit, she joins forces with a police agent (Leslie Banks) working undercover with the crooks to bring the criminal cartel down.

IMPRESSIONS

Not with a bang, but with a whimper.

This is the end to the British era? Could Hitchcock really end such a strong period with such a downer? Sadly, yes. *Jamaica Inn* is nothing short of a disappointment. It is a real shame Alfred Hitchcock left this as his last British film before continuing on his path to greatness in Hollywood—and *Jamaica Inn* can be considered nothing but a failure. It's uninteresting, poorly constructed, and lacks that great Hitchcockian element: suspense. It is a forgettable costume drama (one of only two in Hitch's output), notable because it was Hitch's last British film and only because it was his last British film.

The primary problem here is that Hitchcock had no desire to make *Jamaica Inn* in the first place. He simply wanted to move on with his career and begin anew in America. With the success of films such as *The Man Who Knew Too Much* and *The 39 Steps*, he was garnering attention in the United States. Hollywood producer David O. Selznick (*Gone with the Wind*, 1939) contacted Hitch during the filming of *The Lady Vanishes*, prompting Hitchcock's first trip to America in August 1937, after filming concluded. There, Hitch and Selznick struck a deal to import the Hitchcock genius to Hollywood. But the deal was not set to begin until April 1939, which meant Hitch had time to make one more British film.

Regrettably, that film became *Jamaica Inn*, based on a novel by Daphne du Maurier (who also penned the stories upon which *Rebecca* and *The Birds* were based). This in and of itself was not a problem. The fact that Hitchcock was not interested in making the film was. Hitch had a habit of letting his work suffer when he lost interest in the subject matter, as we have already seen in both *The Manxman* and *Juno and the Paycock*. Like most people, Hitchcock had difficulty giving his best effort when his mind was somewhere else. In this case, it had already moved abroad. One final British film to fulfill a contract—and a costume drama at that—could have been only one thing to a director on the cusp of a wider world: a terrible bore.

And it shows.

The direction is lazy, the story bereft of drama, and the narrative impossible to care about. Throw in unlikable characters and Hitch's most unimaginative camerawork since *Juno and the Paycock*, and you have a real dud on your hands.

The movie is not a dud just because it fails to compel, either. Films like *Easy Virtue* don't mark high points in compelling cinema, yet throughout his British period Sir Alfred almost always managed to salvage even mediocre films with some interesting directorial flourishes. He further developed his ability to frame a shot (the aforementioned *Easy Virtue*), honed his storytelling technique (*The Farmer's Wife*), discovered ways to create tension and suspense (*Blackmail*), or found editing tricks he would use later to great dramatic effect (*Number Seventeen*). Even his lesser works usually boast a redeeming quality or two that make them worth watching.

One would be hard-pressed to point out a single redeeming quality of *Jamaica Inn*.

It is evident that Hitchcock had great reservations about the story even before filming began. "*Jamaica Inn* was an absurd thing to undertake," he told François Truffaut. "It was completely absurd, because logically, the judge should have entered the scene only at the end of the adventure. He should have carefully avoided the place and made sure he was never seen in the tavern."[13] Hitch was correct in his assessment. Charles Laughton, who also served as one of the producers, insisted that his role as the justice of the peace be expanded from du Maurier's novel. Consequently, the viewer is told the identity of the chief villain within the first twenty minutes of the film, leaving us with no mystery, no suspense, and a cast of largely unlikable characters. In the end, we're left only to wonder what the point of it all was. Hitchcock knew this and struggled to get through the film, knowing greener pastures were on the horizon.

Still, Hitchcock by this time was much more than the very capable director he was in his earliest days. He was a man on the verge of full-blown genius, a fully developed talent with superior directorial skills. That's why—even in a project he sleepwalked through—there are small moments of excellence. The

> **WHERE'S HITCH?**
>
> Hitchcock made no cameo in *Jamaica Inn*.

opening shots, for instance, manage to instill in the viewer a sense of foreboding simply through the strength of the editing, lighting, and composition. (It's too bad that sense of foreboding is wasted on this dull film.) His storytelling is crisp, effortless, and visual. (It's too bad the story it tells is, once again, dull.) And the climax of the film caps elements off with a welcome dose of excitement. Very much mirroring the suicide that finishes off Hitch's *Murder!*, the end of *Jamaica Inn* is thrillingly shot and large in scope. (It's too bad it caps off such a dull film.)

That climactic suicide is the film's sole sequence worth watching. Hitchcock could stage explosive drama like few others. In *Jamaica Inn*, the forgettable story and mostly forgettable cast (Charles Laughton as the fat, wealthy villain Sir Humphrey Pengallan is memorable largely because he's so repugnant in the role) come together in pure Hitchcockian fashion. Sir Humphrey, knowing he has been outed as the brains behind a series of ships being grounded and plundered, panics, climbs the mast of a sailing vessel, and, in front of a large crowd, hurls himself to his death. Only the viewer's relief that the movie is over manages to overwhelm the impact of this well-done sequence. Had it been the finish of a better film, it would be more noteworthy.

Jamaica Inn is one of the few films in the Hitchcock library that are simply not worth the viewer's time. Even those looking to study his artistic development will find few insights here. Uninspired and burdened with a serious story flaw, along with *Juno and the Paycock* this is the worst of what Hitchcock's British period has to offer.

But when all is said and done, *Jamaica Inn* was an artistic failure not because Hitchcock was incapable, but because he simply did not care. And why should he have cared? America waited—and with it the fame, wealth, and recognition he so craved. In less than two years' time, Alfred Hitchcock would finally be regarded as one of the top directors of his day.

CONCLUSION

Jamaica Inn was a major misstep for Alfred Hitchcock, a drab and lifeless film that ranks among his least worthy efforts. It's worth watching only if your goal is to see every Hitchcock-directed film.

HITCHCOCKIAN THEMES

Chaos in an Unexpected Location · Man (or Woman) on the Run · Murder · Suicide/Attempted Suicide · Unwelcome New Woman

THINGS TO LOOK FOR

- The suicide by way of a leap from a high place, not dissimilar to the one that ends *Murder!*
- The moody photography of the opening sequences.

TRIVIA/FUN STUFF

- ✦ This was Alfred Hitchcock's final British film before making his move to Hollywood.
- ✦ *Jamaica Inn* is one of three Hitchcock-directed films based on a work by Daphne du Maurier; the others are *Rebecca* and *The Birds*.

DVD RELEASES

RELEASE: Cobra Entertainment (2011)
(Dolby Digital 2.0 Mono, 1.33:1 Black & White)
RATING: ***

RELEASE: Mayflower Pictures Corporation (2010)
(Dolby Digital 2.0 Mono, 1.33:1 Black & White)
RATING: ***

RELEASE: Triad Productions Corporation (2009)
(Dolby Digital 2.0 Mono, 1.33:1 Black & White)
RATING: **1/2

RELEASE: BCI/Sunset Home Visual Entertainment (SHE; 2005)
(Dolby Digital 2.0 Mono, 1.33:1 Black & White)
RATING: *1/2

NOTES: Part of a set with eight other Hitchcock films, *The Essential Alfred Hitchcock Collection.*

RELEASE: Kino Home Video (2003)
(Dolby Digital 2.0 Mono, 1.33:1 Black & White)
RATING: *1/2

RELEASE: Delta (2001)
(Dolby Digital 2.0 Mono, 1.33:1 Black & White)
RATING: *1/2

EXTRAS: Packaged with *Murder!*
NOTES: Available with *Murder!* or as part of the *Alfred Hitchcock: The Early Years* boxed set.

RELEASE: Laserlight (1999)
(Dolby Digital 2.0 Mono, 1.33:1 Black & White)
RATING: *1/2

NOTES: Available as a stand-alone or as part of *The Collection* boxed set

Rebecca
(1940)

FILM FACTS

PRODUCTION YEAR: 1939
RELEASE DATE: March 27, 1940 (U.S.)
STUDIO: Selznick International Pictures
FILMING LOCATIONS: Big Sur, California; Palos Verdes, California;
Point Lobos State Reserve, California; Selznick Studios,
Hollywood, Los Angeles, California
PRESENTATION/ASPECT RATIO: Black & White/1.37:1

SYNOPSIS

Rebecca tells the story of a woman (Joan Fontaine) who marries well-to-do Maxim de Winter (Laurence Olivier) after meeting him while on vacation with her employer, Mrs. Edythe Van Hopper (Florence Bates). After the nuptials, the new Mrs. de Winter moves in with her husband to Manderley, a palatial estate previously occupied by Rebecca de Winter, Maxim's now-deceased first wife. Manderley is also home to housekeeper Mrs. Danvers (Judith Anderson), who had an uncommonly strong affection for Rebecca. The new bride is not welcome at Manderley. She suffers from irrational fears as well as mistreatment at the hands of the staff. Beneath it all lurks a mystery that continues to haunt the household: the truth of what really happened to the first Mrs. de Winter.

IMPRESSIONS

In a career spanning more than fifty years, there are major turning points worth noting. Eleven years prior to 1940's Academy Award–winning *Rebecca*, it was *Blackmail*, marking Alfred Hitchcock's first foray into sound. Just five years prior, *The 39 Steps* served as the thrilling signal that Hitchcock's genius had arrived. It was in 1940, however, that Hitchcock's journey from excellent director to full-blown legend truly began. With *Rebecca*, Hitchcock's filmmaking maturity was clear, and his status as one of the era's great directors was made even clearer. *Rebecca* marks his entry into Hollywood. No longer would he tarry in the respectable but otherwise obscure backwater of British film.

Alfred Hitchcock, world-renowned director, had arrived.

As the anticlimactic finish to his British period, *Jamaica Inn*, clearly displays, when disinterested in a project Hitchcock was content to coast sleepily through his commitment. But when he had a mind to prove he could do something, no obstacle could stand in his way, —not even the heavy-handed, almost dictatorial control of one of cinema's most influential producers. And in the case of Hitch's American debut, the hands of the producer are just as evident as those of the director.

Rebecca is, when all is said and done, as much a David O. Selznick film as it is an Alfred Hitchcock film. Selznick was the most powerful producer of his time, responsible for a laundry list of successes. The best known of his box office smashes, and the film that forever cemented his legacy, was *Gone with the Wind*.

> **WHERE'S HITCH?**
>
> Hitchcock appears near the end of the film, walking by a phone booth after Favell makes a call.

Among the biggest films ever to come out of Hollywood, it is the best example of a simple truth: When Selznick did something, he did it big. *Gone with the Wind* is one of cinema's most beloved and successful films, but one could argue that Selznick's greater long-term contribution to American cinema was bringing Alfred Hitchcock to the United States. That wasn't his goal, of course. It was, as was so much with Selznick, just business. Knee-deep in the production of his Civil War epic, the powerhouse producer had an obligation to United Artists. He had to deliver a film. What better way to fulfill said obligation than by signing Britain's most acclaimed young director to take control of a major production adapting a hugely popular novel?

The move would net Selznick two straight Academy Awards for Best Picture—*Gone with the Wind* in 1939 and *Rebecca* in 1940—and propel Alfred Hitchcock to a level of acclaim heretofore unseen in his career. For the next quarter century, Hitchcock would go on to fortify his place as one of the greatest directors of all time, sometimes with the oppressive Selznick hanging over him, but more often on his own.

Selznick was a firm believer in faithful novel adaptations. Hitch told François Truffaut, "Selznick had just made *Gone with the Wind*. He had a theory that people who had read the novel would have been upset if had been changed on the screen, and he felt this dictum should also apply to *Rebecca*."[14]

If this was Selznick's philosophy, his choice of Hitchcock for this picture was curious; Hitch already had a history of making drastic story changes in his film adaptations. Their clashes began with something simple: a name. Hitch wanted to name the heroine "Daphne," after writer Daphne du Maurier, but Selznick objected and the character is never named. She's referred to only as "Mrs. de Winter" or "the second Mrs. de Winter." This is an intriguing decision, but it makes sense not so much because it's faithful to the novel, but because the character is more pathetic to the viewer—a necessity if we're to believe in her powerlessness at Manderley—when we cannot even associate her with a name of her own.

Despite Selznick's heavy hand, *Rebecca* is a film Hitchcock very much wanted to make even before coming to America, and it shows. Hitchcock had been a fan of du Maurier's novel and had the opportunity to purchase its film rights during the filming of *The Lady Vanishes*, but failed due to the high price. It would have worked, Selznick or not. Hitch's best work is marked by an almost stifling attention to detail, and such is the case here. Unlike in *Jamaica Inn* (also adapted from a story by du Maurier), Alfred Hitchcock was engaged in his work. He had something to prove, and he was intent on showing the world he was a great filmmaker. When Hitch had something to prove, not even the constant meddling of one of Hollywood's biggest meddlers—and if Selznick was anything, he was a meddler—could prevent him from seeing his vision come to fruition. The result is a moody dreamscape of filmmaking, a mystery that unravels slowly and deliberately. The critics loved it.

Still, this remains in many ways more a Selznick film than a Hitchcock film. To start, this is a rare movie for which Hitch had no real script involvement. On the set, his decisions were frequently second-guessed and ultimately overruled by the producer. And even at the peak of his powers, Hitchcock was not immune to the infamous, lengthy, and cumbersome memos of the nightmarishly controlling Selznick. Sir Alfred, as he did throughout his career, wanted to use the novel upon which *Rebecca* was based as a springboard for his own ideas. Selznick would have none of it. He bought the rights to *Rebecca* to make *Rebecca*, he told Hitchcock—and *Rebecca* is what he would make.

With Alfred Hitchcock at the helm, such a firm stance by a producer could have resulted in an artistic disaster. Notoriously pouty, prone to spite, and tending to abandon interest in a film at a moment's notice, an Alfred Hitchcock of another time and in another situation may have simply thrown in the towel and slammed through a workmanlike but otherwise uninspired directing job. But not here. Not now. He had gotten his big break, he had made it to Hollywood, and he was working on a property that would be scrutinized the world over.

Hitchcock had to make it a winner. And he did.

Du Maurier's story of *Rebecca*—a title character we never actually meet—skillfully explores the tragic uncertainty of a woman living under the shadow of another. Joan Fontaine brought her character to life in a performance that may have been helped by Hitch's cruel decision to tell her that everyone else on the film set hated her. Yet that is exactly the sort of feeling Fontaine had to bring to the screen in the role of the second Mrs. de Winter, new wife of the wealthy widower Maxim de Winter. She pulls it off wonderfully, from the cautious, naive young girl at the start of the film to the uneasy, tormented wife at the end. Hitchcock ensured that not a moment of her performance was wasted.

In a technique we'll see in a number of upcoming Hitchcock films, *Rebecca* begins relatively light, an easy romance that appears destined for storybook status. As it is prone to do in the world of Alfred Hitchcock, however, darkness awaits. Soon, the restless spirit of the deceased Rebecca de Winter begins to haunt Fontaine's every waking moment.

Speaking of the heroine, some time must be spent examining the character and Joan Fontaine's extraordinary portrayal of her. This is the best female acting performance in a Hitchcock production to date, and is certainly one of the film's great strengths. Fontaine brilliantly evokes a naive romantic who devolves into a world of fear and misunderstanding. Fontaine's acting was undoubtedly enhanced by her feelings of being disliked by the rest of the cast. And what acting it was. That Fontaine was not awarded an Academy Award for this work, but was for the following year's inferior performance in *Suspicion* (another Hitchcock film), is unfortunate. It has been suggested that the Academy gave her the latter award as recompense for its

A pensive Joan Fontaine is scrutinized by Judith Anderson. (United Artists/Photofest © United Artists)

failure to acknowledge her work here. *Suspicion* is arguably a better overall film, but Fontaine's work in *Rebecca* is superior.

Rebecca is also fortified by strong performances by Laurence Olivier, Judith Anderson, Florence Bates, and, to a lesser extent, George Sanders. Olivier is understated as Maxim de Winter, but he does an excellent job in portraying the heartbreak and turmoil Max suffered. Anderson is positively chilling in her portrayal of Mrs. Danvers, a woman who desperately didn't want the second Mrs. de Winter in her home. Bates is fantastic as the pompous, egotistical Mrs. Van Hopper. This woman is so unlikable, it's easy to understand why our heroine jumps at the chance to marry a man who doesn't even show her affection—anything to get away from her overbearing employer. And Sanders is strong as Favell, the man with whom the titular Rebecca engaged in extramarital relations. As one of our links to the unseen Rebecca, Favell is easy to dislike because we know he is not a man of good intentions.

Rebecca is a dark film, heavy with foreboding. It's the first Hitchcock film to have the kind of intangible "weight" that so defines later thrillers like *Shadow of a Doubt* and *Strangers on a Train*. Throughout, we are made to feel as if we are on the cusp of some great and terrible revelation. The film succeeds exactly where it needs to—and beyond. Visually, it's rich and luxurious. Here, Selznick's heavy hand is clear; *Gone with the Wind* had instilled in him a great love for high production values. Those production values are on display here, too. The actors also help nail down the mood. The performances are excellent almost across the board. Finally, the sustaining of tension, despite Hitchcock's longest running time to date, falters only at the very end.

As already discussed, *Rebecca* was very much a Selznick picture. He controlled the cast and the sets and provided the crew, but Hitchcock still found his way to impart his artistic genius upon this fine film. As seen many times already, Hitch often began his films with a spectacular opening shot. He doesn't disappoint here. Opening the film, we see a terrific shot under the second Mrs. de Winter's narration. This image, first through a set of gates, then up a meandering drive and settling on the mansion estate of Manderley, is stunning. It sets the tone for the film and introduces the foreboding mansion serving as the centerpiece of the film. That it was done using miniatures makes it all the more impressive.

An excellent yet subtle touch in *Rebecca* is in how Mrs. Danvers is filmed. While we see her moving around the mansion, we never actually see her walking. She simply appears alongside our heroine. She is a cold character to begin with; presenting her in this way makes Mrs. Danvers utterly creepy. The viewer easily identifies and understands why Maxim's new bride is fearful and apprehensive, even if Maxim—and initially our leading lady—does not.

The similarities between this film and Hitchcock's work of twelve years prior, *Easy Virtue*, are striking. Both feature a new bride who moves into her husband's home only to find her presence unwelcome. *Rebecca* is the vastly superior film, but this is largely the result of better source material.

The pacing of *Rebecca* is strong. We initially experience a whirlwind romance. When the action returns to Manderley, the pace slows as we are introduced to our heroine's new world. It continues to tread cautiously as we witness her journey through irrational fear. Despite the intentional deceleration, the pace never drags because, at this point, we're thoroughly engaged. We have to understand her emotional decline, and the only way to do so is to dwell in her fears.

The most glaring weakness of *Rebecca* comes in the film's final act, when we learn the truth about who Rebecca really was, and how and why she died. It runs longer than necessary and, despite the ratcheting up of our heroine's paranoia, there is little suspense in the revelation. An earlier conclusion would have better served the narrative.

Alfred Hitchcock's American debut was a winner in all respects. Right out of the gate, he created one of his best early American films.

Maybe more important than the creative victory was how strongly this film and its follow-up, *Foreign Correspondent* (also nominated for Best Picture in 1940), managed to solidify Hitch's reputation as a legitimate force in the world of directing. No longer would he be the local darling of UK cinema. Alfred Hitchcock now belonged to Hollywood. And that meant he belonged to the world.

In the years to come, the world would belong to Alfred Hitchcock.

CONCLUSION

Rebecca may be a notch below the best of Alfred Hitchcock's films, but it is not far below. This is an excellent film to mark the beginning of his Hollywood career, marking his arrival as one of the world's elite filmmakers.

HITCHCOCKIAN THEMES

Blackmail · Dark Secret · Murder · Suicide/Attempted Suicide · Unwelcome New Woman

THINGS TO LOOK FOR

- The depiction of Mrs. Danvers. She is never shown walking; rather, she appears to glide.
- The stunning opening shot that introduces us to Manderley.

AWARDS

- Academy Award Nominations (11): Best Picture (David O. Selznick, Producer); Best Director; Best Actor in a Leading Role (Laurence Olivier); Best

Actress in a Leading Role (Joan Fontaine); Best Actress in a Supporting Role (Judith Anderson); Best Adapted Screenplay (Robert E. Sherwood and Joan Harrison); Best Film Editing (Hal C. Kern); Best Cinematography, Black-and-White (George Barnes); Best Original Score (Franz Waxman); Best Art Direction, Black-and-White (Lyle R. Wheeler); Best Special Effects (Photographic: Jack Cosgrove; Sound: Arthur Johns)

- Academy Award Wins (2): Best Picture; Best Cinematography, Black-and-White

TRIVIA/FUN STUFF

+ This was Hitchcock's first film after coming to the United States in 1939.
+ Hitchcock wanted to purchase the film rights to *Rebecca* during filming of *The Lady Vanishes*, but the price was too high.
+ The second Mrs. de Winter is never named, just as in the novel.
+ This is the second of three Hitchcock films based on a Daphne du Maurier story. *Jamaica Inn* was the first; *The Birds* would be the third.
+ This was the only Hitchcock-directed film awarded with the Best Picture Academy Award.

DVD RELEASES

RELEASE: Criterion Collection (2001)
(Dolby Digital 2.0 Mono, 1.33:1 Black & White)
RATING: *****

EXTRAS: Commentary by film scholar Leonard J. Leff; isolated music and effects track; screen tests for Vivien Leigh, Anne Baxter, Loretta Young, Margaret Sullavan, and Joan Fontaine; excerpts from Hitchcock's conversations with François Truffaut; interviews with Joan Fontaine and Judith Anderson; behind-the-scenes photographs; production notes; deleted scene excerpts; 1939 test screening questionnaire; easy on *Rebecca* by author Daphne du Maurier; 1940 Academy Awards footage; reissue trailer; three hours of radio adaptations; twenty-two-page booklet.

NOTES: Available as a stand-alone disc or as part of a set with seven other Hitchcock films, *Alfred Hitchcock: Premiere Collection.*

RELEASE: MGM (2008)
(1.33:1 Black & White)
RATING: ****

NOTES: Also part of a set with seven other Hitchcock films, *Alfred Hitchcock: Premiere Collection.*

RELEASE: Anchor Bay Home Video (1999)
(Dolby Digital 2.0 Mono, 1.33:1 Black & White)
RATING: ****

Foreign Correspondent
(1940)

FILM FACTS

PRODUCTION YEAR: 1940
RELEASE DATES: August 16, 1940 (U.S.); October 11, 1940 (UK)
STUDIO: Walter Wanger Productions
FILMING LOCATIONS: Various locations, California
PRESENTATION/ASPECT RATIO: Black & White/1.37:1

SYNOPSIS

When Johnny Jones (Joel McCrea) is tapped for a position as a foreign correspondent, he is asked to change his name to Huntley Haverstock and go
to Europe to get information regarding a diplomat named Van Meer (Albert
Bassermann) and a secret treaty. When Van Meer appears to be publicly
assassinated, Jones/Haverstock has a big story on his hands—a story that
only gets bigger when his pursuit of the killer uncovers a den of spies intent
on thrusting Europe into World War II. All this while he falls head over
heels for a young lady named Carol Fisher (Laraine Day), the daughter of
peace advocate Stephen Fisher (Herbert Marshall). But this is an Alfred
Hitchcock film, which means things are not as they seem. Chases, spies, and
intrigue lead up to a climactic plane crash that stands as one of Hitchcock's
most legendary sequences.

IMPRESSIONS

After working closely with the difficult David O. Selznick on *Rebecca*, Hitchcock was lent to producer Walter Wanger to make a film. Where Selznick was notoriously hands-on and demanding, Wanger opened new doors for Hitchcock, giving him a large budget and the freedom to do pretty much whatever he wanted.

So take some fifteen years of experimentation on British sound stages by a director capable of finding innovative technical solutions to "problems" of his own creation—meaning self-imposed technical hurdles created solely to reach further heights of cinematic greatness. Mix thoroughly with a blockbuster budget and the kind of creative freedom he would not enjoy with Selznick, the legendary powerhouse who brought him to Hollywood. The result? Alfred Hitchcock's first American thrill ride, *Foreign Correspondent*.

It was nominated for Best Picture—but the nomination came in the same year *Rebecca* was nominated. That film eventually won, causing this one, in a sense, to live under that film's shadow. (That *Rebecca* is the more historically significant film for Hitchcock scholars does not help matters.) This is too bad. *Foreign Correspondent* deserves to be better remembered. When set side by side with any of his other adventure thrillers, it shows the director at his most creative.

> **WHERE'S HITCH?**
>
> In one of the easiest cameos to spot, early in the film Hitchcock can be seen strolling next to Jones/Haverstock outside his hotel, reading a newspaper.

What makes *Foreign Correspondent* so great? It starts at the beginning, with a long opening shot that sets up the story. From there, it flows into the introduction of Johnny Jones, who will become Huntley Haverstock. Then it's off to London, where a shocking assassination triggers the film's breakneck sprint through one sequence after another.

While the film is known for its audacious set pieces, notably the windmill sequence and the bombastic airplane crash, it is not the big that makes it work, but the small. *Foreign Correspondent* does not rely on any one of Hitchcock's strengths, but on *all* of them. We've got the spy-driven drama he did so well during his British period, a colossal American budget, and, in what gives the film much of its charm, delightful dialogue of the sort that would later become a hallmark of Hitch's best work.

Johnny Jones is the primary reason the audience gets so wrapped up in the tale. He's an everyman, something of a happy-go-lucky goof, but as

Reporter Joel McCrea watches over Eduardo Cianelli (center) and his coconspirators. (United Artists/Photofest © United Artists)

Hitchcock's first real depiction of a common American he's a man with whom we can identify. Sure, he's oblivious to much of the plot, but he's heroic because he's courageous, patriotic, and caring. The audience wants to be on his side.

The increased budget at Hitchcock's disposal shows in the phenomenal production design. From the opening in New York to the crucial scenes in London, the astounding windmill sequence, and all the way through to the climactic plane crash, the set pieces are top-notch, probably the most consistent of any of Hitchcock's films thus far. The setting for the assassination scene, for instance, is inspired, notably the sea of black umbrellas.

And that windmill sequence is a classic. One may wonder why this part of the story was set inside a windmill. Probably for no other reason than for Hitchcock to show off. That may have been the motivation, but the execution cannot be faulted. It never feels forced, it makes sense, and it becomes crucial to the plot. The cinematography—going in and out, up, down, and around the windmill—is a marvel. Even without sound and outside the context of the story, this sequence would be fascinating to watch. That the plot is driven forward by it is almost the icing on the cake. This is an example of a brilliant filmmaker inspired by great ideas and possessing the talent and the resources to make amazing things happen.

Yet the windmill sequence is not the most breathtaking sequence in the film. That honor belongs to the astounding plane crash, which, despite having been filmed almost seventy years ago with primitive technology, remains an extraordinary visual achievement. The plane's impact with the water was ingeniously achieved with a thin rear projection screen in the cockpit applied to the front of a water tank; the tank was opened and the water gushed through the screen, appearing to flood the plane. In slow motion, you can see the screen break, but at normal speed the effect is indeterminable. A believable scene of the wreckage floating in the ocean immediately follows, the survivors clinging onto one of the plane's wings. It was shot in a studio water tank, but it is so well realized that there's no doubt in the viewer's mind it is actually an ocean. This whole sequence is, without a doubt, one of Hitchcock's best.

But *Foreign Correspondent* is more than just great filmmaking technique. It's also a film filled with terrifically funny dialogue. Writers Charles Bennett and Joan Harrison pull out all the stops with great lines like, "You can't run out on your kidnapper like that." The decision to name one of the key characters "Scott ffolliott" (yes—two lowercase *F*s) is irreverent and silly, yet is sold with a great explanation: "One of my ancestors had his head chopped off by Henry VIII and his wife dropped the capital letter to commemorate it," he says. Robert Benchley deserves credit for some of the dialogue, as Hitchcock allowed him to write his own lines. There's a hilarious bit near the end of the film where ffolliott gives Stebbins a laundry list of things to do. Stebbins acts as if he's taking it all seriously, but when ffolliott leaves, Stebbins says to himself, "Two ham sandwiches on rye bread."

This is typical of the best Hitchcock. Look at any one of the classic films he would make in the years to follow: *Shadow of a Doubt, North by Northwest, Rear Window*. With few exceptions (*Psycho* and *Vertigo*, for instance), the drama is always punctuated with clever, witty dialogue. Certainly humor has not been absent from Hitch's films to this point. We saw plenty of playful, dry humor in his British films—*The Lady Vanishes* and *Young and Innocent*, for example, both tempered their drama with humor—but never quite like this. For maybe the first time (*The Lady Vanishes* is the key British exception), the kind of tempo audiences would come to associate with Hitch dialogue is present. In part emboldened by his leap across the Atlantic, Hitch was becoming increasingly involved with his screenwriters. He asked for the kind of scenarios he would most like to direct (a technique taken to its extreme some nineteen years later with *North by Northwest*) and encouraged writers to do their best. Such was certainly the case here. Joel McCrea and Laraine Day rip through quick, cutting lines. McCrea especially is lively, animated and charming; it's hard to imagine the reserved Gary Cooper, Hitchcock's first choice for the role, in this film. In some exchanges, the clever wordplay is so rapid-fire you'd need multiple viewings to catch it all. This punches up almost every scene, tempers a movie that could be heavy with prewar weight, and breathes life into the characters.

In addition to the great job McCrea does in his part, the rest of the cast—led by Day, Herbert Marshall, George Sanders (seen in *Rebecca*), Albert Basserman, Benchley, and Edmund Gwenn (seen in *The Skin Game* and again in *The Trouble with Harry*)—show great chemistry and charisma. It is impossible to overstate how important the supporting cast is to the finished product. Individually, each is excellent; taken in sum, they elevate this film to greatness.

Notably, Bassermann was nominated for an Academy Award for his role as peaceable diplomat Van Meer, despite having scant minutes of screen time. Figuratively and literally, his final appearance is a dark, gut-wrenching scene with one of the great monologues to appear in a Hitchcock film. Van Meer, stubbornly clinging to the notion of peace, hissing and wheezing, defying those who would make war and telling them with weighty conviction that in the end the good people of the world will cast aside the warmongers. It's so powerful that one wonders why the scene is overlooked when great Hitchcock acting moments are discussed.

Rebecca may have been Hitchcock's first Hollywood film, but *Foreign Correspondent* was certainly his first truly *American* film. The earlier film was set in Britain, with a British cast, and could have easily passed as a British movie, but the latter is undoubtedly American in its cast, style, and message. Hitchcock remained loyal to his roots, but his comfort level with his American cast and crew on *Foreign Correspondent* is evident throughout.

Just two films into his Hollywood career, Hitchcock had already directed two Academy Award nominees for Best Picture, quite the achievement for a foreign-born director. That *Foreign Correspondent* failed to win a single Oscar—not even for editing or cinematography—is a shame. It is a well-regarded movie, but it doesn't receive the high level of praise it deserves. The relative lack of star power of its leads, Joel McCrea and Laraine Day, does not help in this regard. Though popular figures in their day, they are not remembered in the same way as contemporaries like Humphrey Bogart and Bette Davis. Yet despite this lack of star power, *Foreign Correspondent* is one of Hitchcock's top films.

It is difficult to pinpoint why this film is so overlooked. Given a big budget and creative freedom, Hitch was firing on all cylinders, tossing out dramatic set pieces and bold ideas as he never had before. It is arguably the best motion picture to this point in his career. Certainly in its day it was well received. *Foreign Correspondent* thrilled audiences and earned a slew of award nominations, giving Hitch the clout to pursue the kind of projects he wanted to tackle. One can only assume that the strength of the films to come ended up relegating *Foreign Correspondent* to second-tier status.

When viewed in the context of his career, however, it is a huge step forward in the filmmaking career of Alfred Hitchcock, a realization of his skills as a director of suspenseful thrillers that British budgets simply could not afford him. It is a forgotten gem, and one that shines all the more brightly for having been forgotten.

CONCLUSION

Foreign Correspondent is one of Hitchcock's most exciting, underappreciated thrillers, showing the director in peak action/adventure form and boasting some of his most audacious set pieces to date. It's clear that by this point in his career, Hitch had made the suspense thriller something of a science. Superior to almost everything preceding it, *Foreign Correspondent* is a further refinement of the kind of work seen in *Murder!*, *The Man Who Knew Too Much*, and *The 39 Steps*. It's not only worth seeing, it's downright essential viewing.

HITCHCOCKIAN THEMES

Blackmail · Chaos in an Unexpected Location · Climactic Showdown at an Iconic Location · Dark Secret · Exotic Location · Ineffectual Authority Figures · MacGuffin · Murder · Spy Syndicate

THINGS TO LOOK FOR

- The stylish and dramatic opening shots, typical of the best Hitchcock films.
- The subtle and clever windmill scenes. Look for the evocative interior design, the stunning photography, and the tense, impressionistic cinematography throughout.

TRIVIA/FUN STUFF

+ If you watch closely during the plane crash, when the aircraft hits the ocean and the cockpit is flooded with water you can see the rear projection screen tear open, allowing water from a tank hidden behind to pour onto the set.
+ Because the film dealt with politics and World War II, the film was not seen in Germany until 1960, and even then only in a highly censored form that saw twenty-two minutes cut. It was not until 1995 that Germans were finally able to see the full, uncut *Foreign Correspondent*.
+ The closing scene, in which Jones/Haverstock makes a radio address during an air raid in England, was added at the last minute. Filmed when European tensions were high but war had not yet begun, *Foreign Correspondent* dealt with the possible start of World War II—but just as the last footage was shot, the war began in earnest.
+ In a rare concession by Hitchcock, Robert Benchley was given leeway to improvise his own dialogue during filming.
+ Preferring an iconic American star, Hitchcock wanted Gary Cooper for the lead, but Cooper declined. Cooper is said to have later regretted his decision.
+ Like Peter Lorre in *The Man Who Knew Too Much*, Bassermann, who played Van Meer, knew no English. His lines were all delivered phonetically.
+ The film was nominated for six Academy Awards, including Best Picture. It lost Best Picture and Best Cinematography to another Hitchcock film, *Rebecca*.

- The climactic plane crash, one of the biggest and most expensive sequences Hitchcock ever filmed.
- The moody, dark look and feel of the scenes in which Van Meer is being interrogated. For the first time in years, Hitchcock's strong German influence is readily apparent.

AWARDS

- Academy Award Nominations (6): Best Picture; Best Actor in a Supporting Role (Albert Bassermann); Best Writing; Original Screenplay (Charles Bennett and Joan Harrison); Best Cinematography, Black-and-White (Rudolph Maté); Best Art Direction, Black-and-White (Alexander Golitzen); Best Special Effects (Photographic: Paul Eagler; Sound: Thomas T. Moulton).

DVD RELEASES

RELEASE: Warner Home Video (2004)
(Dolby Digital 2.0 Mono, 1.33:1 Black & White)
RATING: ****1/5

EXTRAS: *Personal History: Foreign Hitchcock* documentary; theatrical trailer.
NOTES: Available as a stand-alone or as part of *The Alfred Hitchcock Signature Collection.*

Mr. & Mrs. Smith
(1941)

FILM FACTS

PRODUCTION YEAR: 1940
RELEASE DATE: January 31, 1941 (U.S.)
STUDIO: RKO Radio Pictures
FILMING LOCATION: N/A
PRESENTATION/ASPECT RATIO: Black & White/1.37:1

SYNOPSIS

Mr. & Mrs. Smith tells the story of a young, well-to-do couple living a good life in New York City. The Smiths (Robert Montgomery and Carole Lombard) have rules they live by. For instance, once a month, each is allowed to ask a question of the other, and that question must be answered truthfully. With that rule invoked, Mrs. Smith asks her husband if he had to do it all over, would he choose to marry her again? His answer is that he would not. Later that day, Mr. Smith learns his marriage is legally invalid. Faced with this news, he decides he *does* want to remarry his wife. But she has other ideas.

IMPRESSIONS

The screwball comedy is an all but dead genre. Hollywood doesn't produce them anymore, but the 1930s and early 1940s gave the world such classics as

It Happened One Night (1934), *Bringing Up Baby* (1938), and *His Girl Friday* (1940), which were not only great comedies, but terrific films regardless of genre. *Mr. & Mrs. Smith*, Alfred Hitchcock's lone foray in the world of screwball comedy, is not quite up to the level of the better pictures of this forgotten era of American film history. This is unfortunate, because from a technical standpoint, the film is well made. The problem is, it isn't funny. Hitchcock may have been adept at bringing humor to otherwise dramatic films, but in shooting for humor alone, here he falls short. *Mr. & Mrs. Smith* is one of just a small handful of comedies in Hitchcock's career (it's often called his only comedy, but that is inaccurate), and it came hot on the heels of two of his most financially and critically successful films to date, *Rebecca* and *Foreign Correspondent*.

A wacky comedy about a married couple after two of the lushest suspense films of his career? One almost wonders if Hitchcock *wanted* a film that could not stand up to those two major successes in order to "reset" expectations.

"You must understand, it was not really a film for myself," Hitchcock told two French interviewers for a 1972 issue of *Écran* magazine. "I had just finished, in rapid succession, *Rebecca* and *Foreign Correspondent* when Carole Lombard, who had become a friend, said to me, 'Why don't you direct me in a film?' I accepted her suggestion."[15]

He makes it seem blasé, almost as if to defuse suggestions it is a lesser work. He even told François Truffaut accepting the job was a "weak moment."[16]

A weak moment, maybe, but a nice gift for a good family friend. The Hitchcock family—Alfred, Alma, and daughter Patricia—had rented a home from Lombard when they first came to the United States in 1939, and the entire family became friends with Lombard and her husband, megastar Clark Gable. By that point, she was already known as the "Queen of Screwball Comedy," having starred in such hits as *Nothing Sacred* (1937) and *True Confession* (1937). It may have seemed natural for Lombard to have Hitchcock direct her, but this was not natural material for Hitch.

Had she not tragically died in a plane crash in 1942, the year after *Mr. & Mrs. Smith* was released, Hitchcock would likely have cast Lombard as the leading lady in one of his suspense thrillers. She would have been per-

> **WHERE'S HITCH?**
>
> Hitchcock appears about halfway through the film, walking past Mr. Smith in front of his apartment building.

Robert Montgomery and Carole Lombard do their best to keep the comedy screwball. (RKO/Photofest © RKO)

fect. Lombard was a beautiful blonde with a sharp face, and an excellent actress to boot. Yet they only ever made this film together, a film Sir Alfred was not prone to praise. Hitch characterized the filmmaking process matter-of-factly: "I more or less followed Norman Krasna's screenplay. Since I really didn't understand the type of people who were portrayed in the film, all I did was photograph the scenes as written."[17]

If it truly was as simple as that, Hitch's skills as a director at this point in his career were superb indeed. The directing on *Mr. & Mrs. Smith* is crisp and lively, and has punch in all the right places. The film is by no means essential Hitchcock, but it's also far from the dismal failure some consider it to be. If this film is any indication, it is no stretch to say he was unlikely to have become a great purely comedic director, but the man quite simply knew how to put a film together.

Maybe the film feels upbeat and warm because, unlike in other films that strayed too far from what he liked to do, Hitch's mood was positive throughout the filming process. Lombard was not just a friend, she was a misfit and prankster—a perfect fit for the kind of on-set tone Alfred Hitchcock set. She played pranks, encouraged crazy antics, and generally made the experience a good one for all involved. Few were the creative strides in *Mr. & Mrs. Smith*—it's hard to point to any, really—but, lukewarm reviews or not, audiences made it a financial success.

In retrospect, it's true that *Mr. & Mrs. Smith* is rather pedestrian when compared to other Hitchcock works. There are no moments of excitement, little in the way of noteworthy set pieces, and only passable performances (Lombard, who prompted the film in the first place, fails to reach the same level of screwball charm as her costar, Robert Montgomery). Despite this, it succeeds in the moments that need to work. In one memorable scene, the couple returns to the restaurant where they had their first date, only to find it has changed dramatically. Montgomery's obsessing over a cat sleepily lounging on their dinner table while they eat is hilarious. In another scene, Montgomery finds himself in an awkward position as he dines with an overbearing oaf from the local men's club and two graceless tramps. He wants desperately to be somewhere else, and that desire is accelerated even further when his estranged wife shows up on a date with, of all people, his law firm partner. After first embarrassing himself by pretending he is with a beautiful woman, Mr. Smith attempts to give himself a bloody nose. Chaos and further embarrassment, of course, ensue.

The cinematography here is above average, sometimes even amazing for a screwball comedy. The Ferris wheel scene is extremely impressive, with a great combination of outstanding rear projection work, strong character placement, and stellar editing.

It doesn't all work, however. The film's ending feels forced, and the pivotal role of Mrs. Smith's new romantic interest, Jeff Custer (Gene Raymond), is simply bland. In fact, aside from the two leads, the entire supporting cast is nothing but blasé, a near-unforgivable fault for a comedy.

But the biggest flaw here is that, a few humorous sequences aside, *Mr. & Mrs. Smith* just isn't all that funny. And it's a comedy! The lightning wit of *Foreign Correspondent*, which is ostensibly a thrilling suspense and adventure film, offers more genuine laughs than does *Mr. & Mrs. Smith*. So do many of Hitch's later films.

Things start off strong enough. From the very beginning, with its bright, upbeat music, it is obvious that *Mr. & Mrs. Smith* isn't a typical Hitchcock film. It quickly establishes its two main characters and their lives as a well-to-do couple in New York. The potential is there to deliver a mad-cap romp, but once the news of his marital status is delivered to Mr. Smith, the film takes a turn for the bland. The comedy stops delivering because we never really get a sense of why this young couple felt discontented in the first place. Offer up a life-altering event just prior to the news of their invalid marriage, and perhaps there would have been a sense of urgency for the Smiths, something that might humorously drive them toward a conclusion. Instead, we're left to watch and wonder if a tighter story would have made the film more enjoyable. The film has its share of funny moments, but they are scattered all over the place.

In the end, this is a pretty difficult flaw to overlook, considering the very intent of this film was humor. In fact, it's all but fatal.

Alfred Hitchcock clearly considered *Mr. & Mrs. Smith* a footnote in his career. While it's certainly a film worth watching, and not at all the failure some claim, he is correct. Hitch had been known to underestimate the quality of his own work, but in this case, his self-assessment is accurate. *Mr. & Mrs. Smith* is passable, light entertainment—and little more.

CONCLUSION

Mr. & Mrs. Smith is among the least Hitchcockian films of his career. His only venture into screwball comedy is a mild disappointment; simply put, the humor fails to deliver in strong doses. Hitch did an admirable job from a technical perspective, but the film is missing the comic pacing a screwball adventure like this needs. This film is recommended only to those desiring to see everything Hitchcock directed.

HITCHCOCKIAN THEMES

Bathroom Scene/B.M. • Love Triangle • Manipulative Mother

THINGS TO LOOK FOR

- Effective use of rear projection technology during the Ferris wheel scene.
- Strong cinematography throughout the film.

TRIVIA/FUN STUFF

+ *Mr. & Mrs. Smith* was made by Hitchcock at the request of star Carole Lombard, a friend of the family.
+ This is the only straight comedy Hitchcock made in Hollywood.

DVD RELEASES

RELEASE: Warner Home Video (2004)
(Dolby Digital 2.0 Mono, 1.33:1 Black & White)
RATING: ***

EXTRAS: *Mr. Hitchcock Meets the Smiths* documentary; theatrical trailer.
NOTES: Available as a stand-alone or as part of *The Alfred Hitchcock Signature Collection*.

Suspicion
(1941)

FILM FACTS

PRODUCTION YEAR: 1941
RELEASE DATE: November 14, 1941 (U.S.)
STUDIO: RKO Radio Pictures
FILMING LOCATION: N/A
PRESENTATION/ASPECT RATIO: Black & White/1.37:1

SYNOPSIS

Lina McLaidlaw (Joan Fontaine) falls for a charming scoundrel named Johnnie (Cary Grant) after a whirlwind courtship. On the surface, Johnnie appears to love her, but there are clues he may be little more than a manipulative con artist. After Johnnie's friend Beaky (Nigel Bruce) is killed under seemingly suspicious circumstances—and at a time that appears particularly opportune for Johnnie—Lina begins to suspect her new husband is actually a murderer.

IMPRESSIONS

After a brief hiatus with the comedic *Mr. & Mrs. Smith*, Hitchcock returned to more familiar territory in *Suspicion*, a suspenseful drama based on the novel *Before the Fact* by Francis Iles. Here we have a story right up Hitchcock's alley. A young woman, desperate to shed her image as a dour spinster, marries a dashing playboy—only to discover he is not everything he seems. With this story, Hitch was able to explore themes such as love, fear, regret, murder, honesty, naïveté, friendship, loyalty, and, of course, suspicion.

But *Suspicion* is a flawed film that falls short of brilliance thanks to niggling issues. That doesn't mean it isn't strong Hitchcock suspense built around a skeleton of false leads, misleading hints, and tantalizing clues. One would be hard-pressed to argue that *Suspicion* doesn't come on strong with the suspense. It remains, even when viewed in this context, an underappreciated Hitchcock film. Yet the flaws can't help but be noticed.

First, let's backtrack for a moment and take a look at what *Suspicion* meant for the career of Alfred Hitchcock. Although it is a film that, in retrospect, should have ended differently, it remains important because it is the first of several appearances by screen icon Cary Grant. Equaled only by James Stewart, Grant ranks as one of the most important of

WHERE'S HITCH?

Roughly forty-five minutes into the film, Hitchcock can be seen mailing a letter at the post office.

the Alfred Hitchcock players. However, in a twist befitting the film, it is not Grant who anchors *Suspicion*, but the alluring Joan Fontaine, who plays Lina.

At the heart of the narrative are Lina's growing suspicions of her new husband, Johnnie. First, she discovers he's penniless, but, blind in the happiness of her newly discovered love, she dismisses her apprehensions. Time and again, though, Johnnie's actions beg to be questioned. Lina entertains the seeds of doubt, yet she's so desperately in love with Johnnie that she's not willing to give credence to those suspicions, no matter how well founded they seem to be.

From the first scene on the train (yes, Hitch is again on a train, however briefly), when we see Lina reading a book titled *Child Psychology*, we're given the impression she fancies herself an amateur psychologist. Soon, the audience will be amateur psychologists, too. With the story told entirely through her perspective, *Suspicion* is fascinating as a psychological examination of Lina herself. She observes the actions of Johnnie and his friend Beaky, and comments that they are childlike, that they should grow up. This brilliant young woman is keen to analyze the actions of people in her life, yet she's unable to see that her love for Johnnie completely clouds her judgment of him.

Joan Fontaine, Cary Grant, and Nigel Bruce share a lighthearted moment. (RKO Radio Pictures/Photofest © RKO Radio Pictures)

Our judgment of Johnnie is clouded, too. Right from the beginning, Hitch teases us. Johnnie is painted as a sly and charming manipulator, a moocher of the worst sort. Just as quickly, however, we're shown a different side of him. Women swoon over him, the townsfolk love him, and the way he seems to take advantage of Lina is shown to be a big misunderstanding. And then we see yet *another* side of Johnnie—two more, in fact— as Hitch first teases us with what appears to be a murder in progress, and then brings us into the scene to show Johnnie as a carefree romantic with something of a playfully cruel side. All this in the first ten minutes or so. Who is the real Johnnie? That's the question the film plays with for the rest of its running time.

Sometimes the dead ends and audience teasing work, such as during a fabulous conversation about murder over dinner, a common scene in Hitchcock's work. The camera splits characters with well-placed candle holders, focuses on meat being sliced during talk about vivisection, and cuts from character to character in such a way that you can only surmise Johnnie is a murderer—a murderer who has found the perfect way to claim a victim. Other times, the teasing falls flat. At one juncture Johnnie, Lina, and Beaky are playing a game of Anagrams (a word game similar to Scrabble). Lina, suspecting that an upcoming trip Johnnie and Beaky are taking will not end well for Beaky, continues to fret as she plays. She places down the game's tiles to spell a word—and that word is "murder." Rather clumsy and obvious for Hitchcock.

It doesn't help matters that Grant's character is far from likeable. Despite occasional bouts of kindness and love, he is presented as thoughtless, uncaring, selfish, and often mean-spirited and cruel. Leading the audience down the wrong path in order to heighten the tension is one thing. Doing so when it's hard to care whether or not Johnnie is a murderer is quite another.

Yet if it sounds as if these flaws are fatal, they are not. We might dislike Grant's Johnnie, but Joan Fontaine manages to keep the viewer's interest as the kindhearted, terribly naive Lina. Between her performances here and in *Rebecca*, it's easy to fall in love with her. Beautiful yet approachable, elegant yet down-to-earth, she's the kind of actress you just don't see anymore. She was also a remarkably capable performer, able to convey mood and emotion with simple gestures and changes of expression. Fontaine's performance is perhaps the best thing the film has going for it. Others certainly noticed. While *Rebecca* is the better of her two efforts for Hitch, she won an Oscar for *Suspicion*, the only Academy Award ever won by an actor in a Hitchcock film. Many have suggested this award was atonement for not recognizing her astonishing work in *Rebecca* the year before.

Similar praise cannot be given to Cary Grant's performance. Johnnie is supposed to be a smooth playboy with a devilish, somewhat sleazy side, but Grant played this side up too much. One can't help but feel it would have played better had Grant shown more restraint. The personality conflict is distracting; a more nuanced performance could have added layers to this film.

From a technical standpoint, Hitch continued to grow in *Suspicion*. Stylistically, the camera work is some of his strongest to this point. The way he frames shots more often than not does all the heavy lifting when it comes to adding dire subtext to the narrative. Some of his decisions, such as the aforementioned shots during dinner, strike an excellent tone. So, too, is the editing strong. *Suspicion* is heavy with hints and teases, and the editing plays a big role in that. Almost across the board it's effective in bringing the right amount of tension to the table.

And then there is the iconic moment. From *Foreign Correspondent* on, almost every Alfred Hitchcock film has a signature moment (and some, more than one). Here it is a famous shot of Johnnie carrying a tray and glass of milk up a sweeping stairway to a resting Lina. By this point, we're firmly convinced he is a murderer and that Lina is next on his list, about to be a victim of poisoning. In a masterful stroke, Hitchcock arranged to have a small lightbulb inside the glass. As Johnnie carries it up the dark stairway, it glows with an ominous light. This famous Hitchcock moment is recognizable even to people who haven't seen *Suspicion*. It's pure movie magic.

Much has been made about the ending of *Suspicion*. According to Hitchcock, his original concept had Johnnie truly intending to kill Lina. He would then mail a letter she had secretly written about her suspicions to her mother, inadvertently sealing his fate. But, as the story goes, RKO Radio Pictures refused to allow beloved screen idol Cary Grant to be portrayed as a murderer. The audience, the studio claimed, would not stand for it. Thus the ending as we know it was conceived. It's not an entirely unpleasing ending as it is, but given the way Johnnie is portrayed—as a calculating conniver—Hitchcock's suggested ending would have been more in line with the story, not to mention far more satisfying.

But did the studio really order this change? It has been suggested that Hitchcock practiced some revisionist history when he made this claim. "Careful research has shown that the truth of the matter is otherwise," wrote Donald Spoto. According to Spoto, the ending, as seen, was how it was conceived and intended by Sir Alfred, and that the story of RKO's interference was concocted only after the film was not well received upon release. "*Suspicion* is just what [Hitchcock] constructed," wrote Spoto, "and the ingenious disclaimer was put forth only after the picture failed to please critics and audiences and its status among his early American films diminished in time."[18] It's an interesting theory that merits consideration, but its assertion as fact is questionable because the research mentioned is never documented in his book.

Yet, despite the flawed ending, *Suspicion* remains an excellent film—one of the best from Hitchcock's early American period. With this film, Hitchcock launched into a series of dark, psychological thrillers pushed forward not through action and grand set pieces, but with disturbing characters motivated by secrets, dark desires, and a skewed outlook on life. To one degree or another, *Shadow of a Doubt*, *Spellbound*, *Strangers on a Train*, and others all toy with these ideas. *Suspicion* may have some flaws that hold it back from true greatness, but it's still an excellent prelude to this darker stretch in Hitchcock's filmmaking.

CONCLUSION

Suspicion is among the best of the lesser known Hitchcock gems, a film rife with tension and fantastic Hitchcockian moments. It is not flawless, however, burdened by an uneven performance by Cary Grant and a questionable ending, and probably does not rise to the level of "forgotten classic" because of these shortcomings. However, for Joan Fontaine's wonderful turn and the entry of Grant into the world of Alfred Hitchcock, *Suspicion* is a key stop on any journey with Hitch.

HITCHCOCKIAN THEMES

Dark Secret • Discussion of Murder at Dinner • Exotic Location • Murder • Trains • Wrongly Accused

THINGS TO LOOK FOR

- A rare uneven performance by the usually consistent Cary Grant.
- The famous glowing glass of milk.
- The teasing, often misleading musical score.

TRIVIA/FUN STUFF

✦ A lightbulb was hidden inside the glass of milk to make it glow.
✦ According to legend, the intended ending revealed that Johnnie was indeed a murderer. This was changed because a star of Cary Grant's caliber "couldn't" be portrayed that way.
✦ The dog featured in the film was Alfred Hitchcock's own.
✦ Francis Iles, the author of *Before the Fact* (the novel upon which *Suspicion* is based), was a pen name for author Anthony Berkeley.
✦ Joan Fontaine won an Oscar for her performance in *Suspicion*, the only Oscar-winning performance Hitch ever directed.

AWARDS

- Academy Award Nominations (3): Best Picture, Best Actress (Joan Fontaine), Best Scoring of a Dramatic Picture (Franz Waxman)
- Academy Award Win: Best Actress (Fontaine)
- New York Film Critics Circle Award Win: Best Actress (Fontaine)

DVD RELEASES

RELEASE: Warner Home Video (2004)
(Dolby Digital 2.0 Mono, 1.33:1 Black & White)
RATING: ****

EXTRAS: *Before the Fact: Suspicious Hitchcock* documentary; theatrical trailer.

NOTES: Available as a stand-alone or as part of *The Alfred Hitchcock Signature Collection.*

Saboteur
(1942)

FILM FACTS

PRODUCTION YEAR: 1942
RELEASE DATE: April 22, 1942 (U.S.)
FILMING LOCATIONS: Boulder Dam, Nevada;
Red Rock Canyon State Park, Cantil, California
STUDIO: Universal Pictures
PRESENTATION/ASPECT RATIO: Black & White/1.37:1

SYNOPSIS

Barry Kane (Robert Cummings) is a worker in a wartime airplane factory. When he is wrongfully accused of sabotage, he is forced to travel cross-country in an effort to prove his innocence. Along the way, Kane meets Pat Martin (Priscilla Lane), a young lady who doubts his story at first, but later becomes a valuable ally. A climactic confrontation between Kane and the real saboteur occurs atop the Statue of Liberty.

IMPRESSIONS

Hot off the heels of the departure from the norm that was *Mr. & Mrs. Smith* and the mixed reaction received by *Suspicion*, Alfred Hitchcock wasted no time getting back to what had made his reputation: spy-driven espionage thrillers featuring a man on the run.

Saboteur was not the first retread of Hitchcock's career, nor would it be the last. The setup is almost painfully familiar by now. A man is suspected of a crime he did not commit. He goes on the run in an effort to clear his name and meets up with a female companion who isn't altogether on his side. After a series of adventures, they fall in love just prior to a rousing climax.

Despite the familiar territory, if *Saboteur* is more of the same from Alfred Hitchcock, his ability to find innovative solutions to technical problems—problems imposed by the director's own grand imagination—ensures that *Saboteur* is yet another fresh take on an old idea.

This film marks an important step in Hitch's career because it is his first distinctly "American" thriller. His first Hollywood film, *Rebecca*, could hardly be called *distinctly* American. *Foreign Correspondent* featured his first American lead, but all the action is centered in Europe. *Mr. & Mrs. Smith* was a screwball comedy, far removed from his

> **WHERE'S HITCH?**
>
> Hitchcock appears as a man at a newsstand shortly after Barry Kane's arrival in New York City.

usual fare, and *Suspicion* was overtly British. With *Saboteur*, Hitch wanted all-American actors, all-American action, and all-American locations.

That's exactly what he delivered.

World War II was in full swing when *Saboteur* was released; hence war themes play a central role. Fifth columnists intent on sabotaging American industry are the chief villains, setting the narrative in motion with a fire in an airplane factory. Here Hitchcock's German impressionist influence is clear with some wonderfully evocative photography. This doesn't mean *Saboteur* is a "war film" or that the specific war serving as a backdrop is central to the plot. Like *Foreign Correspondent*, the particular nature of the war is almost irrelevant. World War II is a backdrop that could be substituted for just about any international conflict. This was often the case with Hitchcock's films; with only rare exceptions, they were set in the time during which they were filmed, yet were presented in such a way that, even to this day, they call little attention to their period.

With the plot device in place, the narrative launches into familiar territory: the flight of the protagonist, a clue leading him to the real villains, meeting the female lead, the two leads butting heads, "colorful" local characters,

A handcuffed Robert Cummings tries to elicit Priscilla Lane's help. (Universal Pictures/Photofest © Universal Pictures)

a set piece, the two leads growing close, another set piece, the race to the climax, the finale.

Yes, the audience had seen it before. It would be easy to dismiss *Saboteur* as a lesser incarnation of *The 39 Steps*, Hitch's British masterpiece. The rough outlines are practically interchangeable, with *Saboteur* coming in lighter on the chase factor and falling short on several other fronts. Robert Cummings and Priscilla Lane are fine enough actors in the two lead roles, but they lack the kind of charismatic star power needed to push such a set piece–driven film forward. Cummings wasn't an unknown, but he was far from a charismatic box office superstar.

In many ways, Barry Kane is similar to both Richard Hannay in *The 39 Steps* and Johnny Jones in *Foreign Correspondent*. These three characters are all young, vibrant, courageous, and upstanding—the kind of guys anyone would want on their side. Yes, the audience knows from the beginning Kane is innocent, but that is not why it is easy to root for his exoneration. He is easy to root for because he is simply the type you *want* to root for. It was not lost on Hitchcock that likeable characters make for the best kind of heroes. It's too bad Cummings wasn't entirely up to the task. It has been said that Hitchcock wanted Gary Cooper for the lead. Cooper would have fulfilled the star quota, but he would not have been right for the part. Cary Grant? That's easy to envision . . . but audiences would have to wait until *North by Northwest* to see why.

The film falters in other areas, too. As dazzling as the set pieces are, the narrative lacks the urgency of its British cousin. The script is loose and careless, badly in need of tightening. Things should have come together. After all, this is already familiar territory for Hitchcock.

So often in his movies, Hitchcock set a chain of events in motion with a seemingly harmless incident, as in *The 39 Steps*, in which a chance meeting triggers a wild adventure. *Saboteur* also features an otherwise innocuous incident that sets the story in motion—in this case, a dropped wallet. Hitch was fascinated with minutiae, and was aware of how minor events are an intrinsic part of forming a bigger picture, and of affecting lives.

Perhaps *Saboteur*'s biggest shortcoming is that, despite being continuously on the run, Kane is rarely in clear danger of being caught. Sure, the villains are always just a few steps behind him, but the film lacks the urgency so prominent in *The 39 Steps*. Without this, the tension is inconsistent and, as we have learned from Hitch's best thrillers, consistent tension is a must.

Of course, tension is pointless without interesting characters. Hitchcock was infatuated with bizarre, unusual people, as seen with the choice to set a crucial scene aboard a truck loaded with circus freaks. The human skeleton, the bearded lady, the Siamese twins, the fat lady, and the midget are quite a troupe of characters. Yes, Hitchcock exploits their abnormalities, but he simultaneously turns out an effective scene while portraying them in a favorable light. These characters highlight one of the film's most memorable scenes.

Yet, while it's true that *Saboteur* seems like a lesser film when set next to classic espionage thrillers like *The 39 Steps* and later *North by Northwest*, when taken on its own terms it's another solid page out of the Hitchcock thriller textbook. In a technique he began using in Britain and would continue to use until the end of his career, Sir Alfred manages to build a successful film around a series of seemingly unrelated set pieces, with just enough style and pizzazz to turn it into a strong adventure. It worked. In 1942, audiences devoured *Saboteur*, giving Alfred Hitchcock a huge success and solidifying his place in the eyes of many as a Hollywood director.

If there were any doubt that *Saboteur* was more "American" than any Hitchcock film to date, such doubt is cast aside during its iconic climax on the Statue of Liberty. On a purely story-driven level, this famous sequence—with a key villain and the hero having a tense confrontation atop the statue's torch—is something of a small failure. The character in peril is the villain, making it hard for the audience to sympathize with his plight. It's easy to overlook this flawed story decision, however, when presented with the technical bravado of the sequence. Even sixty years later, the special effects look brilliant. Outside the torch, Kane has a showdown with Frank Fry (Norman Lloyd), the man who set the fire at the start of the film. Kane lurches forward with a pistol. The villain steps back, topples over the railing, falls, and catches himself. He clings precariously to the Statue of Liberty's raised hand. Kane attempts to pull him up, to no avail: The villain falls and is killed. Were it not for the dazzling imagery on display here, no one would care—but the imagery is indeed dazzling. Bold angles, dramatic composition, and sharp special effects come together in one of Hitch's most iconic sequences, astonishingly convincing for a film made in 1942. For sheer technical bravado, it's one of the most impressive examples of filmmaking seen from Hitchcock thus far.

Ultimately, it is this technical wizardry that propels the film from a fairly blasé thriller to a worthwhile spectacle. Even when all but painting by the numbers, Hitchcock manages to salvage memorable moments from an otherwise unmemorable film. And that is what makes Alfred Hitchcock such a special director.

CONCLUSION

Saboteur is a motion picture loaded with Hitchcockian themes and Hitchcockian touches. Despite this, it is not entirely successful, though nevertheless enjoyable. The relative lack of star power hinders *Saboteur*, but there are enough of Hitchcock's standard elements, themes, and techniques present to make this a solid effort, if not a true step forward for the Master of Suspense.

HITCHCOCKIAN THEMES

Blonde Leading Lady • Chaos in an Unexpected Location • Climactic Showdown at an Iconic Location • Handcuffed Man and Woman • MacGuffin • Man (or Woman) on the Run • Murder • Spy Syndicate • Trains • Wrongly Accused

THINGS TO LOOK FOR

- The astonishing technical achievement of the Statue of Liberty sequence.
- The entertaining circus troupe sequence.
- The German impressionist influence in the early fire scene.

TRIVIA/FUN STUFF

✦ Hitchcock originally wanted Gary Cooper to play the part of Barry Kane.

✦ The late shot of the floundering ship was an actual shot of the SS *Normandie*, which had capsized as a result of a real case of sabotage. The United States Navy requested the shot be removed from the film, but Hitchcock refused.

✦ The Statue of Liberty sequence required the building of a life-size replica of the hand and torch, as well as the invention of a new camera technique: pulling the camera back from a stationary object to simulate falling.

DVD RELEASES

RELEASE: Universal Studios (2001, 2005, 2006)
(Dolby Digital 2.0 Mono, 1.33:1 Black & White)
RATING: ***1/3

EXTRAS: *Saboteur: A Closer Look* documentary; storyboards: the Statue of Liberty sequence; Alfred Hitchcock's sketches; production notes and photographs; theatrical trailer.

NOTES: Available as stand-alone releases from 2001 and 2006, or as part of *The Alfred Hitchcock Collection* (out of print) and *Alfred Hitchcock: The Masterpiece Collection. The Masterpiece Collection* is recommended. The transfers on all releases appear identical.

WEEK

25

Shadow of a Doubt
(1943)

FILM FACTS

Production Year: 1942
Release Date: January 12, 1943 (U.S.)
Studio: Universal Pictures
Filming Locations: Universal Studios
904 McDonald Avenue, Santa Rosa, California;
Newark, New Jersey
Presentation/Aspect Ratio: Black & White/1.37:1

SYNOPSIS

Young Charlie (Teresa Wright) couldn't be more thrilled when her Uncle Charlie (Joseph Cotten) comes to the Newton household for an extended visit. Things have been down lately, and Uncle Charlie's visit is just what the Newton family needs. Or is it? Young Charlie thinks she shares a personal bond with Uncle Charlie—that is, until she begins to suspect her uncle is carrying a dark secret: He's a serial killer. As she begins her quest to find out the truth, a shadow begins to loom over the Newton household—a shadow only Young Charlie can see. As tension mounts, Uncle Charlie realizes his niece is on to him. She knows the truth. He is, in fact, a killer. And that means for the truth to stay hidden, one of them will have to die.

IMPRESSIONS

"Do you know the world is a foul sty? Do you know if you rip off the fronts of houses you'd find swine? The world's a hell. What does it matter what happens in it?"

—Uncle Charlie

Powerful words for 1943. Powerful words, even today. An excerpt from one of two gut-punch monologues delivered by Joseph Cotten in Alfred Hitchcock's chilling 1943 thriller, it points to darkness deeper than the average person will ever face.

Alfred Hitchcock is best remembered for directing brilliant suspense thrillers, but he was equally adept at creating thoughtful moral dramas. There is no better example of this than *Shadow of a Doubt*, a film with a somewhat dark perspective on the world, yet filled with bright characters and sharp humor. Here we have one of Hitch's absolute best motion pictures.

It is no surprise, then, that *Shadow of a Doubt* was one of Hitchcock's personal favorites. Possibly more than any of his other works, it depicts darkness thrust into a world of light. Ordinary and innocent people confronted with sinister characters. Dark secrets. These are themes Hitch dabbled with as early as *The Lodger*, and something he would continue with until the end of his career. *Shadow of a Doubt* stands among the very best of Hitchcock's works, in large part because not only are the darker aspects of the story well-painted—certainly no surprise at this point in his career, right in the midst of one of his most creative stretches—but because the innocence of sleepy Santa Rosa, the quaint suburban picture of Americana in which the film is set, is so well realized.

The story told in *Shadow of a Doubt*, that of a niece who comes to suspect that her beloved uncle is a serial killer, is unusual for its time. In 1943, American films typically depicted an idealized life, with evil something of an afterthought. Hitchcock brought evil into focus with this film, and he did it in such a way that the viewer must consider it.

What we have here is an Alfred Hitchcock masterpiece.

More than any other factor, the greatest strength of *Shadow of a Doubt* is the performance of Teresa Wright as Young Charlie. In just the fourth film of her fledgling career, Wright is given top billing, and rightfully so. Her acting is astonishing on multiple levels. Her subtle portrayal of a young woman whose life is shattered by a horrible truth is something to behold.

We don't merely observe her character growth, we feel it, too. That she is also a stunning beauty only adds to her allure as one of Hitchcock's greatest heroines, despite the lack of golden locks so typical of Hitchcock's most memorable leading ladies. It is incredible to consider that Wright was Oscar nominated for her first three films (winning for William Wyler's *Mrs. Miniver* in 1942), but would never again be nominated in a career spanning nearly sixty years. She should have been nominated for *Shadow of a Doubt*.

As great as Wright is, she is also surrounded by a terrific supporting cast, led by the brilliant Joseph Cotten. Cotten's Uncle Charlie is chilling, terrifying, charming, and disarming. This is a complex character. Hitchcock needs a strong performance to elicit feelings of stress, distress, and fear from Wright. Cotten delivers in spades. So, too, does the rest of the cast. Highlighted by Henry Travers, Patricia Collinge, Macdonald Carey, Hume Cronyn (who would later collaborate with Hitchcock on a number of projects as a writer), and the kids, Edna May Wonacott and Charles Bates, all are outstanding. This is undoubtedly one of Hitch's best ensembles, and that cast comes together to work with some provocative thematic material.

> **WHERE'S HITCH?**
>
> Near the start of the film, Hitchcock appears playing cards with other passengers on the train. His back is turned to the camera during the entire cameo.

Hitchcock loved dark things: cruel tricks and putting people off their guard. And what else is *Shadow of a Doubt* but a film about a young woman put off her guard, cruelly deceived by her murderous uncle?

It is Uncle Charlie who thrusts the film from great thriller into brooding masterpiece. Hitchcock loved his villains, and throughout his career his films boasted some truly fantastic on-screen evil. Anthony Perkins's Norman Bates in *Psycho* and Robert Walker's Bruno Anthony in *Strangers on a Train* are probably the two most critically acclaimed Hitchcock villains—charismatic, loathsome, and played with terrific abandon by both actors. By any measure, Uncle Charlie stands among them as one of the silver screen's greatest villains. Cotten is not melodramatic or over-the-top. Instead, he is so chillingly believable, he could easily be *your* Uncle Charlie. And such is the power of his performance. He smiles and charms; he seems warm and caring—yet beneath the surface is a man consumed with nihilism and hatred. He does not represent the duality of man; he *is* the duality of man.

Cotten's first great monologue is almost painful to hear. It's delivered with such crisp conviction, such loathsome disdain, that it resonates more than sixty years later.

The cities are full of women, middle-aged widows, husbands, dead, husbands who've spent their lives making fortunes, working and working. And then they die and leave their money to their wives, their silly wives. And what do the wives do, these useless women? You see them in the hotels, the best hotels, every day by the thousands, drinking the money, eating the money, losing the money at bridge, playing all day and all night, smelling of money, proud of their jewelry but of nothing else, horrible, faded, fat, greedy women .... Are they human or are they fat, wheezing animals, hmm? And what happens to animals when they get too fat and too old?

While modern filmmakers do "dark" with shocking visuals, Hitchcock manages to burrow into the core of what we think of our fellow man and expose our inner blackness for all the world to see by injecting it into an otherwise idyllic setting.

The film is also rife with symbolism, the most important being the repeated use of pairs and doubles. There are two Charlies. Two dinner scenes. Two train sequences. Two attempts by Uncle Charlie to murder Young Charlie. Two evening excursions into town. Two discussions of the best murder methods by Young Charlie's father, Joe, and his friend, Herbert. Two younger children. Two sets of two detectives. Two murder suspects. Two garage scenes. Two scenes in which Uncle Charlie grabs Young Charlie by the arm. Two friends of Young Charlie. Two drinks ordered by Uncle Charlie inside the Till Two bar. And on and on and on.

At the center of *Shadow of a Doubt* is the ultimate pairing of Young Charlie and Uncle Charlie. Young Charlie says to her uncle early in the film, "We're not just an uncle and a niece. It's something else. I know you. I know you don't tell people a lot of things. I don't either. I have a feeling there's something nobody knows about. Something secret and wonderful. I'll find out." At this point, we have already learned that Uncle Charlie has a dark past. We also know that despite her adoration for her uncle, Young Charlie is an astute observer and will soon learn the truth.

These pairs are also important because they underline that concept of the duality of man, a central theme of the film. *Shadow of a Doubt* concerns itself with man's capacity for evil. The viewer is clued in to Uncle Charlie's

The two Charlies, Teresa Wright and Joseph Cotten. (Universal Pictures/Photofest © Universal Pictures)

past at the onset, but Young Charlie is left to deduce, discover, and decide the truth about her uncle. When her realization comes, she is horrified by what he has done. She also learns that she herself is capable of murder, telling her uncle, "Go away. I'm warning you. Go away or I'll kill you myself. See . . . that's the way I feel about you." She means it, too. Young Charlie, though repulsed by her uncle's killings, knows she is capable of the same if necessary. It's an astounding character realization that is brilliantly executed by Hitchcock and his players.

And perhaps the instincts of Young Charlie *were* right. The two Charlies *are* alike. Witness her transformation once the knowledge sinks in that her uncle is a terrible man. The sweet, innocently nihilistic (and painfully naive) girl from the start of the film is gone. She has been replaced by a girl with a grim view of what people can be. And is that not what drives Cotten's Charlie—his view of humanity as little more than "swine"?

With a villain this strong, a lead this powerful, and performances that manage to do them justice, it's no wonder *Shadow of a Doubt* was among

Hitchcock's favorites. What's truly Hichcockian here is not simply that Uncle Charlie is a depraved but charming villain, but that his dire evil is thrust into an otherwise normal world. Viewed through the eyes of his niece, Young Charlie—the role that ultimately holds the entire film together—Cotten's character is frighteningly realistic because we can imagine him in our lives. The situation is all the more menacing because Wright's character feels a great connection to her uncle. She loves him and feels drawn to him, but in the end, in a cinematic theme one sees often from Hitchcock (most notably in *Vertigo*), the love she craves is denied her when she realizes Uncle Charlie is not the man he appears to be.

Effectively and powerfully, in *Shadow of a Doubt* Alfred Hitchcock brought an emotionally devoid evil into a world each and every American could understand.

But things are not all dark and serious. In the midst of all this drama and the morality play underlying the entire narrative, there is a tremendous amount of comedy. More than any film we have seen thus far, *Shadow of a Doubt* perfectly melds drama and humor in a way not only effective for the story, but appropriate to its characters. Most enjoyable are two of the pairs: the two young children, and Joe and Herbie.

The children, wise beyond their years, are delightfully funny yet natural. The screenplay was initially written by Thornton Wilder (*Our Town*) and later revised by Hitchcock and his wife, Alma Reville. Hitchcock felt the script needed a little humor to punch it up, so Sally Benson was brought in to rewrite some of the dialogue. The children are given the funniest lines. "Really, Papa, you'd think Mama had never seen a phone," young Charlie's little sister, Ann, says as her mother talks too loudly on the phone. "She makes no allowance for science. She thinks she has to cover the distance by sheer lung power."

Also funny are Joe and his friend, Herbie. These two are fascinated with the concept of the perfect murder method. And not just any murder. These two discuss how they could get away with murdering *each other*. It is morbid, yes, but extremely funny. It is even funnier considering these amateur sleuths are oblivious to the presence of a real serial killer living right under their noses. Joe and Herbie are a pair to rival Caldicott and Charters of *The Lady Vanishes*. When, in defense of their talks about killing people, Joe explains, "We're not talking about killing people. Herb's talking about killing *me* and I'm talking about killing *him*," you can't help but laugh . . . uncomfortably.

It is worth comparing *Shadow of a Doubt* with Hitchcock's drama of two years prior, *Suspicion*. Each features a man with a questionable past coming into the life of a naive young woman, only to have the woman come to suspect he is a murderer. Each is bolstered by outstanding performances by the lead actress. Where they differ greatly is in the ending. We gripe about *Suspicion*'s failure to deliver Cary Grant as a criminal. Such is not the case with *Shadow of a Doubt*, and the film benefits greatly as a result. Young Charlie's emotional journey would not be nearly as satisfying were it based on unfounded suspicions.

Shadow of a Doubt is a veritable smorgasbord of Hitchcockian themes, things we have seen and will continue to see crop up in much of his other work. There are no chase scenes, no wrongfully accused, and no spies here, but otherwise most of the elements that define Hitchcock are present. We have murder, dark secrets, ineffective authority figures, a leading lady involved with a detective investigating the crime central to the plot, discussions of murder over dinner, trains, and music integral to the plot. All of these things are common in his other films.

Hitchcock is said to have asserted that *Shadow of a Doubt* was his personal favorite of all the films he made, but this was apparently not the only answer he gave. Hitchcock told François Truffaut, "I wouldn't say that *Shadow of a Doubt* is my favorite picture; if I've given that impression, it's probably because I feel that here is something that our friends, the plausibles and logicians, cannot complain about."[19] Nevertheless, it is evident Hitch had a sense of reverence for the film.

Fresh off of several strong motion pictures, *Shadow of a Doubt* falls squarely in the middle of one of the greatest stretches of Hitchcock's career, overshadowed only by his amazing run in the 1950s. So much of this film is executed flawlessly, it's a wonder it doesn't turn up more frequently on "best of" lists. Hitch's decision making is remarkably focused throughout; his every shot has purpose. He frames Wright in a doorway at the bottom of a set of stairs, reflecting her decision to box herself off from her uncle. The dramatic pullback shot in the library, when realization first dawns on her, punctuates the isolation she must feel at that moment. At dinner, when Cotten delivers his first monologue, the camera pushes in close, accentuating the intensity of the moment. In one especially clever shot that gives insight into the characters through visuals alone (and via a pair of pairs), at the start of the film Cotten glances out his window and sees two investigators. We can tell by his reaction that they are looking for him. The scene is heavy with paranoia. Later, when he first arrives in Santa Rosa, he again looks out his window in the very same manner. In an almost identical shot, we see not two investigators, but two innocuous old ladies. Uncle Charlie has arrived at a safe haven. He is secure.

It's hard to find something that does not work in this film. Here we see Hitch at the peak of his creative powers. You don't often hear it mentioned with his greatest classics, but make no mistake, it should be. *Shadow of a Doubt* is one of his greatest works and absolutely essential viewing.

CONCLUSION

If *Shadow of a Doubt* is not often mentioned with the best of Hitchcock's work, it is certainly no fault of the film. It belongs there. Not just among his best early American work, but among his best work overall, *Shadow of a Doubt* is a meticulously directed, darkly ominous masterpiece that is as good as domestic thrillers get. Featuring superb direction and remarkable performances, it's an absolutely essential part of Hitchcock's filmography. This is Alfred Hitchcock at the pinnacle of his craft.

HITCHCOCKIAN THEMES

Bathroom Scenes/B.M. • Dark Secret • Discussion of Murder at Dinner • Ineffectual Authority Figures • Murder • Music Plays a Role in Plot • Trains • Woman with Cop Boyfriend

THINGS TO LOOK FOR

- Pairs. In *Shadow of a Doubt*, almost everything comes in, or happens in, twos.
- The film's rich, evocative photography, especially the shots in the library and the framing of Teresa Wright in the doorway.
- The playful banter between Joe Newton and Herb Hawkins. Their incessant talk about how they would murder one another is both grim and hilarious.
- The precocious Newton children, who are seemingly more well grounded than their parents.

TRIVIA/FUN STUFF

+ Many of the film's extras were residents of Santa Rosa.
+ The waltz that torments Uncle Charlie does so for good reason—it is called "The Merry Widow Waltz."
+ *Shadow of a Doubt* was Hume Cronyn's first acting job. He would go on to appear in more than eighty productions, including *Lifeboat* (1944), *Ziegfeld Follies* (1946), *The Postman Always Rings Twice* (1946), two episodes of *Alfred Hitchcock Presents*, and a TV production of *12 Angry Men*.
+ In addition to three other acting jobs for or relating to Alfred Hitchcock, in 1960, Hume Cronyn appeared in a television version of *Juno and the Paycock*.
+ In 1991 the film was added to the National Film Registry by the National Film Preservation Board, which selects films that "are considered to be culturally, historically or aesthetically important."

AWARDS

● Academy Award Nominations (1): Best Writing, Original Story (Gordon McDonnell)

DVD RELEASES

RELEASE: Universal Studios (2001, 2005, 2006)
(Dolby Digital 2.0 Mono, 1.33:1 Black & White)
RATING: *****

EXTRAS: *Beyond Doubt: The Making of Hitchcock's Favorite Film* documentary; production drawings and photographs; theatrical trailer; production notes.

NOTES: Available as stand-alone releases from 2001 and 2006, or as part of *The Alfred Hitchcock Collection* (out of print) and *Alfred Hitchcock: The Masterpiece Collection*. *The Masterpiece Collection* is recommended. The transfers on all releases appear identical.

Lifeboat
(1944)

FILM FACTS

PRODUCTION YEAR: 1943
RELEASE DATE: January 11, 1944 (U.S.)
STUDIO: 20th Century Fox
FILMING LOCATION: 20th Century Fox Studios, Los Angeles, California
PRESENTATION/ASPECT RATIO: Black & White/1.37:1

SYNOPSIS

An American cargo ship is destroyed in a battle with a German U-boat. The survivors, all of varying backgrounds, are brought together aboard a lifeboat, clinging to survival. Before long, they come upon a German sailor who had been aboard the sunken U-boat. They debate what to do with him—Kill him? Cast him overboard?—before eventually allowing him to take control of their craft. But this may not have been the wisest decision, as they soon learn.

IMPRESSIONS

The lack of recognition for Alfred Hitchcock's *Lifeboat* is, in some ways, a little surprising. A technical tour de force of Hitch's ability to work with stringent limitations—the entire film takes place in a single lifeboat—and featuring a dynamic ensemble cast in a tense story set during World War II, it's as deserving of praise as any but the very best Hitchcock films.

The film certainly wasn't overlooked for lack of quality. A tight, tense drama, *Lifeboat* is as easy to appreciate today as it must have been in 1944. It's fascinating not just because of the technical bravado on display, but because it's a good story.

But first in any discussion of *Lifeboat* is a discussion of its technical bravado. This film marks one of the first times Alfred Hitchcock envisioned doing a film solely to see if he could overcome a self-imposed technical obstacle. (The best known example is the forthcoming *Rope*.) Could he set an entire film in the confines of a single small lifeboat? Hitch thought he could, and so he pushed to get a script written that would offer him just such a situation.

After working with Thornton Wilder on the script for *Shadow of a Doubt*, a collaboration that resulted in an artistic triumph, Hitch again wanted to work with a successful American author. He first courted Ernest Hemingway, who declined, but was able to draft John Steinbeck to write a simple story: A group of survivors from a ship sunk by a German U-boat during World War II are stranded together in a small lifeboat. They must survive the elements, the ocean, and one another.

WHERE'S HITCH?

Hitchcock, in perhaps his most creative cameo, appears in a newspaper advertisement for the fictional weight loss drug Reduco. The newspaper is seen about twenty-five minutes into the film.

That is the sum total of the story.

The catch, of course, is that the entire film takes place in a lifeboat. We open with a dramatic shot of the last remnants of an ocean vessel sinking, followed by a slow pan across the wreckage before the camera finally settles into the tiny boat we won't leave for the rest of the picture. The idea was Hitchcock's. He wanted a challenge: to see if he could overcome the technical hurdle of being stuck with one small boat upon one massive ocean. After seeing how effective he was in staging the plane crash in *Foreign Correspondent*, it's no surprise that visually, he succeeds. Something of a surprise is the fact that he manages to sustain the illusion for more than ninety minutes. *Lifeboat* was filmed in a huge studio water tank. This setting is enhanced with constant waves and by the use of simulated ocean mist, rain, and fog. The changing camera angles used in the film accomplish two things: It gives different perspectives on the singular setting, keeping *Lifeboat* visually pleasing despite no change in the setting, and it perpetuates the idea that the boat is in constant motion.

It is striking that the only music heard in *Lifeboat* is during the opening and closing titles. This is atypical of Hitch's work. Many of his great classics are famous for their music, particularly later in his career. One would think Hitchcock would have wanted a score for *Lifeboat*; already constrained by its setting, every little bit could help. Yet the decision to forgo music only serves to enhance the drama, highlighting the desperate situation of the survivors. Ultimately, it was the right decision.

Like Sidney Lumet's brilliant *12 Angry Men* (made thirteen years after *Lifeboat*), the claustrophobic setting is a boon rather than a burden thanks to a strong script built upon the densely woven interplay of a well-drawn cast of characters. We believe in these individuals; we sympathize with them and accept them as who they are. We take their struggles to heart, and we're torn by their conflicts.

The actors are given excellent material to work with. This is not just a sea adventure. The survivors on the lifeboat face not only harsh conditions, but also harsh personal realities. The interplay of the psychological strain of their situation and the moral dilemma the German sailor presents them with is brilliantly constructed.

Steinbeck, who received story credit for *Lifeboat*, wrote most of the first draft of the screenplay, but Jo Swerling was brought in to finish and revise the script, thus receiving screenplay credit. Hitchcock also made revisions of his own. The finished product is one of the best Hitchcock scripts, filled with terrific dialogue. Prophetic dialogue, as well: "Hey, remember that boom we had after the last war? Well, the boom we're gonna have after this one'll make the last look like a mild flurry."

In order to pull off the uniquely limiting set, *Lifeboat* needed the strong direction of Alfred Hitchcock. He could overcome the technical limitations. What he could not do is deliver the performances the script so badly needed in order to succeed. To pull off the strong intercharacter relationships, *Lifeboat* needed a strong array of actors and actresses.

The cast here is wonderful. It seems that with every ensemble film since *The Lady Vanishes*, Hitchcock's ability to allow multiple actors to shine within the same film improved. *Foreign Correspondent* was a great jump forward in this regard, and *Shadow of a Doubt* even better. *Lifeboat* is, on this issue, their equal.

John Hodiak, Walter Slezak, Hume Cronyn, Tallulah Bankhead, Heather Angel, Mary Anderson, Henry Hull, and Canada Lee. (20th Century Fox Film Corp./Photofest © 20th Century Fox Film Corp.)

The ensemble cast in *Lifeboat* is terrific, but Tallulah Bankhead's portrayal of newspaper reporter Connie Porter is the force that drives the film forward. Connie's moral character arc is remarkable. At the film's outset she is self-centered, egotistical, and uncaring, but as she is stripped of her possessions, Connie comes to realize what is important and thus becomes a likeable character.

What Hitchcock and these great actors bring to life is a highly interesting story with elements a little more "modern" than one would expect from a 1944 motion picture. Once again, Hitch was way ahead of his time. During an era when black characters in film were largely limited to porters and comic relief, here we have one of the most thoughtful of the survivors, Joe, cast as a black man. (It's worth noting that Steinbeck did not agree with this assessment; he thought Hitchcock treated the Joe character with condescension.) The film can also be terribly grim for its time. Early on, we're greeted with the shadow of a dead infant, followed closely by the suicide of the baby's mother. Soon after, we get an amputation. Finally, late in the film, we see the brutal murder-by-beating of the German sailor when the survivors gang up and kill him. That we never actually see any of the blows land only makes the killing all the more difficult to watch.

As in *Shadow of a Doubt*, Hitch manages to paint grim, disturbing pictures without ever drifting into the realm of exploitation. An argument could be made that this was largely because he was forced to operate under the strict Hayes Code. He had no choice but to be creative in squeezing limit-pushing darkness out of "acceptable" standards, after all. The Master of Suspense made those limitations work for him. Hitchcock played within a set of arbitrary boundaries as well as anyone. (Remember, we're talking about a film he purposely set within a single boat.)

We have not discussed much in the way of Hitchcock's cameo appearances, mainly because they are generally unremarkable in execution, but such is not the case with *Lifeboat*. By 1943, Hitch's cameos had become expected, and his fans kept a sharp eye out for them. Confronted with his limited setting and the fact that he could not play one of the main characters, Hitch was forced to be creative with his screen appearance. He briefly toyed with the idea of filming himself as a body floating by the boat, but, not wanting to get in the water—better to subject his actors to such trials than himself—he thought better of it. The solution was perhaps his most creative cameo. Sir Alfred had been in the midst of a crash diet, dropping from three hundred to two hundred pounds. He capitalized on this by placing himself in a mock advertisement for Reduco, a fictional weight loss drug, in the newspaper read by one of the men on the boat. This little moment added a much-needed bit of humor and illustrated that no obstacle was too big for Hitchcock's creativity.

Other instances of Hitchcock's humor at work are subtler, intended for himself rather than the audience. He was famously fascinated with bathroom humor. He often staged scenes in bathrooms just because it amused him. When it was not practical to use a bathroom set, Hitch would insert the initials B.M. (for "bowel movement") somewhere within his movies. Similar to the initials engraved on the ring in *Shadow of a Doubt*, Hitchcock achieved this in *Lifeboat* by tattooing B.M. on the chest of John Kovac, one of the survivors. This seemingly trivial point sheds a light on Hitchcock's personality.

Lifeboat was panned by critics when it was released. With its wartime setting, critics and audiences alike had difficulty accepting the notion that the Nazi German sailor was better fit to helm the boat. That the film was staunchly pro-Allies did not seem to matter to some critics. The film never recovered from those sour reviews.

But the truth is, there is little to criticize about *Lifeboat*. There are no flaws in its execution, the acting is uniformly excellent, and the story is compelling. So why isn't *Lifeboat* better remembered as a minor Hitchcock classic?

We just don't know.

CONCLUSION

Lifeboat is one of the most underrated films in the Hitchcock library. It is one of Hitch's most daringly creative works and features an excellent cast, an interesting story, and a strong moral message. This is not a typical Hitchcock film—no trains, spies, blackmail, iconic locations, or even a MacGuffin—but it remains thoroughly entertaining and thought provoking. A must-see film in the Hitchcock canon, and painfully overlooked as one of his secondary classics.

HITCHCOCKIAN THEMES

Bathroom Scene/B.M. • Handcuffed Man and Woman • Murder • Suicide/Attempted Suicide

THINGS TO LOOK FOR

- Connie Porter, the pampered, materialistic, and arrogant celebrity, slowly losing all the possessions important to her.
- Constantly changing camera angles.
- Effective use of waves, boat movement, fog, storms, rain, and mist.

AWARDS

- Academy Award Nominations (3): Best Director (Hitchcock); Best Writing, Original Story (John Steinbeck); Best Cinematography, Black-and-White (Glen MacWilliams)
- New York Film Critics Circle Award Win: Best Actress (Tallulah Bankhead)

TRIVIA/FUN STUFF

+ The lifeboat appears to be in constant motion, but was filmed on a single set.
+ This was the only film Hitchcock made for 20th Century Fox.
+ The first script, by MacKinlay Kantor, was rejected.
+ John Hodiak, who played John Kovac, was later married to Anne Baxter, who played the female lead, Ruth Grandfort, in Hitchcock's *I Confess*.
+ Ernest Hemingway was initially asked to write the story of *Lifeboat*, but he declined.

DVD RELEASES

RELEASE: MGM (2008)
(1.33:1 Black & White)
RATING: ****

NOTES: Available as a stand-alone disc or as part of a set with seven other Hitchcock films, *Alfred Hitchcock: Premiere Collection*.

RELEASE: 20th Century Fox (2005)
(Dolby Digital 2.0 Stereo, 1.33:1 Black & White)
RATING: ****

EXTRAS: Commentary by Drew Casper; *The Making of Lifeboat* documentary; photo gallery.

Bon Voyage
(1944)
and *Aventure malgache*
(1944)

FILM FACTS

PRODUCTION YEAR: 1944
RELEASE DATE: 1993 (UK)
STUDIO: British Ministry of Information
FILMING LOCATION: Elstree Studios, Borehamwood, Hertfordshire, England
PRESENTATION/ASPECT RATIO: Black & White/1.37:1

SYNOPSIS

In 1944 Alfred Hitchcock journeyed to England to do his part for the war effort. There, he filmed two short movies, *Bon Voyage* and *Aventure malgache*, in support of the French Resistance. The former tells the story of a Royal Air Force pilot who escaped from behind enemy lines. Interrogated by French officials, he discovers someone who helped him escape may have been a German agent. The latter focuses on a group of actors about to do a performance when one of the actors relates a story about his time with the French Resistance running an illegal radio operation.

IMPRESSIONS

"I felt the need to make a little contribution to the war effort, and I was both overweight and over-age for military service. I knew that if I did nothing, I'd regret it for the rest of my life."

—Alfred Hitchcock[20]

Hitchcock's contribution to the war effort was two short films, *Bon Voyage* and *Aventure malgache*, made for the British Ministry of Information, with a French cast and crew, in support of the French Resistance. These two shorts, twenty-six and thirty-one minutes in length, respectively, are not technical or artistic masterpieces, but they are worth watching if for no other reason than they are a novelty within the Hitchcock canon.

As the focus of this book is on Hitchcock's artistic development from one film to the next, it must be noted that there is little remarkable about either in this regard. Both are effective in telling a story, but you will not see anything particularly daring. Both films were made in a little more than a month's time. They were not artistic endeavors. They were not intended to entertain or to flex his creative muscle. They were not distributed to the public. They exist almost solely because Hitchcock wanted to contribute to the war effort in the way he was best able—through film.

> **WHERE'S HITCH?**
>
> There are no Hitchcock cameos in these short films.

From that angle, these two short movies, long left in a film archive, are something of a historical curiosity. They've hardly been seen since World War II (they were finally released to the public in 1993), and, outside of the most ardent Hitchcock followers, few Hitchcock fans even know they exist. And why would they? These were two short propaganda films made with the sole purpose of boosting the war effort. Now, decades later, they are novelties on the résumé of a brilliant director. And that is likely what they will remain.

Bon Voyage, the more interesting of the two, tells the story of a Scottish RAF sergeant who escaped a German prisoner of war camp with the aid of the French Resistance. It is a terrific depiction of the sometimes subtle but great differences between perception and reality. Aside from John Blythe, a British actor who played the RAF sergeant, the rest of the cast is simply credited as the Molière Players, as it is with the next picture. This was done for fear the Nazis would harm the actors' families were they credited by their real names.

The short is directed admirably enough. Told almost entirely in flashback, it's a mildly tense story about spies and counterspies—or, to be more accurate, the Gestapo and the French Resistance—during World War II. During its brief twenty-six minutes, we see secret codes, betrayal, murder, and a plot twist or two. Right up Hitchcock's alley, really. Overall, there is a very noir-inspired quality about the film; the photography is dark, with narrow beams of light illuminating the actors' faces. *Bon Voyage* even features a somewhat Hitchcockian moment. The second of two murders in the story plays out with several stylistic cuts before ending in a startling close-up of the victim's face just as he is shot. It's a sudden, unexpected cut, and would not feel out of place in a traditional Hitchcock thriller.

As a whole, this short film has more historical than artistic significance in the Hitchcock filmography, but for what it is, it's certainly well done. In fact, some may find it surprisingly entertaining.

Aventure malgache doesn't fare as well. This story of a member of the Resistance on the island of Madagascar in 1940, told by a member of an acting troupe as he and two others are preparing for a performance, is muddled and murky. It is difficult to make sense of who is who and what is what. The flashback motif returns, but here it's less effective. This is probably because what is being recalled is less interesting. We have some domestic drama, a visit to a courtroom, and plenty of talk filmed in an ordinary, unremarkable manner. Unlike *Bon Voyage*, there is nary a Hitchcockian moment to be found in *Aventure malgache*.

Neither of these shorts is particularly memorable, but by no means are they a waste of time. They offer an insight into Hitchcock's loyalty to the Allies and, despite their length and relative lack of creativity, offer several Hitchcockian themes. Both feature spies, and *Bon Voyage* has a man on the run, murder, and even a sequence on board a train. Ultimately, though, they're significant in the story of Alfred Hitchcock's life, but entirely forgettable in the story of his life as a filmmaker.

CONCLUSION

Bon Voyage and *Aventure malgache* are curiosities in the Hitchcock filmography, more so for how and why they were made than for their artistic noteworthiness. While the latter is bland and forgettable, the former is a surprisingly enjoyable twenty-six minutes. Neither, however, is essential save for those who wish to explore this unique detour in Hitch's career.

HITCHCOCKIAN THEMES

Man (or Woman) on the Run · Murder · Spy Syndicate · Trains

THINGS TO LOOK FOR

● The very Hitchcockian murder scenes in *Bon Voyage*.

TRIVIA/FUN STUFF

✦ *Bon Voyage* and *Aventure malgache* were filmed during World War II to support the French Resistance and the war effort.

✦ All cast members save John Blythe were credited as "The Molière Players" in order to protect their families back home in France from the Nazis.

✦ The films were not released from the British Film Institute archives until 1993, when they were finally made available for public viewing.

DVD RELEASES

RELEASE: Image Entertainment
(French Dolby Digital 1.0, 1.33:1 Black & White)
RATING: **

NOTES: Both short films appear on one disc.

Spellbound
(1945)

FILM FACTS

PRODUCTION YEAR: 1944
RELEASE DATE: October 31, 1945 (U.S.)
STUDIO: Selznick International Pictures
FILMING LOCATIONS: Alta Lodge, Alta, Utah;
Cooper Ranch, Northridge, California
PRESENTATION/ASPECT RATIO: Black & White/1.37:1

SYNOPSIS

Dr. Murchison (Leo G. Carroll) is going to be replaced as chief psychiatrist at the Green Manors mental asylum by the brilliant but unseen Dr. Edwardes. When the man who appears to be Edwardes (Gregory Peck) arrives, Dr. Peterson (Ingrid Bergman), another psychiatrist (a cold woman wrapped up in her work) quickly falls for him. She soon discovers the truth: Edwardes is not who he seems. He is a man posing as the doctor, an amnesiac whose real name is John Ballantine. The real Edwardes is dead. Murdered. Ballantine runs off before he's accused of murdering the real doctor. Peterson follows, and, along with her mentor, Dr. Brulov (Michael Chekhov), sets out to figure out Ballantine's true past and prove his innocence.

IMPRESSIONS

America had been good to Alfred Hitchcock. By the time *Spellbound* was made, he had already proven he was a director to be reckoned with. He had garnered awards recognition and worked with some of America's biggest stars, and his films were consistent box office successes. The decision to leave his native England had reaped him the financial compensation and critical acclaim he so desired.

With success, money, and popularity now under his belt, his directorial efforts were increasingly turning not toward surefire formula-driven thrillers, but experimental endeavors crafted in part to flex his creative muscle. Such was Alfred Hitchcock's mindset when he talked legendary producer David O. Selznick into purchasing the rights to the novel *The House of Dr. Edwardes* by Francis Beeding, a story in which a psychiatrist is not what he appears to be.

> **WHERE'S HITCH?**
>
> Hitchcock appears about forty minutes into *Spellbound*, smoking a cigarette and carrying a violin case as he comes out of an elevator.

It probably wasn't a hard sell. Selznick had a personal interest in psychotherapy, having undergone it himself. In fact, the producer wanted Hitchcock to direct a film based loosely on Selznick's own experiences with therapy, making the book a perfect fit. Because Hitchcock was still under contract, if Selznick wanted such a film to be made, it was going to be made. That film would become *Spellbound*.

If directing *Rebecca* under the watchful eyes and meddling control of Selznick was an unpleasant task for Hitch, the producer's personal connection to the film's subject matter could only mean that directing *Spellbound* would be worse.

And it was. Selznick forced his own therapist into the production as a technical adviser. He was strongly against the Salvador Dali–designed dream sequences Hitchcock so badly wanted (eliminating one, the now legendary "statue" sequence, entirely). He even cut footage—some fourteen minutes or more—from Hitchcock's final product.

While it would be nearly impossible to entirely suppress Sir Alfred's astonishing burst of creativity during his early American period, *Spellbound* is saddled with too much Selznick baggage to be anything other than a fascinating experiment that ultimately fails to entertain despite its innovations. For a mainstream film featuring major stars, it's full of bold cinematic techniques and daring experimentation, but it is also lacking focus, as if it doesn't quite know what it wants to be. With two giants of 1940s cinema playing tug-of-war over the finished product, this should not come as a surprise.

As with *Rebecca*, *Spellbound* is as much a David O. Selznick film as it is an Alfred Hitchcock film. And it shows.

Spellbound is a film not nearly as good as the sum of its parts. A man who assumes the identity of a chief psychiatrist at a mental asylum only to become a suspect in the killing of the real doctor is a hook full of potential. Hitchcock took it in an interesting direction, crafting it into one of his "man on the run" thrillers, but it fails to deliver consistent tension or drama, in large part due to questionable plot points.

Perhaps it played better in the 1940s, but modern audiences would find it difficult to understand why Bergman's Dr. Peterson would fall in love so quickly with the man she believed to be Dr. Edwardes. Yes, he is charming, attractive, and seemingly brilliant, but Peterson is a reserved woman, very much wrapped up in her "man's world" work. After Peterson falls for the man we learn is really John Ballantine, her actions continue to belie the character established early in the film. While smiling, she says, "I keep forgetting you're a patient." Can we believe such dialogue comes from the same serious woman established at the film's outset?

The other serious issue with the narrative is that no explanation is given as to why Ballantine came to take the place of Dr. Edwardes. That Ballantine suppressed the memory of accidentally killing his brother during childhood is certainly reason for him to act strangely, but it does not explain how or why he would assume Edwardes's identity.

The film's story may fall flat, but the film itself does not lack artistic merit. The cinematography, sets, music, and, of course, the Dali dream sequences all make this picture worth watching. Both Gregory Peck and Ingrid Bergman give strong performances that manage to hit all the right notes. Peck, in a role for which he probably was not best suited, is moody and intense in his portrayal of a man overcome by guilt. *Spellbound* benefits from Selznick's love of high production values. The set design and photography are both rich and lush. Even more noteworthy, the film is loaded with evocative imagery and creative camera tricks, beyond even the famous Dali dream sequences. The way Hitchcock films light streaming underneath a doorway, or a simple picnic, or a series of hallucinogenic doors swinging open, or a small child being killed in an accident is as visually compelling as anything in the Hitchcock canon. When we see the fearful way he frames Peck's strange late-night visit with Dr. Alex Brulov, for instance—shot from a low angle, a razor blade slid-

Ingrid Bergman and Gregory Peck embrace while an amused ticket collector (Richard Bartell) watches. (United Artists/Photofest © United Artists)

ing in and out of the frame—we can't help but be impressed with how well Hitch can play the audience. Even the score is at least as strong as anything to this point in his career, striking the right tone throughout.

And yet it doesn't *quite* manage to come together. *Spellbound*'s story gets too bogged down in explanations of psychiatric phenomena, and the audience is never given a truly compelling reason to root for this twist on Hitch's "man on the run" theme. The pacing falters two-thirds of the way through the 110-minute running time, and despite efforts by the film to provide hints of "the truth," the end feels like it comes out of left field. There is a "gotcha" feel here—the entire mystery explained in a quick rush of exposition. The worst of it is that the final confrontation has little connection to anything seen up until that point. Had any of what we learn in the end been set up in the first act, it might work . . . but it wasn't.

Ultimately, *Spellbound* is an interesting exercise in surreal experimentation for Hitchcock with a great deal of directorial flourish, but as pure entertainment, it falls short of the mark.

CONCLUSION

Spellbound is a picture filled with beautifully shot scenes, excellent acting, and memorable Hitchcock flourishes, yet it is ultimately disappointing. Held back by story flaws and the meddling hand of producer David O. Selznick, it is rife with unrealized potential. The clever Dali sequences are rightfully cited as high points, but the film itself falls short of the mark.

HITCHCOCKIAN THEMES

Blonde Leading Lady · Chaos in an Unexpected Location · Dark Secret · Man (or Woman) on the Run · Murder · Wrongly Accused

THINGS TO LOOK FOR

- The Salvador Dali dream sequence.
- Parallel lines over white surfaces, which trigger a reaction from Ballantine.

TRIVIA/FUN STUFF

- ✦ *Spellbound* is based on the novel *The House of Dr. Edwardes* by Francis Beeding. Hitchcock had Selznick purchase the rights to the novel for $40,000.
- ✦ This was the first Hollywood film to focus extensively on psychoanalysis.
- ✦ Selznick wanted the film to be partially based on his own experience in psychoanalysis. He went so far as to put his own doctor on set to serve as a technical adviser.
- ✦ Against Hitchcock's wishes, Selznick deleted about fourteen minutes from the film.
- ✦ Screenwriter Ben Hecht consulted with many real-life psychoanalysts as he wrote the script.

AWARDS

- Academy Award Nominations (6): Best Picture; Best Director (Hitchcock); Best Actor in a Supporting Role (Michael Chekhov); Best Cinematography, Black-and-White (George Barnes); Best Music, Scoring of a Dramatic or Comedy Picture (Miklós Rózsa); Best Effects, Special Effects (Photographic: Jack Cosgrove)
- Academy Award Win: Best Music, Scoring of a Dramatic or Comedy Picture
- New York Film Critics Circle Award Win: Best Actress (Ingrid Bergman; also for *The Bells of St. Mary's*)

DVD RELEASES

RELEASE: MGM (2008)
(1.33:1 Black & White)
RATING: ****

NOTES: Available as a stand-alone disc or as part of a set with seven other Hitchcock films, *Alfred Hitchcock: Premiere Collection*.

RELEASE: Criterion Collection (2001)
(Dolby Digital 2.0 Mono, 1.33:1 Black & White)
RATING: ***1/2

EXTRAS: Commentary by Hitchcock scholar Marian Keane; illustrated essay *A Nightmare Ordered by Telephone* on the Dali sequences; excerpts from interview with composer Miklós Rózsa; complete 1948 *Lux Radio Theatre* radio adaptation; radio piece on the theremin; essays by Hitchcock scholars; photo galleries; theatrical trailer.

NOTES: Recommended. Out of print. Very expensive on the secondary market. Also available as part of the out-of-print boxed set *Wrong Men & Notorious Women*.

RELEASE: Anchor Bay Home Video
(Dolby Digital 2.0 Mono, 1.33:1 Black & White)
RATING: **1/2

Notorious
(1946)

FILM FACTS

PRODUCTION YEARS: 1945–1946
RELEASE DATE: August 15, 1946 (U.S.)
STUDIO: RKO Radio Pictures
FILMING LOCATIONS: Beverly Hills, California
Los Angeles County Arboretum & Botanic Garden
301 N. Baldwin Ave., Arcadia, California
Santa Anita Park
285 West Huntington Drive, Arcadia, California
Exteriors: Rio de Janeiro, Brazil, and Miami, Florida
Presentation/Aspect Ratio: Black & White/1.37:1

SYNOPSIS

When Alicia Huberman (Ingrid Bergman) is asked to spy for the American government after her father is outed as a foreign spy, she accepts only because she has little choice. When she falls hopelessly in love with fellow spy T. R. Devlin (Cary Grant), her mission—to marry and ultimately spy upon an old family friend, Alexander Sebastian (Claude Rains)—becomes an emotional nightmare, as she must pretend to love one man while truly loving another.

IMPRESSIONS

It is evident Hitch loved stories revolving around spies and espionage. He revisited such material time and again. One might think these repetitious themes would lead to stagnation, yet this was anything but the case with the Master of Suspense. *Notorious* was the latest and perhaps the best to date example of Hitchcock's incomparable ability to create something new and fascinating out of oft-used themes.

Perhaps the most critically acclaimed of Alfred Hitchcock's early American work, *Notorious* closes out a seven-year stretch of sustained brilliance—*Rebecca, Foreign Correspondent, Suspicion, Shadow of a Doubt,* and *Lifeboat* all came during this period—all the more astonishing because an even better seven-year stretch was still to come between 1954 and 1960. For most directors, a run of work even as good as Hitchcock's late British period (1933 to 1939) would have been enough to ensure a memorable legacy. That he not only followed it up with a series of films just as good, but actually improved his craft during his early American period, is a testament to his constant growth as an artist.

This take on the spy thriller is built around one of the cleverest of all the Hitchcock MacGuffins, the uranium ore stored in wine bottles in Alexander Sebastian's wine cellar. As was the case in his stretch of films made during World War II, *Notorious* is thoroughly in and of its time (this was set at the dawn of the Cold War), yet the story stands the test of time.

> **WHERE'S HITCH?**
>
> About an hour into the film, Hitchcock appears during the party at Alexander Sebastian's house. He is front and center, drinking champagne.

Notorious finds Alfred Hitchcock in complete control of his craft. From the very start it is clear we're dealing with a focused work of deliberate vision. In a short, effective scene, we get all the backstory we need to get to know our lead, Ingrid Bergman's wonderfully realized Alicia Huberman. It is Alicia who sets the plot in motion. We see her spiraling out of control at a party, but we just as quickly know her fortunes are going to change when Hitch teases us with the identity of a party guest.

Enter Cary Grant. And what an entrance it is. The introduction to Grant's T. R. Devlin is wonderfully executed. Once again, Hitchcock finds a simple yet effective technique to accomplish multiple goals in one shot. After the revelation that Alicia's father was a Nazi spy, we see her throwing

Cary Grant makes life difficult for Ingrid Bergman. (RKO Radio Pictures Inc./Photofest © RKO Radio Pictures Inc.)

a party to help her forget her troubles. Devlin is at this party, but we only see him from behind. Though Alicia speaks to him, he has no dialogue. As Alicia wakes from a bout of binge drinking, we see the room from her viewpoint: blurry, unfocused, and swaying drunkenly. The disorienting camerawork reinforces the state Alicia is in, while also giving superstar Cary Grant the opportunity to have an unforgettable entrance. Alicia is obviously drunk—but this does not stop him from agreeing to go on a car ride with her. This sequence is doubly effective, as it both establishes Devlin's reserved nature and Alicia's escapist attitude.

This is the sort of thing at which Hitch was so good. Time and again, his directorial flourishes serve a purpose beyond mere showing off. He picks his spots and uses otherwise self-indulgent techniques to tell his stories and paint his characters. *Notorious* is positively laden with such moments.

Notorious would not work were it not for the rest of the outstanding cast, which includes Claude Rains and Leopoldine Konstantin. Grant and Bergman were each in their second film for Hitchcock; both took advantage of a better script the second time around and worked brilliantly together as one of Hitch's most troubled yet endearing couples. Rains is also fantastic as the charming yet vile Alexander Sebastian. And Konstantin, in her only American film, is excellent as the mother who conspires with her son to murder her daughter-in-law.

At the heart of *Notorious* is the love story between Devlin and Alicia, and the effect their mission has on the relationship. They quickly fall in love, but each has issues that prevent their love from blossoming. Alicia's history as a party girl, as well as her apparent alcoholism, make Devlin uneasy. Devlin also has difficulty dealing with the demands of their mission; he is unable to prevent Alicia from taking her assignment to the extreme when she agrees to marry the villain she must spy on. The story here is fascinating. We question how far we would be willing to endanger ourselves for the good of our country, weighing the importance of duty versus love. The drama is compelling.

Mr. *Psycho*, Mr. Spy Story, Mr. Suspense . . . Mr. Love?

Without question. Love—usually of the romantic variety, but not always—is a central theme in a great many of Hitchcock's films. (Would *Shadow of a Doubt* be the emotional nail-biter it is without Young Charlie's initial love for Uncle Charlie?) Hitchcock's heroes almost invariably fall for an attractive young lady by the time his films wrap. Love turns villains into heroes, as in the forthcoming *North by Northwest*. It places our leads into terrible situations, as in *Rebecca*. It drives men crazy, as in *Vertigo*. But most of all, it is presented as an essential luxury all good people revel in. Such is the case in *Notorious*, where much of the film's conflict comes not from its uranium MacGuffin or its spy syndicates or its dark plots, but from the simple fact that all these things get in the way of the love Alicia Huberman and T. R. Devlin share for one another. Their love—shown but unspoken, felt but unacknowledged—is the driving force of *Notorious*. Without it, the whole of the film falls apart.

This is brought to life by edgy, layered performances by Bergman and Grant. If Grant's performance in *Suspicion* was something of a disappointment, in *Notorious* he is a walking, talking acting clinic. Curt, cutting, on the edge, Grant does all in his power to portray a man torn between a job with international stakes and his love for Bergman's Alicia. He's a man hiding his feelings behind a hard-edged mask, saying mean things to avoid expressing what he really feels. In the hands of a lesser actor, this could be clunky and awkward, yet with Grant, the layers here are never ambiguous; we hear what he is saying, yet his eyes betray the truth of his feelings. Late in the film, during a scene in which Devlin and Alicia talk on a park bench,

Alicia is swooning from drugs she has unknowingly ingested. Devlin says she looks unwell, and Alicia, knowing Devlin may soon be leaving her, in an effort to let him walk away easily, claims she has been on another bender. Hurt but unwilling to say so, Devlin lashes out with biting remarks; yet Grant's eyes tell the full tale. He doesn't mean a word of it.

So, too, does Bergman shine. While Grant largely has one acting hurdle to leap in the film—a difficult leap, to be sure—Bergman's character has such a distinct arc that the actress is forced to practically be three or four different characters. From the reckless young woman angry at the world, to the girl pulled against her will into spying for the government, to the woman hopelessly in love, to the young lady forced to pretend she loves a much older man, to the woman drugged into a stupor, Bergman has a lot of ground to cover.

Like so many of Hitchcock's best films, *Notorious* is famous for a signature shot. In this case, it is a beautifully executed crane shot. A slow zoom begins above a party in Sebastian's house, pulling in, in, in until we reach the nervous Alicia clutching a key to the wine cellar, a key she had just stolen from her unloved husband. This famous shot hearkens back to Hitch's audacious pan to the drummer's face in *Young and Innocent*. This tremendously effective shot illustrates both Alicia's fear and the magnitude of her deceit.

The legendary extended kissing scene was not only a slap in the face of censorship, it was the ultimate portrayal of the passion between Devlin and Alicia. In 1946, film codes restricted on-screen kisses to only a couple seconds. In a move that was Hitchcock both thumbing his nose at these restrictions as well as illustrating a beautifully budding love, Devlin and Alicia engage in a lengthy sequence of short kisses intertwined with dialogue. One of the true hallmarks of the Hitchcock genius was his unique talent for using the burden of filmmaking restrictions to develop better ways to tell a story. Hitchcock viewed filmmaking challenges as opportunities for improving his craft, not as roadblocks.

It is interesting to observe the lack of humor in *Notorious*. In so many of the films we have seen thus far, Hitchcock peppered moments of humor into even the darkest of his films. This is certainly not the case here. And it works. *Notorious* is a picture better served without laughs. The grave situation in which Alicia finds herself would not have been any more identifiable or realistic had levity been made part of it. Hitch was adept at picking his spots for injecting humor, and here he made the right choice in not including it.

While it does not have the eminent rewatchability of *Foreign Correspondent* or *Shadow of a Doubt*, this flawless film is still a terrific example of the best Alfred Hitchcock had to offer. When seen in this context, it's clear what we're seeing: a director who had spent the last seven years refining a new chapter in his personal textbook, further developing his artistic language in a way that, five years later, would serve as the building blocks for the most remarkable decade of creation any director in the history of cinema has ever enjoyed.

CONCLUSION

There is no disputing that *Notorious* is one of Alfred Hitchcock's most critically acclaimed films, and for good reason. Wonderfully written, beautifully shot, and powerfully acted, it serves as a brilliant crescendo to Hitch's early American period.

HITCHCOCKIAN THEMES

Blackmail · Blonde Leading Lady · Exotic Location · Handcuffed Man and Woman ·Love Triangle · MacGuffin · Manipulative Mother · Murder · Spy Syndicate · Unwelcome New Woman

THINGS TO LOOK FOR

- The Kiss. One of the most famous kisses in film history, the lengthy, code-skirting kiss between Cary Grant and Ingrid Bergman is legendary.
- The Shot. Hitchcock's zoom from a wide balcony view to a small key in Ingrid Bergman's hand is deservedly one of the most famous in the Hitchcock canon.
- The unimportance of the film's MacGuffin. Maybe more than any other, the MacGuffin in *Notorious* displays that the specifics are entirely unimportant; the only important thing is that it prompts the characters into action.
- Continuity errors. *Notorious* is surprisingly full of them, from changing background characters to changing props. But more noteworthy is that none of this much matters because the storytelling is so tight.

AWARDS

- Academy Award Nominations (2): Best Actor in a Supporting Role (Claude Rains), Best Screenplay, Original (Ben Hecht)
- Cannes Film Festival Nomination: Grand Prize of the Festival (Alfred Hitchcock)

DVD RELEASES

RELEASE: Criterion Collection (2001)
(Dolby Digital 2.0 Mono, 1.33:1 Black & White)
RATING: *****

EXTRAS: Commentary by Hitchcock film scholar Marian Keane and film historian Rudy Behlmer; complete 1948 *Lux Radio Theatre* radio adaptation; production photos, correspondence, and artwork; trailers and teasers; script excerpts from deleted scenes and alternate endings; excerpts from *The Song of the Dragon*, which served as source material for *Notorious*; newsreel footage; isolated music and effects track.

NOTES: Out of print. Very expensive on the secondary market. Also available as part of the out-of-print boxed set *Wrong Men & Notorious Women*. Highly recommended.

RELEASE: MGM (2008)
(1.33:1 Black & White)
RATING: ****

NOTES: Available as a stand-alone disc or as part of a set with seven other Hitchcock films, *Alfred Hitchcock: Premiere Collection*.

RELEASE: Anchor Bay Home Video (1999)
(Dolby Digital 2.0 Mono, 1.33:1 Black & White)
RATING: ****

TRIVIA/FUN STUFF

✦ The legendary Bergman/Grant kiss was orchestrated the way it was—short kisses with dialogue interspersed between—because code regulations of the day limited how long an on-screen kiss could be. In typical Hitchcock fashion, he found a way to push the envelope.

✦ Claude Rains, a full seven inches shorter than Cary Grant, was asked to stand on a box for several scenes so that he would not appear shorter than Ingrid Bergman. This is most apparent during a scene with Grant, when the two appear to be nearly the same height.

✦ Hitchcock long claimed that because the film dealt with the potential of uranium before it was a matter of wide public knowledge, the FBI had him watched for several months.

✦ Hitchcock also claimed to have come up with the idea of using uranium as a central plot point on his own, without being aware of its role in the creation of the atomic bomb.

✦ In 2006 the film was added to the National Film Registry by the National Film Preservation Board, which selects films that "are considered to be culturally, historically or aesthetically important."

The Paradine Case
(1947)

FILM FACTS

Production Year: 1946
Release Date: December 31, 1947
Studio: Selznick International Pictures
Filming Location: N/A
Presentation/Aspect Ratio: Black & White/1.37:1

SYNOPSIS

Mrs. Paradine (Alida Valli) is on trial for poisoning her husband, a blind military hero. Anthony Keane (Gregory Peck), a respected British attorney, is called to mount her defense. But Keane becomes infatuated with his new client, which jeopardizes the health of his relationship with his wife, Gay (Ann Todd).

IMPRESSIONS

Alfred Hitchcock's sustained run of greatnesses from 1940 to 1946 could not last forever. The ebb and flow of Hitch's career is not unlike the ebb and flow of his films: a slow but steady build, followed by sharp increases in drama divided by clearly defined "catch your breath" moments.

For the next several years, that's exactly what Alfred Hitchcock would do. He would catch his creative breath: reassessing, reorganizing, and, though he may not have been aware of it at the time, refocusing his artistic vision in preparation for his remarkable 1950s period.

Perhaps it shouldn't be surprising that this adjustment period begins with one of Hitchcock's most disappointing films.

Widely considered one of his weakest efforts, *The Paradine Case* is an ill-advised courtroom drama that plays to none of Hitchcock's strengths. On its own that should not be enough to stymie a director of Hitchcock's talents. Here, however, the flaws pile up so high that no amount of technique can turn this ordinary drama into a winner.

The problem with *The Paradine Case* is that it is simply bland. The script, adapted by Hitchcock's wife, Alma Reville, and written by producer David O. Selznick from the Robert Hichens book of the same name, lacks urgency, a conflict worth caring about, or much of anything to hold the viewer's interest. There is something of a murky love triangle pushing this courtroom drama along—several, in fact—but it's vague and uninteresting, played in hints and implication. Gregory Peck offers a forceful performance as attorney Anthony Keane, but even he cannot sustain our interest when there is nothing to be interested *in*. Hitchcock was a master at setting up a conflict and then maintaining the dramatic tension of said conflict over the course of a film. Here, however, his talents failed him. With a flat script and a long running time (initially released at 132 minutes, it's still overly long in the 114-minute version most common today), there were already two big factors working against *The Paradine Case*. An even bigger factor—yet again—was David O. Selznick.

> **WHERE'S HITCH?**
>
> Hitchcock appears about a third of the way into the film carrying a cello case.

Pushy, insistent on seeing his vision dominate Hitchcock's, and overbearing to the point of taking control of the editing and scoring (which explains the film's bombastic, inappropriate music): that was Selznick. It is no stretch to imagine Hitchcock wanted no part of yet another forced "collaboration" with him. It would be their last. It would also be their worst.

What might have happened had Alfred Hitchcock not accepted producer David O. Selznick's offer to work in America? Surely Hitch would have come to the United States at some point, but the decision to work for Selznick had a profound impact on his artistic output in the 1940s, often for the worse. Selznick afforded Hitch the opportunity to advance his American career, but not without forcing him to endure unnecessary interference. Hitchcock was able to overcome Selznick's heavy-handed influence in *Rebecca* and, to a lesser extent, in *Spellbound*, but certainly not in *The Paradine Case*.

Hitchcock's original deal with the producer called for him to make movies for Selznick exclusively. Luckily, Selznick was often in need of financing for other pictures, so Sir Alfred was loaned out to other studios. These other studios afforded him greater artistic freedom. In their eight-year relationship, Hitchcock and Selznick produced just three films together—three films that were increasingly disjointed and rife with incongruous moments.

For all his talents as a producer (he had back-to-back Best Picture Oscars for *Gone with the Wind* and *Rebecca* to show for it), Selznick was not on the same level as a writer. His screenplay for *The Paradine Case* is lacking polish and burdened with an impossible-to-ignore flaw: Why would Anthony Keane fall for Mrs. Paradine? Mrs. Paradine is portrayed as likeable neither to Keane nor to the audience, giving us no reason to believe in his infatuation.

Selznick's overzealous hand was not involved only in penning the script. His influence is seen throughout the film, rarely in a good way. With shooting taking ninety-two days, among Hitchcock's longest productions, Selznick insisted on editing the film himself to avoid paying Hitch his salary of $1,000 per day. The result is a muddled collection of scenes lacking in cohesion.

The one other major flaw in *The Paradine Case* is in the casting. Other than Ann Todd as Mrs. Keane, it seems as if all the major characters are miscast. As beloved an actor as Gregory Peck was, he is not believable as a British lawyer. Hitchcock wanted Laurence Olivier, who would have been perfect for the part, but Selznick had easy access to Peck and insisted on his casting. Also out of place were Alida Valli as Mrs. Paradine and Louis Jourdan as Latour, her lover. Valli was unlikable in a part that demanded some sense of attraction, while Jourdan was charming in a role that required repulsion. Ethel Barrymore, Charles Laughton, Charles Coburn, and Leo G. Carroll *were* well cast, but with so many important characters off the mark, their efforts fail to overcome the wider casting flaws.

If there is anything noteworthy in Hitch's artistic approach here, it is the active camera. Among the most mobile camera work to date, shots push, pull, pan, slide, and are otherwise all over the place. He wanted the audience to notice, too, with objects carefully placed to glide through the field of vision. It is a sometimes lovely, sometimes forced technique that is intrusive as often as it is effective. It also serves as a bit of creative foreshadowing for the next several films, during which Alfred Hitchcock would experiment boldly with long takes and highly mobile camerawork.

It's not that *The Paradine Case* is terrible. It isn't. Once you unravel the basic courtroom conflict, it's clear there is a strong set of interrelationships at play here. The performances are crisp, and Hitch's camera work is excellent (late in the film he uses the 180-degree swing pan more often associated with Sergio Leone and Akira Kurosawa). It's quite an attractive film to look at, really.

It just isn't very *interesting*.

CONCLUSION

The Paradine Case marked the end of Hitchcock's association with powerful producer David O. Selznick. In what is easily the worst of the three films they made together, the viewer is forced to endure a jumbled mess of a picture with characters and situations that neither make sense nor arouse viewer interest. Containing few Hitchcockian traits and little in the way of quality filmmaking, this is one of Hitch's least enjoyable films.

HITCHCOCKIAN THEMES

Blonde Leading Lady · Dark Secret · Love Triangle · Murder

THINGS TO LOOK FOR

- The ever-moving camera.
- The terribly inappropriate and overdone musical score.

TRIVIA/FUN STUFF

- ✦ Hitchcock originally wanted Laurence Olivier to play the part of Anthony Keane, but producer Selznick insisted on Gregory Peck.
- ✦ Hitchcock also wanted Greta Garbo to play the part of Mrs. Paradine, but Selznick insisted on Alida Valli.

AWARDS

● Academy Award Nomination: Best Actress in a Supporting Role (Ethel Barrymore)

DVD RELEASES

RELEASE: MGM (2008)
(1.33:1 Black & White)
RATING: ****

EXTRAS: Commentary with film historians Stephen Rebello and Bill Krohn; isolated music and effects track; 1949 radio play starring Joseph Cotten; Peter Bogdanovich interviews Hitchcock; restoration comparison; theatrical trailer; still gallery; trailer farm.

NOTES: Available as a stand-alone disc or as part of a set with seven other Hitchcock films, *Alfred Hitchcock: Premiere Collection*.

RELEASE: Anchor Bay Entertainment (1999)
(Dolby Digital 2.0 Mono, 1.33:1 Black & White)
RATING: **

Rope
(1948)

FILM FACTS

PRODUCTION YEAR: 1948
RELEASE DATE: August 28, 1948 (U.S.)
STUDIO: Warner Bros.
FILMING LOCATION: Warner Bros. Studios, Burbank Studios, Burbank, California
PRESENTATION/ASPECT RATIO: Color/1.37:1

SYNOPSIS

Young intellectuals Brandon Shaw (John Dall) and Phillip Morgan (Farley Granger) commit a murder just to see what it's like, then take the bold step of throwing a party in their apartment while the body is hidden in plain view. Their plan goes awry when an old teacher, Rupert Cadell (James Stewart), begins to suspect something is amiss. Over the course of eighty real-time minutes, innovatively shot as if it were done in one long take, Brandon and Phillip's plan slowly crumbles, resulting in a dramatic confrontation with Rupert.

IMPRESSIONS

"I undertook *Rope* as a stunt; that's the only way I can describe it. I really don't know how I came to indulge in it."

—Alfred Hitchcock[21]

In this publicity still for *Rope*, Farley Granger and John Dall seem to keep Alfred Hitchcock distracted, while James Stewart contemplates his next move. (Photofest)

Rope was indeed a stunt: a grand cinematic stunt like no other. Nothing quite like it had ever been attempted, and while the result is at times uneven, it is a fascinating picture remembered as one of Hitchcock's most ambitious movies.

Alfred Hitchcock was always up for taking on technical challenges, something apparent even in his earliest films. Witness the trick photography during the climactic boxing scene in *The Ring* and the shot through a champagne glass in *Champagne*. He would continue challenging himself throughout his career, but during this middle period something seemed to be driving him down a path of self-imposed technical hurdles. In 1944 it was *Lifeboat*, the entire film set on one small vessel. In 1945 *Spellbound*'s dream sequences pushed him forward. *Rope* and its follow-up, *Under Capricorn*, would see Hitchcock experimenting with elaborate sets and extended takes, and, several years after that, Sir Alfred would push elaborate sets as far as he could with his 1954 masterpiece, *Rear Window*.

Rope would be one of his most ambitious undertakings. Who but Alfred Hitchcock would dare attempt to set an entire film inside a single apartment and take the audacious steps necessary to film it the way he did? The entire eighty-minute film consists of just nine shots cut together to appear as a single take (with a few exceptions, discussed below). In order to mask his cuts, Hitchcock closed the camera in on a dark, inanimate object at the end of a take. The next take would pull back from the same position; the illusion is one of seamless photography. It works, but only to a point. Watching for these moments, the cuts become obvious to the point of distraction. This is only a minor criticism, because it would be difficult (if not impossible) to find a better solution considering the circumstances Hitch forced upon himself.

Rope is a technical marvel. In order to avoid appearing like a filmed stage play, the camera was in constant motion. Because of the monstrous size of the color film cameras of the late 1940s, this created a huge technical challenge. The camera could not be easily moved from one room to another—certainly not with continuous action and without cuts. Hitch's solution was to have the set built with its walls on tracks, allowing them to be silently moved out of the camera's way. Considering the choreography involved in maneuvering the cast, crew, walls, and set pieces in takes lasting up to ten minutes, all featuring constant character movements, the accomplishment is amazing. The set even featured a faux New York City skyline in the background designed to seamlessly transition from daytime to dusk to nightfall, said to be one of the film's most lavish expenses.

> **WHERE'S HITCH?**
>
> Just under an hour into the film, the famous profile line drawing of Alfred Hitchcock appears on a neon sign seen through the apartment window. In addition, it appears as if one of the pedestrians outside the apartment during the opening moments of the film might be Alfred Hitchcock. This, however, remains unconfirmed.

What got into him? What drove him? Was he growing weary of one spy-laden thriller after another, desperate to flex his creative muscles between more accessible and mainstream films? Likely the explanation is simple: Alfred Hitchcock liked trying new things. It's as simple as that. That's what he did with *Rope*. He created an intricate puzzle for himself, thought he had a solution, and proceeded to build a film around the idea. It largely works, too, to the point that the casual viewer might not pick up on the long takes. Despite the bold attempt at extended shots set in a single apartment, Hitch's clever and suggestive framing and composition remain intact. He swings the shot around to put a murder weapon in the foreground, or maneuvers the characters in such a way that a background element becomes important, or, in one well-done sequence, lets the camera linger on the chest in which our victim's body is hidden as a housekeeper slowly . . . slowly . . . slowly comes close to revealing the murder for all to see.

But it can also be clunky. The filming of conversations is often awkward, and, despite all his effort, much of *Rope* still screams "stage play." The self-imposed limits ultimately end up limiting the scope of the film, too.

Yet hidden in this flawed technical marvel is a good suspense film built upon an interesting (and entirely Hitchcockian) premise. How often have characters in Hitchcock films discussed killing as if it was the most natural thing in the world? Dinner conversations about murder, such as those in *Shadow of a Doubt* and *Suspicion*, are entirely mundane in Hitchcock's universe. That's why it seemed natural, maybe even inevitable, that he would make a film like *Rope*. In it, two young intellectuals decide to commit murder. As an experiment. For fun. Just because they can. And we get to watch them play out their game of murder. This is right up Hitchcock's alley. Based on a play by Patrick Hamilton titled *Rope's End*, it was inspired by a true life murder committed in 1924 by Nathan Leopold and Richard Loeb, two University of Chicago students who felt their superior intellect made them capable of the perfect crime. This is a theme featured prominently in *Rope*.

There is another element to *Rope* that sets it apart from typical 1948 fare: The two leads are homosexual lovers. This is never explicitly mentioned in the movie, but was unquestionably Hitchcock's intent. The opening murder scene is a not-so-veiled metaphor for sex. Listen to the dialogue between Brandon and Phillip in the moments right after the killing. This is post-coitus conversation. Of course, this makes sense coming from Hitchcock; he was often credited as saying he filmed his love scenes like murder scenes and his murder scenes like love scenes.

Rope represents a number of important firsts for Hitchcock. First, this is his first picture as an independent producer after the end of his seven-year contract with David O. Selznick. Free from Selznick's overbearing demands, Hitchcock was able to be his own producer. He could choose his own projects, casts, and crew, enjoying complete creative control over his film projects. The first two pictures Hitch made during this time, *Rope* and *Under Capricorn*, were both financial disasters, but there is no question they were important steps forward for Sir Alfred. For the first time, he was afforded the opportunity for complete accountability in his work.

Rope was also his first color film. Color film technology had been around for a decade at this point, so it is interesting that it took so long for Hitch—ever the adopter of new filmmaking techniques and technologies—to make his first foray into the world of color cinema. The choice to make *Rope* his first color picture is intriguing because, on the one hand, the challenges created by the "no-cut" style of filmmaking were magnified by the use of a new, unfamiliar technology; on the other, the singular setting and muted tones of the costumes and set design were certainly easier to photograph. *Rope* also marks the first of two films Hitchcock produced in his short-lived partnership with Sidney Bernstein, Transatlantic Pictures. The plan was to produce films alternately in Hollywood and London, but the lack of success of the first two pictures (*Under Capricorn* being the other) led to an early end to this venture.

Finally, and perhaps most significantly, this film marks his first collaboration with James Stewart. The casting of Stewart would prove to be the beginning of a wonderful and fruitful director/actor relationship. The two would go on to make three more highly innovative films together (*Rear Window*, *The Man Who Knew Too Much* (1956), and *Vertigo*). Hitch apparently had Cary Grant in mind to play Rupert Cadell, along with Montgomery Clift as one of the young men, but both passed on *Rope* for fear of being associated with homosexuality. Stewart was not entirely right for the part of Rupert, however; he failed to impart a real emotional background with his two former charges. It has been suggested that Rupert also had a sexual relationship with one of the young men, but, to the film's detriment, Stewart's performance does not betray this.

The other leads, however, are more than up to carrying the film. Farley Granger's Phillip Morgan is suitably shaky and nervous, but it is John Dall as Brandon Shaw who steals the show. Vile, full of himself, and the real mastermind behind the killing, Dall sneers and smirks and glides his way through each scene with pure arrogance. That is, when he's not stuttering awkwardly in the presence of Rupert, whom he wants badly to impress. You hate him, but you're drawn to him, too. Not one of Hitchcock's all time great villains, to be sure, but a fine screen presence who manages to carry a lot of weight on his shoulders.

Throughout the film, Hitchcock delights in his ability to tease the audience, often effectively enough so you forget the "all-in-one-take" gimmick. The teases are, of course, essential to the plot. Brandon Shaw is one of those villains who subconsciously wants to be caught; he wants people to know what he did so they can see how brilliant he is, so he serves dinner on the chest in which his murdered friend's body is hidden, ties up a set of books for a party guest with the same rope used in the murder, and is relentless in dropping veiled hints that something is amiss. All of this serves not only to paint a vivid portrait of the character, but to maintain suspense for the audience. When the climax finally comes, complete with an impassioned Stewart monologue, you forget the gimmick, the awkward staging, and the cardboard supporting cast and find yourself wrapped up in the story, on the edge of your seat, and awaiting a resolution.

And in the end, isn't that what a suspense film is all about?

CONCLUSION

Alfred Hitchcock's bold, daring technical experiment is worthy of accolades despite its flaws, but its place in the pantheon of Hitchcock films is debatable. *Rope* has a lot going for it even beyond its "long take" gimmick. The story has bite, the actors are entertaining (if not entirely convincing), and the filmmaking experimentation is worthwhile. Ultimately, however, small niggles keep *Rope* from being ranked among Hitchcock's best. This adds up to make this one of Hitchcock's most important, but not most artistically successful, pictures.

HITCHCOCKIAN THEMES

Blackmail · Dark Secret · Discussion of Murder at Dinner · Love Triangle · Murder

THINGS TO LOOK FOR

- The long, long takes.
- The slow shift from day to night in the set's backdrop.
- The homosexual subtext between the two main characters, and, to a lesser extent, with Stewart's character.
- In an early conversation during the dinner party, veiled references are made to another Hitchcock film, *Notorious*. Look for a mention of Ingrid Bergman to place the scene.

AWARDS

- Edgar Allan Poe Awards Nomination: Best Motion Picture (Arthur Laurents, Patrick Hamilton)

TRIVIA/FUN STUFF

+ This was Alfred Hitchcock's first film made in color.
+ *Rope* was also Alfred Hitchcock's first independently produced film.
+ The little-seen trailer is staged as a scene set prior to the film during which the murder victim and his girlfriend have a conversation in a New York City park—all, of course, with winks at the upcoming murder.
+ *Rope* is loosely based on an actual murder case, a killing committed by University of Chicago students Nathan Leopold and Richard Loeb. The same murder was the subject of the 1959 film *Compulsion*.
+ While the film is famous for being constructed as if it were done in one long take, in fact there are three traditional cuts in the film.
+ James Stewart was not Hitchcock's first choice for the Cadell role. He initially wanted Cary Grant, but Grant feared being associated with homosexuality.
+ Screenwriter Arthur Laurents did not think the actual murder should be shown on screen. Hitchcock disagreed, and the film opened with strangulation.
+ Along with *Vertigo*, *Rear Window*, *The Man Who Knew Too Much*, and *The Trouble with Harry*, rights issues made *Rope* unavailable—and hence unseen by the public—for decades.

DVD RELEASES

RELEASE: Universal Studios (2001, 2005, 2006)
(Dolby Digital 2.0 Mono, 1.33:1 Color)
RATING: ***1/2

EXTRAS: *Rope Unleashed* documentary; theatrical trailer; production notes.
NOTES: Available as stand-alone releases from 2001 and 2006, or as part of *The Alfred Hitchcock Collection* (out of print) and *Alfred Hitchcock: The Masterpiece Collection*. *The Masterpiece Collection* is recommended. The transfers on all releases appear identical.

Under Capricorn
(1949)

FILM FACTS

PRODUCTION YEAR: 1948
RELEASE DATE: September 8, 1949 (U.S.)
STUDIO: Transatlantic Pictures/Warner Bros.
FILMING LOCATIONS: MGM British Studios, Borehamwood,
Hertfordshire, England; Los Angeles County Arboretum & Botanic Garden,
Arcadia, California
PRESENTATION/ASPECT RATIO: Color/1.37:1

SYNOPSIS

It is 1831, and the Honorable Charles Adare (Michael Wilding) of Ireland
moves to Australia, where his uncle has been named the new governor.
There, Adare meets Sam Flusky (Joseph Cotten), a former convict who pro-
poses to do business with him. At a party, Adare is introduced to Flusky's
wife, Lady Henrietta (Ingrid Bergman), an alcoholic who had been friends
with his sister as a child. He attempts to rehabilitate Henrietta, and in doing
so falls in love with her, creating conflict for everyone in the house, including Milly (Margaret Leighton), the housekeeper, who is secretly in love with
Flusky.

IMPRESSIONS

Despite being one of the most little-known and little-watched films in the Hitchcock canon, *Under Capricorn* has a curious and interesting place in Hitch history. It would be his final period piece/costume drama (and only his second overall), his second color film, the second and final film from his short-lived venture with Sidney Bernstein of Transatlantic Pictures, and his final production with favored actress Ingrid Bergman.

None of this adds up to a great film, only to interesting historical footnotes.

Yet, that said, *Under Capricorn*'s dismal reputation as a failure is probably not well deserved. While far from one of the great Hitchcock productions, it manages to be a passable (and beautifully shot) drama that deserves a second look.

Hot off the heels of his grand experiment with long takes in *Rope*, Hitchcock still had self-indulgent cinematography in mind when he took on this nineteenth-century tale of love both lost and unrequited. This time, rather than burden the entire film with what some would say amounts to a gimmick, the long takes are limited to a few specific scenes. Some of these shots are among Hitchcock's most ambitious and cinematically successful, making it almost tragic that they're lost in a film few beyond Hitch's most devoted fans will ever see.

Under Capricorn puts an unfamiliar set of clothes on themes common in the universe of Alfred Hitchcock. Previously, only *Jamaica Inn*—his dreadful final English film—was set in a period other than the present day. Here, we jump back to 1831, and overseas to Australia—entirely unfamiliar territory in Hitchcock's world. Yet aspects of the story, notably the quartet of lovers, prospective lovers, and aspiring lovers, would be right at home in any number of Hitchcock films.

At the heart of the drama is Sam Flusky and Lady Henrietta Flusky, a married couple living an awkward, sheltered life thanks to Lady Henrietta's apparent drunken insanity. Into the picture strolls Lady Henrietta's childhood friend, Charles Adare, who comes to desire Lady Henrietta for his own, and Milly, the Fluskys' housekeeper, who secretly desires Sam Flusky for *her* own.

We've seen this sort of thing before: Love triangles, and even dual, interwoven triangles, have been a part of Hitchcock's films from the start. *Rich and Strange*, another ambitious but ultimately unsuccessful film, springs

Joseph Cotten and Ingrid Bergman in a rare period thriller from Hitchcock. (Warner Bros./Photofest © Warner Bros.)

to mind. Yet despite its reputation, *Under Capricorn* is more artistically successful than *Rich and Strange*, and by a long way.

So, too, do we see hints of *Rebecca*. In that film's case, it was a female intruder into a house all but ruled by a servant who prompted the turmoil to follow. In *Under Capricorn*, the intruder is male. When Adare arrives on the scene, the servant, Milly, secretly enamored with Sam Flusky and keeping Mrs. Flusky in a constant drunken stupor because of it, adopts the bitter lover-who-could-not-be role Mrs. Danvers plays in *Rebecca*.

The thematic heart of *Under Capricorn* works well enough for what it is. Milly is suitably manipulative, and Adare's intentions are left unclear long enough to leave you guessing, revealed in time to spark Sam Flusky into misguided action. The problem is that this subject matter is simply not Hitchcock's specialty. As we've previously discussed, love is no stranger to the films of Alfred Hitchcock, nor is lost love. But as the focus? This is a character-driven story, and Hitchcock is a plot-driven director. As visually lush as this film is, he falls just short of realizing the tone needed to create an engaging story. And yes, *just* short. *Under Capricorn* has a reputation as one of Alfred Hitchcock's worst films, but it is not a deserved reputation. As a character-driven period piece it may be wildly out of character for Hitchcock, but that doesn't mean there is not worthwhile filmmaking here.

In fact, *Under Capricorn* features some of the most audacious and lush cinematography of his career. The 117 minutes here are worthwhile for the grand dinner introduction scene alone. Over the course of eight or nine minutes, the camera is nothing short of a roving eye, leading us through a dank and dirty kitchen, through a dining room that will play a key role in the film, a foyer that will do the same, then into a side room where Sam Flusky meets guest after guest, all as the camera moves and shapes each conversation. It's incredible work that preceded the famous Copacabana entry shot in Martin Scorsese's *GoodFellas* (1990) by more than forty years. Hitchcock couldn't have pulled this off without the experience provided by *Rope*. With the lessons learned there, he managed to create one of the single most spectacular shots of his career, on par with the wonderful zooms in *Young and Innocent* and *Notorious*.

We also get a less audacious long take in Lady Henrietta's confession scene, but one that may be even more impressive than the dinner scene because it's so focused on raw *performance*. For just short of nine minutes, Ingrid Bergman puts on an acting clinic. No cuts. No breaks. No pauses.

> **WHERE'S HITCH?**
>
> Hitchcock appears on the steps in front of a government building, about thirteen minutes into the film.

Just Ingrid Bergman revealing that the drunken, sick Lady Henrietta was a more tortured soul than we previously imagined, letting unfold the entire story of how the Flusky couple came to be: their tragedy, their turmoil, the dark days that made Sam who he is. All of it. It's a powerful, well-acted, tastefully staged scene.

These two standout long takes are part of a larger tapestry that includes more fine camerawork. At one point—twice, actually—Sam Flusky and Charles Adare are talking in front of Flusky's estate, the camera following them as they walk, when it suddenly sweeps upward to the second floor to reveal Lady Henrietta gazing painfully from a balcony above. Beautiful.

Yet the film's reputation suggests it is terrible cinema. Conventional wisdom says it's widely considered among the worst of Alfred Hitchcock's career, an entirely forgettable costume drama better passed over for more traditionally Hitchcockian films.

To an extent, conventional wisdom is wrong. *Under Capricorn* is lush like *Rebecca* without feeling hollow, artistically daring like *Rope* without stumbling over its own boldness, and beautifully acted by the whole cast. It may not be traditionally Hitchcockian, and it falls far short of being a masterpiece, but it has far more going for it than critics over the years would have you believe.

But what about the traditional school of thought? Is there merit to the notion that *Under Capricorn* is, in fact, not worth seeing? It is a legitimate and defensible viewpoint.

Under Capricorn is a beautiful picture, to be sure—with elaborate sets, stunning costumes, and outstanding photography—but too often the beauty is overshadowed by talk with little substance and a murky narrative that never seems to hit its stride. To keep the viewer engaged, a drama built around multiple love stories demands urgency in its conflict. The drive to the rather lackluster conclusion is slow, uneven, and unable to convey the depth of the characters' internal conflicts.

Bergman, Cotten, Wilding, and Leighton form the core of an excellent lead cast. It's just too bad this terrific group of actors were forced to work with a scattershot script by Hume Cronyn, who also worked on the script for *Rope* and acted in both *Shadow of a Doubt* and *Lifeboat*. The dialogue is wordy and lacks force. Hitchcock had asked his friend Cronyn to write this script, but later realized this was a mistake. Hitch said, "I wanted him because he's a very articulate man who knows how to voice his ideas. But, as a scriptwriter he hadn't really sufficient experience."[22]

The ending to *Under Capricorn* is perhaps its biggest disappointment. It's so anticlimactic and so lacking in punch that one has difficulty taking it seriously. How can a story like this end so cleanly? It begs for betrayal and heartbreak, but, aside from Milly's downfall, we get none of that. A story this dark and gloomy should not end on such a positive note.

Additionally, the music in this picture is not right for the story. It's cartoonish and distracting. Though often adept at choosing appropriate music for his films, Hitchcock failed here.

It would be inaccurate to call *Under Capricorn* a complete failure; it truly does have a lot going for it. The photography, set designs, costumes, and cast are all wonderful elements, but problems with dialogue, pacing, and story tend to cloud what otherwise might be a compelling movie.

CONCLUSION

While *Under Capricorn's* overall quality is debatable, this picture has a lot that makes it worth seeing. The audacious long takes, stunning photography, and excellent performance by Bergman play tug-of-war with a poor script and wooden dialogue. It will never be seen as one of Hitchcock's great works, but this is certainly not for lack of effort or filmmaking merit.

HITCHCOCKIAN THEMES

Blonde Leading Lady • Dark Secret • Love Triangle • Murder

THINGS TO LOOK FOR

- The ever-moving camera.
- Three extended long takes.
- The cartoonish and inappropriate musical score.

TRIVIA/FUN STUFF

✦ One of two period pieces made by Hitchcock; the other was *Jamaica Inn*.
✦ This was the third and final pairing of Hitchcock and screen legend Ingrid Bergman.

DVD RELEASES

RELEASE: Image Entertainment (2003)
(Dolby Digital 2.0 Mono, 1.33:1 Color)
RATING: ***

Stage Fright
(1950)

FILM FACTS

Production Year: 1949
Release Date: April 15, 1950 (U.S.)
Studio: Warner Bros.
Filming Location: N/A
Presentation/Aspect Ratio: Black & White/1.37:1

SYNOPSIS

When actress Charlotte Inwood (Marlene Dietrich) comes to Jonathan Cooper (Richard Todd) for help—she has just killed her husband and doesn't know what to do—he is so taken in by her charm, he agrees to help make it look like an accident. But Cooper is spotted at the scene of the crime, making him a suspect in the killing and sending him on the run. He enlists the aid of his friend Eve Gill (Jane Wyman), who helps him elude Detective Wilfred Smith (Michael Wilding) and gather evidence to clear his name. That is, until he reveals that he can't clear his name because his story was a lie from the very start. He was the real killer all along. Eve, as well as the audience, have been lied to.

IMPRESSIONS

After the grand experiment with color and long takes in *Rope* and *Under Capricorn*, Alfred Hitchcock moved back to a more traditional approach with *Stage Fright*. Back was black-and-white photography; gone were gimmicks.

At first glance, it would be understandable to think Hitchcock took an artistic step backward with *Stage Fright*, returning to a seemingly straightforward "innocent man" thriller after a series of films that pushed his craft forward. Like *Stage Fright*'s first look into the story at hand, however, that first glance is unreliable. This film finds Alfred Hitchcock playing with a technique he had never used before (in the "unreliable narrator"), showcasing how his experiments with long takes can be used effectively in a mainstream thriller, and continuing down the road of ever-darkening villains that began roughly with *Shadow of a Doubt*. While it fails to rise to the level of Hitch's best—it lacks an intangible *something*—*Stage Fright* is a better-than-average thriller.

Perhaps the most noteworthy aspect of the film is its "unreliable narrator." The opening flashback showing the film's murder is at the end revealed to be false; our "innocent" man is, in fact, the murderer. This ran contrary to traditional storytelling methods of the time, and apparently Hitchcock regretted the decision. "I did one thing in that picture that I never should have done; I put in a flashback that was a lie,"[23] Hitch told François Truffaut. This is a case where

> ### WHERE'S HITCH?
>
> In one of his most obvious cameos, Hitchcock is seen on the street walking past our leading lady, turning to look at her while she is disguised as a maid.

time has been good to a movie like *Stage Fright*. More than fifty years later it has become just another cinematic device, such as in modern cult classics like *The Usual Suspects* (1995), but in its day it was a remarkably risky decision. It has been said that Hitchcock did not even realize what he was doing until after he saw the finished picture, and by then it was too late to change. Modern audiences benefit from his alleged error. Hitch may have regretted the decision, but it ultimately works well and adds to the film's mystery.

More important than his experiments with story were how his technical skills had grown. Not ten minutes into the film we see how the ambitious experiments of *Rope* and *Under Capricorn* added new techniques to his directorial arsenal. Jonathan Cooper is about to enter the home of friend and actress Charlotte Inwood. His plan—or so the audience thinks—is to tamper with evidence proving she has just killed her husband. Our shot begins outside the home, with Cooper on the street, facing the front door. He walks toward the door, the camera following. Opens the door. Enters. The camera seamlessly trails him inside. He closes the door behind himself, but rather than the door closing in the viewer's figurative face, we find we're now in the home, too. A wonderful little shot crafted in part by the lessons (the breakaway sets especially) learned from the prior two films. And yet that's just the start. The camera has yet to cut away. Cooper, nervous, tense, and potentially in over his head, must make his way upstairs to find Mr. Inwood's body in order to cover up the murder. The stairway winds upward, beginning on Cooper's right and spiraling around the room to a doorway above, on the left. So, now in the house, the shot still unbroken, he climbs the stairway—around, around, around—until he is framed by the doorway of the room in which the murder took place, the camera rising and following the whole way. This long, unbroken shot would look like a steadicam shot to a modern viewer (years before the steadicam was invented), but was in fact accomplished with bulky, unwieldy technology of the early 1950s.

And it isn't showboating. Like so many of Hitchcock's directorial flourishes, this one serves a purpose. In this case, the tension of the scene, as well as Cooper's own nervousness, is heightened tenfold by the technique. We feel as if we're creeping into the house with him, making the viewer complicit in his crime.

The cast, featuring Jane Wyman, Marlene Dietrich, and Michael Wilding (who played Charles Adare in *Under Capricorn*), is excellent. Wyman is asked to do a lot because her character is something different to every other character, and she does a great job playing the extremes of confidence and hesitance. Legendary screen star Dietrich was an inspired choice to play Charlotte Inwood, a conniving woman who was well aware of the power of her stardom. And Wilding turned in another strong performance for Hitchcock as the detective who falls in love with a woman who is not all she seems.

In addition to the strong leads, *Stage Fright* is blessed with a fantastic supporting cast. Returning once again to London as the setting for a film, Hitch populates *Stage Fright* with a slew of character actors from Britain, little known in the United States but respected in his home country. Particularly memorable are Eve's parents (Alastair Sim and Sybill Thorndike), a quirky couple who maintain separate residences, and Nellie Goode (Kay Walsh), Charlotte Inwood's blackmailing dresser, who takes advantage of her situation when Eve's position becomes treacherous. These characters, especially Eve's father, work well with the heavily British humor: dry, a bit

Richard Todd and Jane Wyman backstage. (Warner Bros./Photofest © Warner Bros.)

wacky, even slightly slapstick. This is most evident in the hilarious carnival scene with Joyce Grenfell working the shooting stand. The scene is entirely unessential, yet is so full of character and charm you can't help but love it. Arguably, it is the wide-ranging supporting cast that truly gives *Stage Fright* its strength, keeping the viewer interested from scene to scene more than the somewhat lacking story.

That's a tightrope Hitchcock had walked from the beginning of his career. Even the most ardent Hitchcock supporter would have a difficult time arguing against the notion that some of the stories he told were, at their core, relatively simplistic in structure. For a largely plot-driven director like Alfred Hitchcock, one might think this would sound the bells of doom. Hitch, however, was adept at letting his characters—leading and supporting alike—drive his narratives forward.

But doesn't that mean Alfred Hitchcock was, in fact, a character-driven director?

No, it does not. An examination of his films reveals that, by and large, most are contingent upon a very specific set of plot points, plot points that could (and would) take place regardless of the characters being dragged through them. His stories do not unfold by virtue of the characters' nature, but because his plots would die without characters to serve as chess pieces for those stories. (A generalization, of course, with notable exceptions; *Shadow of a Doubt*, for instance, is very much a character-driven film.) Yet as *Stage Fright* clearly shows, Hitchcock was ever cognizant of the fact that audiences need interesting characters to root for, to root against, to amuse them, to intrigue them. And that's what we get here: a rich cast to elevate the film to greater heights than it might otherwise reach.

She does not have a particularly memorable or important role, but it is worth noting that *Stage Fright* marks the first screen appearance for Sir Alfred's daughter, Patricia Hitchcock. Here she plays Chubby Bannister, one of Eve's friends at the Royal Academy of Dramatic Art, where Patricia herself was in real life studying the craft of acting. She would later appear in two other Hitchcock films, *Strangers on a Train* and *Psycho*, both in more prominent roles.

Prevalent themes turn up time and again throughout the Hitchcock filmography. *Stage Fright* is no different. Here we have multiple love triangles (between Charlotte, Jonnie, Wilfred, and Eve), the wrongfully accused, a man on the run, murder, blackmail, a female lead falling in love with a police officer investigating a murder committed by someone she knows, and a less-than-flattering portrait of a mother, to name just a few. These themes appear in multiple Hitchcock films, but again, he always finds new and interesting ways to insert them into his work. Never do his recurring themes seem tired or passé.

After having directed more than thirty films, most directors would have been on the decline. Not Alfred Hitchcock. *Stage Fright* is far from his best work, but it is nevertheless a tense picture with a lot to recommend.

What's even more amazing is that Hitch still has at least ten films to come that are better than this.

CONCLUSION

It would be an exaggeration to call *Stage Fright* a forgotten Hitchcock classic. The film simply does not rise to that level of greatness. It would not be an exaggeration, however, to call *Stage Fright* a fine thriller true to the Alfred Hitchcock spirit, a well-crafted film that proves even Hitchcock's mid-level work makes for better than average viewing.

HITCHCOCKIAN THEMES

Blackmail · Chaos in an Unexpected Location · Dark Secret · Ineffectual Authority Figures · Man (or Woman) on the Run · Murder · Music Plays a Role in Plot · Woman with Cop Boyfriend

THINGS TO LOOK FOR

- The false flashback creates an intriguing twist on what might otherwise be a straightforward suspense thriller.
- Continued use of longer takes.
- The outstanding supporting cast made up of primarily British players.

TRIVIA/FUN STUFF

- ✦ Marlene Dietrich insisted her costumes be supplied by Dior, with Dior receiving a listing in the credits. Paramount complied with this request, but only after insisting on—and receiving—a 25 percent discount on costume costs.
- ✦ The first of three Alfred Hitchcock films featuring his daughter Patricia (followed by *Strangers on a Train* and *Psycho*).

AWARDS

- Edgar Allan Poe Awards Nomination: Best Motion Picture

DVD RELEASES

RELEASE: Warner Home Video (2004)
(Dolby Digital 2.0 Mono, 1.33:1 Black & White)
RATING: ***

EXTRAS: *Hitchcock and Stage Fright* documentary; theatrical trailer.

NOTES: Available as a stand-alone or as part of *The Alfred Hitchcock Signature Collection*.

Strangers on a Train
(1951)

FILM FACTS

PRODUCTION YEAR: 1950
RELEASE DATE: June 30, 1951 (U.S.)
STUDIO: Warner Bros.
FILMING LOCATIONS: Danbury, Connecticut;
Los Angeles, California; Washington, D.C.
PRESENTATION/ASPECT RATIO: Black & White/1.37:1

SYNOPSIS

Tennis player Guy Haines (Farley Granger) meets psychopathic playboy Bruno Anthony (Robert Walker) aboard a train, where they lunch during travel from New York City to Washington, D.C. Haines is in love with socialite Anne Morton (Ruth Roman), the daughter of a senator (Leo G. Carroll), but his estranged wife (Laura Elliott) will not grant him the divorce he needs in order to be with his true love. Bruno, who suffers from an overbearing father, suggests they swap murders—he will kill Guy's wife if Guy will kill Bruno's father. Guy does not take this discussion seriously—but Bruno does, killing Guy's wife and setting off a spiral of tragic events.

Farley Granger considers Robert Walker's proposal. (Warner Bros./Photofest © Warner Bros.)

IMPRESSIONS

Alfred Hitchcock loved his villains. Make a list of the top ten—or even top five—most memorable characters in Hitchcock's filmography and a majority of them will be villains. He knew that if made loathsome yet charismatic, a good villain could captivate an audience.

Arguably the most menacing, memorable, and vile of those villains is Robert Walker's twisted Bruno Anthony, the focal point of the madness that is *Strangers on a Train*. It would be impossible to underestimate Walker's role in making *Strangers*—widely considered one of the best mid-period Hitchcock films, and indeed one of his best films overall—the classic it is. While the film is well directed, featuring a compelling story and boasting a solid cast of characters, Walker's performance quite simply *is Strangers on a Train*.

Is it any wonder Hitch was attracted to this story, based on a novel by the then-unknown Patricia Highsmith (whose novel *The Talented Mr. Ripley* was the basis for an excellent—and most Hitchcockian—film of the same name in 1999)? It was loaded with themes common in Hitchcock cinema. And it is not just the themes that would have piqued the director's interest—there was also a genuinely interesting and thrilling story to be told.

In classic Hitchcock fashion, with Guy Haines we have a seemingly ordinary man who gets caught up in a situation out of his control. That situation, however, has nothing to do with spy syndicates and secret plans. It has to do with his relationship with another man.

And that man is a psychopath.

As littered with iconic directorial touches as *Strangers* is, the whole film hinges on this man. Are we charmed by him? Are we disgusted by him? Are we both repulsed and fascinated by him? If the answer to these questions is yes—and it is—then we have a classic on our hands. A film like this cannot survive on grand set pieces. It must have an edge. Anything less than a perfect villain in this case brings the film down with it.

But we don't have anything less than a perfect villain. This is as unsettling an individual as you're likely to find on screen: a man with no boundaries and no morals, save the pursuit of that which pleases him. We first saw this kind of lunatic with Uncle Charlie in *Shadow of a Doubt*. We return to that inner darkness—a man entirely out of touch with how people interact with one another—with Bruno Anthony. Here we have a charming, intelligent, charismatic man who is also as twisted, detached, and (arguably) evil as they come. The world around him is a game—a test to see how far he can push, how he can exploit others. With this film Sir Alfred goes down a road he was prone to from time to time, exploring the inner workings of a man on the fringe of society who looks at the world askew from a veil of inner darkness.

Biographers like Donald Spoto hint that maybe folks like Bruno were a window into Hitchcock's own mind—into his thoughts, his twisted fascinations. We've precious little evidence beyond Hitchcock's body of work to back such a theory, yet it can't be denied that said body of work often peaked when a sociopathic villain with an inability to interact with the world around him was on the scene. We could attribute this to an affinity in Hitchcock toward, shall we say, antisocial thinking.

Instead let's attribute it to something simpler: that such twisted villainy stands out most in Hitchcock's career because such twisted villainy stands out most *anywhere*. Individuals of such a depraved nature will always be more fascinating than a generic "bad guy," and thus are much more capable of manipulating an audience. Hitchcock's love for audience manipulation is well established; hence his forays into exploring the minds of depraved individuals. He could use these villains to deftly tug his audience's strings, always his ultimate goal. These individuals are more likely to be fascinating not simply because of Hitchcock, but by virtue of their very nature.

But take that with as large a grain of salt as you should take any other Hitchcock writer willing to psychoanalyze. At the end of the day, all we can judge by—and all that truly matters—are the films. And what a film *Strangers on a Train* is.

Like so many of his better works, the tone for *Strangers on a Train* is set at the outset. A brilliant opening sequence introduces the two leads, Guy and Bruno. We see what appear to be two random pairs of legs—one adorned with pinstriped pants and flashy two-toned shoes, the other in more conservative gray pants and black shoes—each on their way to catch a train. We do not see the faces of the men attached to these shoes until a chance encounter sets the plot in motion. This introduction immediately highlights how different these characters are, while also illustrating how incidental events can lead to unexpected intrigue. Hitchcock loved how seemingly small things could have a profound impact on one's life. Few films display that more than *Strangers on a Train*.

The rest of the cast is overshadowed by Walker's performance, but that is no criticism of the acting of Farley Granger and Ruth Roman. Neither Guy Haines nor Anne Morton is the type one would remember over Bruno Anthony, not because the actors are anything less than competent in their roles, but because of the purposely ordinary nature of their characters. Their work is not to the film's detriment. Neither is the work of Patricia Hitchcock, in a much larger role here than in *Stage Fright*. This time around she was given a meatier character, one she could really get into—and she does. She's funny and charming in one of the few sources of comic relief in an otherwise dark film.

Strangers on a Train is typical Hitchcock in that it is replete with his directorial touches. This is Hitch at his most engaged, a uniquely talented director thoroughly excited by the opportunity to tell a story that interested him. Hitchcock was at his best when he was excited by his work. We see this clearly with *Strangers on a Train*.

Two sequences stand out above the rest. Both are worth special attention. First is the scene that depicts the murder of Guy's wife, Miriam. Instead of simply filming a strangulation, which would have had to be brief to satisfy the censors, Hitchcock chose to film the murder reflected on the lens of Miriam's broken glasses. The result is a lingering, disturbing killing that could not have appeared on film had it been shot using traditional methods. The Master of Suspense ingeniously made the scene less violent, but at the same time even more intense and shocking.

The other great sequence takes place when Bruno goes to watch Guy play tennis. The viewer is treated to the fantastic image of Bruno sitting amid a large crowd of tennis fans. They are engrossed in the match, moving their heads from left to right to follow the action on the court. But Bruno's head does not move with the crowd's. His gaze is transfixed on Guy. It is a powerful indicator of what a psychopath Bruno Anthony really is.

Brimming with dark, dark thoughts and an ever-growing sense of menace, *Strangers on a Train* is as disturbing a look into as twisted a mind as you'll see prior to the 1970s, matching—and maybe even exceeding—the brooding work in *Shadow of a Doubt*. On the heels of the plot-driven *Stage Fright*, Hitch lets this film work at its own pace, pushed forward less by pivotal plot twists and more by the growing tension between our two leads. It is, again, much like *Shadow of a Doubt* in that respect. As it becomes increasingly clear to Guy that he is dealing with a maniac, it also becomes clear he's dealing with a *brilliant* maniac who has played his hand perfectly. There are moments when you want to lose sympathy for Guy. He makes poor decisions. But as Bruno slithers his way out of the shadows and stalks Guy, we forget Guy's bad choices and remember that we're scared for him.

The grim look into the workings of a deranged mind has shown up a few times prior to *Strangers*. The theme is not alien to Hitchcock's work, yet here

---

WHERE'S HITCH?

Hitchcock appears about eleven minutes into the film, carrying a double bass fiddle case as he boards a train, recalling his cameo in *The Paradine Case*.

---

he seems to have reached a turning point. *Strangers on a Train* delights in its darkness in a way *Shadow of a Doubt* does not. If in *Shadow* we're repulsed by the sociopathic cynicism, in *Strangers* we *embrace* it. It's a sign of things to come: Henceforth, Hitchcock's work will show an increasing fascination with minds on the edge of sanity.

Indeed, the similarities between *Strangers on a Train* and *Shadow of a Doubt* are considerable. In both films, Hitchcock set innocent, likeable characters (Guy and Young Charlie) against charmingly evil madmen (Bruno and Uncle Charlie), but made the bad guys easy to root for. We are satisfied by their ultimate demise, but not before finding ourselves thoroughly fascinated by them. As with *Shadow*, in *Strangers* Hitchcock took great pains to introduce as many instances of doubles or pairs as possible in order to depict the duality of man. While it is not something that will jump out at the viewer as important, it is this attention to detail that makes Hitchcock's best work so rewarding upon multiple viewings. We have two strangers meeting on a train, two scenes of tennis, two Morton sisters, two scenes of strangulation, two scenes at the carnival, two boyfriends for Miriam, two men assigned to keep an eye on Guy, and two scenes where Bruno is impacted by the sight of eyeglasses, to name just a few. That he would add seemingly minor things to an already intriguing story is a testament to Hitch's storytelling creativity.

This was Hitchcock's most impeccably directed film in five years, riding high on moment after moment of directorial genius. And those moments come furiously: the strong homosexual subtext in the meeting of Bruno Anthony and Guy Haines; the grim murder-seen-through-reflection of Guy's wife, Miriam, which is one of the most memorable and difficult murder scenes in the Hitchcock filmography; the disturbing scene when Bruno passes out while choking a partygoer; and of course, the climactic showdown at the carnival.

If *Strangers on a Train* has faults, they are minor. A vital tennis match during the film's climax probably goes on for too long, swapping tension for tedium. With so much on the line, why didn't Guy throw the match? In addition, Farley Granger is a great "aw-shucks" actor, but he fails to carry scenes with strong emotion. And that's about it.

In many ways, this film was a signal that Alfred Hitchcock had not only returned to form after a handful of mediocre films, he had come back stronger than ever.

Over the course of the next ten years, he would go on to prove exactly that.

CONCLUSION

Strangers on a Train is not one of Hitchcock's most well-known movies, but it is certainly one of his best. Overflowing with Hitchcockian themes and directorial flourishes, not to mention a thrilling story, likeable characters, and one of the most memorable of all of Hitch's villains, this picture is an essential part of any examination of his work.

HITCHCOCKIAN THEMES

Blackmail • Chaos in an Unexpected Location • Dark Secret • Discussion of Murder at Dinner • Ineffectual Authority Figures • Man (or Woman) on the Run • Manipulative Mother • Murder • Trains • Wrongly Accused

THINGS TO LOOK FOR

- The opening sequence introducing the two leads.
- The filming of murder reflected on the victim's broken eyeglasses.
- Bruno at the tennis match, his eyes locked on Guy while the crowd watches the match.
- Numerous instances of doubles or pairs.

TRIVIA/FUN STUFF

- ✦ Hitchcock bought the rights to the novel anonymously and was thus able to secure them for the low price of just $7,500.
- ✦ Raymond Chandler (who wrote, among other things, the brilliant *Double Indemnity*), is given screenplay credit, but the vast majority of the screenplay was rewritten by Czenzi Ormonde, an assistant to frequent Hitchcock collaborator Ben Hecht, from a detailed treatment by Hitchcock.

AWARDS

- Academy Award Nomination: Best Cinematography, Black-and-White (Robert Burks)
- Directors' Guild of America Nomination: Outstanding Directorial Achievement in Motion Pictures

DVD RELEASES

RELEASE: Warner Home Video (1997, 2004)
(Dolby Digital 2.0 Mono, 1.33:1 Black & White)
RATING: ****1/5

EXTRAS: Audio commentary by Peter Bogdanovich, Joseph Stefano, Andrew Wilson, and others; 103-minute preview version of the film; *Strangers on a Train: A Hitchcock Classic* documentary; three featurettes: *The Hitchcocks on Hitch, Strangers on a Train: The Victim's P.O.V.*, and *Strangers on a Train: An Appreciation by M. Night Shyamalan*; *Alfred Hitchcock's Historical Meeting* newsreel footage.

NOTES: The out-of-print 1997 release features text bios and the newsreel footage. The two-disc special edition released in 2004 features the slightly recut British print, which has a more overt homosexual subtext at the film's opening, as well as the above-listed extras. Available as a stand-alone or as part of *The Alfred Hitchcock Signature Collection*. This DVD release is one of the best available for any Hitchcock film.

I Confess
(1953)

FILM FACTS

PRODUCTION YEAR: 1952
RELEASE DATE: March 22, 1953 (U.S.)
STUDIO: Warner Bros.
FILMING LOCATIONS: Québec City, Québec, Canada; Warner Bros. Studios,
Burbank Studios, Burbank, California
PRESENTATION/ASPECT RATIO: Black & White/1.37:1

SYNOPSIS

When the poor, elderly Otto Keller (O. E. Hasse) is caught robbing a
man, he kills him in a panic. Keller later confesses his crime to Father
Michael Logan (Montgomery Clift), a Catholic priest. Father Logan's
religious vow to remain silent about the confession becomes more than
just a burden, however, when a police inspector (Karl Malden) pegs Logan
himself as the murderer. Matters are not helped when a past affair with
the beautiful Ruth Grandfort (Anne Baxter) appears to give Logan motivation to commit the murder. He must clear his name without breaking
his sacred oath.

IMPRESSIONS

I Confess is both typical and atypical Alfred Hitchcock. On one hand, it is dark, brooding, and populated with themes like murder and betrayal. On the other, it is completely lacking in humor and is built upon perhaps the most contrived plot in the entire Hitchcock filmography. The result is a film very difficult to judge. Is this a worthwhile thriller or a misguided failure? The answer lies somewhere in between.

A flawed film is most tragic when those flaws keep it from reaching the heights it could have reached. Such is the case with *I Confess*, a bleakly shot, powerfully acted drama whose bold themes cannot quite overcome a script with too many contrived plot devices. The flaws are not quite fatal, but they do mar what could have been one of Hitch's most harrowing looks at a conflicted mind.

With a plot that leaves one wondering what Hitch was thinking, it's left to Montgomery Clift and the rest of the cast to carry the film's weight. Pity the weight is not as heavy as it could have been.

The cast is indeed a great strength. Clift, Anne Baxter, Karl Malden, Brian Aherne, Roger Dann, O. E. Hasse, and Dolly Haas are uniformly outstanding. Clift is terrific in the part of Father Michael Logan. His amazing screen presence was never better suited for a role than this one. His face—particularly his eyes—tells more of the story of Father Logan's inner struggles than the dialogue or on-screen action. It is around his masterful acting that the entire film revolves. Without Clift's great lead work, *I Confess* would likely be an afterthought in Hitchcock's career. One of the earliest method actors, Clift was said to have exasperated Hitchcock on the set, sometimes balking at Hitch's instructions if they did not meet with his vision for the character. If their working relationship was rocky, however, the results certainly are not. His way of expressing volumes without saying a word; the depth of pain and resolve in his eyes; his tense, tight, and tortured manner—Clift shines in the role.

Also worth special mention are Hasse and Haas, two German actors brought in to play the Kellers, German immigrants living in the church rectory. Hasse is mesmerizing, especially in his bookend confession scenes, while Haas is understated but memorable as the woman who betrays her husband to save another man.

Acting is not this picture's sole strength. The camera work is also excellent. *I Confess* is beautifully shot, the black-and-white photography highlighted by fantastic use of shadows; this is some of Hitchcock's best looking work, helped along by location shooting. The decision to film exteriors in Québec was against the norm in the studio system, but it works wonders for the finished product. Hitch does a great job of utilizing the beauty of Québec City, notably in the opening shot (which recalls both *Rebecca* and *Shadow of a Doubt*) and the climactic sequences. Hitchcock was not known for location shooting, being much more comfortable shooting in a studio, yet, recognizing the importance of capturing Québec's essence, he took great advantage of the opportunities the location shoot afforded.

But then there is the matter of plot.

On paper, the story of a Catholic priest who hears a murder confession and must then conceal his knowledge of said murder even as he himself becomes a suspect is certainly intriguing. There is little doubt it would have appealed to Hitchcock's fascination with the aftermath of murder, especially in light of his stern Catholic upbringing. The notion that a priest must never reveal the secrets of a confession, and in fact must never even acknowledge to the confessor what was heard, is a fascinating precept around which to build a plot. Not only does it make for great drama, it also makes for an intriguing tale when someone decides to take advantage of the situation.

Yet screenwriters George Tabori and William Archibald, with considerable input from Hitchcock, made the terrible mistake of adding complexity to the narrative in their adaptation of a play by Paul Anthelme. What could have worked beautifully as a simple story of a priest's struggles to deal with a confession is muddled by an overly

> **WHERE'S HITCH?**
>
> Hitch appears in the distance at the top of a flight of stairs in the first minutes of the film.

contrived plot. In order to make Logan a plausible suspect to police by creating a motivation for him to kill, Hitchcock introduced the notion of blackmail. A reasonable addition to the story? Maybe. But the way it is executed borders on ridiculous. That Logan and a former lover, Madame Villefort, would meet for the first time in years to discuss being blackmailed—blackmail perpetrated by the murder victim, no less—on the same night as the murder is too fantastic to believe. Suspension of disbelief can stretch only so far. To trust this confluence of events is too much to ask of an audience.

The series of coincidences around which the plot is built are implausible and wholly unnecessary. Clift's brooding performance is enough to carry the film without them. *I Confess* would have been a greater artistic success had Hitchcock allowed exactly that. Instead, the old love triangle card is

Dolly Haas and Montgomery Clift. (Warner Bros./Photofest © Warner Bros.)

once again played, creating a subplot that grows to be larger than what should be the heart of the film—Father Logan's struggle to keep his vow of silence even as he is falsely accused of a crime. This side story of long-suppressed love, told at times in flashback, is not only distracting, it's an example of glaringly unfocused storytelling by a director not usually prone to such wanderings.

The weighty subject matter is further lessened by a climactic finish that arguably should not have been. Father Logan is put on trial for murder and is ultimately found innocent. The people of Québec City, however, have no love for a man they see as a priest who got away with murder. A mob scene unfolds. Alma Keller, wife of the actual murderer, cannot stand by and watch as violence looms. She moves to reveal to all that it was her husband who did the murder, and, in front of a crowd of hundreds, he shoots her to keep her silent. This sparks a chase. Otto Keller shoots several more people, then falls into a suicidal madness, finally dying under the guns of the police. A tragic end for a tragic man. While Otto Keller was not painted as a wholly innocent man, this sudden outburst feels out of character, and is far from keeping with the moody tone of the film.

With a cast as strong as this, the script flaws are unfortunate. When the film's stark, impressionistic photography is taken into account, they're downright criminal. *I Confess* is superbly shot and crisply directed, brimming with shadowy, angular imagery and deft look-cut-reaction editing. There is little question Hitchcock was engaged here. This motion picture shows all the hallmarks of an Alfred Hitchcock interested in his subject matter.

Thematically, *I Confess* is right up Hitchcock's alley, with its central themes of murder, betrayal, and the wrongfully accused. He explored these themes repeatedly in his films, and, as always, here he finds new ways to explore the material. It is a shame that such a promising concept is ultimately denied greatness by its convoluted plot.

If this sounds harsh, understand that this is an enjoyable film. It has quite a bit to like, but only if the viewer can ignore its impossibilities and suspend disbelief. It remains a good film, undoubtedly worth watching, but in this case Hitchcock's inability to break away from favored plot devices—climactic chase scenes, unrequited love triangles—works against the finished product.

Maybe he realized this, too, because in the coming years he would endeavor to break the mold of the typical Hitchcock thriller . . . to amazing results.

CONCLUSION

I Confess is haunted by plot flaws that do the film no favors, notably in a script that tries to do too much when the simplicity of Father Logan's dilemma has weight enough to carry the film. Strong thematic elements, powerful acting, and starkly beautiful photography, however, rescue *I Confess* from failure and make it a film worth watching.

HITCHCOCKIAN THEMES

Blackmail · Blonde Leading Lady · Chaos in an Unexpected Location · Dark Secret · Love Triangle · Murder · Wrongly Accused

THINGS TO LOOK FOR

- The stark, angular photography.
- Clift's surprisingly Hitchcockian method acting—which annoyed Hitchcock.

TRIVIA/FUN STUFF

✦ In the play upon which this film was based, the priest is hanged. This would not fly with the censors and was changed for the film.

AWARDS

- Cannes Film Festival Nomination: Grand Prize of the Festival (Alfred Hitchcock)

DVD RELEASES

RELEASE: Warner Home Video (2004)
(Dolby Digital 2.0 Mono, 1.33:1 Black & White)
RATING: ***

EXTRAS: *Hitchcock's Confessions: A Look at I Confess* documentary; premiere newsreel; theatrical trailer.
NOTES: Available as a stand-alone or as part of *The Alfred Hitchcock Signature Collection*.

Dial M for Murder
(1954)

FILM FACTS

PRODUCTION YEAR: 1953
RELEASE DATE: May 29, 1954 (U.S.)
STUDIO: Warner Bros.
FILMING LOCATION: Warner Bros. Studios, Burbank, California
PRESENTATION/ASPECT RATIO: Color/1.37:1

SYNOPSIS

Former tennis player Tony Wendice (Ray Milland) lives the good life in London on his wife Margot's (Grace Kelly) money. When he discovers she is cheating on him with an American writer, Mark Halliday (Robert Cummings), he conspires to blackmail an old college acquaintance, Charles Swann (Anthony Dawson), into murdering Margot so he can keep her money. Things go awry when Margot kills Charles in self-defense. She is charged with murder herself as Tony attempts to cover up his secret.

IMPRESSIONS

Enter Grace Kelly.

If Ingrid Bergman defined the early Hitchcock blonde as the iconic actress of his black-and-white era, Grace Kelly unquestionably defines the later Hitchcock leading lady, the singular actress of his color period. Maybe more than any other actress, Grace Kelly is *the* Hitchcock leading lady. A case can be made that Bergman is just as deserving—a fair case indeed—but for the next several years Kelly would define what Hitch looked for in a leading lady: Stunning beauty; an exuberant sense of fun; energy; a sense of humor, but the ability to be serious when the scene calls for it.

She makes her entrance into the world of Alfred Hitchcock here, in *Dial M for Murder*.

Dial M for Murder is one of Alfred Hitchcock's most beloved films, starring one of his most beloved actresses. It marks the start of his great color era of the 1950s, a tightly plotted and paced thriller that manages to defy the limitations of its single-apartment setting in a way *Rope* was unable to do.

But we're getting ahead of ourselves. It is important to first discuss Grace Kelly and her role in the Hitchcock canon. Here, she stars in one of his most popular films. She'd go on to star in a film considered among his very best in *Rear Window*, and did her final work with Hitchcock in *To Catch a Thief*, which features as much star power (it costars Cary Grant) as any-

> **WHERE'S HITCH?**
>
> Hitchcock appears about thirteen minutes into the film, in the reunion photograph Tony shows to Swann.

thing else on his résumé. Those three films constitute the sum total of her work with Alfred Hitchcock. A mere three films, yet, for such a slim lady, the shadow she casts is long indeed.

And with good reason. She was incomparably beautiful and possessed a charm that won her the desire of men and admiration of women everywhere. It is no wonder she had such a profound impact on Hitchcock's life and work. The introduction of Grace Kelly to Alfred Hitchcock began not just a rich and rewarding professional relationship, but a strong personal friendship. This would impact Hitch for the better over the next few years, and, according to some biographers, would ultimately leave him feeling a sense of loss and longing after her eventual retirement from acting.

At least one biographer has suggested that Hitchcock's treatment of his leading ladies changed after Kelly left the scene. Their role in his films and the manner in which they were portrayed—as objects of obsession and manipulators of men—certainly changed. Kelly was, without question, a tremendous part of his life, arguably helping invigorate him with creative drive at an age when other directors might be expected to begin slowing down. Her unexpected departure from Hollywood injected bleakness into his later work.

It has been suggested, most notably by author Donald Spoto, that Hitchcock was in love with Kelly and took her leaving the acting profession as a personal rejection. Indeed, there is ample evidence he attempted to replace her in future films with other beautiful but often icy blondes. Look no further than *Vertigo*, *North by Northwest*, and *The Birds* for examples. There is little doubt that Kelly's presence in Hitchcock's life affected his future films.

It all started with this, *Dial M for Murder*, Hitchcock's first color film since *Under Capricorn*, and the most artistically successful stage adaptation of his career. This is a film remembered fondly because it pushes all the right buttons. Its look, feel, and pacing are simple and elegant, and, most important of all, it's a thriller that keeps you on the edge of your seat. *Dial M* brims with that key word: suspense.

Suspense . . . and Grace Kelly. She plays a cheating wife, but the sheer force of her charm ensures the audience is always on her side.

In turn, the sheer force of Alfred Hitchcock's directorial powers ensures the film works despite being hampered with some of the same limitations of his other stage adaptations. Save for a few very brief scenes, the entire film takes place in one apartment. Aside from the famous attempted murder scene—evocatively shot; one of Hitchcock's best—the film contains no real action, leaning instead on heavy dialogue and long, information-heavy conversations. None of this, however, ends up being a burden on the film. Rather, Hitchcock relishes in the limitations, finding inventively stylish ways to photograph the set and bleeding dialogue-driven information to the audience with a clockwork punctuality that keeps the tension high. And without question, tension is nothing less than essential here. We have no chases. No ruthless villains of the sort we saw in *Strangers on a Train*. No MacGuffin to string us along. Only a man trying to have his wife killed using an elaborate plan, and later trying desperately to keep his secret even as an inspector comes closer to the truth—all built on a misleadingly simple batch of ideas.

Little things. That's what the film, the suspense, is built on. Little things that add up to a complex whole. A key. A stocking. A letter. An item left where it doesn't belong. A framed picture. A stray comment.

Dial M for Murder's real joy is in watching Alfred Hitchcock set all these things up one by one, constructing an elaborate house of cards in the process, then watching as each one of these plot devices come back later to haunt our antagonist. The structure is tight and focused. Everything is in

A distraught Grace Kelly, a scheming Ray Milland, a deceased Anthony Dawson. (Warner Bros./Photofest © Warner Bros.)

its place for a reason, and is all paid off before the end. If his previous film, *I Confess*, suffered from too much script, *Dial M* certainly does not. There is no fluff, no filler, no elements aside from the vital components needed to create, build, and maintain suspense. Finally, after the dismal failure of *Juno and the Paycock* and the ambitious disappointment of *Rope*, Hitchcock showed he could take a simple stage play and make it much more. After a short string of artistic experiments that didn't quite work, Hitch found his stride and his touch for suspense, becoming, in name and practice, the *Master* of Suspense.

Pay close attention to the editing work on this film. It will inform the look-shot-reaction editing of *Rear Window* and almost every Hitchcock film to follow. Also note the deliberate way in which you, the viewer, are offered information. Extraneous details are slim; everything is there to advance the plot, often not paying off until much later in the film. We'll see this again in films like *Vertigo*.

Even the story itself is economically structured. Consider just two short, masterfully executed sequences that drive the film inexorably forward: the opening twin kiss scenes and Margot's trial.

Rather than wasting time with opening exposition to establish Margot's duplicitous relationship with Mark Halliday, Hitch simply provides two short scenes, one featuring Margot and her husband, Tony; the other featuring Margot and Mark. These brief scenes, no more than a few minutes in total, set the story in motion with a brisk pace that will not slow for the rest of the film.

The same can be said for the trial sequence, which was not even in the stage play. Instead of slowing things down with courtroom melodrama, economy again rules. We merely see Margot's face in close-up against a solid background as charges are brought against her; she's convicted of murder despite her plea of self-defense. It's a brilliant addition to the stage narrative, moving the story miles forward in an incredibly short time. Hitchcock realized he had a great suspense story on his hands, but at the same time, he had to be creative with exposition or risk losing the audience to uneven pacing or even boredom.

It is no wonder the stage play *Dial M for Murder* would appeal to Hitchcock. It is chock-full of Hitchcockian themes: murder, blackmail, a love triangle, deception, and the wrongfully accused. Hitch again turned to familiar elements, but, as always, found new and inventive ways to feature them in his movies. This creativity in reusing common themes is really astonishing because one would think—especially within the context of watching his films in chronological order—that his constant retreading of these story elements would hinder the enjoyment found in these films. Yet Hitchcock was almost always inventive enough that the repetitious thematic ground never grew stale—quite the testimony to his creativity.

Yes, *Dial M for Murder* is filled with great suspense, an intriguing story, attractive players, and impeccable direction, but despite so many positives, it is not bereft of minor flaws that prevent it from rising to the level of artistic greatness that marks Hitch's best work.

For instance, there seems to be no reason for Margot to want Mark rather than her husband. Cummings, similar to his bland performance in *Saboteur*, fails to win the viewer's affection. Why would she choose him over Tony Wendice? If there is something to like about Mark, the audience does not see it.

Further, it seems at least a little unreasonable that Charles Swann would fall for Tony's blackmail scheme. Swann appears intelligent and capable of moving on at a moment's notice. Why would he feel compelled to kill a stranger's wife as a result of blackmail he could have simply ignored? Perhaps it can be explained that he did it for the promise of the money, but that would have necessitated desperation on Swann's part, something we do not see.

Finally, it seems unlikely that Tony would not have discovered he had taken the wrong key from Swann's pocket after his untimely death. Margot's trial is only given brief screen time, but we have the impression that months have gone by. It seems difficult to believe Tony would not once have looked under the carpet on the steps during that time.

These flaws are minor points that may keep *Dial M for Murder* out of the upper echelon of Hitchcock films, but they do not keep the picture from being one of Sir Alfred's most enjoyable experiences. This may be considered a minor Hitchcock classic, but a classic it is—an entertaining and engrossing thriller that is all but a lesson in Hitchcockian suspense.

CONCLUSION

Dial M for Murder is widely regarded as one of Alfred Hitchcock's better films. And no wonder. There is an awful lot to like here, from the story, to the execution of suspense, to the cast, including the unforgettable Grace Kelly, and excellent direction. Some minor flaws prevent *Dial M for Murder* from achieving a place among his landmark thrillers, but that does not make it anything less than a thoroughly enjoyable motion picture experience.

HITCHCOCKIAN THEMES

Blackmail · Blonde Leading Lady · Dark Secret · Love Triangle · Murder · Wrongly Accused

THINGS TO LOOK FOR

- The outstanding photography despite the limitations imposed by a single primary set.
- Margot's progressively changing clothing colors, reflecting her state as the film progresses.
- Little things—such as a key, a letter, a stocking, and a pair of scissors—that play huge roles in the development of the story.

● The film was shot to take advantage of the new 3-D film technology. Notice a number of shots at low angles and a focus on objects such as lamps.

TRIVIA/FUN STUFF

✦ *Dial M* was based on a stage play by Frederick Knott, who also wrote the screenplay. Hitchcock suggested a number of changes to the story, including the addition of the trial sequence.
✦ The film was shot in just thirty-six days.
✦ This was the first of three consecutive Hitchcock films starring the legendary Grace Kelly. It was the second film featuring Robert Cummings, who was previously seen in *Saboteur*.
✦ In an early scene, Kelly mistakenly calls Cummings by his first name, Bob, rather than his character's name, Mark.

AWARDS

● National Board of Review Wins: Best Actress (Kelly, also for *The Country Girl* and *Rear Window*), Best Supporting Actor (John Williams, also for *Sabrina*)
● New York Film Critics Circle Award Win: Best Actress (Kelly, also for *The Country Girl*)
● Directors Guild of America Nomination: Outstanding Directorial Achievement in Motion Pictures (Hitchcock)
● British Academy of Film and Television Arts Awards Nomination: Best Actress (Kelly)

DVD RELEASES

RELEASE: Warner Home Video (2004)
(Dolby Digital 2.0 Mono, 1.33:1 Color)
RATING: ****

EXTRAS: *Hitchcock and Dial M* documentary; *3D: A Brief History* documentary; theatrical trailer.

NOTES: Available as a stand-alone or as part of *The Alfred Hitchcock Signature Collection*. Also available in Warner's *The Leading Ladies Collection*.

Rear Window
(1954)

FILM FACTS

PRODUCTION YEAR: 1953
RELEASE DATE: August 1, 1954 (U.S.)
STUDIO: Paramount Pictures
FILMING LOCATION: Paramount Studios
5555 Melrose Ave., Hollywood, Los Angeles, California
PRESENTATION/ASPECT RATIO: Color/1.66:1

SYNOPSIS

Globe-trotting photographer L. B. Jefferies (James Stewart) has a problem: He's been stuck in a wheelchair for weeks, recovering from a broken leg. With little to do when not spending time with his girlfriend, high-class jet-setter Lisa Carol Fremont (Grace Kelly), he takes to watching the colorful and eclectic neighbors in his apartment complex courtyard. His peeping grows serious, however, when he begins to suspect one of the neighbors, Lars Thorwald (Raymond Burr), may have killed his wife. Jeff, as he's nicknamed, gets his girlfriend wrapped up in his peeping, and he and Fremont watch for clues, hoping to prove once and for all that Thorwald is a murderer.

IMPRESSIONS

Everyone is a voyeur. As human beings, we are hard-wired to observe others. We watch movies because we like to watch other people. We enjoy catching glimpses of their private lives. Yet, despite being part of human nature, there is a stigma attached to voyeurism. Though we all possess a desire to peep to some extent or another, society says we should not spy on others. And so we don't. Alfred Hitchcock knew this better than anyone. His *Rear Window* is among the very best films that touch on voyeurism, a motion picture that still resonates more than fifty years later in both its message and its ability to entertain.

Alfred Hitchcock was a master at audience manipulation. Virtually everything he did with his films was calculated with audience reaction in mind. There is perhaps no better example of this than *Rear Window*, a picture so concerned with making the viewer part of what takes place on screen that the entire story is depicted from the perspective of its primary character. All but a few shots originate within L. B. Jefferies's apartment. This is done to emphasize the theme of voyeurism. By limiting the scope of the film to Jeff's perspective, the viewer is taken along on his path of discovery. As a result, the viewer becomes complicit in his voyeurism. If we participate in his actions, we see him as a less pathetic character, a man with whom we can relate.

> **WHERE'S HITCH?**
>
> Roughly thirty minutes into the film, Hitchcock appears in the apartment of the composer, winding a clock, his back turned toward the audience.

Few films in the Hitchcock canon boast the kind of reputation enjoyed by *Rear Window*. Widely cited as among his greatest achievements, it stands with his most discussed, studied, and examined work. By now, its every frame has been analyzed, its every edit put under the microscope. All this analysis, study, and examination is appropriate when you consider that *Rear Window* is the ultimate manifestation of a common Hitchcock theme: The people around you are not necessarily what they seem. They may be hiding dark secrets. Worse still, the mere act of observing them may pull you into their world.

Thematically, this is the core of *Rear Window*. What's so fascinating about the film is not so much the theme, but how Hitchcock makes Jeff's voyeurism seem almost mundane. Yes, Lisa and his nurse, Stella (Thelma Ritter), scold him for spying on his neighbors, but Hitch makes it so comfortable and

Thelma Ritter, Grace Kelly, and James Stewart (Paramount Pictures/Photofest © Paramount Pictures)

entertaining for the viewer—again, the ultimate voyeur—that it becomes easy to forget Jeff is peering in on some very private moments. We're peering into those moments, too, watching, in an example of brilliantly intricate scripting, what amounts to a series of short films interwoven into the larger whole.

Rear Window's story is impeccably constructed. Jeff is an interesting character who had led an exciting life prior to his injury, but how to make him worthy of our attention when he is wheelchair-bound and stuck in a cramped apartment for the entire movie? Give him an uncertain romance with a beautiful woman and a limited view of an outside world featuring an astounding assortment of unusual characters, that's how. All within the confines of that little apartment, he is able to experience a personal crisis while also becoming wrapped up in the lives of complete strangers. It is an amazing dynamic Jefferies experiences: one the viewer, the ultimate voyeur, also experiences while observing his actions.

Jeff's apartment life—with Lisa and Stella dropping by to care for him—is separated from the world he watches outside, yet these two worlds play off of and complement each other. Each apartment in the courtyard represents an element of L. B. Jefferies's relationship with Lisa Fremont. He loves Lisa, but is unsure of how he wants her as part of his future. When he looks into each apartment, he sees different possibilities for that future, uncertain what she would become to him. Would she be a nag, like Mrs. Thorwald? A woman who ignores him while fussing over a pet? A woman he quickly tires of? A woman who attracts the attention of all sorts of men, like Miss Torso? Or would he spurn her, causing her to become an old spinster like Miss Lonelyheart? Could he deal with that? It's a terrific dichotomy, wonderfully built and executed to perfection.

Rear Window is positioned as a comic thriller, but even as such, it is much funnier than would be expected when one considers that its plot hinges on a suspected murder. The story is speckled with comedy; the dialogue is consistently biting and humorous. John Michael Hayes's screenplay, based on a short story by Cornell Woolrich, does an exceptional job of keeping the tone relatively light in the face of a somewhat dark plot. Virtually every line of dialogue in the script reveals something about a character or advances the story. It's insightful dialogue, too. "What people ought to do is get outside their own house and look in for a change," Stella says early in the film. This is undoubtedly some of the best writing we have seen—or will see—in a Hitchcock film.

The pacing here is different than one might expect from a typical Hitchcock thriller. Instead of opening with a bang and sending the viewer off on a thrill-a-minute ride to the end, we are instead treated to a slow beginning. It is against the grain for Hitchcock, who often started his films at a sprint, but the slower pace is extremely satisfying. The deliberate start allows the viewer to become familiar with the characters and involved in the story. The pace then steadily picks up as the film progresses to its inevitable climax.

In a strange way, *Rear Window* is among Hitchcock's most unfocused films, at least on the surface. At almost every juncture in the story, Jeff—distracted, bored and immobile as he is—absently scans the apartments around him. Time and again we drift away from the mystery that drives the narrative forward, instead poking and prodding at side characters we never see save from a distance. The film wanders as much as Jeff's mind. Yet that unfocused feel is an illusion, carefully crafted to not only add life to the bustling apartment complex, but to emphasize the voyeuristic boredom felt by Jeff.

That thematic element—voyeurism—could easily have felt forced. Clumsy. Heavy handed. The sight of a sweaty man leering silently through a camera lens could have been too much, losing the audience and making our protagonist someone impossible to relate to, much less *like*. Instead, the myriad stories that unfold—Ms. Lonelyheart's inability to find love, the composer's struggle to finish a song, the newlywed couple for whom the honeymoon does not last, Miss Torso's endless stream of fawning men and ultimate love for a diminutive, awkward lover—make us as interested in Jeff's neighbors as he is, complicit in his voyeurism.

Pulling this off meant more than tight scripting and crisp editing. It meant a technical achievement the likes of which Hollywood had never before seen. *Rear Window* was shot on set, not on location, which meant constructing the entire apartment complex from scratch. Hitchcock was no stranger to leaping technical hurdles. In 1929, after all, he was among the first in the world to produce a sound film. Productions like *Foreign Correspondent*, *Lifeboat*, and *Rope* all forced Hitch to make innovative use of the technology available to him. Here, he went big. The indoor set of *Rear Window* was the largest ever created for a Paramount film up until that time, some six stories tall at points (the floor had to be dug out of the studio to accommodate the size), boasting more than a thousand arc lights, and, in an almost outlandish display of excess, featuring thirty-one apartments, including eight that were completely furnished and utilized full electricity and running water.

All that for a film in which almost every last frame is shot from a single location.

No amount of scripting, technical achievement, or thematic content can overcome a lackluster cast, however. Not that there was a danger of that here. Stewart shines in his second Hitchcock role, equal parts lovable cad and cynical loner. The entire house of cards—or, shall we say, apartment of cards—collapses if he fails to draw us in. He does not fail. Kelly is equally fantastic. She manages to play a flighty socialite struggling to love an incorrigible Scrooge with surprising subtlety. When she smiles broadly while attempting to woo her boyfriend, her uncertainty about the relationship is apparent beneath the surface. This dynamic is yet another pleasing subplot, one that allows the audience to grow fond of Lisa Fremont, a feeling that becomes vital as the climax approaches. Wendell Corey as Detective Thomas Doyle is suitably sarcastic as Jeff's cop friend who doesn't believe his stories of murder, but the real star of the otherwise small supporting cast is Thelma Ritter as Stella, Jeff's nurse. She is, in a word, hilarious, playing up the black humor just as Patricia Hitchcock did three years before in *Strangers on a Train*. All the best lines in the film are hers.

The casting of James Stewart as L. B. Jefferies was somewhat against type, yet Stewart was a perfect choice. Stewart had cultivated an everyman image in such films as *Mr. Smith Goes to Washington*, *You Can't Take It With You*, and *Harvey*, but in *Rear Window* (as well as his other three films with Hitchcock) he proved he was more than adept at playing darker characters in darker films. His performance here is understated on the surface, but below, it is wrought with unexpressed emotion. Stewart's work in *Vertigo* was his best for Hitchcock, but this is nearly on the same level.

On the other hand, the casting of Grace Kelly was *not* against type. Kelly, as discussed when we looked at *Dial M for Murder*, was a transcendent beauty with great charm and charisma who could make even the most mundane of movies worth watching. Given the opportunity here to really exercise her acting skills, she absolutely shines in one of the best performances of her career. Kelly's Lisa Fremont is a woman of stunning looks and great success in the fashion industry—just the type of woman we would expect from her—but she is also a woman torn by love and fear of rejection. Her pain does not go unnoticed.

With all his pieces in place—set, cast, and script—the final piece of the puzzle for Hitchcock was to put together the finished product. Save for a few brief images, the entire movie is shot from Jeff's apartment, either focusing on him or showing the audience what he is seeing. Because *Rear Window* is so much about viewpoint—what else is voyeurism but a kind of unclean viewpoint?—editing choices are vital. The narrative is driven entirely by what is seen through Jeff's eyes. Every piece of information we receive mirrors the information our lead character receives. This is a surprisingly rare trait for a Hitchcock film, as the Master of Suspense delighted in teasing the audience and mounting the tension by offering them a tantalizing glimpse of something the lead characters did not know. Here, we only know as much as Jeff. Despite this, *Rear Window* is a textbook example of Hitchcock editing: We see a character looking at something, we get a shot of that something, we then return to the character for a telling reaction shot. On its surface, it sounds remarkably simple. In practice, it's a delicate balancing act of timing, implication, and suggestion. Hitch is able to convey a lot of story and subtext through editing alone, maybe more so than in any other of his films to date.

For the average viewer, though, *Rear Window* ultimately earns its reputation simply by being a superbly enjoyable experience. The characters are funny and layered and likeable. The story is gripping; the plot, compelling. The whole picture is grounded in a reality easy for the average person to understand.

All this being said, *Rear Window* at times misses the mark. As mentioned earlier, the pace steadily increases throughout the film. This shouldn't be a problem, but at the end it speeds up a notch too far. The rapid-fire pace of Thorwald coming after Jeff, Jeff toppling from his window, and the police scurrying to the scene is completely at odds with the rest of the film. We need time to absorb the energy of the climax, but instead of events unfolding at a natural pace, Hitchcock plays things out at the end in an almost slapstick style. As a result, the finale is overly comic and somewhat ill fitted. One other significant problem with the ending is that Jeff defends himself with flashbulbs from his camera. On one hand, it perfectly illustrates just how helpless he is, but on the other, its execution is distracting. Perhaps film audiences in 1954 would have been more accepting, but this sequence does not age well.

In the grand scheme of things, these flaws are minor. This is a complex film that can be viewed on many levels: suspense thriller, comedic drama, and dense social commentary. Hitchcock earned his unofficial title of Master of Suspense, and *Rear Window* is a prime reason why. This is a compulsory Hitchcock title: boundlessly fun, thoroughly suspenseful, technically daring, and featuring two of the iconic stars of its generation. *Rear Window* is easily on the short list of Alfred Hitchcock's greatest accomplishments.

Maybe it comes back to voyeurism. When watching a film, you are watching someone else's life unfold. You're observing events that are not yours, yet, in a distant way, becoming part of those events. This is true of all film, yet in *Rear Window*, with its unique presentation and viewpoint and heavy sense of Peeping Tomism, the strange contradiction of acceptably seedy voyeurism is pushed to the forefront. It *is* the film. We watch because we are compelled by what we see, even when we know we shouldn't be looking. Alfred Hitchcock knew this, exploited this, and, in doing so, left us with one of the great classics of cinema.

CONCLUSION

Rear Window is widely considered among Alfred Hitchcock's best films, and with good reason. It is suspenseful, features stellar star power, and boasts a clever premise almost anyone can relate to, grounding the film in a reality the average person can understand. In addition to being an enjoyable thriller, the film is also a technical marvel and a veritable clinic on Hitchcockian editing. No journey through the work of Alfred Hitchcock, whether intensive or casual, is complete without a viewing of *Rear Window*.

HITCHCOCKIAN THEMES

Blonde Leading Lady • Dark Secret • Ineffectual Authority Figures • Murder •
Music Plays a Role in Plot

THINGS TO LOOK FOR

- The tiny stories that play out in the courtyard.
- Grace Kelly's legendary entrance scene, among the most memorable in cinema.
- The remarkable technical complexity of the set, built entirely indoors especially for this film.

TRIVIA/FUN STUFF

- ✦ When it was rereleased to theaters in 1983, *Rear Window* had been absent from the public eye for nearly thirty years; Hitchcock bought back the rights from the studio in the 1950s and hadn't shown it since.
- ✦ *Rear Window* contains no soundtrack. All of the sound and music is diegetic, or sourced within the film set itself.
- ✦ In its day, it featured the largest indoor set ever built at Paramount Studios.
- ✦ Several of the apartments were actually functional; Hitchcock worked out of one, and the actress who portrayed Miss Torso all but lived in hers during shooting days. These apartments had electricity and running water.
- ✦ In 1997 the film was added to the National Film Registry by the National Film Preservation Board, which selects films that "are considered to be culturally, historically or aesthetically important."
- ✦ Rank on American Film Institute Top 100 Films (1997): 42.
- ✦ Rank on American Film Institute Top 100 Films (2007): 48.

AWARDS

- Edgar Allan Poe Award Win: Best Motion Picture (John Michael Hayes)
- National Board of Review Win: Best Actress (Grace Kelly, also for *The Country Girl* and *Dial M for Murder*)

- Director's Guild of America Nomination: Outstanding Directorial Achievement in Motion Pictures
- Academy Award Nominations (4): Best Director (Hitchcock); Best Writing, Screenplay (John Michael Hayes); Best Cinematography, Color (Robert Burks); Best Sound, Recording (Loren L. Ryder)
- Writers Guild of America Nomination: Best Written American Drama (John Michael Hayes)
- British Academy of Film and Television Arts Awards Nomination: Best Film from any Source

---

DVD RELEASES

RELEASE: Universal Studios, Universal Legacy Series (2008)
(Dolby Digital 2.0 Mono, 1.66:1 Color)
RATING: *****

EXTRAS: Two-disc set includes feature commentary with John Fawell (author of *Hitchcock's Rear Window: The Well-Made Film*); production photographs; production notes; theatrical trailer; rerelease trailer narrated by James Stewart; *Rear Window Ethics: An Original Documentary*; a conversation with screenwriter John Michael Hayes; *Pure Cinema: Through the Eyes of the Master* documentary; Hitchcock/Truffaut interview excerpts; *Breaking Barriers: The Sound of Hitchcock* documentary; *Alfred Hitchcock Presents* episode "Mr. Blanchard's Secret"

RELEASE: Universal Studios (2001, 2005, 2006)
(Dolby Digital 2.0 Mono, 1.66:1 Color)
RATING: *****

EXTRAS: *Rear Window Ethics: An Original Documentary*; interview with screenwriter John Michael Hayes; production notes and photographs; theatrical trailer; rerelease trailer.

NOTES: Available as stand-alone releases from 2001 and 2006 or as part of *The Alfred Hitchcock Collection* (out of print) and *Alfred Hitchcock: The Masterpiece Collection*. *The Masterpiece Collection* is recommended. The transfers on all releases appear identical.

To Catch a Thief
(1955)

FILM FACTS

PRODUCTION YEAR: 1954
RELEASE DATE: August 5, 1955 (U.S.)
STUDIO: Paramount Pictures
FILMING LOCATION: Côte d'Azur, France
PRESENTATION/ASPECT RATIO: Color/1.85:1

SYNOPSIS

Reformed jewel thief John Robie (Cary Grant) lives a quiet life on the French Riviera. That is, until his past crimes are duplicated, prompting police to seek him as a suspect. In an effort to prove his innocence and catch the real thief, Robie seeks help from insurance man H. H. Hughson (John Williams), whose clients include Jessie Stevens (Jessie Royce Landis) and her daughter, the beautiful Francie (Grace Kelly), with whom Robie becomes involved romantically.

IMPRESSIONS

Add up the sum of its parts, and one would assume *To Catch a Thief* would have an easy time scaling to near the summit of Hitchcock's best work. It has the charismatic star power of two silver-screen icons in Cary Grant and Grace Kelly. It has the lush, luxurious imagery of the French Riviera. And it has Alfred Hitchcock at the peak of his 1950s power directing a film about beautiful people and cat burglary.

A surefire formula for artistic success? Not quite. It's remarkably light fare during a time when Hitchcock's films were growing increasingly dark. This is crowd-pleasing adventure, and little more. But that doesn't make *To Catch a Thief* a failure. It is crowd pleasing, offering up witty dialogue, clever situations, two legendary performers, and a well-rounded cast of excellent supporting players.

When we discussed *Dial M for Murder*, we mentioned the importance of Grace Kelly's entrance into the life of Alfred Hitchcock. She was, in many ways, his perfect leading lady, able to do exactly what he wanted on screen— all with an alluring beauty few can deny—and, like Ingrid Bergman, she also became a dear friend off the set. She brought an energy to his motion pictures and to his life that several biographers claim he never forgot. This 1955 film would be Hitch's last with Kelly, however, and one of her last overall. In 1956 she married Prince Rainier of Monaco, becoming Princess Grace of Monaco and retiring from acting. The move, biographers claim, broke Hitchcock's heart. It may be no coincidence that three years later he would direct *Vertigo*, a film about a man's obsessive need to reshape a woman in the image of a lost love—and that, in the years to follow, actresses like Vera Miles and Tippi Hedren would suffer under an almost maniacal level of control from the acclaimed director.

> **WHERE'S HITCH?**
>
> Hitchcock appears about ten minutes into the film, sitting next to Cary Grant on a bus.

You'd never know such a dark future was ahead based on this film, however.

Sunlight drenches the day shots, awash in color so that scenes look like a painting, while the night shots are anything but shadowy and ominous. Cinematographer Robert Burks, who worked with Hitchcock on almost every film between *Strangers on a Train* and *Marnie* (*Psycho* being the lone exception), won his only Academy Award for *To Catch a Thief*. Stylistically, the photography doesn't do much to stand out from the crowd, but of course it doesn't need to when the scenery is so beautiful.

The same, almost down to the adjective, can be said of the cast. This is a film revolving around burglary, but it's far from the seedy thievery associ-

Cary Grant, Grace Kelly, and Hitch on location during filming of *To Catch a Thief*. (Paramount Pictures/Photofest © Paramount Pictures)

ated with the word. Our characters are charming, charismatic, beautiful, and always well dressed. While the humor in *To Catch a Thief* isn't necessarily among Hitchcock's best—though it is quite endearing—it doesn't need to be when delivered by performers like Grant, Kelly, John Williams, and the hilariously expressive Jessie Royce Landis (whom we'll see a few years later in an even better role).

Speaking of the cast, all discussions of *To Catch a Thief* must include talk of its leads.

Grant and Kelly were each favorite players of Hitchcock's, and with good reason. There were no two bigger stars in the mid-1950s, and never was there a more attractive or charming on-screen couple than these two. That this is fundamentally remembered as something less than the best work of either actor—or of Hitchcock, for that matter—is inconsequential. The movie, despite pretensions of mystery and suspense, is ultimately a romance story. And who better to star opposite one other in a romance than

Cary Grant and Grace Kelly? These were two huge, beautiful stars who remain popular to this day. With leads this strong, it is no surprise that *To Catch a Thief* was a box office success.

Get beyond the beautiful stars and gorgeous setting, however, and something becomes abundantly clear: This film is artistically unremarkable. A classy, funny thriller, yes—but when set next to the body of work Hitchcock had amassed up until this point, there is little to push it above the rest save star power. It's an entertaining ride with a small handful of noteworthy moments—the suggestive discussion Grant and Kelly have over a lunch, with chicken parts becoming allusions to sex, is a standout—but coming in the middle of the most creatively successful decade of Hitchcock's career, *To Catch a Thief* comes across as rather pedestrian.

Despite a general lack of suspense and its generally light tone, *To Catch a Thief* is still notable for presenting a number of elements common to Hitchcock's work. Its opening shot of a woman screaming at the camera after discovering her jewels were stolen recalls *The Lodger* and looks ahead to *Psycho*. We also see a wrongfully accused man on the run, murder, a blonde leading lady, an exotic setting, a chase, ineffective authority figures, and chaos in unexpected locations—all elements shared with other Hitchcock films. It is incredible how often these themes come up, yet despite their familiarity, they rarely feel overdone.

In the end, Hitchcock makes no great artistic strides here. *To Catch a Thief* stands instead as a minor landmark in his personal life, the end of the all-too-brief Grace Kelly era. Her departure from the Hitchcock landscape would impact his future creative endeavors, not because it broke new directorial ground for him, but because it changed his overall demeanor.

Yet *To Catch a Thief* itself reflects none of this. There is nothing wrong with the film; it just isn't all that remarkable. *To Catch a Thief* is a light thriller—a pretty entertaining one at that—and no more.

CONCLUSION

To Catch a Thief is an enjoyable entry in the Hitchcock filmography, but despite its beautiful setting, wonderful stars, and a story loaded with Hitchcockian elements, it does little to advance the art of the Master of Suspense. It is light but enjoyable Hitchcock.

HITCHCOCKIAN THEMES

Blackmail · Blonde Leading Lady · Dark Secret · Ineffectual Authority Figures · Wrongly Accused

THINGS TO LOOK FOR

- The beautiful French Riviera setting highlighted by Robert Burks's excellent cinematography.

TRIVIA/FUN STUFF

- ✦ This was Grace Kelly's last of three films for Alfred Hitchcock. She retired from acting the following year and married Prince Rainier of Monaco.
- ✦ The voice of Charles Vanel, a French actor who plays Bertani, had to be dubbed whenever his character speaks English in the film. Several times he turns away to "deliver" his lines or his mouth is clearly closed while he "speaks."
- ✦ Cinematographer Robert Burks won his only Academy Award for *To Catch a Thief*.

AWARDS

- Academy Award Nominations (3): Best Cinematography, Color (Robert Burks); Best Art Direction/Set Decoration, Color (Hal Pereira, J. McMillan Johnson, Sam Comer, Arthur Krams); Best Costume Design, Color (Edith Head)
- Academy Award Win: Best Cinematography, Color (Robert Burks)
- Writers Guild of America Nomination: Best Written American Comedy (John Michael Hayes)
- Venice Film Festival Nomination: Golden Lion (Alfred Hitchcock)

DVD RELEASES

Release: Paramount Home Video, Special Collector's Edition (2007)
(Dolby Digital 2.0 Surround, 1.85:1 Color)
Rating: ***1/2

EXTRAS: Theatrical trailer; photo and poster gallery; *Writing and Casting To Catch a Thief; The Making of To Catch a Thief; Alfred Hitchcock and To Catch a Thief: An Appreciation; Edith Head: The Paramount Years;* commentary by Peter Bogdanovich.

RELEASE: Paramount Home Video (2002)
(Dolby Digital 2.0 mono, 1.85:1 color)
RATING: ***1/2

Extras: Includes theatrical trailer; photo and poster gallery; *Writing and Casting To Catch a Thief; The Making of To Catch a Thief; Alfred Hitchcock and To Catch a Thief: An Appreciation; Edith Head: The Paramount Years.*

The Trouble with Harry
(1955)

FILM FACTS

PRODUCTION YEAR: 1954
RELEASE DATE: October 3, 1955 (U.S.)
STUDIO: Universal Studios
FILMING LOCATIONS: Barre, Vermont; Craftsbury Common, Vermont
PRESENTATION/ASPECT RATIO: Color/1.85:1

SYNOPSIS

The trouble with Harry? The trouble with Harry is that he's dead. He's dead, the residents of a small New England town keep stumbling over his body in the woods—and no one seems to care! Captain Albert Wiles (Edmund Gwenn) thinks he accidentally shot Harry. Sam Marlowe (John Forsythe) agrees to help bury the body. Jennifer Rogers (Shirley MacLaine) and her son, Arnie (Jerry Mathers), shrug off finding Harry's corpse, even though Harry and Jennifer were married. And Miss Ivy Gravely (Mildred Natwick) treats the existence of a dead body as a matter of course. The trouble with Harry is that he's dead, and these folks don't know what to do with him.

IMPRESSIONS

Alfred Hitchcock was notorious for his dark sense of humor, but rarely were his films straight comedies. Rather, he interspersed moments of humor throughout his suspenseful, tension-filled movies. A fair amount of dark humor has already been seen in Hitchcock's work, but only two of the nearly forty films prior to *The Trouble with Harry—The Farmer's Wife* and *Mr. & Mrs. Smith*—were out-and-out comedies. It was not that Hitchcock was averse to this type of picture; he simply worked better within the realms of suspense and drama. *The Trouble with Harry* does not follow any of the typical Hitchcock movie formulas—no spies or a man on the run, for instance—but it is one of his more enjoyable films, and arguably the funniest.

Yes, this may indeed be the funniest film Hitchcock ever made. It is dark humor—how could it not be, with its story revolving around a dead body?—but very real humor nonetheless. The absurdity of the entire concept is so over-the-top, the viewer is compelled to suspend disbelief and simply appreciate it for what it is. How can these people be so unconcerned over the death of a man? How can so many people think they caused his death? The situation is ridiculous, but this is not a bad thing. In fact, that is the point. It is supposed to be full of inanity, and it succeeds in this pursuit.

> **WHERE'S HITCH?**
>
> Roughly twenty minutes into the film, Hitch can be seen walking behind the limousine parked in front of the painting stand.

The success of *The Trouble with Harry* begins with its screenplay. John Michael Hayes, in the third of four scripts he wrote for Hitchcock during a wonderful partnership, did a terrific job of playing up the absurdity of Jack Trevor Story's novel while delivering fantastic dialogue. When Miss Gravely happens upon the captain dragging Harry's body, rather than acting shocked, surprised, or bewildered, she nonchalantly says, "What seems to be the trouble, Captain?" Throughout, Hayes's dialogue—as it was in *Rear Window* and *To Catch a Thief*—is one of the true highlights of the film. It is consistently biting, revealing of its characters, and genuinely funny.

Another of Hitchcock's strongest working relationships began here, this time with composer Bernard Herrmann. In the first of eight scores he did for the Master of Suspense, Herrmann was at the top of his craft from the very beginning. He was a master at viewing a scene and creating music to accompany it in a way that did not dominate the action, but enhanced it. If

Little Arnie Rogers (Jerry Mathers) is just one of many who stumble on the inconvenient body of Harry. (Universal Pictures/Photofest © Universal Pictures)

you have not seen *The Trouble with Harry* but are familiar with Hitchcock's later, more successful films such as *North by Northwest* or *Psycho*, you will certainly recognize that the music is from the same artist.

In the long term, it would be Herrmann's touch that would prove most significant to Hitchcock's final surge of growth as an artist. Sir Alfred showed an appreciation for how important a score was to a film early in his career, famously clashing with producer David O. Selznick, for instance, over musical choices. In Herrmann he found a kindred spirit: a man remarkably devoted to coaxing every last bit of drama, emotion, suspense, and humanity from a film; a man as devoted to the small details as to the larger strokes.

Also contributing to the success of *The Trouble with Harry* is its outstanding ensemble cast, led by Edmund Gwenn (Mr. Hornblower in *The Skin Game* and Rowley in *Foreign Correspondent*), John Forsythe (famous as the heard but never seen voice of Charlie in *Charlie's Angels*), and, in her first screen appearance, Shirley MacLaine. The cast is rounded out in strong fashion by Mildred Natwick, Mildred Dunnock, Royal Dano, and a young Jerry Mathers (Beaver Cleaver himself) in a funny role. This great cast works extremely well together; the chemistry is evident in the delivery of the often absurd dialogue.

But it is more than these elements that make *The Trouble with Harry* a worthwhile film. Any number of things could have gone wrong. *Mr. & Mrs. Smith* proved that Hitch could fall short with comedy, that no amount of wonderful photography can save a poor script, and that an excellent score is wasted if not attached to an entertaining film. In the end, Hitchcock's experiment with dark comedy would utterly fail if it did not deliver the laughs. In this case, the laughs are plentiful.

This comes as little surprise when one considers the subject matter at hand. A small group of people matter-of-factly trying to figure out what to do with a corpse, talking as if it were little different than disposing of a troublesome piece of furniture. It's safe to suggest that when confronted with such an outlandish hook, most directors would treat the audience to winks, nods, and nudges, as if to say, "Well *this* is an unbelievable situation, isn't it?" Chalk it up to dry British humor, a shrewd directorial decision, or his own twisted sense of humor, but Alfred Hitchcock did not do that. Instead, he played the story of a corpse people keep burying and digging back up again relatively straight, as if there were nothing at all unusual about the situation. That is the heart of the humor.

Hitchcock adored absurd situations that pushed the bounds of good taste—not just on film, but in his personal life, too. The Hitchcock legend is filled with stories about his tasteless, often mean-spirited practical jokes. Friends and acquaintances have frequently noted Hitch's bleak means of finding laughter. Because of his lifelong delight in making light of all things dark, it's fair to say he was uniquely suited to directing a film like *The Trouble with Harry*. The funniest moments in Sir Alfred's films come when humor is contrasted with something serious. The gleeful conversations about murder in *Shadow of a Doubt* are the best example of this sense of humor at work. Such is the case here, too. The humor comes not from the corpse—let's face it, all poor Harry does is lay around and be dead—but in the reaction (or lack thereof) people have to the corpse. It's putting a dead man at a dinner table and pretending he's not there. Situations like that scream Alfred Hitchcock.

Of course, one would be hard-pressed to make the case that *The Trouble with Harry* breaks significant new ground for Hitch. It successfully distills his humor into a feature-length gag, brings to the fray the musical genius of Herrmann, features pastoral photography right out of a Norman Rockwell painting, and just plain entertains—but a groundbreaking work of artistic achievement? Not for Alfred Hitchcock, who had dabbled with this sort of humor his whole life. On the other hand, if bringing the public a film about casually dealing with a corpse—and doing so in 1955, no less—isn't groundbreaking in its own small way, it sure comes close.

The Trouble with Harry is not one of Hitchcock's most renowned films, and it is far from the standard Hitch formula, but it is nevertheless an excellent picture. Even with its place as a straight but dark comedy, it remains loaded with Hitchcockian themes like murder, dark secrets, and ineffective authority figures. This is Sir Alfred taking a break from his standard fare, yet it never feels like anything but a Hitchcock film. *The Trouble with Harry* is a hilarious romp.

CONCLUSION

Perverse, dark, yet hilariously funny, *The Trouble with Harry* is a noteworthy entry in Alfred Hitchcock's filmography not because it pushed his craft forward in significant ways, but because it's just plain enjoyable. Even casual Hitchcock fans are likely to enjoy this fun, funny, and absurd film.

HITCHCOCKIAN THEMES

Dark Secret • Discussion of Murder at Dinner • Ineffectual Authority Figures • Love Triangle • Murder • Wrongly Accused

THINGS TO LOOK FOR

- The lush New England location shooting.
- An early appearance by Jerry Mathers, child star of television's *Leave It to Beaver*.
- The music. This was the first collaboration between Hitchcock and Bernard Herrmann, a working relationship that would result in several classic films—with scores to match.

AWARDS

- Director's Guild of America Nomination: Outstanding Directorial Achievement in Motion Pictures
- British Academy of Film and Television Arts Awards Nominations: Best Film from any Source, Best Foreign Actress (Shirley MacLaine)

TRIVIA/FUN STUFF

+ *The Trouble with Harry* was among five films (the others were *Vertigo*, *Rear Window*, *Rope*, and the 1956 version of *The Man Who Knew Too Much*) called the "lost Hitchcocks," films unavailable for decades due to rights issues. It was not until 1984 that these movies were again available to be seen by the public.

DVD RELEASES

RELEASE: Universal Studios (2001, 2005, 2006)
(Dolby Digital 2.0 Mono, 1.85:1 color)
RATING: ****

EXTRAS: *The Trouble with Harry Isn't Over* documentary; production notes and photographs; theatrical trailer.

NOTES: Available as stand-alone releases from 2001 and 2006, or as part of *The Alfred Hitchcock Collection* (out of print) and *Alfred Hitchcock: The Masterpiece Collection*. *The Masterpiece Collection* is recommended. The transfers on all releases appear identical.

Alfred Hitchcock Presents
(1955–1957)

INTRODUCTION

In the fall of 1955 Alfred Hitchcock parlayed his success on the silver screen into a television show bearing his name, *Alfred Hitchcock Presents*. This anthology program, which aired for seven seasons, featured suspense and mystery stories in the vein one would expect of a Hitchcock creation. Over the course of the first six seasons, Hitchcock directed seventeen of the episodes himself. Here we will look at the first eight of these episodes, which aired between 1955 and 1957.

"REVENGE"
(ORIGINALLY AIRED OCTOBER 2, 1955)

The title of this premiere episode alone screams Alfred Hitchcock. More so even than the title and related subject matter, though, this installment of his popular crime/mystery series is noteworthy because of just how Hitchcockian it is. A man believes his wife was attacked in their home, yet the attacker is nowhere to be found. Consumed with fury, he seeks revenge, ultimately finding and killing the man who committed the crime.

Or does he?

Stylistically, "Revenge" hearkens back to the peak of his British years; several instances of impressionistic photography (notably during the revenge murder) remind one of compositions from *The Lodger*, while the twist ending is given impact through audio alone, the repetition of a word (or in this case a phrase) acting as the red flag that something is amiss, à la *Blackmail*. There isn't much in the way of plot—just setup, brief climax, and twist. Here, that twist ending is everything, giving this simple story about a man's revenge for an attack on his wife tremendous impact in its final moments.

"BREAKDOWN"
(ORIGINALLY AIRED NOVEMBER 13, 1955)

This was the second television episode directed by Hitchcock. It concerns the aftermath of a car accident involving William Callew (Joseph Cotten), an unsympathetic businessman who had earlier terminated a loyal employee. Callew is left paralyzed by the accident and appears dead to several people who stop by the scene. But he is not dead. He is very much alive, but completely unable to move. As time goes on, Callew is left alone in his thoughts, knowing he still lives, yet unable to communicate to those around him. Eventually, he spends the night in a morgue before it is finally discovered in the morning that he is alive.

The story told in "Breakdown" is as implausible as they come—surely someone could see he was breathing—but it is nevertheless a wonderful television program. Cotten (who we saw earlier in *Shadow of a Doubt* and *Under Capricorn*), one of the great Hitchcock actors, is fantastic as the man stuck in his thoughts. Though unable to convey his anguish through facial expressions, Cotten does a marvelous job expressing his emotions through his voice. This powerful little morality tale forces the viewer to consider how they would react in such a situation, whether as the victim or as someone who comes across the scene. As a dark look into the mind of a man who cannot control his own fate, it is easy to see why it would have appealed to the director.

"THE CASE OF MR. PELHAM"
(ORIGINALLY AIRED DECEMBER 4, 1955)

This episode from the first season of *Alfred Hitchcock Presents* is less concerned with directorial tricks than it is with disorienting, slightly disturbing subject matter. In a curious story that still resonates today, Mr. Pelham begins to suspect someone is impersonating him when the people in his life report seeing him in places he could not have been, doing things he never did. What begins as confusion or maybe a simple misunderstanding grows darker as he finds aspects of his life all but taken away, until one day, Mr. Pelham discovers that, for all intents and purposes, his life has been stolen by a look-alike.

Much more than a forward-looking take on identity theft, "The Case of Mr. Pelham" is very much about *becoming* someone, about changing who you are in order to assume a new identity. Made just a couple years before he would make *Vertigo*, the subject matter has a lot to offer when exploring themes of self, memory, experience, and reality. One suspects that if given an opportunity, Hitchcock could have used "The Case of Mr. Pelham" as an opportunity to explore themes of identity and perception over the course of a feature-length film. The way he offers the audience information, piece by piece, building the mystery until the stunning close, is effective despite the short running time. It is a clever episode right up Hitch's alley.

"BACK FOR CHRISTMAS"
(ORIGINALLY AIRED MARCH 4, 1956)

The last of the first-season episodes Hitchcock directed, this is the tale of Herbert Carpenter (John Williams), a man who conspires to murder his wife and bury her in the basement before setting off for a California vacation. Once in America, Carpenter receives a letter addressed to his wife. The letter indicates she had planned to have a wine cellar professionally installed in the basement. The program ends with the realization that Carpenter's crime is to be discovered and he is powerless to prevent it.

This episode is particularly Hitchcockian in that it revolves around murder and deceit, two themes common in his feature films. And with Williams, who we have already seen in *The Paradine Case*, *Dial M for Murder*, and *To Catch a Thief*, we have a favorite Hitchcock player in a story that was surely intriguing to Hitch. It is a story without depth, but the interaction between Mr. & Mrs. Carpenter and their neighbors makes for enjoyable television, as does his vacation life afterward.

"WET SATURDAY"
(ORIGINALLY AIRED SEPTEMBER 30, 1956)

Here, Hitchcock directs a particularly grim episode—not because it is explicit, but because the black humor is very black indeed. A young girl in love with her teacher kills said teacher. Her apparently wealthy family attempts to cover up her crime and protect the family name by setting up another person to take the fall. "Wet Saturday" looks and feels like one of Hitchcock's early American films, the small sets made to look like one of the wealthy homes we saw in *Suspicion*, *Rebecca* or *Notorious*. The directorial style is much the same.

Hitch often dealt with stories showing the rich to have rather twisted morals. Such is the case here. The distant, antisocial behavior of the Princey family is in keeping with the disturbingly oblivious family life of Bruno Anthony in *Strangers on a Train* or the murderers of *Rope*. The tone is lighter for television than in those films, but not by much. A family gathering together to nonchalantly plan the covering up of a murder, including disposal of a corpse? Humor or no, it's dark for a 1956 broadcast. One gets the sense Hitchcock was getting back to directorial territory he had left behind by the mid-1950s.

"MR. BLANCHARD'S SECRET" (ORIGINALLY AIRED DECEMBER 23, 1956)

Babs Fenton (Mary Scott) is a nosy neighbor. After watching her new neighbor, Mr. Blanchard (Dayton Lummis), through her window, Babs becomes convinced Mrs. Blanchard (Meg Mundy) has been killed at the hands of her husband. Babs tries to convince her own husband (Robert Horton) of what she believes is the truth until Mrs. Blanchard shows up at her door to introduce herself. Later, Babs is again convinced Mr. Blanchard has killed his wife when she sees him carrying something out of his home, but she is once again proven wrong when Mrs. Blanchard again turns up at Babs's door. Mrs. Blanchard tells Babs that Mr. Blanchard has left her after a squabble. Later, after a lighter is found missing, Babs becomes convinced Mrs. Blanchard is a thief. In the end, Mrs. Blanchard returns with the news that she has reconciled with her husband—along with the lighter, which has been fixed by Mr. Blanchard.

This is a somewhat convoluted story for a half-hour program and it features far from the tightest direction we've seen from Hitchcock, but it is an enjoyable tale for the viewer. In many ways, it is reminiscent of *Rear Window*, focusing on a Peeping Tom who becomes convinced their neighbor is a murderer. Of course, there is one major difference—no crime is actually committed by the neighbor.

"ONE MORE MILE TO GO"
(ORIGINALLY AIRED APRIL 7, 1957)

A wonderfully Hitchcockian opening highlights "One More Mile to Go," a 1957 episode of *Alfred Hitchcock Presents*. We peer in through a cottage window, watching a fight unfold between a married couple. Their voices are muffled. We can't hear what they are saying, but we can see the fight is growing serious. The husband picks up a fireplace poker, the wife turns and walks out of frame, and he strikes. Sixty seconds into the episode, and we have a murder. Not a single clear line of dialogue. No motivation or plot. Just a classic Hitchcock murder.

The next few moments are spent in relative silence as Sam Jacoby (David Wayne), the murderer, labors to put his wife's body in the trunk of his car. Once secure, he drives off to dispose of the corpse. All of this takes place in just the first few minutes of the program. We need not know who these people are or exactly why he killed her; it's little more than setup. As long as there is a body in the trunk of the car, the details are irrelevant.

What follows is an exercise in extended tension. There is little of substance here as far as story is concerned, but there doesn't need to be. Hitchcock offers the audience suspense via minimalism. Long, static shots of scenery rolling by. Speedometers. The gentle curves of the road. Innocuous conversations with a police officer (Steve Brodie) that border on leaving the murderer exposed, but never quite get there. Every moment screams, "Is this when Jacoby will be caught?" Every line of dialogue comes tantalizingly close to exposing the murder. "One More Mile to Go" is a mere television series episode, but with nothing more than bare-bones cinematic technique, the Master of Suspense shows clearly how he earned the title.

"THE PERFECT CRIME"
(ORIGINALLY AIRED OCTOBER 20, 1957)

Charles Courtney (Vincent Price) is an egotistical detective, convinced of his own greatness because he has never met a crime he could not solve. He keeps mementos of his cases on a set of shelves. On those shelves, he leaves one spot open, saving it for the "perfect crime." One night, while Courtney is sipping brandy and reveling in his own genius, a defense attorney, James Gregory (John Gregory), stops by to reveal that Courtney made a mistake that resulted in the execution of an innocent man. Rather than sully his reputation by allowing this to become known, Courtney kills Gregory and bakes his body in a kiln.

This story is particularly enjoyable in the way it pokes fun at a detective who is not as great as he thinks. The episode takes place almost entirely within a single room, but it does not want for suspense. Additionally, the acting is top-notch. The best part is, just when it appears that Courtney has committed the perfect crime and the episode ends, Hitchcock comes out to give his epilogue. There, he reveals that Courtney was caught when his housekeeper knocked over a vase Courtney made out of Gregory's remains.

Hitchcock, ever disdainful of detectives and police, could never have allowed Courtney to come out of this story a victor.

CONCLUSION

These eight episodes of *Alfred Hitchcock Presents* not only offer Hitchcock a chance to experiment with techniques on sustaining tension and play with audience manipulation, they offer us a wonderful diversion at this point in our journey with Hitchcock. Here we see a man capable of switching gears from high profile, big-budget motion pictures to low-budget television programs without missing a beat. That Hitchcock could alternate between these programs (he would continue to go back and forth between television and movies) and maintain such a high level of quality in his feature films is truly phenomenal, a feat unmatched by any other director before or since.

AWARDS

- 1956 Emmy Win: Best Editing of a Television Film (Edward W. Williams, "Breakdown")
- 1956 Emmy Nominations: Best Director, Film Series (Hitchcock, "The Case of Mr. Pelham"); Best Action/Adventure Series
- 1957 Emmy Win: Best Teleplay Writing, Half Hour or Less (James P. Cavanaugh, "Fog Closing In")
- 1957 Emmy Nomination: Best Series, Half Hour or Less
- 1957 Directors Guild of America Nomination: Outstanding Directorial Achievement in Television (Robert Stevens, "Never Again")

DVD RELEASES

Alfred Hitchcock Presents—Season One
RELEASE: Universal Studios (2005)
(Dolby Digital 2.0 Mono, 1.33:1 Black & White)
3 Discs
39 Episodes:

1. "Revenge" (directed by Alfred Hitchcock)
2. "Premonition"
3. "Triggers in Leash"
4. "Don't Come Back Alive"
5. "Into Thin Air" (aka "The Vanishing Lady")
6. "Salvage"
7. "Breakdown" (directed by Alfred Hitchcock)
8. "Our Cook's a Treasure"
9. "The Long Shot"
10. "The Case of Mr. Pelham" (directed by Alfred Hitchcock)
11. "Guilty Witness"
12. "Santa Claus and the Tenth Avenue Kid"
13. "The Cheney Vase"
14. "A Bullet for Baldwin"
15. "The Big Switch"
16. "You Got to Have Luck"
17. "The Older Sister"
18. "Shopping for Death"
19. "The Derelicts"
20. "And So Died Riabouchinska"
21. "Safe Conduct"
22. "Place of Shadows"
23. "Back for Christmas" (directed by Alfred Hitchcock)
24. "The Perfect Murder"
25. "There Was an Old Woman"
26. "Whodunit?"
27. "Help Wanted"
28. "Portrait of Jocelyn"
29. "The Orderly World of Mr. Appleby"
30. "Never Again"

31. "The Gentleman from America"
32. "The Baby Sitter"
33. "The Belfry"
34. "The Hidden Thing"
35. "The Legacy"
36. "Mink"
37. "Decoy"
38. "The Creeper"
39. "Momentum"

EXTRAS: *Alfred Hitchcock Presents: A Look Back* documentary.
RATING: ****

Alfred Hitchcock Presents Volumes 1–4
RELEASE: Universal Studios (1999, 2001)
(Dolby Digital 2.0 Mono, 1.33:1 Black & White)
RATING: ****

NOTES: Hitchcock-directed episodes spread over four discs, all out of print. Discs one and four were only available in *The Alfred Hitchcock Collection*, Vol. 1 and Vol. 2. These discs are out of print but are available on the secondary market.

Alfred Hitchcock Presents—Season Two
RELEASE: Universal Studios (2006)
(Dolby Digital 2.0 Mono, 1.33:1 Black & White)
5 Discs
39 Episodes:

1. "Wet Saturday" (directed by Alfred Hitchcock)
2. "Fog Closing In"
3. "De Mortuis"
4. "Kill with Kindness"
5. "None Are So Blind"
6. "Toby"
7. "Alibi Me"
8. "Conversation Over a Corpse"
9. "Crack of Doom"
10. "Jonathan"
11. "The Better Bargain"
12. "The Rose Garden"

13. "Mr. Blanchard's Secret" (directed by Alfred Hitchcock)
14. "John Brown's Body"
15. "Crackpot"
16. "Nightmare in 4-D"
17. "My Brother, Richard"
18. "The Manacled"
19. "A Bottle of Wine"
20. "Malice Domestic"
21. "Number Twenty-Two"
22. "The End of Indian Summer"
23. "One for the Road"
24. "The Cream of the Jest"
25. "I Killed the Count: Part 1"
26. "I Killed the Count: Part 2"
27. "I Killed the Count: Part 3"
28. "One More Mile to Go" (directed by Alfred Hitchcock)
29. "Vicious Circle"
30. "The Three Dreams of Mr. Findlater"
31. "The Night the World Ended"
32. "The Hands of Mr. Ottermole"
33. "A Man Greatly Beloved"
34. "Martha Mason, Movie Star"
35. "The West Warlock Time Capsule"
36. "Father and Son"
37. "The Indestructible Mr. Weems"
38. "A Little Sleep"
39. "The Dangerous People"

Alfred Hitchcock Presents—Season Three
RELEASE: Universal Studios (2007)
(Dolby Digital 2.0 Mono, 1.33:1 Black & White)
5 Discs
39 Episodes:

1. "The Glass Eye"
2. "Mail Order Prophet"
3. "The Perfect Crime" (directed by Alfred Hitchcock)
4. "Heart of Gold"
5. "Silent Witness"
6. "Reward to Finder"

7. "Enough Rope for Two"
8. "Last Request"
9. "The Young One"
10. "The Diplomatic Corpse"
11. "The Deadly"
12. "Miss Paisley's Cat"
13. "Night of the Execution"
14. "The Percentage"
15. "Together"
16. "Sylvia"
17. "The Motive"
18. "Miss Bracegirdle Does Her Duty"
19. "The Equalizer"
20. "On the Nose"
21. "Guest for Breakfast"
22. "The Return of the Hero"
23. "The Right Kind of House"
24. "The Foghorn"
25. "Flight to the East"
26. "Bull in a China Shop"
27. "Disappearing Trick"
28. "Lamb to the Slaughter" (directed by Alfred Hitchcock)
29. "Fatal Figures"
30. "Death Sentence"
31. "The Festive Season"
32. "Listen, Listen!"
33. "Post Mortem"
34. "The Crocodile Case"
35. "Dip in the Pool" (directed by Alfred Hitchcock)
36. "The Safe Place"
37. "The Canary Sedan"
38. "The Impromptu Murder"
39. "Little White Frock"

Rear Window (Universal Legacy Series, 2008): This 2-disc set includes the episode "Mr. Blanchard's Secret" from *Alfred Hitchcock Presents*

Vertigo (Universal Legacy Series, 2008): This 2-disc set includes the episode "The Case of Mr. Pelham" from *Alfred Hitchcock Presents*

WEEK
———
41

The Man Who Knew Too Much
(1956)

FILM FACTS

PRODUCTION YEAR: 1955
RELEASE DATE: June 1, 1956 (U.S.)
STUDIO: Paramount Pictures
FILMING LOCATIONS: Paramount Studios
5555 Melrose Ave., Hollywood, Los Angeles, California
Various locations, Morocco; Royal Albert Hall, London, England
PRESENTATION/ASPECT RATIO: Color/1.85:1

SYNOPSIS

When the McKenna family goes on vacation to Morocco, the last thing they expect is trouble. A chance encounter with a Frenchman on a bus brings exactly that, however, when he dies in the arms of Dr. Ben McKenna (James Stewart). In his dying breaths, the Frenchman whispers news of an assassination plot. In order to protect their plan, those behind the plot kidnap young Hank McKenna (Christopher Olsen), prompting the doctor and his wife, Jo (Doris Day), to race to England, hoping to rescue their son and maybe prevent an assassination. While the surface details differ, the plot is nearly identical to Hitchcock's 1934 film of the same name.

IMPRESSIONS

Alfred Hitchcock's remake of his 1934 *The Man Who Knew Too Much* is clearly the better of the two films of the same name. By 1956 Hitch was an established filmmaking star, with one great success after another on his résumé. The original is one of Hitchcock's most memorable and enjoyable British pictures, but in comparison with its remake, its luster fades. After three decades in the motion picture industry, Hitch had developed unmatched skills as a director, and he used those skills to great effect in this version of the film.

That this film is a remake of a film previously made by Hitchcock presents a unique opportunity to assess Sir Alfred's growth as an artist over the course of more than two decades. As far as story is concerned, the differences between the two films are superficial. The execution is another matter altogether. Here we have the same director telling what is essentially the same story, but doing so far more impressively, with a sense of confidence that comes across in every frame. Hitchcock improved upon almost every aspect of the film he made just over twenty years prior.

Aside from relatively minor changes to the settings, changing the central family from British to American and the child from girl to boy, and increasing the length by nearly forty-five minutes, the stories are quite similar. The plot again hinges on a MacGuffin (the reason the villains want to assassinate a diplomat) that results in a child being abducted to prevent a secret from being revealed. It again features a family willing to go to all lengths to save one of their own. It again presents a mother figure with a unique talent (this time, Doris Day's singing voice instead of Edna Best's shooting skills). It again places a lengthy scene of tension in Royal Albert Hall, which is again followed by an overdone climactic sequence. The differences in the story are important and largely serve to improve the film, but on the whole the stories are structurally the same. Where the films differ is in the execution.

When it comes to Hitchcock's finely honed craft, perhaps what is most telling comes not in the big things, but in the small. First, the simple, elegant titles at the start of the film—a Hitchcock staple by this point—amount to an extended tease, winking at the audience as it hints at the famous Royal Albert Hall climax. As the production opens, we're treated to an example of how Hitchcock gives the audience a great deal of information with the simplest of shots. We open with a man (James Stewart in his third role for Hitchcock), a woman (American icon Doris Day), and a young boy: a model American family. They sit in the back of a bus, a nondescript landscape behind them. As the camera pulls away, however, we see the passengers surrounding the family. A model American family, but they are not in America. With this simple shot, devoid of dialogue, we are introduced to the McKenna family and informed of their Moroccan vacation.

Their short bus ride will be important, as it employs a storytelling device Hitchcock used time and again: the chance meeting with dire consequences. The McKenna family is unaware at the time, but their encounter with a friendly Frenchman on the bus will prove disastrous.

Unlike 1934's rapid-fire *The Man Who Knew Too Much*, in the 1956 version of the film Hitchcock builds to the murder that sets the plot in motion. We spend time with the characters, get to know them, care about them. Because of this, we're far more invested in their fate. This slower build also succeeds in creating increased tension. When the street stabbing of the Frenchman and kidnapping of young Hank McKenna finally take place, we feel a sense of urgency sometimes missing from the earlier film. Rather than just minutes into the film being thrust into the search for this family's child, the sense of calm before the storm serves to heighten the drama. Clearly Hitch had learned a thing or two about suspense in the previous twenty years.

James Stewart, moments after he learns too much. (Photofest)

This slow build also allows one other thing: A standout scene for Doris Day, whose performance is surprising and emotional. When Stewart reveals to her that their son has been taken, she breaks down into tears, near hysterics. Her pain and anguish are tangible. The same is true again later in the film as she sings her famous song, a tune that leads her husband to their captured son. With Day working alongside Stewart, the epitome of the "ordinary American," we never doubt for a moment that this is a real American family in real crisis.

The leads also provide a stark contrast between the two films. There was nothing wrong with Leslie Banks or Edna Best in the original, but Stewart and Day are ideal for these roles. Stewart was the epitome of the American everyman, just what is needed here. He is understated but serious, confident and able to convey the complex emotions he experiences as he is thrust into a situation completely out of his control. Stewart makes Dr. Ben McKenna much more than just a doctor from the Midwest. This is a heroic yet vulnerable character. Day is equally important to the success of this film, if not more so. She is completely believable and compatible with Stewart (something that, as great as Grace Kelly was, cannot be said about *Rear Window*). Day's performance in *The Man Who Knew Too Much* is outstanding, the work of an actress and singer at the top of her game.

> **WHERE'S HITCH?**
>
> Early in the film, Hitchcock can be seen watching acrobats, his back to the camera.

Speaking of her singing, Day's contribution of the song "Whatever Will Be, Will Be (Que Sera, Sera)" to the film's soundtrack leaves an indelible impression. It truly is a wonderful song, sung by a woman whose voice is able to match her acting talents. "Que Sera, Sera," written for the film by Jay Livingston and Ray Evans, won an Academy Award for Best Song, the only Oscar for *The Man Who Knew Too Much*. The song is surprisingly in tune with the film's theme. The McKennas are in a situation beyond their control, but the song encourages people to live in the moment rather than stressing about the future.

The most remarkable sequence in the film is the twelve minutes spent inside the Royal Albert Hall. There is not a word of spoken dialogue throughout its duration, but, through Hitchcock's incredible planning and execution, it turns into a mesmerizing and suspenseful sequence, requiring

124 separate shots. Hitchcock, ever the meticulous planner, had the entire sequence storyboarded and edited in his mind before it was shot. For its achievements in editing and creation of near-silent suspense, it calls to mind the great crop duster sequence in the forthcoming *North by Northwest*.

Yet make no mistake: *The Man Who Knew Too Much* is not without faults. This film is marred by unfortunate pacing problems, especially in the final act. In this area the remake offers only a marginal improvement over the original. Both are uneven, and both falter in third acts that drag on too long. *The Man Who Knew Too Much* fails to keep up the near-relentless pace the story requires, but more damaging to the finished product is the exceedingly lengthy finale. The Royal Albert Hall scene is nothing short of brilliant, a textbook example of how image and sound can result in dramatic suspense. Too bad the film could not have ended here. While the scenes that follow include the famous sequence during which Doris Day sings "Que Sera, Sera"—and a fine scene it is—the pacing is downright tedious. We've experienced the McKenna's quest, we've seen a rousing climax—but rather than rush Hank back into the arms of his parents, Hitchcock drags us through to this final bit of closure. An ending that plods along well after the tension has subsided lessens the impact of the preceding Royal Albert Hall sequence.

This relatively minor flaw is one of the few things that mar Hitchcock's otherwise excellent return to *The Man Who Knew Too Much*. It's not his best work, considered a minor classic by some—more for Day and Stewart than anything else—but it's a fine example of how Sir Alfred's craft improved over the years. Most critics rate the second *The Man Who Knew Too Much* as better than the first, but still a notch below Hitchcock's best work. It is easy to agree with this sentiment.

CONCLUSION

The Man Who Knew Too Much is one of Hitchcock's more popular works, in part because of its magnificent star power, in part because of its memorable song, and in part because it's an exciting thriller. It features almost all the elements of classic Hitchcock filmmaking. In addition, for those studying Hitchcock's craft it presents a unique opportunity to see how his approach changed between the 1930s and 1950s.

HITCHCOCKIAN THEMES

Blackmail • Blonde Leading Lady • Chaos in an Unexpected Location • Climactic Showdown at an Iconic Location • Dark Secret • Exotic Location • Ineffectual Authority Figures • MacGuffin • Murder • Music Plays a Role in Plot • Spy Syndicate

THINGS TO LOOK FOR

- Doris Day's moving portrayal of a mother who has lost her son.
- The tense twelve-minute Royal Albert Hall scene, which features no dialogue yet remains one of the most recognizable Hitchcock sequences.

TRIVIA/FUN STUFF

- ✦ The man conducting the orchestra at Royal Albert Hall is Bernard Herrmann, who scored the film.
- ✦ One of five Hitchcock films unavailable for decades due to rights issues. The others were *The Trouble with Harry*, *Vertigo*, *Rear Window*, and *Rope*.
- ✦ The climactic musical number during which the assassination is supposed to take place is the same piece featured in the first version of the film. Herrmann chose not to rewrite this piece because he felt it was already the right choice.
- ✦ Doris Day did not like the tune she sings in the film, "Whatever Will Be, Will Be (Que Sera, Sera)," but it went on to win an Academy Award and became the best-known hit of her career.

AWARDS

- Academy Award Win: Best Music, Original Song, "Whatever Will Be, Will Be (Que Sera, Sera)" (Ray Evans, Jay Livingston)
- Directors Guild of America: Outstanding Directorial Achievement in Motion Pictures
- Cannes Film Festival Nomination: Golden Palm (Alfred Hitchcock)

DVD RELEASES

RELEASE: Universal Studios (2001, 2005, 2006)
(Dolby Digital 2.0 Mono, 1.85:1 Color)
RATING: ***1/2

EXTRAS: *The Making of The Man Who Knew Too Much* documentary; production notes and photographs; theatrical trailer; rerelease trailer.

NOTES: Available as stand-alone releases from 2001 and 2006, or as part of *The Alfred Hitchcock Collection* (out of print) and *Alfred Hitchcock: The Masterpiece Collection. The Masterpiece Collection* is recommended. The transfers on all releases appear identical.

The Wrong Man
(1956)

FILM FACTS

PRODUCTION YEAR: 1956
RELEASE DATE: December 22, 1956 (U.S.)
STUDIO: Warner Bros. Pictures
FILMING LOCATIONS: New York, New York;
Warner Bros. Studios, Hollywood, California
PRESENTATION/ASPECT RATIO: Black & White/1.66:1

SYNOPSIS

Nightclub bass player Manny Balestrero (Henry Fonda) lives a quiet, frugal life with his wife, Rose (Vera Miles), and their two young boys. One night after work, he is picked up outside his home by the police on suspicion of armed robbery. Manny is innocent, but circumstantial evidence is squarely against him. What follows is a tragic ordeal for Manny as he is put through the legal system and convicted of a crime he did not commit. The charges against him are eventually dropped after the real criminal is caught, but not before Rose falls victim to extreme paranoia as a result of the terrible circumstances of Manny's case.

IMPRESSIONS

A man falsely accused of a crime he did not commit must prove his innocence, even as the accusation throws his life into turmoil. On its surface, *The Wrong Man* is your typical Alfred Hitchcock film, telling the story of a man caught up by forces beyond his control, desperate to clear his name and return a semblance of normality to his life.

The Wrong Man is not your typical Hitchcock film, however. It is an atypical film not because it tells a true story (more on that later), but because stylistically it bears little resemblance to other works in the Hitchcock canon, despite the similarity of themes and plot. Taken by an Italian film movement called neorealism, a stripped-down kind of cinema grounded in a tangible reality and usually featuring working-class characters, Hitch sought to emulate this new style, which was popular among young European directors. His motion picture would feature a paycheck-to-paycheck musician barely able to make ends meet; drab, sparse sets; and a matter-of-fact cinematic style. Artistically, his experiment was a success. He created a film that feels like no other in his filmography. In Europe the film was a critical success, too, garnering the attention of French film scholars and elevating Hitchcock to a new level of admiration among the artistic elite.

> **WHERE'S HITCH?**
>
> Hitchcock, by this time comfortable as the host of his own television program, appears at the outset of *The Wrong Man* to introduce the film and tell the audience that the story is true.

The Wrong Man was not a box office success, however, and has not enjoyed the long-term recognition of the other Hitch productions of its era. In fact, despite starring screen legend Henry Fonda, it is probably the least well-known film from this period of his career.

Why the relatively modest recognition for *The Wrong Man*? It's certainly not for lack of quality. Though something of a distant cousin to Hitchcock films sharing the "wrong man" theme, it is a movie that works well within the narrow framework in which it was created. As a neorealist film, the focus here is on presenting an everyday reality unfiltered by the gloss of Hollywood. Dialogue is terse, believable. Plots are untouched by screenwriting clichés. Sets, if any (real-world locations are preferred), are lived-in, gritty, and dank. Stylization is minimal and not

Henry Fonda as real-life wrong man Manny Balestrero. (Warner Bros./Photofest © Warner Bros.)

at all flashy. It was a far cry from the flashy, dynamic work Hitch had become known for.

To tackle this style of filmmaking, Hitchcock chose to do something he had never done before. He told a true story.

The Wrong Man tells the tale of one Christopher Emmanuel Balestrero, a man of modest means earning a living as a bass player at New York's Stork Club. Manny is mistaken for a man who has committed a series of robberies in the area. The police question him, and Manny, though nervous and scared, cooperates. Mounting circumstantial evidence compounds the case of mistaken identity, Manny is charged with armed robbery, and his life begins to unravel.

It is easy to understand why Hitchcock would have wanted to film the story of Manny Balestrero. It featured two likeable, everyday characters with no control over their fate. This is a concept seen repeatedly throughout Hitch's films, usually with great success. This compelling true story is made all the stronger by its leads, Henry Fonda and Vera Miles, yet the element of truth serves as both a strength and a hindrance to the ultimate success of the picture.

On one hand, knowing the tale is true makes it more interesting for the viewer. It is easy for the common person to identify with the Balestreros. The narrative—unfolding with the harshness of the circumstances, the helplessness of the participants, and the seemingly insurmountable odds they face—offers up a nightmare the average viewer would never want to endure.

On the other hand, the fact that it is a true story prevents the Master of Suspense from introducing the elements that make his best thrillers so enjoyable, most notably, humor. Hitchcock's most enduring films almost always contain humor to lighten the mood. There is none of that here. After all, how could he inject humor into a story such as this? It just would not work.

Hitchcock never made a more depressing film than *The Wrong Man*. Even with its studio-mandated ending (in real life, the family did not live happily ever after), it is still a tough movie to watch. Manny is trapped in a terrible situation. With circumstantial evidence piling up against him, Rose, the ever-loving and adoring wife, plunges into a world of paranoia and disaffection as a defense mechanism against the harsh reality that faces her. This is both interesting and believable, but low on the excitement scale. And as a filmgoing experience, excitement is just what *The Wrong Man* could use. As common as these themes have been throughout Hitch's career, never has one of his "wrong man" tales been this mundane. There is nothing fanciful or fantastical about the series of events we see unfold. No stylish murder. No dead body. No iconic locations. Just an ordinary man caught up in unfortunate circumstances.

Unlike *I Confess*, his slow-burning black-and-white "wrong man" production of three years prior, *The Wrong Man* features little to no eye-catching photography or innovative camera work. Hitchcock's direction is so sparse here, a strong performance is essential to carrying the deliberately paced film. Casting Fonda in the role of Manny Balestrero was a choice that washes these concerns away. Probably the only actor capable of matching James Stewart's status of the "everyman," Fonda brings a grounded humanity to the role in spite of his superstar status. His performance is riveting yet not flashy. He's just a man out of his element, innocent of the crimes of which he has been accused.

Thematically, it is not hard to see why Hitchcock was drawn to the story. In his biography *Alfred Hitchcock: A Life in Darkness and Light*, author Patrick McGilligan recounts in detail Hitch's apparent fear of authority figures. He was nothing less than terrified of the police and the power they could hold over a man's life. This sort of story—going about your business and suddenly being pulled into a police investigation—fascinated and terrified Hitchcock. He'd grapple with this subject matter for his entire career, though rarely with the air of seriousness found here. Hitchcock often portrayed police as inept and bumbling, but rarely in an entirely negative light. Here they are seen as overbearing, uncompromising, and even dishonest. Hitch clearly had distrust for figures of authority; this is never more evident than it is in *The Wrong Man*.

Elements of *The Wrong Man* arise in the classics to follow, but in far more dramatic fashion. He explores the madness of Rose Balestrero in *Vertigo* (and, later, in *Marnie*), in *North by Northwest* "wrong man" themes are once again given the sense of rollicking adventure they once had, and isolation and bleak scenery appear once again in *Psycho*.

There are some high points. A film focused so strongly on its two central characters and devoid of flashy filmmaking and Hitchcockian touches (save a minor few), *The Wrong Man* is utterly dependent on strong performances from its lead actors. Ever the consummate professional, Fonda is excellent in his portrait of a man consumed with quiet desperation, while Vera Miles is truly outstanding as the woman overcome with despair. Here, Miles, who would later play Lila Crane in *Psycho*, gives one of the best performances of her long and varied career.

Also a great strength of *The Wrong Man* is the musical score by Bernard Herrmann. Here, in the third film on which he would collaborate with Hitchcock, his haunting score does an outstanding job of establishing and maintaining a dark tone. After just three films together, it becomes obvious that Hitchcock and Herrmann are perfect complements to one another's talents. Herrmann would go on to experience great success with a number of other prominent directors, but it is his work with Hitchcock that would cement his name on the list of great film composers.

None of this is to suggest *The Wrong Man* is an undiscovered classic. While the artistic experiment is indeed largely a success, the film suffers from drag in the second act, bogging down in an uninteresting subplot (Mrs. Balestrero's aforementioned nervous breakdown). In addition, that the camera work is *supposed* to be stark makes it no more compelling. Lastly, as a viewer, it's hard to suppress the urge to scream at Fonda, "Run away! Flee and prove your innocence!" It's the reaction Hitchcock has trained viewers to have over the years, after all, making Fonda's lack of initiative in that respect veer dangerously close to disappointing. Yes, offering a glimpse into reality was the point of the exercise. But when has Alfred Hitchcock ever offered us reality?

Yet that it lacks the excitement, adventure, and pure creativity seen in Hitch's best work does not prevent *The Wrong Man* from being worth watching. It is not at all representative of the work that made him famous, but as an experiment in style it's a noteworthy film in the Hitchcock filmography.

CONCLUSION

The Wrong Man is unlike any other film in the Hitchcock canon. Here we have an experiment in neorealism, offering a stripped-down, bare-bones approach to filmmaking. Its true story and dark subject matter are not offset by humor and excitement, as seen in Hitch's better-known "wrong man" thrillers, but ultimately *The Wrong Man* is a fine, if slow, film worth seeing despite its depressing subject matter.

HITCHCOCKIAN THEMES

Ineffectual Authority Figures • Wrongly Accused

THINGS TO LOOK FOR

- The real armed robber can be seen at least three times during the film: outside the Stork Club, in the Victor Moore Arcade, and outside one of the liquor stores.

TRIVIA/FUN STUFF

- ✦ Warner Bros. insisted on the ending of the film, which depicts the Balestreros moving away as a happy family once again. In fact, the Balestreros never recovered from these tragic events.
- ✦ For dramatic purposes, Hitchcock chose to leave out information from Manny's story that would have pointed at his innocence earlier in the film.

DVD RELEASES

RELEASE: Warner Home Video (2004)
(Dolby Digital 2.0 Mono, 1.85:1 Black & White)
RATING: ***

EXTRAS: *Guilt Trip: Hitchcock and The Wrong Man* documentary; theatrical trailer.

NOTES: Available as a stand-alone or as part of *The Alfred Hitchcock Signature Collection.*

Vertigo
(1958)

FILM FACTS

PRODUCTION YEAR: 1957
RELEASE DATE: May 9, 1958 (U.S.)
STUDIO: Paramount Pictures
FILMING LOCATIONS: San Francisco, California; Los Angeles, California;
Hollywood, California; San Juan Bautista, California;
Boulder Creek, California; Big Basin, California
PRESENTATION/ASPECT RATIO: Color/1.85:1

SYNOPSIS

San Francisco police detective John "Scottie" Ferguson (James Stewart) develops a fear of heights when a fellow officer falls to his death during a chase. Scottie suffers from vertigo as a result, effectively making him useless in the field. He chooses to retire rather than take a desk job. When an old schoolmate, Gavin Elster (Tom Helmore), asks Scottie to follow his suicidal wife, Madeleine (Kim Novak), he reluctantly accepts the work. In the coming days, Scottie falls in love with Madeleine, but when he is unable to save her from an apparent suicide, he suffers a mental breakdown. Later Scottie meets Judy, a woman who looks strikingly similar to Madeleine. He begins a relationship with Judy, making her over to look just like Madeleine. Then Scottie discovers the truth: Judy *is* Madeleine.

IMPRESSIONS

Other than *Psycho*, no Alfred Hitchcock film has been as analyzed, examined, deconstructed, and dissected so much as *Vertigo*, Hitch's deeply personal treatise on obsession. Film critic Roger Ebert called it Hitchcock's most personal film, an intimate look into the director's psyche. It has been hailed by some as one of the great achievements of American cinema, a haunting portrayal of a man so obsessed with a lost love that he endeavors to remake another woman in her image. It is widely praised and widely respected—yet it is far from the most accessible Alfred Hitchcock film.

But then, one gets the sense that Alfred Hitchcock made *Vertigo* more for himself than for an audience. The result is a captivating yet not always satisfying film.

If biographical accounts of his life and times are even partially accurate, the notion that this film is a personal one should come as no surprise. From his later years, most notably after the departure of Grace Kelly from his life, tales spring forth of a controlling, forceful man intent on "creating" his ideal actress. Their clothes. Hair. Style. Demeanor. He forced his wishes for all this and more onto a series of aspiring actresses, sometimes (according to some accounts) making their working (and occasionally nonworking) experiences miserable. Tippi Hedren's time with Hitchcock was rigorous; Sir Alfred was demanding and specific in his views on how she presented and conducted herself. Vera Miles received much the same treatment until she became pregnant, after which she was cast aside. Other actresses, some of whom languished in obscurity, are reported to have had similar experiences with Hitchcock in his waning years. This sort of behavior, this drive to make someone over in your desired image, is at the heart of *Vertigo*.

In Hitch's legendary masterpiece, James Stewart returns for his fourth, final, and arguably finest role in a Hitchcock film. He plays John "Scottie" Ferguson, a detective on leave after suffering from a sudden fear of heights. An old friend hires Scottie to investigate his wife, Madeleine, to see if he can discover what is at the root of her strange fascination with deceased relatives, the past, and dying. Already, we're delving into the big theme of obsessive behavior. Madeleine lives her life repeating patterns, going through the same motions again and again; afraid to break routine, she is fixated on symbolic imagery from years long since passed. In that respect, she is not unlike Alfred Hitchcock, a man said to have been unusually set in his ways, almost ritualistic in the way he ate, drank, worked, and recreated. This is reflected even in his work. He was a man who, over the course of fifty years of filmmaking, returned time and again to the same themes and motifs.

At the heart of *Vertigo* is Scottie's obsession with Madeleine, first when he falls in love with her after saving her life, and later when he transforms Judy into the image of his lost love. It is a compelling tale and an honest look at a difficult subject for its creator. Scottie, like Hitchcock, is a sympathetic character—but his actions, particularly in his transformation of Judy, are reprehensible, to say the least. Understandable, yes, but difficult to forgive. It is this mistreatment of a beautiful woman (albeit a woman guilty of misdeeds herself) that makes *Vertigo* difficult to enjoy.

It is evident that *Vertigo* is not a film to be enjoyed, but rather a film to be absorbed and cogitated. Hitchcock saw himself in Scottie; he likely identified more with Scottie than with any other character in his entire filmography. Hitch felt the need to create the perfect leading lady after Grace Kelly left show business. It is well documented that Hitchcock controlled the

> **WHERE'S HITCH?**
>
> Hitchcock appears about eleven minutes into the film, walking across the screen in front of Elster's shipyard.

dress of his leading ladies, much as Scottie did with Judy. Extensive wardrobe tests were completed with Vera Miles for the part of Madeleine/Judy before she was forced to leave in the preproduction phase after becoming pregnant. It is interesting to note that Hitchcock's desire to dress his women shows itself as far back as *The Lodger*, with Ivor Novello's character choosing clothing for Daisy.

For Scottie, it's not enough to follow this woman and discover what she's all about. He is attracted to her mystery, to her air of being something *other*. She is beyond his grasp, beyond truly understanding. In some ways, unobtainable. Yet obtain her he does. They enjoy a whirlwind romance, a quick and secretive affair upon which hangs the air of impending doom. When Madeleine throws herself from the top of a bell tower shortly after the kiss that consummates their love, that doom arrives, and Scottie's strangely exhilarating love is lost.

But, as we learn halfway through the film, Madeleine was living a lie. As has so often been the case in our journey with Hitchcock, things are not as they seem. Scottie will learn the truth—and he will learn it the hard way.

Kim Novak disorients James Stewart. (Paramount Pictures/Photofest © Paramount Pictures)

Lost in despair and suffering from a nervous breakdown, he sees a woman on the street who stirs something in him, a woman named Judy. She's a tough-talking brunette, nothing like the delicate and proper blonde, Madeleine. There is something about her, though—something that drives him. It's as if he can see parts of his lost love in her, and so he pushes and pushes, demands she dress a certain way, styles her hair a certain way, forces her to act a certain way, comport herself a certain way. He shapes and molds every aspect of Judy until he has re-created his beloved Madeleine.

Judy, of course, *is* Madeleine—a twist Hitchcock boldly revealed to the viewer not in a shocking climactic revelation at the end of the film, but midway through this new, twisted relationship. In some ways, Hitchcock's decision is a puzzling one. He gives up the game early, wiping away the mystery of Judy before it has a chance to build steam, going so far as to detail the elaborate plot through which Scottie was deceived with nothing more than a simple voiceover. Why go through the trouble of building up a mystery only to tear it down prematurely? Because, at its heart, *Vertigo* is not about Scottie's fear of heights, nor is it about the mystery of Madeleine's apparently delusion-driven suicide. Rather, it is about Scottie's all-consuming obsession, and how that obsession drives him to once again lose the one he loves. Love is a fickle, dangerous thing; it can push you to joyous heights, but can also bring you to the brink of madness if you let it overwhelm you. Scottie does exactly that. Small wonder that Roger Ebert calls this a deeply personal film for Alfred Hitchcock. Sir Alfred was deeply hurt by the "loss" of Grace Kelly, and would endeavor for much of the rest of his career to craft a new ideal leading lady. Hitchcock's very *life* was a quest for perfection. The perfect film. The perfect food. The perfect wine. And the perfectly unobtainable woman.

This fertile thematic ground is brought to life with an almost dream-like cinematic approach. The film is heavy with a hazy, druggy atmosphere. The people and places seem to linger on the edge of reality, shadows beyond Scottie's notice. They move in slow motion, faceless. Early in the film, when Scottie first pursues Madeleine, the pace is slow and deliberate. The pace quickens as their love reaches its climax in the barn near the tower from which Madeleine plunges, a sense of urgency in the air both before and after, but just as quickly shifts back to a staggering, dazed pace, reflecting Scottie's state of mind following her apparent death. In addition to pacing, Hitchcock utilized color to great effect in achieving the film's almost mystical quality: Deep, bold reds; eerie, ghostly greens; and wavering, watery blues evoke Scottie's state of mind and add texture to the subtle tapestry of moods Hitchcock was trying to weave. *Vertigo* is all stylization, venturing back into more accessible territory only when Scottie is with his peppy friend, Midge (Barbara Bel Geddes), and rarely at any other time.

The incredible stylization comes to full bear during *Vertigo*'s legendary kiss scene, a Hitchcock kiss rivaling even the one in *Notorious*. In this remarkable piece of cinematic technique, Scottie sits in a hotel room on the cusp of finally accomplishing his impossible goal: transforming Judy into his lost love, Madeleine. Judy steps out of the bathroom, wearing Madeleine's clothes, her hair styled like Madeleine's, her very demeanor the picture of Madeleine. Scottie, of course, does not know that Judy *is* Madeleine. All he sees is his love returned, the payoff to his obsessive need to re-create the woman he lost. Bathed in the ghostly green light of a neon sign, she steps forward like something from another world, truly like a woman returned from the dead. They embrace. They kiss. The camera whirls about them, and for a fleeting instant the room transforms into the barn where Scottie and Madeleine's love was finally realized with a passionate kiss. It's a symbolically powerful shot, bringing to fruition Scottie's twisted efforts, and encompassing the journey of the film in one masterful stroke.

Such a journey cannot end happily. Driven as Scottie was, possessed as he was, as unsympathetic as his forceful handling of Judy was, it would be hard to imagine anything other than a tragic ending. No man so driven can truly attain happiness. We feel for Scottie, yet, in a way, we are also repulsed by his actions. James Stewart walks a tightrope here in one of the greatest performances of his career, simultaneously portraying an everyman plagued by fears he cannot control (thus drawing our sympathy) and a man so tormented by his lost love that he is driven to psychologically controlling and abusing a new girlfriend, actions that can only be described as utterly distasteful. Yet Stewart manages the trick. When Scottie leads Judy/Madeleine up the steps of the bell tower that second time, we, as an audience, both loathe him for what he is doing and plead with him not to do it because we don't want to see him make a terrible mistake. We can see an even greater tragedy is coming. We like Scottie; we feel for him; we don't want to see it happen again. We're torn, though. Since losing Madeleine, he has been unlikable and controlling, even villainous.

And so, when Madeleine once again plunges from the top of the bell tower, this time in truth, our worst fears are realized. We're left stunned, exhausted by the tragic inevitability of it all. But Hitchcock does not allow us time to reflect. He ends the film with Scottie still gazing down upon the body of the woman he loves. The credits roll. And we are dumbstruck. It is almost as if Hitchcock knew his own real-life efforts to create the "perfect" leading lady were futile, that they could only end in pain. Yet, like Scottie, he would plunge forward despite the futility, manipulating women to get what he wanted, and ultimately dying alone and misunderstood for it.

Hitchcock was not known for his writing, but he was notorious for the precise demands he made of his screenwriters. *Vertigo* is perhaps the best example of this. The novel *D'Entre les Morts*, written by Frenchmen Pierre Boileau and Thomas Narcejac with the intention of selling the rights to Hitchcock, was never even read by screenwriter Samuel Taylor. Alec Coppel is also credited for the screenplay, but only for contractual reasons; his script, also unread by Taylor, was quickly scrapped. Instead, Taylor worked off meticulous notes from Hitchcock in creating a realization of Hitch's inner demons. "I deliberately did not read the original novel or screenplay," Taylor recalled in Donald Spoto's *The Art of Alfred Hitchcock*. "The story had already been worked out by Hitchcock, and I wanted to concentrate on what he wanted, not what the book had."[24] The famed director had a history of deviating greatly from his source material. *Vertigo* was a major example of that. The Midge character was invented for the film, for instance, as was the decision to reveal the truth about Judy/Madeleine to the viewer before Scottie figured it out.

The decision to reveal the truth in the middle of the film instead of at the end goes entirely against traditional formula, particularly for a film released in the late 1950s, yet it works to *Vertigo*'s advantage. With the truth known, the viewer is left to wonder what will happen when Scottie learns of Judy's actual identity. We are better able to examine and contemplate Scottie's anguish and observe how it manifests itself.

Scottie's anguish is key. With any other actor in the part, *Vertigo* might fall flat on its face, but Stewart's portrayal of a man consumed by both grief and obsession is outstanding, the motor that drives this dark film forward. Scottie's actions, particularly later in the film, are unforgivable and ultimately make him unlikable, but Stewart manages to evoke compassion from the audience.

Kim Novak, too, carries a lot of weight. It has been suggested by critics, and also by Hitchcock, that Novak was not right for the part of Judy/Madeleine: that she was too naive to play such a complex character. This notion is flawed. Novak was not a particularly accomplished actress, but what she brought to the part was perfect. Judy was a simple girl from Kansas swept up in a desperate situation out of her control. Novak's naïveté was well suited for this role, and did not prevent her from illustrating the pain experienced by her character.

Of course it helps that Novak and Stewart were given great material to work with. Taylor's aforementioned script is one of the best in the Hitchcock filmography. The story is impeccably constructed, and while the dialogue is at times economical, it is nevertheless biting:

> JUDY: Couldn't you like me, just me the way I am? When we first started out, it was so good; w–we had fun. And . . . and then you started in on the clothes. Well, I'll wear the darn clothes if you want me to, if, if you'll just, just like me.
> SCOTTIE: The color of your hair . . .
> JUDY: Oh, no!
> SCOTTIE: Judy, please, it can't matter to you.

This exchange is heartbreaking, powerfully illustrating the depths to which these characters have sunk. This beautiful young woman, so desperate to be loved, is willing to give up her identity for Scottie even as she realizes his love is not really for her, but rather for the memory of someone she has been made to resemble. And Scottie, not entirely conscious of the torment his demands have placed on Judy, is so consumed with his obsession that he is willing to place his own desires above her pain.

Taylor delivers another sequence of biting dialogue at the conclusion, after Scottie finally puts aside his obsession to call Judy out on her deception at the scene of Madeleine's faked suicide:

> He made you over, didn't he? He made you over just like I made you over, only better. Not only the clothes and the hair, but the looks and the manner and the words. And those phony trances! And then what did he do? Did he train you? Did he rehearse you? Did he tell you exactly what to do and what to say? You were a very apt pupil, weren't you? You were a very apt pupil!

Scottie's anger at both Judy and himself is realized in dramatic fashion.

With *Vertigo*, Hitchcock began a trilogy of films (along with *North by Northwest* and *Psycho*) concerned with the loss of identity. It is phenomenal to consider that all three films—each decidedly different from each other in genre, tone, and style—are widely regarded among the greatest movies of all time. No director is able to match this stunning output of three timeless films in three years. Maybe Francis Ford Coppola can make an argument with *The Godfather*, *The Conversation*, and *The Godfather: Part II* from 1972 to 1974, but Hitch's diversity in his stretch separates him from the rest. What other director could follow a timeless psychological mystery drama with an even better adventure film and then an unforgettable horror flick? Nobody but Hitchcock.

Vertigo may not be thoroughly enjoyable—Scottie's actions are simply too difficult to sympathize with—but it is perpetually fascinating, one of the most intriguing stops on a journey through Hitchcock's films.

Ultimately, *Vertigo* ends as it begins, with Scottie dangling from a great height, his own psyche his worst enemy. By most accounts, so, too, was Alfred Hitchcock's own psyche his worst enemy.

CONCLUSION

Alfred Hitchcock never made a more honest film, a picture that reflects his own deep-seated fears, anxieties, and apprehensions in a way no other work in his filmography does. An exceedingly intimate movie, *Vertigo* easily ranks among his very best works. Featuring great acting, a terrific script, deft direction, and a thought-provoking story, *Vertigo* is one of the most important films in Hitchcock's filmography.

HITCHCOCKIAN THEMES

Blonde Leading Lady · Chaos in an Unexpected Location · Dark Secret · Love Triangle · Murder · Music Plays a Role in Plot · Suicide/Attempted Suicide

THINGS TO LOOK FOR

- The famous push-pull shots (a new invention for *Vertigo*) used to simulate the feeling of vertigo for the viewer.
- Numerous instances of mirror reflections and repeated imagery.
- The change in lighting from light to dark, and vice versa, from scene to scene.
- Hitchcock's use of color to establish mood and paint characters.
- The hotel room kiss scene.

TRIVIA/FUN STUFF

- ✦ Hitchcock originally intended the role of Judy/Madeleine for Vera Miles, and even completed wardrobe tests with her, but she was forced to leave the production when she became pregnant.
- ✦ Tom Helmore, who played Gavin Elster, previously appeared uncredited in Hitchcock's *The Ring* as one of Carl Brisson's opponents, and in *Secret Agent* as Colonel Anderson.
- ✦ The Spanish mission San Juan Bautista did not have a bell tower. It was created through trick photography. The mission originally had a steeple, but it was destroyed in a fire.
- ✦ In 1989 the film was added to the National Film Registry by the National Film Preservation Board, which selects films that "are considered to be culturally, historically or aesthetically important."
- ✦ Rank on American Film Institute Top 100 Films (1997): 61.
- ✦ Rank on American Film Institute Top 100 Films (2007): 9.
- ✦ Ranking in *Sight and Sound* magazine's survey of the Top Ten Films of All Time: 1982: 7; 1992: 4; 2002: 2.

AWARDS

- Academy Award Nominations (2): Best Art Direction/Set Decoration, Black-and-White or Color (Hal Pereira, Henry Bumstead, Sam Comer, Frank R. McKelvy); Best Sound (George Dutton)
- Directors Guild of America Nomination: Outstanding Directorial Achievement in Motion Pictures
- San Sebastián International Film Festival Wins: Silver Seashell (Alfred Hitchcock), Best Actor (James Stewart; tied with Kirk Douglas for *The Vikings*)

DVD RELEASES

Release: Universal Studios, Universal Legacy Series (2008)
(Dolby Digital 2.0 Mono, 1.85:1 Color)
Rating: *****

Extras: Two-disc set includes feature commentary with associate producer Herbert Coleman, restoration team Robert A. Harris and James C. Katz, and other *Vertigo* [participants; feature commentary with director William Friedkin; foreign censorship ending; The *Vertigo* Archives; production notes; original theatrical trailer; restoration theatrical trailer, *Obsessed with Vertigo: New Life for Hitchcock's Masterpiece*; *Partners in Crime: Hitchcock's Collaborators*; Hitchcock/Truffaut interview excerpts; *Alfred Hitchcock Presents* episode "The Case of Mr. Pelham"

Release: Universal Studios (2001, 2005, 2006)
(Dolby Digital 2.0 Mono, 1.85:1 Color)
Rating: *****

Extras: *Obsessed with Vertigo* documentary; commentary by associate producer Herbert Coleman; alternate ending; Vertigo Archive Restoration Team; production notes; theatrical trailer; restoration trailer.
Notes: Available as stand-alone releases from 2001 and 2006, or as part of *The Alfred Hitchcock Collection* (out of print) and *Alfred Hitchcock: The Masterpiece Collection*. *The Masterpiece Collection* is recommended. The transfers on all releases appear identical.

North by Northwest
(1959)

FILM FACTS

PRODUCTION YEAR: 1958
RELEASE DATE: July/August 1959 (U.S.)
STUDIO: MGM
FILMING LOCATIONS: Bakersfield, California; New York, New York;
Chicago, Illinois; Los Angeles, California; Mount Rushmore National
Memorial, Keystone, South Dakota; Long Island, New York
PRESENTATION/ASPECT RATIO: Color/1.85:1

SYNOPSIS

Advertising executive Roger O. Thornhill (Cary Grant) lives a successful but ordinary life. That is, until a spy syndicate mistakes him for a top-secret government agent. Suddenly, his life spirals out of control. Thornhill escapes their initial attempt to kill him, but all his escape manages to do is set him on a cross-country journey to find out the truth, clear his name, and, of course, to just plain survive. His flight takes him to the United Nations, desolate cornfields, and, in the film's climactic sequence, to Mount Rushmore. Along the way, he meets up with Eve Kendall (Eva Marie Saint), a stunning beauty initially working for the spies, but who eventually joins with Thornhill to unravel their machinations and clear his name.

IMPRESSIONS

North by Northwest is the single film that best exemplifies the work of Alfred Hitchcock. It is an endlessly entertaining motion picture, exceptionally well written, exquisitely acted, gorgeously shot, impeccably edited, and beautifully scored. This is the quintessential Hitchcock, the culmination of thirty-five years of ever-improving filmmaking. Hitch would make several outstanding pictures after *North by Northwest*, but none so perfectly executed and none so representative of his larger body of work.

For those engaging in artistic endeavors, doing the same thing over and over again might be approaching creative suicide, signaling a lack of new ideas and new creations. For a filmmaker, treading the same ground again and again is a recipe for stagnation. At best, it's a recipe for boredom.

For Alfred Hitchcock, it was an invitation to the world of borderline perfection.

Any discussion of *North by Northwest* must begin with the screenplay by Ernest Lehman, a prolific writer who was nominated six times for an Academy Award, but was never a winner. Unlike *Vertigo*, based on a novel and thoroughly outlined by Hitchcock before screenwriter Samuel Taylor began work, *North by Northwest* was largely Lehman's brainchild. He and Hitch worked closely together, but aside from the "man on the run" concept and the idea that the film would begin at the United Nations and end at Mount Rushmore, the scenarios were entirely generated by Lehman. The result is the best screenplay Hitchcock ever filmed.

Lehman's script efficiently blends suspense, mystery, drama, sexual innuendo, and humor. The story of a Madison Avenue adman who gets caught up in a case of mistaken identity, forced to go on the run to prove his innocence, is absurd to say the least. The entire premise is ridiculous. Because the characters are so entertaining and the situations exciting, that matters not one bit. At 136 minutes, this is Hitchcock's second-longest film, but it never feels long because virtually every moment drives the story forward. Even the famous crop duster sequence, slow as it is to develop, is a tour de force of filmmaking genius.

North by Northwest is, by any objective measure, a bigger, flashier rehash of movies Alfred Hitchcock had done before. The themes, situations, and general narrative structure are all but interchangeable with films like *Saboteur*, *Young and Innocent*, and *The 39 Steps*. Those films, however, were made by a director still exploring his own creative world, still finding and refining the techniques he would use to thrill audiences for years to come. *North by Northwest*, on the other hand, was made by a director at the peak of his powers, a man so intimately familiar with the intricacies of his craft he was often finished with a great motion picture before getting the first shot to film. In the midst of one of the most remarkable stretches of filmmaking in cinema history—and that's no hyperbole—Alfred Hitchcock returned to ground he had tread before and created a masterpiece, utilizing every film-making lesson he had learned in the previous thirty-plus years.

North by Northwest came together in a way that, on the surface, would seem to be fare for glitzy but empty Hollywood summer blockbusters. Hitchcock had in mind a series of set pieces: locations and events he had always wanted to film. He gave them to Lehman, who fit the pieces together into a narrative. Cobbled together like Frankenstein's monster, they called it a story. By all rights, it should have failed. It should have been vapid. It should have barely held together. Instead, it stands as one of Alfred Hitchcock's greatest achievements.

As in *Vertigo*, the viewer is offered the truth of a situation—in this case that Eve is a double agent—well before the protagonist. It's an interesting choice to not delay the revelation of such a major truth in a suspense film, but in this case it works beautifully. The adventure is strong enough that the viewer is left to enjoy the ride rather than ponder the mystery.

> **WHERE'S HITCH?**
>
> During the opening credits, Hitchcock can be seen trying to catch a bus . . . and failing.

Most enjoyable is Lehman's dialogue, which is equal parts satirical, indicative of its characters, and full of wit and humor. When Thornhill is told to wait in the library at the Townsend residence, he quips to Vandamm's henchman, "Don't hurry, I'll catch up on my reading." Shortly after, he tells Vandamm, "Not that I mind a case of abduction now and then, but I have tickets to the theatre this evening, to a show I was looking forward to, and I get, well, kind of unreasonable about things like that."

Throughout the film, there are repeated references to theatre and play-acting. The three central characters, Thornhill, Vandamm, and Eve Kendall, all play different roles to one another in this absurd tale. Vandamm, thinking Thornhill is really the faux government agent George Kaplan, says to him, "Has anyone ever told you that you overplay your various roles rather severely, Mr. Kaplan?" He later says, "Seems to me you fellows could stand a little less training from the FBI and a little more from the Actor's Studio." The meta-commentary is both a sly wink at the audience and appropriate to the story.

Adam Williams, Martin Landau, and Robert Ellenstein force Cary Grant to take a drink. (MGM/Photofest © MGM)

As we have seen so many times, *North by Northwest* again features a strong opening. This time it is not an amazing shot that draws the viewer in to the story, but the outstanding Saul Bass titles and Bernard Herrmann theme. Bass, who for nearly fifty years designed Hollywood's most attractive titles, worked on just three Hitchcock films (*Vertigo* and *Psycho* being the others), but his work here is particularly strong. The opening credits cascade on top of what becomes a New York City skyscraper, a clever assemblage of geometric patterns and letters. Combine these titles with Herrmann's memorable theme and viewers are instantly clued in that they are in for an exciting ride.

Not only is Herrmann's main theme excellent, the rest of his score does a fabulous job of driving the story forward. It would be difficult to pick the best score Herrmann did for Hitchcock, but this one has to be high on the list. The music is always right for the moment, whether it is serious, suspenseful, or playful. Of all of his collaborators, the teaming with Herrmann during Hitch's most successful period was fortuitous. He certainly deserves a great deal of credit for the variety of work he brought to the Hitchcock catalog.

First and foremost on a list of reasons why Hitchcock managed to elevate his already formidable directorial talent during this period is that not only did he show an uncanny knack for picking the right performers and collaborators, he now had the pull to get exactly who he wanted. Auteur theory aside, making films is a project of collaboration, even with a man of vision such as Hitchcock at the helm. Without other talented people involved, his films would never have realized their full potential. At the forefront of this were the amazing performers he secured for his motion pictures.

Enter, for the fourth and final time, the incomparable Cary Grant.

It has been suggested that James Stewart (who appeared in four Hitchcock films) played the characters in which Hitch saw himself reflected, while Cary Grant (who also appeared in four Hitchcock films) played the characters Hitch wished he could be. There is credence to this theory. Stewart portrayed the man who casually discusses murder (*Rope*), the inquisitive voyeur (*Rear Window*), the loving husband and father (*The Man Who Knew Too Much*), and the hopelessly obsessed romantic (*Vertigo*), while Grant played the carefree playboy (*Suspicion*), the savior of the beautiful blonde (*Notorious*), the wrongfully accused hero (*To Catch a Thief*), and the sophisticated man who overcomes all sorts of danger to win the beautiful woman (*North by Northwest*).

Whether or not Thornhill was someone Hitchcock wished he could be, Grant was indeed the ideal man for the part. Never was there a better fit between movie and movie star. Grant had been a superstar for more than twenty years by this time, perfecting the image of the suave, sophisticated man whom women adored and men admired. Here he plays a man who may have a checkered past (two divorces), but he's eminently likeable. Grant's charm and class make him the ultimate hero. We want to see Thornhill trapped in one difficult circumstance after another because we know he will entertain the heck out of us extricating himself from danger. It is little wonder why the character of James Bond was created in the mold of Cary Grant.

Yet if Cary Grant is wish fulfillment, he is an approachable brand of wish fulfillment. While a handsome man adored by women, he is far from the muscular, machine-gun toting screen heroes who would come to populate cinema in the coming decades. He takes on incredible odds not because he's extraordinarily brave or talented, but because he is *forced* to take on incredible odds. With better clothes, a better job, and a bit of charm, we could overcome the same obstacles. That is important. More than making Thornhill a sympathetic character, it repeats (and refines) a theme we've seen time and again in Hitchcock's work: It takes but a coincidental crossing of paths for an ordinary person to be caught up in machinations much bigger than himself. It was as if Hitchcock both feared the prospect of getting pulled into some such thing and savored it at the same time. Like the best of Hitchcock's protagonists, Thornhill is an everyman—albeit a much different breed of everyman than James Stewart's L. B. Jefferies, or Ben McKenna, or Scottie Ferguson. Even with a project like this, with Hitchcock thinking in broad brush strokes and ambitious set pieces, the notion of the everyman remains a vital theme. In this, Hitchcock's ultimate "wrong man" film, we still need our heroes to be somewhat down-to-earth. That's exactly what Grant manages—without diminishing his star.

Helping bring Grant's star down-to-earth is his own willingness to be the butt of jokes and a cast that manages to keep the mood light without undermining the tension inherent in the tale. A lively script can help a motion picture shine, but in the hands of Alfred Hitchcock this dialogue just sings. Yet we should credit Grant more than Hitchcock; his whimsy and charm are infectious. The charismatic Grant is what elevates this over another set piece–driven picture, the somewhat similar *Saboteur*. The same can be said for other Hitchcock films that tread similar thematic ground, such as *The 39 Steps* and *Young and Innocent*. Not only had the director's craft improved since those films, so, too, did his ability to get the perfect star. *North by Northwest* is essentially more of the same from Alfred Hitchcock—but better.

To complement the screen presence of Grant, Hitchcock needed a beautiful woman. MGM wanted to cast Cyd Charisse, but Hitchcock, whose contract stipulated he had complete creative control, insisted on Eva Marie Saint, an elegant beauty best known for her star-making turn opposite Marlon Brando in *On the Waterfront* (1954). Saint became the epitome of the icy Hitchcock blonde, duplicitous yet fallible. We have discussed the importance of Grace Kelly on Hitchcock's films, but aside from her adultery in *Dial M for Murder*, Kelly was exclusively portrayed in a positive light. With Saint's Eve Kendall, Hitch gives us not just a graceful beauty, but a tough, intelligent, and deceptive woman torn by the conflict of her commitment to her country and the love she feels for Thornhill—shades of the conflict experienced by Alicia Huberman in *Notorious*. It is a difficult part, but Saint succeeds admirably.

And what would a Hitchcock thriller be without a charming villain? James Mason was up to the challenge of playing opposite the formidable Cary Grant. Mason may not match Joseph Cotten or Robert Walker for pure screen presence, but his Vandamm is still one of the indelible villains in the Hitchcock canon. It's arresting when a villain maintains his cool during times of crisis, and Vandamm is the ultimate cool customer.

The supporting cast, particularly Leo G. Carroll, Jessie Royce Landis, and Martin Landau, is also excellent. Carroll, as we have come to expect through his multiple appearances in Hitchcock's work, is an imposing authority figure, a man never unsure of himself. Landis, playing Grant's mother despite being just seven years older than him, is delightful as a source of comic relief. "You gentlemen aren't really trying to kill my son, are you?" she says to two of Vandamm's henchmen on the elevator. And with his chilling demeanor and dark eyebrows, Landau is creepy as Vandamm's right-hand man, Leonard. These actors are critical to the success of the film; anything less than perfection would distract from the frenetic enjoyment found in *North by Northwest*.

Editing is almost always a strength in Hitchcock's work, and such is the case with *North by Northwest*, which contains one of the single best edited sequences in his filmography: the crop duster scene. This ten-minute sequence is a textbook example of how editing can be used to propel a story forward despite a relative lack of dialogue. It is a legendary film moment that came about through meticulous planning. Hitchcock was notorious for his detailed storyboarding. Here it has never been more evident. Every cut has purpose; every shot pushes this absurd yet riveting sequence forward.

The ending is typically Hitchcockian, featuring both an iconic location and chaos in that setting. The audacious decision to set the climactic scene not just at Mount Rushmore, but on the face of the sculptures, is something only Hitch would have considered. The U.S. Department of the Interior would not let Hitchcock shoot on the actual face of Mount Rushmore, so the entire setting was meticulously re-created in the studio. Even decades later, it looks realistic, making it a wild setting for the struggle for life, death, and the ultimate MacGuffin: the microfilm hidden inside Vandamm's sculpture.

Since this is a comic adventure, it is appropriate to end the film on a light note. Just as Thornhill is pulling Kendall to safety on the face of Mount Rushmore, Hitch jump cuts to a scene aboard a train where Thornhill is pulling Kendall into his bed. They are now married. Hitchcock then cuts to an image of the train moving up-screen into a tunnel, the ultimate sexual metaphor.

Looking at the films surrounding this one, it comes as no surprise that *North by Northwest* is impressively directed. The creative peak Hitch hit in the 1950s, knocking out classic after classic, is nothing short of astonishing. How did Alfred Hitchcock come to this stunning achievement after more than thirty years of filmmaking? By honing every aspect of his craft to razor-sharp perfection. No director in history has ever had a run of sustained genius as constant, successful, consistent, and impressive as Alfred Hitchcock during this period. Here was a man who, for all intents and purposes, had "figured it out."

Did Hitch feel he had something to prove at this late stage of his career? Did he feel a need to prove his worth as an artist and his growth as a director? After all, he had recently remade *The Man Who Knew Too Much*, a solid but not overly innovative thriller from his days as a British director. It was almost as if he was saying, "You do not realize how good I have become. Watch, and I will show you. I will do what I have always done, but now you will finally recognize the accomplishment in what I do." He was a man, after all, who never won an Academy Award for Best Direction, and whose sole Best Picture award (for *Rebecca*) was as much a David O. Selznick picture as an Alfred Hitchcock picture. He had some respect as a visionary in Europe, largely in French cinema circles, but in Hollywood he was recognized as little more than a crowd-pleasing moneymaker. This had to grate. From this point of view, it is entirely possible that Hitch was revisiting old ground with something to prove.

More likely, however, is that he simply had some big ideas he wanted to see come to fruition—nothing more, nothing less. He wanted his crop duster chase and his confrontation on Mount Rushmore. And so he made it. To suggest any more is posthumous mind reading.

No matter his motivations, conscious or not, one thing is clear: *North by Northwest* represents all that is good in Alfred Hitchcock's work.

CONCLUSION

If there is a single film that best exemplifies all that made Alfred Hitchcock an enduring, successful entertainer, it is *North by Northwest*. Whether or not it is his "best" film is inconsequential; it represents almost all of what made him stand out from his peers. Visually inviting, impeccably directed, suspenseful and engaging, wonderfully acted, boasting innovative special effects, and laden with themes Hitchcock dealt with his entire career, *North by Northwest* is Alfred Hitchcock cinema defined.

HITCHCOCKIAN THEMES

Blonde Leading Lady • Chaos in an Unexpected Location • Climactic Showdown at an Iconic Location • Ineffectual Authority Figures • MacGuffin • Man (or Woman) on the Run • Manipulative Mother • Spy Syndicate • Trains • Wrongly Accused

THINGS TO LOOK FOR

- The crop duster sequence, arguably the second most famous Hitchcock sequence (next to *Psycho*'s shower scene) and one of cinema's most iconic moments.
- The innovative special effects used to bring the Mount Rushmore scene to life. For the climactic pursuit, the entire monument was re-created in the studio.
- The daringly sexual banter between Grant and Saint on the train. The dialogue was highly risqué for 1959, and was, in fact, censored. If you watch closely, you can see Saint's lips say, "I never make love on an empty stomach," while the audio says, "I never discuss love on an empty stomach."

AWARDS

- Academy Awards Nominations (3): Best Writing, Story and Screenplay–Written Directly for the Screen (Ernest Lehman); Best Art Direction/Set Decoration, Color (William A. Horning, Robert F. Boyle, Merrill Pye, Henry Grace, Frank R. McKelvy); Best Film Editing (George Tomasini)
- Directors Guild of America Nomination: Outstanding Directorial Achievement in Motion Pictures
- Edgar Allan Poe Awards Win: Best Motion Picture (Ernest Lehman)
- San Sebastián International Film Festival Win: Golden Seashell (Alfred Hitchcock)
- Writers Guild of America Nomination: Best Written American Comedy (Ernest Lehman)

TRIVIA/FUN STUFF

◆ Due to a misunderstanding, for a time James Stewart thought he was set to star in the film.

◆ Early prints included thanks to the Department of the Interior and the National Parks Service. Those thanks were subsequently removed at their request, as Hitchcock ignored their request that no violence be shown on Mount Rushmore.

◆ The park scenes near the end of the film were not shot on location; all those dozens and dozens of trees were painstakingly planted on a soundstage.

◆ Jessie Royce Landis's role as Thornhill's mother—one of the film's standout performances—would not be possible in real life; she was only seven years older than Cary Grant.

◆ The scenes outside the United Nations were shot covertly, since Hitchcock was denied permission to shoot there. The interior shots were filmed on a soundstage.

◆ The idea of a man being mistaken for a secret agent who did not exist was inspired by comments journalist Otis L. Guernsey Jr. made to Hitchcock. The plot of the film itself was cobbled together by screenwriter Ernest Lehman.

◆ Leo G. Carroll makes his sixth and final appearance in a Hitchcock film, the most of any actor. His other Hitchcock roles were in *Rebecca, Suspicion, Spellbound, The Paradine Case,* and *Strangers on a Train.*

◆ In 1995 the film was added to the National Film Registry by the National Film Preservation Board, which selects films that "are considered to be culturally, historically or aesthetically important."

◆ Rank on American Film Institute Top 100 Films (1997): 40.

◆ Rank on American Film Institute Top 100 Films (2007): 55.

DVD RELEASES

RELEASE: Warner Home Video (2002, 2004)
(Dolby Digital 5.1, 1.85:1 color)
RATING: *****

EXTRAS: *Destination Hitchcock: The Making of North By Northwest* documentary; commentary by screenwriter Ernest Lehman; photo gallery; trailer gallery; TV spot; isolated film score.

NOTES: Available as a stand-alone or as part of *The Alfred Hitchcock Signature Collection*.

RELEASE: Warner Home Video, 50th Anniversary Special Edition
Blu-ray Disc (2009)
(Dolby Digital 5.1, 1.85:1 Color)
RATING: *****

EXTRAS: Commentary by screenwriter Ernest Lehman; new 2009 documentary: *The Master's Touch: Hitchcock's Signature Style*; feature-length career profile: Cary Grant: A Class Apart.

Alfred Hitchcock Presents
(1958–1961)

INTRODUCTION

By 1958 Alfred Hitchcock's television show, *Alfred Hitchcock Presents*, was a bona fide success, making the director a household name and propelling him into a level of stardom he still enjoys three decades after his death. The anthology program, which aired for ten seasons, featured suspense and mystery stories in the vein one would expect of a Hitchcock creation. Over the course of the first six seasons, Hitchcock directed seventeen of the episodes. Here are Hitch-directed episodes of the show shot between 1958 and 1961.

"LAMB TO THE SLAUGHTER"
(ORIGINALLY AIRED APRIL 13, 1958)

Food and murder, two of Alfred Hitchcock's favorite subjects, are brought together in "Lamb to the Slaughter" for a low-key thriller bordering on black comedy. In it, Mary Maloney (Barbara Bel Geddes, who also appeared in *Vertigo*), confronted with the unexpected revelation that her husband wants to leave her, takes matters into her own hands and clubs him to death with an uncooked lamb roast. A crime of passion? Not quite. It is clear that there is something askew in Mrs. Maloney's mind. She's insane. But she's also a shrewd woman. If the murder weapon was a roast, what better way to destroy the evidence than by cooking it? That's just what she does, prepar-

Barbara Bel Geddes serves up murder. (CBS/Photofest © CBS)

ing dinner even as the police mill about her home, investigating the break-in she falsely reported.

One can imagine Hitchcock laughing with delight at this script. If "Lamb to the Slaughter" fits with any of Hitch's cinema work, it belongs alongside a film like *The Trouble with Harry*: funny despite its dark subject matter. It's lighthearted and generally lacking in suspense, drama, or directorial flourishes, instead reveling in its humorous take on a macabre subject. The episode should be suspenseful—a police officer asking questions of a murderer while the incriminating weapon lies in plain sight is classically Hitchcockian in nature, hearkening to the teasing of *Rope*—but the premise is so silly, it feels more natural to grin. That was clearly Hitchcock's intention, too. The final shot—police officers eating the murder weapon—is just the sort of humor Sir Alfred delighted in. "Lamb to the Slaughter" may lack technical brilliance, but it more than makes up for it in offering the audience a glimpse at Hitchcock's morbid sense of humor.

"A DIP IN THE POOL" (ORIGINALLY AIRED JUNE 1, 1958)

William Bobitol (Keenan Wynn) is a compulsive gambler aboard a cruise ship to Europe with his wife, Ethel (Louise Platt). Ethel is aware of their limited funds, but is anxious to make the most of their European excursion. Bobitol, who has never met a bet he would not take, befriends Mr. Renshaw (Philip Borneuf), a man of higher class who informs Bobitol of a betting pool to guess the distance the ship will travel within a day's time. Bobitol, convinced that the ship will be slowed by storms, bids heavily for the lowest field in the pool, hoping to win the £10,000 pot. When the storms pass and it appears he will lose money he cannot afford to lose, he finds a woman to witness his jump into the ocean, thinking she will have the ship stopped so he can be rescued, thus slowing down the ship's progress and securing his winning bid. But fate is against Bobitol. His chosen witness is a woman of unstable mind. She does nothing to save him after he jumps.

This is a story of dark, morbid humor to say the least. The entire tale is told at the expense of Bobitol, a man of good intentions who cannot help himself when presented with the possibility of great reward for a sizeable gamble. As in "The Perfect Crime," Hitchcock takes delight in revealing in his epilogue that there is a happy ending, with a twist—Bobitol won the pool, but the winnings were enjoyed by Mrs. Bobitol and her *second* husband.

"POISON" (ORIGINALLY AIRED OCTOBER 5, 1958)

The first episode of the fourth season is a grim, at times mean-spirited piece of work, but is among the most thematically rich of the Hitchcock-directed episodes. *Poison* centers on Mr. Woods (Wendell Corey), who awakes to find that a deadly snake has slithered into his bed and is now sleeping on his stomach. If he moves, if he even attempts to lift the sheets, the snake is likely to strike, dooming him to a painful death. Sweating, frightened, and on edge, this apparent alcoholic's only way out of the situation is to rely on a two-faced friend and a local doctor.

"Poison" is just the sort of episode that tied Hitchcock's name to "twist endings." As in *Suspicion*, we spend much of our time wondering if our lead character is truly in jeopardy or if he (or, in the case of *Suspicion*, she) is simply imagining things. The bulk of the story focuses on both that uncertainty and on figuring out how to get rid of the snake—if it actually exists. Painfully close shots of Woods's face bring an air of dread, even if we ultimately doubt his story.

The end—or what is actually a precursor to the end—is predictable. No snake. Once again, our lead's fears are misplaced. Or are they? In the show's final moments, we see there is a snake after all. We cringe as his friend laughs at Woods's seemingly misplaced panic, and get a final dose of suspense as we wait for him to be bitten. And, in a final piece of grim poetic justice, bitten he is.

"BANQUO'S CHAIR"
(ORIGINALLY AIRED MAY 3, 1959)

Another in a string of "twist ending" episodes, "Banquo's Chair" takes a murder investigation and sets it at that most Hitchcockian of places, the dinner table. Inspector Brent (John Williams, who appeared in *To Catch a Thief*, *Dial M for Murder*, and an uncredited role in *The Paradine Case*) suspects that years prior, John Bedford (Kenneth Haigh) murdered his aunt in order to collect inheritance money. Bedford got away with the crime, but Brent has a plan to finally twist a confession out of him. Bedford is invited to a dinner party held in the very room in which the murder took place. There, the inspector has arranged for the culprit to be tormented by his slain aunt's ghost—a fake played by a Brent-hired actress. Bedford is briefly driven mad by the ghostly vision, and, in an outburst, admits his crime. The twist comes in the episode's final moments, when it is revealed that the actress was not on hand to play the part of the apparition. The ghost, it seems, was real.

"Banquo's Chair" is unremarkable but entertaining, sustaining itself on a single extended hook—Bedford's on-screen mental breakdown. The dark photography, dinner table setting, and fine performances by Williams and

Haigh give this somewhat light episode more punch than it may have otherwise had.

"ARTHUR"
(ORIGINALLY AIRED SEPTEMBER 27, 1959)

Arthur (Lawrence Harvey) is an egomaniac who searches for ways to run his chicken farm without the help of others. When his fiancée, Helen (Hazel Court), breaks off the engagement to run off with another man, Arthur is relieved to be alone again. A year later, Helen returns, having been dumped by her new husband. Penniless, she hopes to reunite with him, but when Arthur rebuffs her, she states she would rather be dead than be left to fend for herself. Arthur grants Helen's wish, strangling her and disposing of the body by mixing it with chicken feed to fatten his flock.

This episode, the first of the fifth season, is interesting for several reasons. First, after Hitch's usual introduction, the episode starts with Arthur breaking the fourth wall in a monologue to the audience. In the monologue, he admits to his murder with an arrogance that is both charming and off-putting. Second, it goes back to a favorite Hitchcock theme: the perfect murder. Arthur is convinced he will not be caught if he smartly disposes of her body. Similar to "Lamb to the Slaughter," where the murder weapon was cooked and served to police investigating the crime, "Arthur" finds the protagonist feeding one of his chickens (enlarged on the feed made from his ex) to police investigating Helen's death. It is a morbid notion, but one can easily see the appeal to Hitchcock's sense of humor.

"THE CRYSTAL TRENCH"
(ORIGINALLY AIRED OCTOBER 4, 1959)

This 1959 episode of *Alfred Hitchcock Presents* opens with a narrative device little-used by Hitch: a voiceover. It's clumsy, and the device remains so every time it is used during this somewhat out-of-place episode. The entire episode, in fact, is clumsy, an unfocused tale spanning decades; it lacks tension, suspension, and a story worth caring about. With so many clever scripts at his disposal, one wonders why Hitchcock chose to direct this one. In "The Crystal Trench," a woman discovers that her husband has been killed in a mountain climbing accident. During the attempt to recover his body, the corpse is trapped in a glacier—lost. The woman has a new suitor, a man who wants to marry her, but she insists on waiting until her husband's body is found before again committing to marriage. Forty years go by. The body is found. And the deceased has a locket with a picture of another woman inside. End of story.

Presumably the message is supposed to tell us, "People are not all they seem, and even the best of people have secrets." (Ending, of course, with a cruel twist.) A common Hitchcock theme, to be sure, but the way the message is delivered is hardly Hitchcockian, and the story itself is a bore. There are no impressive directorial flourishes to salvage this brief misstep for Hitchcock.

"MRS. BIXBY AND THE COLONEL'S COAT" (ORIGINALLY AIRED SEPTEMBER 27, 1960)

The first episode of the sixth season, this story stars Audrey Meadows (of *The Honeymooners*) as Mrs. Bixby, the cheating wife of a dentist (Les Tremayne). She travels to Baltimore under the guise of visiting her aunt. There her lover, The Colonel (Alden Chase), breaks up with her, but not before bestowing on her the gift of an extremely expensive mink coat. Afraid to come home with the luxurious gift but not wanting to get rid of it, either, Mrs. Bixby sells the coat and takes the pawn ticket home to her husband, claiming she found it in a taxi. Dr. Bixby promises to pick up the item at the pawn shop. He tells her he has a surprise for her and presents her with a mink stole, much to her disappointment. Mrs. Bixby thinks the pawnbroker ripped off her husband—that is, until she sees her husband's female assistant walking out of his office wearing the coat.

This is another fun episode, because the guilty party gets her just deserts. The twist ending is tremendously satisfying. There isn't a whole lot of Hitchcockian flair here, yet it's entertaining nonetheless. Meadows is excellent as the duplicitous wife whose plan goes awry. She would have made a wonderful leading actress for Hitch earlier in her career.

"THE HORSEPLAYER" (ORIGINALLY AIRED MARCH 14, 1961)

It is always a pleasure to see the esteemed Claude Rains on screen. In his first Hitchcock role since *Notorious*, "The Horseplayer" sees him donning the robes of a man of the cloth. Rains confronts a parishioner who has been especially generous when donating to the church. The man, it seems, has been inspired to pray while betting at the horse track—and it's working. He is winning and winning, and passing a portion of his winnings on to the church. This puts Rains in a dilemma. He can't encourage the man to pray for winning horses—it just doesn't work that way, he explains—but presiding over a destitute church, he cannot turn down the donations, either. Eventually, the parishioner convinces Rains to bet some of the church's funds on a "sure thing" horse, hoping to use the winnings to repair the church's leaky roof. Rains regrets his decision and prays for the horse to lose, but, in a final twist, ends up winning the money he needs anyway. Meanwhile, the parishioner who could not lose . . . does. He ends up broke, and the church gets the money it needs.

No murder, no real suspense, and nary a hint of the Hitchcockian, but an entertaining and mildly playful look at the power of prayer all the same. There is nothing overly special about Hitchcock's direction—it's capable and effective, but not distinctive—but the story is warm and enjoyable, a far cry from the drudgery of "The Crystal Trench."

"BANG! YOU'RE DEAD"
(ORIGINALLY AIRED OCTOBER 17, 1961)

The last episode of *Alfred Hitchcock Presents* directed by the Master of Suspense himself does not stand the test of time. Uncle Rick (Stephen Dunne) has just returned from a trip to Africa and promises he has a surprise for his nephew, five-year-old Jackie (Billy Mumy). Jackie finds Uncle Rick's revolver and ammunition, and, thinking it is a toy and the surprise his uncle brought him, loads the gun with live ammunition before running off to the grocery store to buy some candy. Uncle Rick discovers that his gun is missing, and, along with Jackie's family, they search after the boy, hoping to avoid disaster.

Likely the least appealing of the Hitch-directed episodes of this program, "Bang! You're Dead" comes off as hokey public service announcement to warn of the dangers of guns and children. In his closing remarks, Hitchcock even warns parents to keep guns away from their children. We're not even offered some directorial flourishes to save the dismal story; there is little creativity to be found in this episode. Requisite Hitchcock viewing this is not.

CONCLUSION

Alfred Hitchcock Presents may have been the most significant element in Hitch's transformation from a successful director to a household name, a personality as recognizable and popular as the stars of his films. He had always made profitable movies, but now more than ever his name alone was a selling point. The show also afforded him an opportunity to get back to filmmaking basics, experimenting with techniques that would inform the shocking style of *Psycho*, the endless tension of *The Birds*, and the bleak suspense of *Frenzy*. It was a creative outlet for the Master of Suspense, an outlet from which viewers benefited.

AWARDS

- 1958 Emmy Win: Best Director, Half Hour or Less (Robert Stevens, "The Glass Eye")
- 1958 Emmy Nomination: Best Dramatic Anthology Series
- 1959 Emmy Nominations: Best Direction of a Single Program of a Dramatic Series, Less Than One Hour (Hitchcock, "Lamb to the Slaughter"); Best Writing of a Single Program of a Dramatic Series, Less Than One Hour (Roald Dahl, "Lamb to the Slaughter"); Best Dramatic Series, Less Than One Hour
- 1960 Emmy Nomination: Outstanding Achievement in Film Editing for Television (Edward W. Williams, "Man From the South"); Outstanding Achievement in Art Direction and Scenic Design (John J. Lloyd, Art Director)
- 1961 Emmy Nomination: Outstanding Achievement in Film Editing for Television (Edward W. Williams, "Incident in a Small Jail")
- 1964 Emmy Nomination: Outstanding Writing Achievement in Drama, Adaptation (James Bridges, "The Jar")

DVD RELEASES

Alfred Hitchcock Presents—Season Three
RELEASE: Universal Studios (2007)
(Dolby Digital 2.0 Mono, 1.33:1 Black & White)
5 Discs
39 Episodes:

1. "The Glass Eye"
2. "Mail Order Prophet"
3. "The Perfect Crime" (directed by Alfred Hitchcock)
4. "Heart of Gold"
5. "Silent Witness"
6. "Reward to Finder"
7. "Enough Rope for Two"

8. "Last Request"
9. "The Young One"
10. "The Diplomatic Corpse"
11. "The Deadly"
12. "Miss Paisley's Cat"
13. "Night of the Execution"
14. "The Percentage"
15. "Together"
16. "Sylvia"
17. "The Motive"
18. "Miss Bracegirdle Does Her Duty"
19. "The Equalizer"
20. "On the Nose"
21. "Guest for Breakfast"
22. "The Return of the Hero"
23. "The Right Kind of House"
24. "The Foghorn"
25. "Flight to the East"
26. "Bull in a China Shop"
27. "Disappearing Trick"
28. "Lamb to the Slaughter" (directed by Alfred Hitchcock)
29. "Fatal Figures"
30. "Death Sentence"
31. "The Festive Season"
32. "Listen, Listen!"
33. "Post Mortem"
34. "The Crocodile Case"
35. "A Dip in the Pool" (directed by Alfred Hitchcock)
36. "The Safe Place"
37. "The Canary Sedan"
38. "The Impromptu Murder"
39. "Little White Frock"

Alfred Hitchcock Presents Volumes 1–4
RELEASE: Universal Studios (1999, 2001)
(Dolby Digital 2.0 Mono, 1.33:1 Black & White)
RATING: ****

NOTES: Hitchcock-directed episodes spread over four discs, all out of print. Discs one and four were only available in *The Alfred Hitchcock Collection*, Vol. 1 and Vol. 2. These discs are out of print but are available on the secondary market.

Alfred Hitchcock Presents, Season Four
RELEASE: Universal Studios (2009)
(Dolby Digital 2.0 Mono, 1.33.1 Black & White)
4 Discs

1. "Poison" (directed by Alfred Hitchcock)
2. "Don't Interrupt"
3. "The Jokester"
4. "The Crooked Road"
5. "The Two Million Dollar Defense"
6. "Design for Loving"
7. "A Man with a Problem"
8. "Safety for the Witness"
9. "Murder Me Twice"
10. "Tea Time"
11. "And the Desert Shall Blossom"
12. "Mrs. Herman and Mrs. Fenimore"
13. "Six People, No Music"
14. "The Morning After"
15. "A Personal Matter"
16. "Out There"
17. "Total Loss"
18. "The Last Dark Step"
19. "The Morning of the Bride"
20. "The Diamond Necklace"
21. "Relative Value"
22. "The Right Price"
23. "I'll Take Care of You"
24. "The Avon Emeralds"
25. "The Kind Waitress"
26. "Cheap Is Cheap"
27. "The Waxwork"
28. "The Impossible Dream"
29. "Banquo's Chair" (directed by Alfred Hitchcock)
30. "A Night with the Boys"
31. "Your Witness"
32. "The Human Interest Story"
33. "The Dusty Drawer"
34. "Curtains for Me"
35. "Touché"
36. "Invitation to an Accident"

Psycho
(1960)

FILM FACTS

PRODUCTION YEARS: 1959–1960
RELEASE DATE: June 16, 1960 (U.S.)
STUDIO: Paramount Pictures
FILMING LOCATIONS: Los Angeles, California; Phoenix, Arizona
PRESENTATION/ASPECT RATIO: Black & White/1.85:1

SYNOPSIS

Marion Crane (Janet Leigh) wants to marry her boyfriend, Sam (John Gavin), but first they must escape from his crushing alimony debt. In a weak moment, Crane steals $40,000 from a client of her employer and flees the state. Her flight brings her to a remote motel, where she meets Norman Bates (Anthony Perkins), a disturbed young man overly attached to his mother. When Crane is suddenly murdered in the shower, Bates appears to hide the evidence. Meanwhile, her disappearance sparks a search by her friends and family. The trail ends at the motel. There they discover that Bates is an insane murderer who killed Crane and has been living with a dual identity since killing his mother ten years before.

IMPRESSIONS

Has there ever been a motion picture that has received the scrutiny of *Psycho*? In a larger-than-life career, this is *the* larger-than-life film—a bold, influential breakthrough that became an instant legend. If there is one Hitchcock film even casual enthusiasts know, it is this. In 1960 Alfred Hitchcock was coming off an unparalleled decade of success, enjoying one achievement after another. He was not only a wildly successful Hollywood director, but his hugely popular *Alfred Hitchcock Presents* had made him a celebrity in his own right. What could he possibly have left in his bag of tricks? How could he sustain the level of greatness film audiences had come to expect? The expectations were astronomical, but the Master of Suspense enjoyed his biggest hit to date in *Psycho*, a film with massive audience appeal and a lasting impact on the motion picture industry. The film solidified Hitchcock's legend for the ages. First he was an applauded director. Then he was a household name. Now he was an icon.

Psycho was the final entry in Hitchcock's unofficial trilogy of films centered on the loss of identity. Despite vast differences in style, tone, and content, each of these three films—*Vertigo*, *North by Northwest*, and *Psycho*—is considered among the very best in its respective genre. Where *Vertigo* offered a look at Hitch's dark obsessions in a romantic mystery and *North by Northwest* offered a glimpse at the heroic man he daydreamed of being, *Psycho* revealed a growing frustration with and disdain for women. In the mid-to-late 1950s, Hitchcock had secretly longed for leading ladies Grace Kelly and Vera Miles, only to see them both leave him: Kelly to become a princess, Miles to have a child. (Miles would return to play Lila Crane in *Psycho*.) From this point forward, women in his work—particularly the leading characters—were seen as less than virtuous.

> **WHERE'S HITCH?**
>
> Shortly after the start of the film, Hitchcock can be seen outside Crane's office, in a cowboy hat.

More noteworthy than the shift in tone, however, is his radical shift in production quality. As Hitchcock productions go, the film is far from elaborate. "It was an experiment in this sense: Could I make a feature film under the same conditions as a television show?" he related to François Truffaut. "I used a complete television unit to shoot it very quickly. The only place where I digressed was when I slowed down the murder scene, the cleaning-up scene, and the other scenes that indicated anything that required time. All of the rest was handled in the same way that they do it in television."[25] To suggest that Sir Alfred learned a lot from directing episodes of *Alfred Hitchcock Presents* would seem foolish, considering that *Psycho* came on the tail end of one of the most astonishing directorial stretches in cinema history, yet that is undeniably the case. Throughout his career Hitch sought big production values, elaborate sets, and expansive designs. Had he not been so adept at directing films quickly, efficiently, and on time, he probably would have broken more than a few budgets in his day. However, a "mere" television series offered him a chance to work in new ways and with new techniques—or, more accurately, with minimalist techniques he was intimately familiar with from his days directing in Britain, where he learned how to make much out of little. This was a relatively low-budget picture, at just $800,000, though it never looks like it. Something sparked in Hitchcock a desire to step back from lavish productions and to get back to filmmaking at its most basic, using his bare-bones television crew for a major motion picture. That stark minimalism helped make the impact of *Psycho*'s shocking imagery and themes all the more powerful for its 1960s audiences.

Despite these restraints, the production quality is excellent, featuring great set design, creative camerawork, and outstanding editing by Hitchcock's regular editor, George Tomasini, who had been working with Hitch since *Rear Window*. The result was a sparse-looking film.

That is one of the most striking aspects of *Psycho*: how sparse it is. Until this point, Hitchcock films had historically been lush affairs, even the most mundane settings presented beautifully. Lavish costumes, luxurious sets, beautiful locations—none of those traits are present. Instead, Hitch opted to strip things down. Using his television crew was a bold move for a man who had just made the expansive *North by Northwest*, yet there is no denying the artistic success that is *Psycho*. The camera work is striking in its simplicity; meticulously composed shots and carefully chosen movement punctuate scenes, heighten tension, and drag the viewer along on a roller coaster of emotions. Take, for instance, the early scene in which Marion Crane is purchasing a car. A police officer looks on, suspicious. He is framed from a distance, a long shot of the officer gazing from across the street. Hitch uses minimalism to create a sense of dread. Such shots are common throughout the film. Nothing flashy, nothing he couldn't do for a half-hour television show—just deliberate, effective filmmaking.

Aside from Norman Bates, the characters in *Psycho* seem almost inconsequential to the story. Extremely economical in its structure, every element

Anthony Perkins as Norman Bates. (Paramount Pictures/Photofest © Paramount Pictures)

drives the story forward, even the red herring of the stolen money. There
are virtually no wasted moments in the film. With the exception of Bates
and Crane, none of the characters are given much depth, only the sparse
details necessary to engage the plot.

Bates is given plenty of expository background, however, and he's one
of the most captivating characters in the entire Hitchcock filmography. Like
Strangers on a Train's Bruno Anthony, he is another charming villain with a
twisted mother-son relationship. Bates was not tall and handsome in the
novel upon which *Psycho* is based; this was Hitchcock's addition to the story.
Because Bates is attractive and seemingly normal on the surface, we wonder why he lives the life he does, and wonder why he is so suffocatingly close
to his mother. This he willingly admits to Marion Crane. "Well, a boy's best
friend is his mother," he tells her.

Anthony Perkins's Norman Bates is one of Hitchcock's three most
enduring, disturbing villains, joining Joseph Cotten's Uncle Charlie (*Shadow
of a Doubt*) and Bruno Anthony in the pantheon of great cinematic antago-

nists. He fidgets, gesticulates; he is, from the start, a man clearly battling personal demons. Perkins's performance is layered and affecting. His lengthy dinner scene with Leigh alone is worth a thousand accolades. Once again, a man and a woman having a conversation over dinner reveals the deepest corners of a troubled soul.

Without a bona fide superstar holding things down, it was up to Hitchcock to bring this untraditional narrative together into a cohesive, compelling whole. Here he pushes all the right buttons. His ability to find the right pacing—accelerating time when the audience needs a jolt, dwelling in a scene when the audience needs a breather or, more ominously, when he wants them to dwell in horror—keeps the suspense high from the start. It never lets up. Not until the very moment when the full depths of Bates's depravity is revealed. From the rapid-fire, vertigo-inducing editing of the infamous shower scene to the plodding, meticulous cleanup scene that follows, Hitchcock is in complete control.

Pyscho's structure is abnormal. There are few movies in which the star is killed less than halfway through, never to be seen again. *Psycho* does just that. The speed with which *Psycho* turns into a different film is riveting. For thirty minutes we think we're watching a "woman on the run" film—a crime drama, and a pretty good one at that. We watch Marion's crime unfold, root for her to elude the authorities, and see her find what we think is safe haven for the night. But with nary a bit of foreshadowing, we take a sudden left turn. Before we have the chance to contemplate her fate, she is savagely killed. As viewers, we are shocked, but, having just met the fascinating character of Bates and not yet fully understanding his relationship with his mother, we cast aside our concern for Crane and instead yearn to find our way into the house on the hill. Without warning, we're watching a different film, with a different lead.

The private investigator trying to track down the missing money, Arbogast, provides us with our first opportunity to enter the Bates household. Very quickly, he meets an untimely death at the apparent hands of Mrs. Bates. We're no longer watching a film about stolen money; we're watching a murder mystery.

There was something else at work, too—something more significant than the Master of Suspense's foray into less bombastic cinema. Darker themes were arising, or at least darker, grimmer takes on the themes he had long worked with. *Psycho* returns to the bleak portrait of humanity we saw in *Shadow of a Doubt*, but this time, rather than existing only in the twisted mind of Uncle Charlie, it's out in the open for all to see. Rather than seeing someone talk about the depraved side of humanity, we see it in action. Brutal murders. Theft. Oedipal longings. Cross-dressing. Split personalities. Evil hiding behind an unassuming, normal face. It was daring stuff for Hitchcock to tackle during this still very conservative era.

Audiences reacted.

Hitchcock was often heard to say that one of his favorite aspects of filmmaking was audience manipulation. There is no greater example of this than *Psycho*. After Arbogast's death, we know that Marion's lover, Sam, or her sister, Lila, will need to enter the house for us to discover the truth. Because Hitch has manipulated us in making us complicit in Bates's voyeurism, observers of his crimes as we are, we want to find the truth that lies inside the Bates home. Yet we are only viewers. We cannot actually go inside the house, and so we are willing to pay any price to learn the truth—even the death of Sam or Lila.

This is audience manipulation at its finest.

Hitch would boast that he could control an audience the way a musician controls his instrument. Here was an opportunity to do exactly that. It was provocative. It demanded a response. It shocked in ways few films to this time had ever shocked. From the barely contained sexuality of the opening scene to the stunning finish, *Psycho* was designed to keep audiences on edge: to show them things—or make them *think* they saw things—they had never seen before. Hitch took delight in his trick. Audiences were amazed by what they saw, not because of the sheer spectacle of it all—spectacle being one of Hitchcock's great talents, yet one not on display here—but because all the cinematic conventions they knew, all they were comfortable with, were thrown out the door. Hitch loved it.

As an extension *Psycho*'s audience manipulation, Hitchcock developed an ingenious marketing stratagem. Trailers for the film included messages that the viewer must see the picture from the very beginning in order to enjoy it and that theater patrons would not be allowed to enter the theater once a screening began. Hitch insisted that this rule be enforced at theaters. He got just what he wanted: packed crowds of theatergoers abuzz with excitement. No such ploy had ever been attempted before. The resulting anticipation from the prerelease trailers led *Psycho* to become Hitchcock's biggest box office success to date.

Of all the great work that Bernard Herrmann did with Alfred Hitchcock, *Psycho* is likely his most memorable. Herrmann's main theme is incredibly effective in driving audience emotion, particularly in the early sequences when Marion is on the run. The music here makes what would otherwise be mundane scenes of a woman driving utterly effective in securing the viewer's support for Marion's well-being. But if there is any cue remembered in *Psycho*, it is Herrmann's work with the shower scene. Hitch initially intended to run the scene without music. The only audio would be the sound of water and the stabbing knife. Herrmann scored the scene anyway, and when he showed it to Hitchcock, the Master of Suspense quickly realized it played better with the shrieking sounds of a string section.

About that shower scene. Of all of the great scenes in all of Hitchcock's great films, this one is the most famous. And for good reason. It is difficult to imagine that a nearly fifty-year-old film could contain such a shocking scene, but it does. Not only is it startling and brutal, it is a phenomenal example of planning and execution. The entire scene, just forty-five seconds on screen, contains more than seventy shots and required a full week to shoot. Interestingly, Anthony Perkins does not appear in the scene; he was in New York preparing for a play during the filming. His part was played by a double.

Psycho can rightly be called a horror film, a unique distinction in Hitchcock's works. Most of his output falls in the genres of mystery, gothic romance, and suspense thriller. Nevertheless, *Psycho* is awash in common Hitchcockian elements. It features murder, a woman screaming directly at the camera, a blonde leading lady, a manipulative mother, dark secrets, a chase, and ineffective authority figures. This is a movie that, while set apart from his other work when it comes to approach, is indicative of its author in its thematic traits.

The climax is among the most satisfying in the Hitchcock canon, an incredible realization of multiple story elements executed in breathtaking fashion. Lila has entered the Bates household without Norman's knowledge. Seeing him coming up the steps, on the verge of being caught, she hides under the interior stairs, then enters the cellar. There, she sees who she thinks is Mrs. Bates in a chair, her back to the camera. And in fact, it *is* Mrs. Bates. But Norman's mother isn't what Lila was expecting. She is dead. Long deceased and preserved by Norman, who enjoys taxidermy as a hobby (as if he's not creepy enough already), his mother is a grinning, leering corpse. The revelation of the truth, Mrs. Bates's empty eye sockets appearing to move in the swinging ceiling light, is a phenomenal payoff on this part of the mystery. But it is not yet over. The viewer is given no time to digest this bombshell before Norman comes into the cellar brandishing a knife and wearing a dress and wig to look like his mother. The woman we long thought was his insane mother was Norman all along.

In the ultimate cruel portrayal of a mother figure, Mrs. Bates is revealed to have been an awful woman whose new love was unbearable for Norman. He killed her, then preserved the body because he could not bear to live with the knowledge that he killed her. Already deranged, the murder pushed Norman over the edge. She becomes part of his personality. Sometimes he assumes the role of Mrs. Bates; sometimes he is part mother, part Norman; but never is he simply Norman, for his "mother" persona dominates over all. The very last scene shows that "mother" has completely taken over. Norman is likely to never be seen again.

Psycho ended up being a landmark work in Alfred Hitchcock's career. It was the film that solidified his stardom for the ages and that hammered into place his reputation as a director who could shock audiences. For good or ill, it has become his best-known picture and, for many, the movie that best defines who Alfred Hitchcock was. It was an instant legend.

But more than that, it was just a damn fine film.

CONCLUSION

Alfred Hitchcock's most successful, influential, famous, and popular film earns its accolades and popularity by being as crisp and shocking a thriller as you'll find, even nearly fifty years later. *Psycho*'s influence cannot be understated, and its popularity is enduring. Further, as a pure example of his craft—the editing, photography, and storytelling are highly refined throughout—*Psycho* stands among the very best Hitchcock films. Some thirty-five years into his career, he created a masterpiece that is studied by film scholars to this day.

HITCHCOCKIAN THEMES

Bathroom Scene/B.M. • Blonde Leading Lady • Dark Secret • Discussion of Murder at Dinner • Ineffectual Authority Figures • MacGuffin • Man (or Woman) on the Run • Manipulative Mother • Murder • Unwelcome New Woman • Woman Screaming Directly at Camera

THINGS TO LOOK FOR

• The shower scene, an example of impeccably choreographed editing and one of the most famous scenes in film history.

- *Psycho*'s minimalism is worth noting. From a technical standpoint, Hitchcock had not directed a film this simple in years.
- In 1960 this film featured the word "transvestite," probably the first ever broaching of the subject on film.

TRIVIA/FUN STUFF

✦ Hitchcock abandoned his normal feature film crew, instead filming *Psycho* with the crew from his television show, *Alfred Hitchcock Presents*.

✦ Though filmed in black and white, colors play an important role in the film. Prior to Crane's theft, she wears white undergarments; after, they are black, reflecting her changed state of "grace." The same holds true for her purse.

✦ Anthony Perkins did not take part in the famous shower scene; he was away preparing for a play at the time it was filmed.

✦ The shower scene was intended to be silent. Herrmann scored the scene anyway. Hitchcock liked the music and kept it. The music remains one of cinema's signature compositions.

✦ The shower scene was sent back for editing because censors thought they saw Janet Leigh's nipples. They did not. The scene was sent back to them untouched, and they approved it on the second pass.

✦ Though a mere forty-five seconds, the shower scene consists of more than seventy cuts.

✦ Saul Bass, famed for creating the magnificent title sequences of *Vertigo* and *North by Northwest*, claimed to have designed and directed the famous shower scene. Others who worked on the film, however, dispute the claim.

✦ The blood in the shower scene was nothing more than simple chocolate syrup.

✦ The close shots of the showerhead spraying water do not depict an actual showerhead, but a gigantic fixture designed to shoot water around the camera. It was some six feet in diameter.

✦ The film spawned several sequels—none of them directed by, or endorsed by, Hitchcock. Perkins returned as Norman Bates in all three sequels (he even directed *Psycho III*, Vera Miles reprised her role as Lila Crane for *Psycho II*, and Janet Leigh had cameos in two of the films.

+ Hitchcock was so pleased with Bernard Herrmann's score that Herrmann's salary was doubled for the effort.
+ In terms of pure budget-to-revenue ratio, *Psycho* ranks among the most successful films of all time. Filmed for just $800,000, it has earned tens of millions of dollars over the years.
+ The trailer features Vera Miles, who played Leigh's sister, screaming in the shower.
+ The last shot of Bates features a split second of disturbing imagery—his mother's skull superimposed on his face.
+ The story was inspired by real-life murderer Ed Gein, also the rough basis for the killers in *The Silence of the Lambs* (1991) and *The Texas Chainsaw Massacre* (1974).
+ *Psycho* is said to be the first American film to show a flushing toilet.
+ When the film was released, theaters were instructed not to permit viewers to enter the theater once the film had started. They complied, thus ensuring the film's shocking plot twist was, indeed, shocking.
+ In 1992 the film was added to the National Film Registry by the National Film Preservation Board, which selects films that "are considered to be culturally, historically or aesthetically important."
+ Rank on American Film Institute Top 100 Films (1997): 18.
+ Rank on American Film Institute Top 100 Films (2007): 14.

AWARDS

- Academy Award Nominations (4): Best Director; Best Actress in a Supporting Role (Janet Leigh); Best Cinematography, Black-and-White (John L. Russell); Best Art Direction/Set Decoration, Black-and-White (Joseph Hurley, Robert Clatworthy, George Milo)
- Directors Guild of America Nomination: Outstanding Directorial Achievement in Motion Pictures
- Edgar Allan Poe Awards Win: Best Motion Picture (Joseph Stefano, Robert Bloch)
- Golden Globe Award Win: Best Supporting Actress (Janet Leigh)
- Writers Guild of America Award Nomination: Best Written American Drama (Joseph Stefano)

DVD RELEASES

RELEASE: Universal Studios, Universal Legacy Series (2008)
(Dolby Digital 2.0 Mono, 1.85:1 Black & White)
RATING: *****

EXTRAS: Two-disc set includes feature commentary with Stephen Rebello (author of *Alfred Hitchcock and the Making of Psycho*); newsreel footage; The Release of *Psycho*, The Shower Scene, The Shower Scene: Storyboards by Saul Bass; the *Psycho* archives; posters and *Psycho* ads; lobby cards; behind-the-scenes photographs; production photographs; production notes; theatrical trailer; rerelease trailers; *The Making of Psycho* documentary, *In the Master's Shadow: Hitchcock's Legacy*, Hitchcock/Truffaut interview excerpts, *Alfred Hitchcock Presents* episode "Lamb to the Slaughter."

RELEASE: Universal Studios (1998, 2001, 2005, 2006)
(Dolby Digital 2.0 Mono, 1.85:1 Black & White)
RATING: *****

EXTRAS 2001: *The Making of Psycho*; censored scene; theatrical trailers; production photos and drawings; The Shower Scene with and without music; newsreel footage.

EXTRAS 2005: Newsreel footage; The Shower Scene; The *Psycho* Archives; production photographs, art, notes, and more; theatrical trailer; rerelease trailer; Shower Scene storyboards by Saul Bass.

NOTES: Available as stand-alone releases from 1998 and 2001, or as part of *The Alfred Hitchcock Collection* (out of print), and as part of *Alfred Hitchcock: The Masterpiece Collection*. *The Masterpiece Collection* is recommended and includes additional extras. The transfers on all releases appear identical.

RELEASE: Universal 50th Anniversary Edition Blu-ray Disc (2010)
(Dolby Digital 2.0 Mono, 1.85:1 Black & White)
RATING: *****

EXTRAS: The Making of *Psycho*; *Psycho* Sound; In the Master's Shadow: Hitchcock's Legacy; Hitchcock / Truffaut Interview Excerpts; Newsreel Footage: The Release of *Psycho*; The Shower Scene: With and Without Music; The Shower Scene: Storyboards by Saul Bass; The *Psycho* Archives; Lobby Cards; Behind-the-Scenes Photographs; Production Photographs; Theatrical Trailer; Re-release Trailers; Feature Commentary with Stephen Rebello.

The Birds
(1963)

FILM FACTS

PRODUCTION YEAR: 1962
RELEASE DATE: March 28, 1963 (U.S.)
STUDIO: Universal Pictures
FILMING LOCATIONS: Bloomfield, Sonoma County, California;
Bodega Bay, California; Bodega, California; San Francisco, California;
Universal Studios, Universal City, California;
Valley Ford, Sonoma County, California
PRESENTATION/ASPECT RATIO: Color/1.85:1

SYNOPSIS

Melanie Daniels (Tippi Hedren), a young and carefree San Francisco socialite, meets Mitch Brenner (Rod Taylor), a brash young attorney, in a pet store as he shops for a pair of lovebirds for his sister on her birthday. Seeking to impress and surprise him, Melanie drives north to Mitch's Bodega Bay home to deliver the birds. There a seagull attacks her. It is a seemingly isolated incident. That is, until another bird attack takes place. And then another. The attacks mount, birds swarm the town, and soon Bodega Bay finds itself under siege.

IMPRESSIONS

In 1960 Hitchcock enjoyed the biggest hit of his career with *Psycho*, a film that shocked audiences and solidified his place in cinema legend. He would follow that success not by diving back into directing, but by taking a few years off. He was growing older, after all, and had just finished a ten-year stretch during which he made eleven films, among them enduring classics like *Strangers on a Train*, *Dial M for Murder*, *Rear Window*, *The Man Who Knew Too Much*, *Vertigo*, *North by Northwest*, and the aforementioned *Psycho*. Never before or since has a director had such voluminous artistic success in so short a span. One imagines the aging director was simply tired.

Hitchcock would return to movie theaters in 1963 with an all-new thriller. Refreshed and full of energy (could it have been the "discovery" of a new leading lady?) his next project would be a tour de force of technical prowess, and, arguably, his last bona fide classic. It was *The Birds*, and, despite nary a human murderer in sight, it would scare people half to death.

Adapted from a short story by Daphne du Maurier, whose stories also provided the framework for *Jamaica Inn* and *Rebecca*, *The Birds* offers up an increasingly apocalyptic story about nature rising up against man. It is a film about the comfortable world man has created decaying into a primal, chaotic thing. It is about beautiful things hiding the potential to cause great pain, a subject Hitchcock knew well. It is about internal upheaval and personal demons, symbolized by the attacks. It is about transformations: gentle to savage; strangers to family; a love story to a horror story.

"Horror story" is no exaggeration. *The Birds* keeps you in a state of unease. It is not the birds themselves that are unsettling so much as the idea of Mother Nature's unexplainable wrath. Ever uncontrollable, never fully understood, beyond mankind's full control no matter our efforts to contain her, the rising up of nature against us is an ancient and primal fear.

Yet, watch *The Birds* with a discerning eye and you will see you are not unsettled so much by fear, but from sustained, prolonged tension. The entire motion picture is an exercise in establishing and sustaining tension, utterly transforming the film even as the town of Bodega Bay itself is transformed. Through a slowly unfolding story and precise editing, the structure of the film undergoes the very same changes as the town: from calm, charming, and warm to claustrophobic, violent, and tense. Shots early in the film that on the surface may have dragged on too long were, in fact, a means of setting a pace intended to be shaken by the intrusion of the birds. Long shots of Melanie Daniels crossing the street or driving down the road or tooling along in a boat seem to linger a touch too long. Their length makes the later change in tone all the more effective. When we switch to quick cuts during the increasingly frequent bird attacks, the violence is that much more jarring because the pace had been so subdued moments before. The deliberate pacing of Sergio Leone's classic Western epic *Once Upon a Time in the West* (1968) springs to mind; in it, slow, plodding drama is punctuated by quick and sudden violence. The same holds true with *The Birds*. When the first gull swoops down and claws at Melanie, it shouldn't be a shocking moment. After all, it's just a bird. Take a simple day trip to the beach and you will see dozens of gulls swooping near people. They're not scary. But the prior sequences had been so low-key that the first attack momentarily shakes you. You get an early sense that something isn't right.

Then Hitchcock slips us back into the quaint "boy meets girl" story that opened the film. Safe ground. We feel at ease again . . . until the next time. Cue another round of steady tension building, this one shorter than the last. By the time Melanie and the Brenner family are bunkered down in the house late in the film, the birds swirling outside like an unnatural storm, we have forgotten that less than two hours ago we were watching the opening scenes of a classic light romance. By the time we reach the film's end, a scene that should be little more than visually interest-

ing—a shot of a car driving slowly through thousands of birds does not on its surface inspire much dread—the effect is unsettling and apocalyptic. Piece by piece, Hitchcock managed to tear down a world—a familiar world, a comfortable, seemingly safe world—right before our eyes.

The film's transformation from unthreatening innocence to nightmarish circumstances is a great achievement. How did we get from a lighthearted "boy meets girl" to an oppressive, apocalyptic terror? More importantly, what does it mean?

Hitchcock provides no easy answers. One of his characters, a hysterical woman in a diner, might. Melanie Daniels is a young, attractive woman. Rich. Often in the tabloids. The subject of scandalous rumors. She is, by every indication, anything but innocent. Without a thought or care in the world, she brings her barely contained sexuality to this tiny, quaint hamlet by the sea. It seems to react to her, lashing out with increasing ferocity the closer she grows to Mitch Brenner and his family. Save the first attack—a warning salvo, if you will—each strike is preceded by a conversation about relationships, of people retreating from the pain of the past and sinking back into a quiet life where troubles are kept to yourself. Melanie's presence is bringing out long-repressed emotions, emotions some would rather leave repressed. Eventually, something has to give.

But this being a Hitchcock film, interpreting the film around Lydia Brenner, the reserved, distant mother played by Jessica Tandy, may be most appropriate. Once again, in a Hitchcock picture a mother figure is portrayed in a less-than-flattering light. Lydia Brenner is seen as a mother willing to sabotage her son's love life to avoid the prospect of losing him. Could this be at the root of the bird attacks? The question allows for an interpretation worth examining. The film opens with birds: lovebirds, to be specific. As a prank, Melanie drives to Bodega Bay and places the lovebirds in the Brenner household. Minutes later, a gull attacks her. As before, a warning shot. Just after the attack, Melanie and Lydia meet. It is clear Lydia is not comfortable with her presence, but when Mitch presses to have Melanie over for dinner, Lydia relents. The dinner is tense, but Mitch and Melanie grow closer. The next day, when Melanie "intrudes" on young Cathy Brenner's birthday party, the first major bird attack takes place. Later Lydia tells Melanie that she is unsure of her, and does not know if she likes her. Another attack follows, more violent than the last. Melanie is forced to flee into the Brenner home with the family, where, once again they are attacked. Facing this great terror together, the family appears to draw closer. But there is one final test. Melanie, caught unaware, is attacked alone, brutalized and savaged by the creatures in an upstairs room. The attacks subside, the family is able to flee the house, and only then does Lydia finally accept Melanie. The attacks cease as Lydia becomes comfortable with Melanie's closeness to her son. The birds are symbolic of Lydia's own struggle to come to grips with her son's love for another woman, and of her suppressed rage at being unable to let go of her son. She is, figuratively speaking, hovering over him, and she will attack any woman she sees as wrong for her son.

There is a difference between Lydia and most Hitchcock mothers, though. She is a sympathetic character. Unlike the most unlikable mothers of Hitch's films, we're offered a glimpse of what troubles Lydia through the backstory of her lost husband. With this information at our disposal, we may not at first like how Lydia treats Melanie, but we at least are able to understand it. Of course, Tandy, the wife of frequent Hitchcock collaborator Hume Cronyn, is essential in delivering the outstanding performance needed to turn Lydia into a character for whom we can care.

Bringing these increasingly nightmarish attacks to life is a display of technical bravado as impressive as Hitchcock has ever put on, featuring stunning special effects for the era.

When it comes to special effects, Hitchcock's visual sensibility has always been at the fore. Here, his audio choices, though subtle, may be even more impressive than the layered blue screen work on the visual effects. *The Birds* does not feature a traditional soundtrack. Instead, like *Rear Window*, we have nothing but sounds from the environment. Gentle piano. Schoolchildren singing. And birds, birds, birds. In this case, the densely textured sound of thousands of birds in lieu of a rousing score probably left audiences unsettled—and they probably did not even know why. Most audiences would not pick up on a lack of score, but they would *feel* it. Things would feel somehow "off," but the reason would be a mystery.

The decision to produce *The Birds* without music is fascinating. Surely Bernard Herrmann, at the height of his craft after creating so many memorable scores for Hitchcock, could have come up with something stirring to augment the fear and terror of the picture, but one cannot fault Hitch's reasoning here. The lack of music, especially on repeated viewings, is particularly unsettling. This also allows the sound effects, most importantly the sound of the birds, to play to the front of the stage. Chirping, clucking, flapping, cawing, all becoming increasingly sinister, haunting on their own merit because the sound of birds begins to signal the start of a new round of terror. The sound of thousands of gulls making their soft gull noises should not be disturbing, but we are subtly trained to react to it with dread. Music never steps on the sound effects. Music never conflicts with the sound effects because there are *only* sound effects.

Of course, the film's technical achievements are not only in the realm of audio. This being a Hitchcock film, the movie's big moments are punctuated with impressive visuals. The special effects in *The Birds* do not age particularly well, but if we consider what Hitch had available to him at the time, it is impossible to ignore what he accomplished. Consider that this 1963 film contained 370 different effects shots, and that the final shots are comprised of thirty-two separately filmed elements. Yes, the effects do not compare favorably with what filmmakers give us today, but they are no less impressive because of it. Hitchcock was one of cinema's great innovators, always working with the newest advancements in filmmaking technology. Several moments stand out.

First, there is the centerpiece attack on Bodega Bay. It begins when a man at a gas station is knocked down, spilling gasoline. A fire breaks out, a car explodes into flames, and we switch to a sweeping aerial shot of the town, a quaint California oasis with a fire blazing in the middle. Then a bird flies into the frame, wheeling downward. For a moment that's all we have. One bird. And then there is another. And then two more. And then another two. And suddenly they are coming from all corners of the frame, perfectly placed, swooping down, until it becomes a hailstorm of birds. It's a dynamic, masterfully executed shot (not to mention a great technical achievement for a 1963 film).

Even better is a scene in the house near the end of the film. With the sound of the apocalypse swirling outside, the camera peers to the ceiling, taking in the fury just beyond the walls. Lydia is pulled into the frame, centered, looking above as the sound of the birds slowly fades. The camera begins to pull back, and she grows smaller and smaller on screen, the ceiling above growing larger and larger until it becomes something menacing, about to crash in on her. We know that something is lurking out there, and that she is a very small thing compared to it. The camera keeps pulling back, now opening the left side of the frame. She keeps drifting back until she becomes a frail old woman huddled in the corner, helpless. Melanie comes into the frame at left, followed quickly by Mitch. All gaze upward at the departing sound of the birds. The camera movement ends with a perfectly lit and composed shot: the three lined up, peering into the unknown.

The technical achievements in *The Birds* are most talked about, but the story structure is arguably one of the picture's overlooked strengths. Evan Hunter's screenplay is a model of genre splicing, in this case mixing light romance with suspense/horror. If the romance had been dropped in favor of a greater emphasis on the terror of the birds, the humanity of the film would have been lost, to its great detriment. If the love story had been expanded and the tale of the birds excised, perhaps it would have made a decent film, but certainly not as interesting. Hunter, who achieved great success as the crime fiction writer Ed McBain, does a terrific job of blending these elements in a way that makes for an especially entertaining story, but is also effective in manipulating the audience's emotions—the primary goal of any Hitchcock movie.

From the start, *The Birds* is strong in the narrative department. The introduction of Melanie Daniels gives us an excellent glimpse of who she is: a young, beautiful, carefree socialite who is used to getting what she wants. The scene in the pet shop featuring Melanie and her newest love interest, Mitch Brenner, is bright and breezy, quickly establishing a foundation for potential romance. Rod Taylor lends a sense of intelligence and principle to Mitch. We instantly like him, and we can see why Melanie does, too.

Usually one to inject humor into otherwise dark and dreary films, Hitchcock tones it down with *The Birds*. Only passing moments of comedy are on display. An early light moment is also one of the only light moments. When Melanie is driving up the coastal highway to deliver lovebirds to Mitch's sister, she drives at high speed on sharply curving roads. In the middle of this sequence, Hitch cuts to a shot of the birdcage inside Melanie's car. We see the birds swaying left to right and back again as

Hitch amuses Tippi Hedren on the set of *The Birds*. (Universal Pictures/Photofest © Universal Pictures)

Melanie maneuvers her car along the twisting roadway. This shot serves two purposes: It helps to demonstrate the reckless abandon of Melanie's driving, offering an insight into her character, and it elicits an easy chuckle from the viewer.

Perhaps the best scene takes place in the diner after the attack on the schoolchildren. There is a terrific array of characters on hand to discuss the situation, particularly the elderly ornithologist, Mrs. Bundy, played brilliantly by Ethel Griffies. She decries the possibility that birds could attack humans en masse. Yes, she speaks logically and with great authority, but after having seen take place the very things she thinks impossible, we can only dislike her. When another attack happens right after this scene, we desperately want to see this woman again so we can say, "I told you so."

But bit parts do not a film make. Here, *The Birds* does not falter. Hedren is radiant in the part of Melanie Daniels. Hitchcock's latest discovery—he had seen her in a diet soft drink advertisement—brings everything to the screen necessary to sell the story. She is equal parts cool and confident, yet able to portray fear and, later, the shattered sense of a completely lost woman. Hedren won a well-deserved Golden Globe for Most Promising Newcomer for her work on *The Birds*.

The mark of a great horror/thriller is found when, after repeated viewings, we still root for the character to do something different. One can see *The Birds* countless times and still urge Melanie, "Don't do it!" when watching her walk up the stairs for the final attack. That is the mark of outstanding character and story development. That it still has that kind of impact after repeated viewings speaks to its ability to capture an audience.

After an absence of several years, Hitchcock came back as strong as ever, once again thrilling audiences as only he could.

What audiences could not know was that *The Birds* would be one of the last great films he would ever make.

CONCLUSION

After three years without releasing a film, Alfred Hitchcock came back with a bang with *The Birds*. Both a technical marvel (especially considering its age) and a study in brilliant story structure, it ranks on the short list of the Master of Suspense's best work. Terrifying and memorable, it stands as one of his best known and most popular films, and with good reason.

HITCHCOCKIAN THEMES

Blonde Leading Lady • Chaos in an Unexpected Location • Love Triangle • Manipulative Mother • Unwelcome New Woman

THINGS TO LOOK FOR

- Each bird attack is preceded by a lull in the action.
- There is no musical score. The only music heard in the entire film is the song sung by the schoolchildren.
- There are multiple references to Santa Rosa, California, home of another Hitchcock classic, *Shadow of a Doubt*.
- When one of the children stumbles and falls to the ground as they flee a bird attack, her glasses fall to the ground and break. The shot of her glasses recalls the broken glasses seen in *Strangers on a Train*.
- In the scene when Lydia goes to Dan Fawcett's house and sees the carnage inside, Hitchcock illustrated part of the destruction by showing a row of broken teacups hanging from a shelf. While a minor quibble, it is difficult to believe the teacups would have broken without also falling off their hooks. Surprising that this got past Hitchcock's intensive planning.

TRIVIA/FUN STUFF

- ✦ Tippi Hedren actually suffered cuts from one of the birds during filming.
- ✦ Despite the lack of a musical score, frequent Hitchcock collaborator Bernard Herrmann is credited as Sound Consultant.
- ✦ The final bird attack on Melanie took a week to film. Birds were attached to her suit by long nylon threads so they could not fly away.
- ✦ The film features 370 effects shots.
- ✦ The final shot is composed of thirty-two different elements.
- ✦ Melanie wears the same green suit throughout the film; she was given six identical suits for the shoot.

AWARDS

- Academy Award Nomination: Best Effects, Special Visual Effects (Ub Iwerks)
- Edgar Allan Poe Awards Nomination: Best Motion Picture (Evan Hunter)
- Golden Globe Win: Best Promising Newcomer (Tippi Hedren, along with Ursula Andress and Elke Sommer)

DVD RELEASES

RELEASE: Universal Studios (2000, 2005, 2006)
(Dolby Digital 2.0 Mono, 1.85:1 Color)
RATING: ****

EXTRAS: *All About the Birds* documentary; deleted scene; the original ending; storyboard sequence; Tippi Hedren's screen test; *The Birds Is Coming* newsreel; *Suspense Story: National Press Club Hears Hitchcock* newsreel; production notes and photographs; theatrical trailer.

NOTES: Available as stand-alone releases from 2000 and 2005, or as part of *The Alfred Hitchcock Collection* (out of print) and *Alfred Hitchcock: The Masterpiece Collection. The Masterpiece Collection* is recommended. The transfers on both releases appear identical, as are the extras.

Marnie
(1964)

FILM FACTS

PRODUCTION YEAR: 1963–1964
RELEASE DATE: July 22, 1964 (U.S.)
STUDIO: Universal Pictures
FILMING LOCATIONS: 30th Street Station
3001 Market Street, Philadelphia, Pennsylvania;
Various locations, Pennsylvania; Atlantic City Racetrack,
Atlantic City, New Jersey
PRESENTATION/ASPECT RATIO: Color/1.85:1

SYNOPSIS

Marnie Edgar (Tippi Hedren) is a thief, a liar, and a woman not to be trusted. After robbing her most recent employer, she flees to Philadelphia, where she finds employment with Mark Rutland (Sean Connery). He is in a position to be her next victim, but little does she realize that Mark suspects she is up to something. The thieving plans of this mentally disturbed woman—she is terrified of the color red, and of thunder—are about to go astray. Mark catches her stealing, recognizes that she is a troubled woman, and, in an effort to get to the root of her problems, blackmails Marnie into marrying him. She resists all his efforts to break down the barriers she has thrown up around herself. Marnie hates and resents Mark's push to discover her dark secrets. Finally, in the home of Marnie's mother, the truth is discovered: As a child, Marnie was molested by a client of her prostitute mother, and when the client turned on the mother, Marnie killed him. She has been a disturbed, troubled woman ever since.

IMPRESSIONS

There are two primary schools of thought on *Marnie*. Some critics are quick to dismiss it, claiming that *The Birds* was Alfred Hitchcock's last important film. Others see greatness in it while recognizing that it may not rise to the level of his greatest works.

It would be unfair to punish *Marnie* for its place in Alfred Hitchcock's filmography. His 1964 motion picture comes on the heels of perhaps the most sustained run of directing greatness in the history of cinema, more than a decade during which he made classic after classic without pause. This is no hyperbole.

Yet, fair or not, this picture suffers for coming at the end of such a long stretch of great films, the most recent his 1963 thriller, *The Birds*. This is not to say *Marnie* is a picture unworthy of praise, but rather that as strong as it may be, it is a film that can only signal the start of the weakest period of Hitchcock's career. Here we have a film that is a Frankenstein's monster of Hitch themes, aspects of several stories brought together in a portrayal of a psychologically damaged woman. Elements of *Spellbound* and *Vertigo* are combined with oft-used Hitchcock themes like suspicion, theft, and being on the run, all of it cobbled together to create a larger whole.

Fresh off the success of *The Birds*, Hitch was eager to use his "pet project," Tippi Hedren, in another film, this one undoubtedly more challenging than the last. She was up to the challenge, turning in a nuanced portrayal of a complex character despite reputedly difficult working conditions. And, if rumor is true, "difficult" is generous. Throughout filming, Hitch's obsession with Hedren grew. She was engaged to marry her agent upon completion of filming, but Hitchcock told her daily about his dreams. In his dreams, she was in love with him. Hedren was uncomfortable with these advances. Despite this, there is certainly no negative effect evident in her performance. And that is to her everlasting credit.

Marnie is another film about the crisis of and changing of identities. Like *Vertigo*, *Marnie* is about the transformations of a woman, but this time the woman herself initiates the transformations. Again Hitch is repeating themes, but in keeping with his modus operandi, he always finds new and intriguing ways to connect these themes in his story.

While Hitchcock managed to mine the same territory repeatedly with his "wrong man on the run" films, a genre he continued to refine right up to the masterful *North by Northwest*, the two most noteworthy of his previous psychological thrillers are on opposite sides of the coin when it comes to approach and artistic success. Those two are *Vertigo* and *Spellbound*. While *Vertigo* was inspired and complex and strikingly personal, *Spellbound* fell short of its lofty aspirations, in part due to the interference of producer David O. Selznick and in part due to a mix of crime thriller and character study that never clicks. *Marnie* is a middle ground, more consistent than the uneven *Spellbound*, but falling far short of the mark set by *Vertigo*. In terms of technique and plot devices, it draws heavily on both. Tippi Hedren's Marnie is shaken by the sight of the color red in the same way Gregory Peck's Dr. Edwardes is disturbed by straight lines on a white background in *Spellbound*. Sean Connery's Mark Rutland, meanwhile, has an almost obsessive compulsion to reshape Marnie into the person he wants her to be, not unlike Scottie Ferguson's obsessive behavior in *Vertigo* and Hitchcock's own conduct with his leading ladies, particularly Hedren.

Marnie's biggest failure is that as a psychological examination of a young woman with a troubled past, it lacks the subtle depths mined by *Vertigo*. The characters and their inner turmoil do not resonate, not even unconsciously. We see Marnie troubled by a variety of phobias—lightning, the color red, sex—

WHERE'S HITCH?

Hitchcock appears in a hotel just five minutes into the film.

but these phobias add to the plot, not the character. And in a film like this, character is vital. Even after we discover the details of her past, we're left no closer to truly understanding who she is—or even caring. Her almost uncontrollable compulsion to steal is the glue that binds her to Mark Rutland, yet one never feels an understanding of why she lives her life in this way. It serves as a convenient means by which to lock the characters together, sowing the seeds of mistrust and setting the plot in motion, but not as a believable extension of the character. In *Vertigo*, we know exactly what drives Scottie. We know his insecurities and his unspoken desires. In *Spellbound*, John Ballantine's (aka Dr. Edwardes's) aversion to lines on a white background is but one element of a richer character rife with feelings of uncertainty regarding his place in the world. Even in films not as focused on pure character study, Hitchcock does a better job of letting us into the mind of twisted people. Bruno's parent-driven mania is fleshed out with precise subtlety in *Strangers on a Train*, and the characters in *Rebecca* and *Suspicion* seem to inhabit a living world in which people think, act, and feel outside the needs of the plot. This is largely absent from *Marnie*. The ultimate explanation—that as a young girl Marnie had been nearly raped and then killed a man trying to protect her mother—is too simple. Too easy. So easy, it ventures perilously close to lazy. We're meant to sympathize with her when all is revealed, yet we are still left with an unlikable thief with no clear motivation for her actions and no clear core around which her character circles. Tippi Hedren is a chess piece.

But is that too harsh an assessment? Does *Marnie* succeed at all in breathing real life into this disturbed woman? To an extent. Hitchcock paces the story well, offering the audience new revelations about Marnie in a steady, deliberate flow. When we're introduced to her, she seems a fairly normal (albeit sticky-fingered) woman. It appears that we're in store for another Hitchcock thriller. He lays on the first hints of her instability in the most appropriate of places: at her mother's home. As the film wears on, each new piece of the Marnie puzzle is snapped into place with increasing intensity, one after another, each more disturbed than the last, until finally the portrait is complete. It's an effective means of showing us the depths of her antisocial behavior.

Throughout the film, Marnie is often troubled by the appearance of red items: the gladiolas in her mother's house, a small drop of red ink on her blouse, red polka dots on a jockey's coat, the solid red of the horse rider's coat during the hunt. In yet another great reveal at the end, we learn the reason these things set her into a craze. It reminds her of the horrifying sight of the sailor's blood after she killed him, a memory she had completely suppressed.

Hedren's excellent performance, script flaws or not, is supported by the rising star of Sean Connery. While Connery is slightly miscast as a Philadelphia gentleman, his performance is also top-notch. Mark Rutland is, in his own way, as troubled as Marnie. Why else would a man who could seemingly have any woman he wants desire a woman who stole from the company he owns?

Because it is a fetishistic love for him.

It is not enunciated in the script, but for Mark, the attraction is in bedding a thief. Connery, freshly minted as a box office star with the James Bond films, betrays this in his eyes and facial expressions. Were it not for

Marnie (Tippi Hedren) prepares to kill the only thing she ever loved. (Universal Pictures/Photofest © Universal Pictures)

Connery's acting, this would be lost on the viewer, though there are hints dropped throughout the film. There are many references to animals and the taming of the wild. Mark's avocation is zoology. He makes reference to having tamed a jaguarundi. It seems obvious that Mark views Marnie as another animal he can tame. She says to him, "You don't love me. I'm just something you've caught. Some kind of wild animal you've trapped!"

But Marnie is not so easy to tame, for she is a mind-numbingly frigid woman. We later learn that Marnie's mother, Bernice, was ashamed of her prostituting ways; she raised Marnie to be a "decent" woman. Marnie takes it to heart—too much to heart. She says to her mother at the film's close, "Oh, Mama! You've surely realized your ambition. I certainly am decent. Of course, I'm a cheat and a liar and a thief, but I *am* decent."

In *Marnie* we once again see what appears to be a negative portrait of a mother figure in Bernice Edgar. Early in the film, Marnie says to her, "Why don't you love me, Mama? I've always wondered why you didn't. You never give me one part of the love you give Jessie." Bernice provides care for a neighboring child, Jessie, and appears to be a loving caregiver, but when confronted with this statement from her own daughter she does nothing to allay Marnie's pain. Yet, in keeping with what we saw in Lydia in *The Birds*, another seemingly cold mother who cannot express her true love, when the truth is revealed at the end of *Marnie* we are better able to understand Bernice. She redeems herself when Marnie says to her, "You must have loved me, Mama. You must have loved me." Bernice replies, "Well, you're the only thing in the world that I ever did love." It is an effective scene and a terrific payoff on a generally strong character arc.

Despite his reputation, perhaps Hitchcock really did have a heart for mothers.

As he always had, Sir Alfred adapted with the changing times, dealing more frankly with sexuality than he ever had before. Even just a year before, in *The Birds*, Hedren as an object of desire was contained, relatively conservative. Here, the sexual talk is open, steering away from innuendo and into the kind of frank conversation only then becoming commonplace in cinema. In this, Hitchcock remained a director who kept pace with the times. His unceasing efforts to expand his subject matter and approach with each new era are front and center throughout *Marnie*.

That's why a growing school of thought says this film is a heretofore undiscovered gem, a fascinating look at a well-developed and extremely complex character. It plays like a Hitchcock film, yet ventures into entirely new psychological territory. It is not a mystery film, per se, but the climactic scene plays out like the grand revelation of a complex puzzle. This climax is a terrific payoff on what is sometimes a difficult film to watch. And no wonder. It was a very personal film for Hitchcock. He probably saw himself in the Connery role, with Hedren as his object of desire.

In the end, *Marnie* is a fine enough film with plenty of ambition, yet, unfair as it may be, it represents a regression in form for the Master of Suspense, an ambitious but flawed attempt at grappling with deeper subject matter.

Alfred Hitchcock's golden years as a director were over.

CONCLUSION

Marnie is arguably one of Alfred Hitchcock's last great films, filled with techniques and thematic content worth experiencing. It is also a flawed film, suffering from an array of niggles great and small. No matter which belief you subscribe to, or even if you think *both* are true, one thing is certain: *Marnie* is an important film in the legacy and story of Alfred Hitchcock. To brush it off as unimportant or unworthy of the great Hitchcock would do it a disservice. *Marnie* is an essential Hitchcock picture.

HITCHCOCKIAN THEMES

Bathroom Scene/B.M. • Blackmail • Blonde Leading Lady • Dark Secret • Handcuffed Man and Woman • Man (or Woman) on the Run • Manipulative Mother • Murder • Suicide/Attempted Suicide • Unwelcome New Woman

THINGS TO LOOK FOR

- Hitchcock's use of color to give the Marnie character added depth. Hitchcock was among the first filmmakers to creatively use color for in-story purposes, something he did right up until his final film.
- The photography during the late "revelation" scenes of Marnie's past. A special camera was used to get the foggy, fish-eye effect.
- The film's striking thematic similarities to *Vertigo* and *Spellbound,* and how the subject matter may have reflected on Hitchcock's own state of mind during this period.

TRIVIA/FUN STUFF

+ Grace Kelly was initially selected for the role of Marnie, but was forced to withdraw because of political pressures at home. (She was Princess of Monaco by this time, and the country would not tolerate her in such a role.)
+ Hedren and Hitchcock had a massive falling-out during the filming, a falling-out that has been the subject of rumor and innuendo ever since.
+ *Marnie* marked the end of Hitchcock's working relationship with Bernard Herrmann.

DVD RELEASES

RELEASE: Universal Studios (2000, 2005, 2006)
(Dolby Digital 2.0 Mono, 1.85:1 Color)
RATING: ***1/2

EXTRAS: *The Trouble with Marnie* documentary; the *Marnie* archives; theatrical trailer; production notes.

NOTES: Available as stand-alone releases from 2000 and 2005, or as part of *The Alfred Hitchcock Collection* (out of print) and *Alfred Hitchcock: The Masterpiece Collection. The Masterpiece Collection* is recommended. The transfers on all releases appear identical.

```
  ┌──────────────┐
  │  W E E K     │
  │  ───────     │
  │   4 9        │
  └──────────────┘
```

Torn Curtain
(1966)

FILM FACTS

PRODUCTION YEAR: 1965–1966
RELEASE DATE: July 14, 1966 (U.S.)
STUDIO: Universal Pictures
FILMING LOCATIONS: Berlin, Germany; Los Angeles, California;
Universal City, California; Copenhagen, Denmark
PRESENTATION/ASPECT RATIO: Color/1.85:1

SYNOPSIS

Professor Michael Armstrong (Paul Newman) is an American scientist in Copenhagen, there for a scientific convention with his assistant/fiancée, Sarah Sherman (Julie Andrews). After observing Armstrong's curious behavior, Sherman follows him to East Germany against his wishes, where it appears he is attempting to defect from the United States. The defection is a ruse, however. Armstrong is actually attempting to steal a mathematical formula from a communist professor in Leipzig.

IMPRESSIONS

With *Torn Curtain* we enter the final stage of Hitchcock's career, a period covering ten years in which he made just four films, none of them reaching the heights of his greatest success from the previous decade.

337

By 1966 Alfred Hitchcock was firmly established as a household name, beloved filmmaker, and living legend. He had set the bar so high that living up to his own standards had become an all but impossible task. It is under the weight of such lofty heights already established by Hitchcock that *Torn Curtain* suffers. It is a fine—at times even excellent—1960s thriller held in modest esteem in part because it had so much to live up to.

As was the case throughout his career, Sir Alfred's latest was in keeping with the times. Here, nuclear secrets are the MacGuffin being chased by our protagonists. The Cold War was booming, fear of communists was a daily part of life, and thoughts of nuclear war loomed over all. Yet, while Hitchcock's spy syndicates had changed loyalties and goals over the years, from Nazi spies to vague communist threats, their means of gripping the audience had changed little.

Once again, we're treated to a story of spies, dark secrets, a man on the run, the wrongly accused, murder, and MacGuffins. Four decades after directing his first picture, Hitchcock was still relying on the same themes he had at the outset of his career. Of course, by this time these themes had become familiar; *Torn Curtain* does not fail because of this. In fact, the story told in *Torn Curtain* is interesting and was certainly ripe with potential at the hands of one of cinema's greatest creators. It ultimately fails as a classic for reasons we will discuss below.

> **WHERE'S HITCH?**
>
> Hitchcock appears a little more than eight minutes into the film, sitting in a hotel lobby with a baby on his knee. The music changes briefly during this sequence to "Funeral March of a Marionette," the theme song to *Alfred Hitchcock Presents*.

Torn Curtain's first hour is stronger than the film's lackluster reputation would suggest, teasing viewers with a slow trickle of often misleading information and red herrings. Professor Michael Armstrong, played by then-rising superstar Paul Newman, does not initially offer the audience a glimpse of the big picture. We see him receiving secret information, evading his fiancée, defecting to communist East Germany (bringing America's nuclear secrets with him), and generally leading the viewer through a series of false starts. The first hour of *Torn Curtain* is a prime example of Hitch's ability to set audience expectations and then knock them over, again and again.

When we are finally allowed a look at the real events unfolding before us—Armstrong did not defect to the communists, but rather is spying on them in an effort to extract vital secrets from a German scientist—the audience is left little time to take it in. Once we finally understand the big picture, a tense confrontation injects danger into the proceedings. The confrontation culminates in one of the most intense and graphic killings in Hitchcock's filmography, a slow, lingering death that includes a stabbing, strangulation, and asphyxiation. The final throes of Gromek, the German security agent, are grim and disturbing. They are also well beyond what would have been allowed on screen a mere ten years prior.

Once again, Hitchcock sought to push the envelope.

Too bad, then, that *Torn Curtain*'s second hour does not fare as well. Hitch had long been a master of pacing, bleeding information to the audience with a tempo designed to sustain suspense. As his career wore on, he began to linger in scenes, his films growing incrementally longer. His days of telling a brisk story in ninety minutes were over; now he was afforded the luxury of stretching his stories out, often to their detriment. Such is the case here. Tension-filled sequences, such as a slow but engaging escape from the police on a bus filled with spies, are undermined by poorly placed (and paced) character interactions that grind the plot to a halt. Specifically, an encounter with a not-very-sober Polish woman washes away all the urgency the bus escape built. In his prime, Hitchcock knew that by this point in a film, maintaining a sense of urgency is paramount. Once Armstrong and his fiancée are in clear danger, plot points should come quickly and ceaselessly. They do not. There are fine bits of directorial technique—the rapid close-ups on a dancer's face, for instance, set the stage well for the final push for escape—but by and large, Hitchcock's own slowing pace (he was sixty-six when he made *Torn Curtain*) shows itself on screen.

At times, Hitchcock's weaker work has been rescued by a strong cast, but despite the superstar names, such is not the case here. The casting of Julie Andrews in particular was a curious choice. She was certainly a star in the mid-1960s after leading roles in the megahit musicals *Mary Poppins* (1964) and *The Sound of Music* (1965), but she had no experience working in suspense thrillers. She was not your typical Hitchcock blonde—and arguably, this film could have used the stereotypical Hitchcock blonde.

Torn Curtain is notable as the film that ended Hitch's relationship with composer Bernard Herrmann, a man he enjoyed a harmonious relationship with since *The Trouble with Harry* in 1955. Herrmann composed a score for *Torn Curtain*, but, as the story goes, Universal Pictures executives wanted something more upbeat. This led to a terrible disagreement between Hitchcock and Herrmann, and the two never worked together again. The replacement score by John Addison is playful and light, and works well at times, especially at the beginning, but at other times is out of harmony with the on-screen suspense. One can only wonder what kind of impact a Herrmann score would have had on the finished film. His work had been so effective in punctuating key moments in Sir Alfred's films, who can say how much better *Torn Curtain* would have been with a similar treatment?

Despite the low esteem in which it is held, *Torn Curtain* is, in the end, an engaging, if flawed, Hitchcock thriller. How engaging is a matter of debate, but certainly *Torn Curtain* contains some worthwhile viewing. One might argue that this fails to deliver as a suspense thriller; were it directed by any other man it might have been seen in a more positive light, but against the backdrop of Hitch's career, it suffers. One might also argue that while it's no groundbreaking piece of work by any measure and does exactly nothing to advance the sweep of his art, it nonetheless displays clearly that even when in his mid-sixties, Hitchcock was still capable of spinning a yarn with the best of them.

CONCLUSION

Torn Curtain is a suspense thriller in the Hitchcockian tradition, but is not up to the Hitchcock standard of greatness. Brief moments of directorial flair and an excellent first half are not enough to overcome problems with pacing, an inappropriate score, and a story that does not age well. It's worth seeing for the Hitch completist, but largely forgettable for the casual fan.

HITCHCOCKIAN THEMES

Chaos in an Unexpected Location · Dark Secret · MacGuffin · Man (or Woman) on the Run · Murder · Spy Syndicate · Wrongly Accused

THINGS TO LOOK FOR

• The stark realism of the killing scene.

TRIVIA/FUN STUFF

✦ Longtime Hitchcock collaborator Bernard Herrmann wrote an original score for *Torn Curtain*, but it was not used. Universal Pictures executives wanted something more upbeat. This led to a disagreement between Hitchcock and Herrmann, and they never worked together again.

✦ The scene where Armstrong and the farmer's wife kill Gromek was written and filmed as it was to show just how difficult it can be to kill a person.

DVD RELEASES

RELEASE: Universal Studios (2001, 2005, 2006)
(Dolby Digital 2.0 Mono, 1.85:1 Color)
RATING: **1/2

EXTRAS: *Torn Curtain Rising* documentary; scenes scored by Bernard Herrmann; production notes and photographs; theatrical trailer.

NOTES: Available as stand-alone releases from 2001 and 2006, or as part of *The Alfred Hitchcock Collection* (out of print) and *Alfred Hitchcock: The Masterpiece Collection*. *The Masterpiece Collection* is recommended. The transfers on all releases appear identical.

Topaz
(1969)

FILM FACTS

PRODUCTION YEARS: 1968–1969
RELEASE DATE: December 19, 1969 (U.S.)
STUDIO: Universal Pictures
FILMING LOCATIONS: Copenhagen and Frederiksberg, Denmark; New York,
New York; Salinas, California; Washington, D.C.; Universal Studios,
California; Paris, France; Wiesbaden, Hessen, Germany
PRESENTATION/ASPECT RATIO: Color/1.85:1

SYNOPSIS

A Russian defector. A secret spy ring code-named "Topaz." The start of the
Cuban Missile Crisis. Cold War escalations and government machinations.
Alfred Hitchcock's *Topaz* is a dense political thriller with as complex a plot and
large a cast as any picture in his filmography. In this lengthy drama, American
officials hope to get information on a French leak—Topaz—through a Russian defector, but the defector does not cooperate as hoped. Forced to take matters into their own hands, they uncover plans that point to a Soviet missile
buildup in Cuba. After a series of betrayals and counter-betrayals, the Cuban
situation escalates, leaving American officials empty-handed. When the source
of the Topaz leak is finally uncovered, it is too late to capture the culprit.

IMPRESSIONS

Grainy archival footage of Soviet armies followed by a text blurb setting the stage for the story to follow? This is hardly an Alfred Hitchcock opening, yet it is how we're introduced to *Topaz*, Hitch's 1969 Cold War thriller.

Topaz is not what one expects from a Hitchcock picture. This is a suspenseful film, but not in the mold we've come to expect. Aside from a few inspired action sequences, *Topaz* is a lengthy, talkative political drama; at 142 minutes, the longest film on Hitch's résumé. It is also among the most maligned. Viewed by the majority of critics as a disaster, the film was a box office failure. The decade Hitchcock had started so strongly with *Psycho* ended on a sour note. Time has also been unkind to it—the consensus is that this is bottom-tier Hitchcock—but lurking beneath the surface is a better film than one might expect given its reputation.

Critics are quick to dismiss *Topaz*, citing its overly complicated plot and notoriously difficult production, but the picture is admirable in some sense *because* of these traits. Yes, the story is complex and there are myriad important characters to keep tabs on, but if you pay close attention this is not a difficult film to follow. While the third act is less satisfying than the first two, the plot structure is impressive. That it all came together under such difficult circumstances makes that all the more commendable.

It is well documented that the problems with the production of *Topaz* were many, chief among them the screenplay. When the film rights were sold, Leon Uris, who wrote the novel upon which *Topaz* is based, was given the opportunity to write the script as part of his deal with Universal Pictures. His working relationship with Hitchcock, who often worked closely with his writers, was poor. The director ultimately claimed the resulting script was virtually unshootable and severed ties with Uris. Samuel Taylor, who had written *Vertigo*, was called in at the last minute to do a massive rewrite. Filming began well before the screenplay was completed, and some scenes were written just hours before they were filmed. An aging Hitchcock, notorious for his intense preproduction planning, struggled to adapt to these filming conditions.

Once again we plunge into the Cold War, using issues of the day—Communism, defections, and the threat of nuclear war—to pull together a slow-burning suspense film. This was not unusual. Throughout his career, Hitchcock had dealt with contemporary times and contemporary fears. From post–World War I Britain to World War II to postwar America and beyond, Sir Alfred's films often reflected the times. Unlike *Torn Curtain*, which was also centered on the ongoing Cold War, *Topaz* does not suffer for being a film of its time. This story, which has elements based on the real-life events of the Cuban Missile Crisis, ages better simply because it is framed by historical events.

If *Topaz* reflects the always-current sensibilities of Alfred Hitchcock, it certainly does not reflect the heightened level of intrigue so typical of his other espionage thrillers. The pace is not deliberate, it is *slow*. We're twenty-three minutes into the film before we even get our first hint of the MacGuffin central to the plot, the code name "Topaz." Thirty minutes into the film, and the plot has inched forward barely a step. It is an hour before any real forward motion begins and the narrative develops a sense of drama. Hitch is taking his sweet time. If there is a single notable change in Hitchcock's style in his waning years, it is in this. Whereas he previously showed a remarkable focus in tone and an almost impeccable sense of pacing, *Topaz* exemplifies the greatest flaws in his later films. Its style and presentation is indistinct, lacking the intangible stamp of the auteur. Rather than feeling like a singular artistic vision, *Topaz* is by-the-book storytelling. Couple this mundane approach with a crawling pace that sucks all urgency from the story—quite

> **WHERE'S HITCH?**
>
> In a late cameo, Hitchcock can be seen about a half hour into the film, getting out of a wheelchair at an airport.

an achievement, considering all that is at stake in the plot—and one gets the sense that Hitchcock was sleepwalking through the production, interested in a few brief scenes and little more.

The characters, however, are decidedly more interesting than the film's reputation would suggest. André Devereaux (Frederick Stafford) is a charming French intelligence agent with an air of mystery about him. His son-in-law, François Picard (Michel Subor), is a newsman who both interviews and sketches his subjects. Rico Parra (John Vernon) is the uncompromising top Cuban official who does not take betrayal lightly. Philippe Dubois (Roscoe Lee Browne) is the smooth and confident West Indies flower shop owner who deftly maneuvers his way into an opportunity to steal Cuban secrets. Michael Nordstrom (John Forsythe, *The Trouble with Harry*'s Sam Marlowe) is the American intelligence agent who conspires with Deveraux to learn what the Cubans are doing. And of course Juanita de Cordoba (Karin Dor) is the beautiful Cuban woman who loves Devereaux and her country, yet leads an effort to thwart her government.

There are a number of Hitchcock touches scattered throughout the movie. The early scene where the Kusenovs, a pair of Russian defectors, make their escape from a department store in Copenhagen (yes, like *Torn Curtain*, the film opens there) is typically understated Hitchcockian action, doing an outstanding job of establishing the characters and their situation in an efficient manner. Another great sequence is the Harlem hotel scene, in which Dubois photographs secret Cuban papers and narrowly escapes with his life. This is clearly a scene in which Hitchcock was engaged; it's rife with tension, efficiently advances the plot, and is thoroughly entertaining. There are also the opening shots, which include a swinging pan to a mirror reflecting a grim-faced onlooker, then a further pan to a family exiting a house. It's a well-choreographed shot that tells a story without saying a word. In another scene, two men step behind a glass door; a conversation takes place in silence, the audience kept unclear on the details of the exchange. A later, lengthier sequence is played the same way, body language and gestures the only indication of how the conversation is unfolding. This helps inject a badly needed sense of intrigue into the proceedings. It is not enough to lift the film from the realm of the ordinary, but enough to prove that Hitchcock had not totally lost his ability to make movie magic out of very little.

In fact, when *Topaz* is good, it is very good indeed. The film's "blooming dress" execution scene is its most famous, and deservedly so. It is tense, powerful, and beautifully shot—not to mention preceded by a harrowing interrogation scene. As a whole, the fifty minutes or so of the second act are borderline brilliant.

The visual design of *Topaz* is also noteworthy. Hitchcock chose to film characters in specific colors. The French characters are associated with yellow, the Cubans (the communists) with red, and lavender is associated with death. Matching colors with people and themes is nothing new to Hitchcock—earlier examples include *Dial M for Murder* and *Psycho*, in which apparel is a window into a character's state of mind—and while this does nothing to move the plot forward, it speaks to Hitchcock's meticulous planning.

Ultimately, however, the film never quite manages to come together as a cohesive whole. The lack of preproduction planning was a major roadblock in realizing the full potential of Hitchcock's directorial skills, the screenplay was too burdened and too unfocused, and the big, sprawling story never seems quite clear what it wants to tackle. We have a solid Cuban Missile Crisis story, a decent spy story, and even an interesting love story. But they do not come together as a satisfying whole.

It is difficult to deny that by this point, Hitchcock's skills as an innovative director were on the wane. He was older, slower, and less focused. All this is reflected in his later films—but he had one last trick up his sleeve. It was called *Frenzy*, and it would be Hitchcock's final masterpiece.

CONCLUSION

Topaz is a big, ambitious film that tackles weighty political issues and deep intrigue. It may in fact be too ambitious for its own good. Hitchcock was not able to do the preproduction planning he was so well known for, making *Topaz* a noble but failed experiment in creating a sprawling political drama. *Topaz* joins *Torn Curtain* and *Family Plot* as capable late Hitchcocks that fall disappointingly short of greatness. Hitch was still a master, as his next film, *Frenzy*, clearly displays, but here we see only hints of that mastery. *Topaz* is among the few Hitchcock films fans can skip without feeling they've missed out on something essential.

HITCHCOCKIAN THEMES

Chaos in an Unexpected Location · Dark Secret · Exotic Location · Ineffectual Authority Figures · Love Triangle · MacGuffin · Murder · Spy Syndicate

THINGS TO LOOK FOR

- *Topaz*'s most famous shot, the "flowering dress" assassination scene, which proves that even in a lesser work, there are Hitchcock touches worth seeing.
- The tense document theft set in New York City, a fine example of Hitchcock's ability to sustain tension and build to an explosive finish.

AWARDS

- National Board of Review Wins: Best Director, Best Supporting Actor (Philippe Noiret)

TRIVIA/FUN STUFF

✦ Probably the most haphazard of Hitchcock's generally meticulous scripts, the initial screenplay (by Leon Uris) was thrown out at the last minute. In a manner out of character with Hitch's usual careful planning, some scenes were written on the same day they were shot.

✦ There are three versions of *Topaz*, with three different endings. The initial ending featured a duel in an empty stadium, during which the leader of the spy ring, Jacques Granville, is shot in the back by a sniper. This was changed after test audiences rejected it. In the German version, Granville commits suicide. And finally, there is the version North American audiences are familiar with.

DVD RELEASES

RELEASE: Universal Studios (2001, 2005, 2006)
(Dolby Digital 2.0 Mono, 1.85:1 Color)
RATING: ***

EXTRAS: *Topaz: An Appreciation* by critic Leonard Maltin; three alternate endings; storyboards; production notes and photographs; theatrical trailer.

NOTES: Available as stand-alone releases from 2001 and 2006, or as part of *The Alfred Hitchcock Collection* (out of print) and *Alfred Hitchcock: The Masterpiece Collection. The Masterpiece Collection* is recommended. The transfers on all releases appear identical.

Frenzy
(1972)

FILM FACTS

Production Year: 1971
Release Date: June 21, 1972 (U.S.)
Studio: Universal Pictures
Filming Location: London, England
Presentation/Aspect Ratio: Color/1.85:1

SYNOPSIS

Richard Ian Blaney (Jon Finch) is a down-on-his-luck bartender. After he loses his job and his ex-wife (Barbara Leigh-Hunt) is found murdered, he becomes a suspect in the "Necktie Murders" terrorizing London. While he is on the run to prove his innocence, it is discovered that the real murderer is his friend Bob Rusk (Barry Foster).

IMPRESSIONS

Then in his early seventies, it would not have been untoward to suggest that in 1972, Alfred Hitchcock's best days were behind him. No longer delivering strings of outstanding films, Hitchcock had faltered in the mid-to-late 1960s. His last three films would have been fine efforts in the hands of any other director, but these were Alfred Hitchcock films. The public expected—nay, *demanded*—more from the Master of Suspense, a man by now as famous as any of his biggest stars. *Marnie, Torn Curtain*, and *Topaz* each had fine moments, but all were modest successes at best, and at worst were critical failures. The man who had been thrilling, entertaining, and shocking audiences for nearly five decades appeared to be a dim shadow of his former self.

When you're a man with the uninhibited, inspired vision of Alfred Hitchcock, however, it is never safe to count you out, as the world would soon learn. Hitch had one more masterpiece left. Once again invigorated by a story he wanted to film, Hitch was able to summon those legendary directorial skills that had made him famous so long ago. And this would be among the most chilling, disturbing, and graphic films he had ever made.

In 1972 Alfred Hitchcock released *Frenzy*—and, in an astonishing turn for a man arguably long past his prime, it was unlike anything he had ever done before, even while mining classic Hitchcock territory.

Take a glance at the elements that create the core of *Frenzy*'s plot, and it sounds remarkably familiar. A man is seen in the wrong place at the wrong

WHERE'S HITCH?

Hitchcock appears early in the film, in the crowd listening to a political speech. He is the only person not applauding the speaker.

time, with all evidence suggesting he is a murderer. He is not, of course. He is our latest (and our final) Hitchcock "wrong man." On the run he goes, while the actual culprit, a depraved serial killer who strangles women with neckties, continues to plague London.

Yes, London. We're back. Again we are living in fear of a serial killer, on the hunt for the man who has been murdering young women. The situation looks much like that in *The Lodger*, a film Hitch made forty-nine years earlier.

But the public would never have seen a film as graphic as this in the 1920s.

At a reportedly depressed time in his life, Hitch shows a side of his personality heretofore unseen in his work. He had always been fascinated by the perverse and the unsightly, but, due to the restrictions of film production codes and societal mores, these things were either left hidden or filtered through a lens of self-censorship. *Frenzy* is not like this in any regard. It is packed with raw violence, coarse language, immoral thoughts, and perversions. Hitchcock was invigorated by the freedom provided by the relatively lax standards of the early 1970s. One can only imagine what he would have done with films like *Strangers on a Train* or *Psycho* had they been made at this time.

From the start, we see classic Hitchcock at work. A camera sweeps over the city to soaring music, coasts in over a crowd, and locks into place, bringing us near a political speech in progress. It's a bold shot that tells the audience they are about to see the Hitchcock of old at work. Cut to a nude body floating along the river, reminiscent of the body washed upon the shore in *Young and Innocent*, but this time the imagery is more graphic. Sinister, even. We then have more cuts, talk about a "Necktie Killer" informs the audience of the mood in the city, and a cut to a new scene that immediately teases us with an image of a man fiddling with a tie. The camera silently follows him like a stalker . . . and we're off and running.

Right from the start, *Frenzy* is laced with Hitchcockian bravado.

Hitchcock's audience manipulation continues unabated from here. We follow this man as he is fired from his job and wanders to a nearby pub. There, two businessmen discuss the grisly details of the necktie killer—including frank, salacious sexual talk—while the man we are following is framed conspicuously in the background. As the discussion grows more graphic, he moves to the front of the frame as if to emphasize a link between the man and the conversation.

Alfred Hitchcock is showing us who our killer is.

In a brisk series of interconnected scenes, we learn that this man has a violent temper, that he is broke and desperate, and that his marriage ended in a bitter, resentful divorce, his relationship with his ex-wife anything but friendly. His name is Richard Blaney. And he is not a nice man.

Then Hitchcock comes to it. While alone in her office, this man's ex-wife is raped, strangled, and murdered—not by Blaney, but by a bit-part character. The culprit is Robert Rusk, whom we briefly met earlier in the film. For the last half hour, Hitch had been teasing us. The man we had been following was not the murderer at all.

Naturally enough, however, he will soon be *suspected* of being the murderer. This is, after all, a Hitchcock film.

Starkly different from Hitchcock's traditional "man on the run" tales is that Richard Blaney is not a likeable character. Blaney is no Roger Thornhill (*North by Northwest*), nor even a Barry Kane (*Saboteur*). Those fellows were good people. It is easy to root for protagonists like that. Not Blaney. He's irresponsible, a drunk, and a poor husband. And, at first glance, he may also be guilty of murder. When we discover he is innocent, it is easier to root

Jon Finch as Richard Blaney, Hitchcock's last man on the run. (Universal Pictures/Photofest © Universal Pictures)

for his exoneration, but the empathy comes without the fervor we would have for Thornhill or Kane, because Blaney is a lowlife. One might argue that Hitchcock, who often pictured his leads as representations of himself, made Blaney a down-on-his-luck kind of guy because that was how he viewed himself at the time. After all, it had been nearly a decade since he had experienced any kind of critical or commercial success.

But let us take a step back for a moment—back to the rape and murder. This scene is impossible to ignore because it is unlike anything in the Hitchcock canon. Even today, it would be considered difficult to watch, and as graphic as anything one would expect to find in mainstream twenty-first-century cinema. It is a long scene. Slow, with lingering shots punctuated by quick cuts and startling visuals. A woman is forced onto a couch, violently. Her blouse is torn away, then her bra, revealing her breasts. She is pleading. Begging. Crying. Finally, she gives in to the inevitable rape and begins to pray, looking away from the horror she is being put through. Murmuring quietly. Her eyes empty. The attacker is upon her, and in verbal mimicry of penetration and climax he sickeningly repeats, "Lovely, lovely, lovely, lovely." He climaxes. Removes his tie. And, in a sequence worthy of *Psycho*'s shower scene, extending the already unbearable brutality we've witnessed, he strangles her. Our final shot is of her bulging eyes, lolling tongue, and dead face. It's exhausting.

This scene, long and slow and realistic to the extreme, is reminiscent of the killing seen in *Torn Curtain*. The method is different and the motives entirely at odds, but the execution of the filmmaking is almost identical. Both sequences are brutal yet bloodless, and both are among the most memorable of their respective films. It was said that the killing in *Torn Curtain* was filmed as it was to illustrate just how difficult it is to kill a man. After a career of presenting such things in a stylized manner, it could be said that in the first rape and murder in *Frenzy*, Hitchcock illustrates just what terrible crimes both rape and murder are.

Alfred Hitchcock had always played with implication. *Suggestion.* Here, he lays bare the darkest corner of the crimes that so often lay at the root of his films and chills his audience to the bone. Disturbing is an understatement.

With *Frenzy*, Hitchcock was clearly pulling out all the stops. Inspired by its subject matter, intent on proving he was still the Master of Suspense, he took almost every trick he had used over the previous five decades and used them in the most extreme way possible. Take, for instance, Hitch's love of having his characters discuss murder and death while eating. Here we have several scenes during which one of the inspectors into the Necktie Killer, Chief Inspector Oxford (Alec McCowen), discusses the case while staring at some of the most grotesque, nausea-inducing food you'll ever see: horrid fish heads and scaled things floating in icky brown liquid. All quite gross. Gratuitously so, in fact. So is the nudity. In not one, not two, but three scenes Hitchcock indulges in showing on-screen nudity, a first for his career. And in two of those scenes the nudity was entirely unnecessary.

Yet it would be unfair to suggest that *Frenzy*'s impact relies solely on shock and exploitation. Far from it. Hitch shows himself to be equally adept at using subtlety and suggestion to move an audience. The best example comes in the form of the film's second rape and murder, a sequence during which the audience neither sees nor hears an act of violence, but knows full well what took place. Here, Rusk takes in Barbara Milligan (Anna Masay), Blaney's girlfriend, and offers her a place to stay. The camera follows as they enter the building in which he lives, coasts along with them up the stairs, and pauses as Rusk leads Milligan into his apartment. The camera, still in an unbroken shot, then coasts back down the stairs, outside, and across the street, framing the building we had just entered.

We know what is happening inside that apartment. Having shown it so graphically the first time, holding back here serves only to enhance the horror.

Hitch again capitalizes on subtlety and implication later in the film, when Blaney is tried and wrongly convicted as the Necktie Killer. The camera is positioned outside the courtroom, peering through a glass door at the proceedings. Blaney's back is to the camera. The audience cannot hear what is going on inside. Twice a bailiff opens the courtroom door, each time just long enough to give the audience the information it needs: that Blaney was found guilty, and the results of his sentencing. Other than those two brief instances, we are but outside observers, the proceedings a vague and unclear process. It is reminiscent of the trial in *Dial M for Murder*, in which Hitchcock gives us only enough information to know what happens with the trial.

Hitch's return to time-tested techniques did not end with his handling of the trial. In *Frenzy*, he once again injects humor into a dark film—humor with a grim subtext. The chief inspector's discussions of his investigations while he struggles to consume his wife's repulsive food are both hilarious and appropriate to the plot. In fact, the entire film is peppered with references to food, one of Hitchcock's greatest loves and excesses in his private life. These numerous eating scenes illustrate the connections between food and sex and murder. For Bob Rusk, rape and murder *are* his food. It is what he lives for.

But food also becomes Rusk's enemy as he is forced to endure a harrowing excursion aboard a truck full of potatoes as he searches for his lost tie pin, which would connect him with the Necktie Killer murders. It's a terrific scene as it ties together adventure, morbid humor, and nerve-racking suspense.

Every trick. Every technique. Every means of audience manipulation. All of it is on display.

Frenzy is constructed with steady, effective pacing; interesting if not sympathetic characters; and a terrific blend of dark humor and an even darker plot. Much credit should go to screenwriter Anthony Shaffer for his adaptation of Arthur La Bern's novel *Goodbye Piccadilly, Farewell Leicester Square*, but in typical Hitchcock fashion, the director had equal, if not more, influence on the shaping of the story. After the disappointing screenplays for *Torn Curtain* and *Topaz*, Hitch once again took control of the story he wanted to tell, guiding the way toward a superb script.

Coming after Hitch's golden period as it did, *Frenzy* is sometimes lost in the shuffle, lumped in with his later, lesser films. Yet make no mistake: *Frenzy* is not a lesser Hitchcock work. This is unquestionably the final great work of Alfred Hitchcock's career. It is solidly among the top films of cinema's greatest director, and clearly shows that Hitch still had his skills even in his seventies, an achievement unmatched by all but a few of his peers. His last great film was a tour de force of directorial technique, wrapping up a slew of the key elements that had come to define Hitchcock's career and putting them together in a decidedly modern, forward-thinking, and entirely contemporary context.

In short, *Frenzy* is essential Alfred Hitchcock.

CONCLUSION

Frenzy is the last of the great Hitchcocks, a film unlike any of his other works when it comes to its explicit gruesomeness, yet littered with tried-and-true Hitchcockian themes. Here we have a newly energized Hitch pulling one last hurrah from his bag of directorial tricks. After nearly a decade without a critical success, *Frenzy* marked a great comeback for the Master of Suspense. He again reached great heights—heights he would never see again.

HITCHCOCKIAN THEMES

Bathroom Scene/B.M. • Chaos in an Unexpected Location • Dark Secret • Discussion of Murder at Dinner • Ineffectual Authority Figures • Love Triangle • Man (or Woman) on the Run • Murder • Woman Screaming Directly at Camera • Wrongly Accused

THINGS TO LOOK FOR

- The stark realism of the first rape and murder scene.
- The way Hitchcock teases us as to the identity of the killer at the start of the film.
- The outstanding reverse-tracking shot that travels outside of Rusk's apartment, down the stairs, out the door, and onto the street.

- The incredibly perverse, comical yet uncomfortable scene in the back of a potato truck.
- Numerous appearances of and references to food.

TRIVIA/FUN STUFF

+ Henry Mancini was hired to write the original score, but was fired from the project when Hitchcock was displeased with what had been written. Mancini's title theme is available on a compilation of his film music excerpts.
+ Elsie Randolph, who portrays a worker at the hotel, appeared more than forty years earlier in Hitchcock's *Rich and Strange* as an old maid.
+ *Frenzy* is the first and only Hitchcock film to feature nudity.

AWARDS

- Golden Globe Nominations: Best Motion Picture (Drama); Best Director, Motion Picture; Best Screenplay (Anthony Shaffer); Best Original Score (Ron Goodwin)
- Edgar Allan Poe Awards Nomination: Best Motion Picture (Anthony Shaffer)
- Cinema Writers Circle Awards (Spain) Win: Best Foreign Film

---

DVD RELEASES

RELEASE: Universal Studios (2001, 2005, 2006)
(Dolby Digital 2.0 Mono, 1.85:1 Color)
RATING: *****

EXTRAS: *The Story of Frenzy* documentary; production notes and photographs; theatrical trailer.

NOTES: Available as stand-alone releases from 2001 and 2006, or as part of *The Alfred Hitchcock Collection* (out of print) and *Alfred Hitchcock: The Masterpiece Collection*. *The Masterpiece Collection* is recommended. The transfers on all releases appear identical.

Family Plot
(1976)

FILM FACTS

PRODUCTION YEAR: 1975
RELEASE DATE: April 9, 1976 (U.S.)
STUDIO: Universal Pictures
FILMING LOCATIONS: Pioneer Cemetery, Sierra Vista Park,
Sierra Madre, California;
Southwestern Law School
3500 Wilshire Blvd., Los Angeles, California;
Grace Cathedral Episcopal Church
1100 California St., San Francisco, California;
Angeles Crest, Angeles National Forest, California;
Various locations, Los Angeles and San Francisco, California
PRESENTATION/ASPECT RATIO: Color/1.85:1

SYNOPSIS

Alfred Hitchcock's final film is a light comedic thriller about two couples
who are up to no good crossing paths. Scam artists Blanche (Barbara Harris) and George (Bruce Dern) agree to help an elderly widow find a long
lost nephew; the nephew is her last remaining heir. Meanwhile, a pair of
thieves, Arthur (William Devane) and Fran (Karen Black), have been kid-

napping wealthy people and holding them ransom for diamonds. When the kidnappers are found out by the scam artists, a figurative tug-of-war between them begins.

IMPRESSIONS

If *Family Plot* is unforgettable, it is only because it holds the distinction of being the final film in a long and astonishingly successful career. Otherwise, one would be forgiven for not being able to recall much about this too often mundane movie experience. It's not that this is a terrible movie. It's not even a *bad* movie. As Alfred Hitchcock's last picture, it has developed a reputation as lackluster, but it has its share of entertaining moments. In fact, it displays a remarkable amount of energy and humor for a film directed by an elderly man with health issues. Yet as an Alfred Hitchcock film it cannot help but disappoint.

At the age of seventy-six, Hitchcock had slowed down, having directed only one other film in the previous seven years. He received a pacemaker for his heart in late 1974, and when filming began in May 1975, he was in a great deal of physical pain. He was understandably distracted and, according to those on the set, at times seemed disinterested in the project. "I had to buck him up a little every morning, to get him ready for the day's work," Bruce Dern told documentary filmmaker Laurent Bouzereau. "He was so tired and so bored with the whole thing. But when he was feeling better, there was no one better on the set. He noticed everything . . . . Just when we thought he had no idea what was going on, he'd snap us all to attention with the most incredible awareness of some small but disastrous detail that nobody would have noticed until it got on screen."[26]

> **WHERE'S HITCH?**
>
> About forty-five minutes into the film, Hitchcock can be seen behind a curtain. He is seen in silhouette only, not unlike the famous opening to *Alfred Hitchcock Presents.*

Once again working with screenwriter Ernest Lehman, who had written the script for *North by Northwest*, Hitchcock was given a well-constructed screenplay with an interesting plot and an amusing array of characters. Hitch had, of course, been meticulous in helping Lehman craft the script. It is far from Lehman's best work—considering he also penned *Sabrina*, *West Side Story*, *The Sound of Music*, and *Who's Afraid of Virginia*

Bruce Dern contemplates the significance of a headstone in *Family Plot*. (Universal Pictures/Photofest © Universal Pictures)

Woolf? that is no great knock—but it remains a solid effort. The dialogue is lively and often witty, and the plot is tightly constructed, though the narrative lacks the kind of punch needed to sustain a steady interest over this film's 120 minutes. There is nothing wrong here, per se, it's just that what is right rarely rises above "pretty good."

Thematically, *Family Plot* shares a number of obvious traits with other Hitchcock films, but none more important than people pretending to be something they're not, as also seen in *The 39 Steps*, *Spellbound*, *Stage Fright*, *Vertigo*, *North by Northwest*, *Psycho*, and *Marnie*, among others. We have Blanche assuming the role of a psychic, Fran playing the role of a blonde, Lumley the actor pretending to be a taxi driver and a lawyer, and Adamson playing the part of a jeweler.

The cast, unfortunately, is one of *Family Plot*'s weaknesses. The studio reportedly wanted Hitchcock to cast major stars, but Hitch instead chose relative unknowns because he didn't want to pay star salaries, which might have cut into his profits. The result is a cast that is competent at best. These actors lack the radiance a star-studded cast could have brought to the production. The studio apparently wanted Liza Minnelli in the part of Blanche, but Hitch refused. Barbara Harris is adequate in her portrayal, but she lacks the screen presence Minnelli would have contributed.

Some of the directing is weak, too. Scenes that a Hitchcock of even a few years earlier would have made sing instead fail miserably. For example, late in the film Blanche struggles as Arthur tries to inject her with a hypodermic needle. The editing is rapid-fire, but the cuts lack precision and purpose, a random montage of sloppy footage rather than the work of the man who brought us *Psycho*'s shower scene.

That said, it would be unfair to suggest *Family Plot* is awful. The issue is that it's an *Alfred Hitchcock* film. Critics might have been more forgiving of this work coming from another director, but we demand more from Hitchcock. Like eating an apple for dessert instead of ice cream, *Family Plot* is fine for what it is, but doesn't satisfy the palate the way one last dose of Alfred Hitchcock perfection would.

But who can fault the man for trying at the age of seventy-six? *Family Plot* is light and enjoyable, not quite what one might expect, but not a complete waste of time.

After an entire career of fantastic thrillers, stunning sights, and cinematic legend, if the end note is mundane rather than monumental . . . well, they say half the fun is getting there, right?

CONCLUSION

At age seventy-six and in poor health, Alfred Hitchcock's energy was on the wane and his filmmaking days were coming to a close. With *Family Plot*, it shows. There are hints of his past glories, but hints are all you'll find in this ordinary comedic thriller, a capable but ultimately uninteresting last hurrah from a man who directed more certifiable classics than any other director in the history of cinema. If *Family Plot* is noteworthy, it is only because it is the final film by the Master of Suspense. But it is exactly for that reason that Hitchcock fans should take in a viewing of *Family Plot*—to see the final work of the master.

HITCHCOCKIAN THEMES

Chaos in an Unexpected Location • Dark Secret • MacGuffin • Murder

THINGS TO LOOK FOR

- Hitchcock's still obvious ability to plant the seeds of intrigue, as evident in the film's opening scenes.
- The unfocused editing of the hypodermic needle scene, quite unlike the usually sharp efforts of previous work.
- The frantic mountain highway sequence, hearkening back to *North by Northwest*.

TRIVIA/FUN STUFF

✦ Some scenes of the film were shot with Roy Thinnes, who was originally cast as Arthur Adamson. When William Devane became available, Thinnes was quickly fired and his scenes reshot.

✦ Hitchcock permitted some of his actors to improvise their lines, a rarity in a Hitchcock production.

✦ Jack Nicholson was offered the role of George Lumley, but he was already committed to shoot *One Flew Over the Cuckoo's Nest* (1975). Al Pacino was also considered for the role, but his salary had grown too high for Hitch.

AWARDS

- Writers Guild of America Nomination: Best Comedy Adapted from Another Medium (Ernest Lehman)
- Edgar Allan Poe Awards Win: Best Motion Picture (Ernest Lehman)
- Golden Globe Awards Nomination: Best Motion Picture Actress, Musical/Comedy (Barbara Harris)

DVD RELEASES

RELEASE: Universal Studios (2001, 2005, 2006)
(Dolby Digital 2.0 Mono, 1.85:1 Color)
RATING: **1/2

EXTRAS: *Plotting Family Plot* documentary; storyboard: The Chase Scene; production notes and photographs; theatrical trailers.

NOTES: Available as stand-alone releases from 2001 and 2006, or as part of *The Alfred Hitchcock Collection* (out of print) and *Alfred Hitchcock: The Masterpiece Collection. The Masterpiece Collection* is recommended. The transfers on all releases appear identical.

Appendix A
Hitchcockian Themes

BATHROOM SCENE/B.M.

Hitchcock was a notorious fan of bathroom humor. He thought it was funny to set otherwise innocuous scenes in bathrooms for no other reason than the humor it brought him. The setting of these scenes rarely had anything to do with the plot, but were instead merely an inside joke for Hitch. In addition to scenes set in bathrooms, Hitchcock also placed the initials B.M. (short for bowel movement) in places the casual viewer would likely never notice.

Seen in *Murder!*, *Mr. & Mrs. Smith*, *Shadow of a Doubt* (B.M. on ring), *Lifeboat* (B.M. tattoo), *Psycho*, *North by Northwest* (hides in train bathroom), *Marnie*, and *Family Plot*.

BLACKMAIL

Blackmail is a popular theme in the Hitchcock film archives, appearing in no fewer than fourteen pictures. Hitch recognized the benefits of blackmail as an element of suspense and used it repeatedly. The blackmail situations in such films as *Strangers on a Train*, *Dial M for Murder*, and *Marnie* are crucial to their ongoing suspense. Hitchcock was fascinated with portraying victims of blackmail—most importantly, how they reacted to being blackmailed—as it tied strongly with the running theme of characters who lose control of their lives. The loss of control, the feeling of being swept up into something beyond oneself, is common in Hitchcock's work. What better way to nudge it along than with some well-placed blackmail?

Seen in *Blackmail*, *The Skin Game*, *The Man Who Knew Too Much* (1934), *Rebecca*, *Foreign Correspondent*, *Notorious*, *The Paradine Case*, *Rope*, *Stage Fright*, *Strangers on a Train*, *I Confess*, *Dial M for Murder*, *To Catch a Thief*, *The Man Who Knew Too Much* (1956), and *Marnie*.

BLONDE LEADING LADY

Grace Kelly. Eva Marie Saint. Tippi Hedren. Ingrid Bergman. Kim Novak. Hitchcock was famous for the beautiful blondes who so often dominated his films. While the leading lady is blonde in fewer than half of Hitchcock's pictures, in almost all of his widely regarded classics there is a blonde at the forefront. Hitch clearly loved his blonde leads and is reputed to have made over the appearances of both Hedren and Saint in much the same way James Stewart's Scottie Ferguson makes over Kim Novak's Madeleine/Judy in the brilliant *Vertigo*. But the blondes in Hitchcock's films are more than just objects; they are often strong, resourceful, independent women who are equal to their male counterparts.

Seen in *The Lodger, Champagne, Blackmail, Rich and Strange, The Man Who Knew Too Much* (1934), *The 39 Steps, Saboteur, Spellbound, Notorious, The Paradine Case, Under Capricorn, I Confess, Dial M for Murder, Rear Window, To Catch a Thief, The Man Who Knew Too Much* (1956), *Vertigo, North by Northwest, Psycho, The Birds,* and *Marnie.*

CHAOS IN AN UNEXPECTED LOCATION

Hitchcock often set a scene of great chaos in an unexpected location—and to great effect. The placement of these events in what we expect to be calm, quiet places served to heighten the impact of the chaos, delivering a jolt of energy to the proceedings. The carousel scene in *Strangers on a Train* and the murder of the ambassador at the United Nations in *North by Northwest* are perfect examples of this. Their settings greatly enhance the suspense and drama of the situations because we simply do not expect to deal with these things when we're in these places. Unpredictability is a key element in the perpetuation of suspense. Alfred Hitchcock not only knew this, he exploited it.

Seen in *The Man Who Knew Too Much* (1934), *The 39 Steps, Young and Innocent, Sabotage, Jamaica Inn, Foreign Correspondent, Saboteur, Stage Fright, Strangers on a Train, I Confess, The Man Who Knew Too Much* (1956), *Vertigo, North by Northwest, The Birds,* and *Family Plot.*

CLIMACTIC SHOWDOWN AT AN ICONIC LOCATION

Similar to the theme of Chaos in an Unexpected Location, Hitchcock often set a climactic showdown in an iconic location both because it would be unexpected and, far more importantly, because the setting would make the climax memorable. Who could forget the Royal Albert Hall climaxes in the two versions of *The Man Who Knew Too Much* or the Statue of Liberty showdown in *Saboteur*? Take these sequences and put them in an ordinary setting and the films' climactic moments are merely good; set them in a memorable locale and they instantly jump to the level of unforgettable.

Seen in *Blackmail*, *Murder!*, *The Man Who Knew Too Much* (1934), *Foreign Correspondent*, *Saboteur*, *The Man Who Knew Too Much* (1956), and *North by Northwest*.

DARK SECRET

Everybody has secrets. Many of us have dark secrets. Depending on the severity or harshness of the truth, we may be willing to go to great lengths to make sure those secrets remain secrets. Hitchcock clearly recognized this as a valuable element for both story and character development, most especially in establishing and maintaining suspense. What would an average person do to protect a piece of vital information? Is he willing to go beyond his normal limits? Is she willing to lie, cheat, or even kill to save herself? It's a timeless theme—and one that Hitchcock repeatedly exploited.

Seen in *Easy Virtue*, *Blackmail*, *The Skin Game*, *The Man Who Knew Too Much* (1934), *Sabotage*, *Rebecca*, *Foreign Correspondent*, *Suspicion*, *Shadow of a Doubt*, *Spellbound*, *The Paradine Case*, *Rope*, *Under Capricorn*, *Stage Fright*, *Strangers on a Train*, *I Confess*, *Dial M for Murder*, *Rear Window*, *To Catch a Thief*, *The Trouble with Harry*, *The Man Who Knew Too Much* (1956), *Vertigo*, *North by Northwest*, *Psycho*, *Marnie*, *Topaz*, *Frenzy*, and *Family Plot*.

DISCUSSION OF MURDER AT DINNER

This common element in Hitchcock films is almost entirely grounded in his extremely dark sense of humor (and his famous love of food). Most people avoid discussions of unpleasant matters, especially murder and death, when eating. It is considered impolite, not to mention uncomfortable. That is exactly why Hitchcock found it so humorous, and in most cases in which we see it in his films, it is indeed quite funny. The discussion of killing between Joseph Newton and Herbie Hawkins in *Shadow of a Doubt* is among the highlights of what is one of Hitchcock's best pictures. Their discussions border on the absurd—they do not simply discuss the perfect murder, they discuss the perfect murder of *each other*. This is traditionally inappropriate conversation to have over a meal, and is all the more entertaining because of it.

Seen in *Blackmail*, *Secret Agent*, *Suspicion*, *Shadow of a Doubt*, *Psycho*, *Rope*, *Strangers on a Train*, *The Trouble with Harry*, and *Frenzy*.

EXOTIC LOCATION

Would *To Catch a Thief* have been as good a film as it was if it were set in northern California instead of the French Riviera? Perhaps, but it surely would not have been as much fun. Hitchcock used exotic locations in his films on occasion, not so much because they were crucial to the story, but because he could. Hitchcock loved to travel when he was not working, so when he could find a way to incorporate an exotic locale into a film without creating too much location work, he took advantage. While not an important theme when set next to the others, it does offer an insight into Hitch's personality.

Seen in *Rich and Strange*, *The Man Who Knew Too Much* (1934), *Secret Agent*, *Foreign Correspondent*, *Notorious*, *Under Capricorn*, *To Catch a Thief*, *The Man Who Knew Too Much* (1956), and *Torn Curtain*.

HANDCUFFED MAN AND WOMAN

A man and a woman who do not wish to be together have conflict. A man and a woman who do not wish to be together, but who are held together by means out of their control, have exponential conflict. In the case of Richard Hannay and Annabella Smith in *The 39 Steps*, they are literally handcuffed together, leading both to comic results and, when they get to know each other better, to teamwork. In *Notorious*, the handcuffing is figurative; Alicia Huberman is stuck with Alexander Sebastian against her wishes. Viewing her actions in light of the terrible situation is not only fascinating, it adds a layer of dramatic tension to an already suspenseful film. This is a device Hitchcock often used to force characters together.

Seen in *The Lodger*, *Number Seventeen*, *The 39 Steps*, *Young and Innocent*, *The Lady Vanishes*, *Lifeboat*, *Foreign Correspondent*, *Saboteur*, *Notorious*, *Under Capricorn*, *North by Northwest* (handcuffed to a villain), and *Marnie*.

INEFFECTUAL AUTHORITY FIGURES

Hitchcock was famously distrustful of the police, telling stories of being deathly afraid of the authorities. It is no wonder, then, that he often portrayed authority figures—especially police officers—as bumblers. From the inept police on both coasts in *Shadow of a Doubt* to the completely wrong authorities in *The Wrong Man*, this is a common theme in Hitchcock's work, appearing in nearly one-third of his pictures.

Seen in *The Lodger, Murder!, The Man Who Knew Too Much* (1934), *Foreign Correspondent, Saboteur, Shadow of a Doubt, Stage Fright, Strangers on a Train, Rear Window, To Catch a Thief, The Trouble with Harry, The Man Who Knew Too Much* (1956), *The Wrong Man, North by Northwest, Psycho, Topaz, Frenzy,* and *Family Plot.*

LOVE TRIANGLE

Another common theme in the Hitchcock canon, the love triangle is a highly effective tool for introducing conflict into an otherwise innocuous story. *The Ring* is entirely structured around this theme. *North by Northwest,* despite countless other brilliant aspects, is dependent on its Thornhill/Kendall/Vandamm triangle to provide conflict and motivation for Thornhill in the later stages of the film. *Dial M for Murder*'s nefarious plot would never take place were it not for a cheating spouse. In almost all cases, the triangle involves one woman and two men.

Seen in *The Lodger, The Ring, Champagne, The Manxman, Rich and Strange, Mr. & Mrs. Smith, Spellbound, Notorious, The Paradine Case, Rope, Under Capricorn, Strangers on a Train, I Confess, Dial M for Murder, The Trouble with Harry, Vertigo, North by Northwest, The Birds, Topaz,* and *Frenzy.*

MacGUFFIN

The ultimate Hitchcock invention, the MacGuffin isn't so much a theme as a common element in his films. Simply defined, the MacGuffin is an item that is of utmost importance to the story's characters, but of precious little concern to the audience. What the MacGuffin is rarely matters; all that matters is that the characters are willing to go to great lengths to get it. In every case, the item or information in question could easily be replaced by something else with no adverse consequence to the story. Such is the nature of the MacGuffin. The most famous MacGuffins include the uranium ore in *Notorious* (it ultimately does not matter the secret Sebastian hides, as long as he's hiding *something*) and the contents of the microfilm in *North by Northwest* (again, the specifics do not matter). These things mean nothing to the viewer, but are of singular importance to the film's characters.

Seen in *The Man Who Knew Too Much* (1934; specifics of assassination), *The 39 Steps* (mathematical formula), *Young and Innocent* (jacket and scarf), *The Lady Vanishes* (code in song), *Secret Agent* (state secret), *Foreign Correspondent* (secret clause in treaty), *Saboteur* (spy plans/real saboteur identity), *Notorious* (Uranium), *The Man Who Knew Too Much* (1956; specifics of assassination), *North by Northwest* (microfilm), *Psycho* (stolen money), *Torn Curtain* (secret code), *Topaz* (the identity of Topaz), and *Family Plot* (diamonds).

MAN (OR WOMAN) ON THE RUN

One of the most important Hitchcock themes, the man (or woman) on the run is central to many of Hitchcock's greatest classics. What better way to get a story going than to set the main character on a run for his life, or to clear his maligned name, or for any number of reasons? To prove his innocence (*Saboteur*) or to find the truth (either version of *The Man Who Knew Too Much*), the man on the run is a story element that Hitch used repeatedly, a means with which to keep the audience at the edge of their seat—but, despite returning to this theme time and again, he always utilized it in a fresh way.

Seen in *The Lodger*, *The Man Who Knew Too Much* (1934), *The 39 Steps*, *Young and Innocent*, *Jamaica Inn*, *Saboteur*, *Shadow of a Doubt*, *Bon Voyage*, *Spellbound*, *Stage Fright*, *Strangers on a Train*, *To Catch a Thief*, *The Man Who Knew Too Much* (1956), *North by Northwest*, *Psycho*, *Marnie*, *Torn Curtain*, and *Frenzy*.

MANIPULATIVE MOTHER

Throughout the Hitchcock filmography, mothers are often portrayed in a negative light. More specifically, mothers are often shown to be calculating and controlling. From the mother in *Notorious*, who conspires to murder her new daughter-in-law, to the mother in *Marnie*, who suppresses a horrific incident from her daughter's memory, mothers are rarely shown in a positive light. Even upbeat, humorous mothers, such as in *North by Northwest*, exert undue control over their sons. Some biographers suggest that Hitchcock had issues with his own mother, and it manifested itself in his work.

Seen in *Easy Virtue*, *Mr. & Mrs. Smith*, *Notorious*, *Strangers on a Train*, *North by Northwest*, *Psycho*, *The Birds*, and *Marnie*.

MURDER

From the start of his career all the way through to the end, Hitchcock was obsessed with murder and its portrayal on film. From the different ways in which to depict it, to the consequences faced by those close to the victims, to the effects on the perpetrator, murder is an important part of more than half of the films seen on this journey. The act of murder does not even need to be committed for its importance to be clear. Take *Dial M for Murder*, for instance. No actual murder takes place (the one killing is done in self-defense), yet murder is the theme around which all revolves. Murder is not an original theme for Hitchcock—much of cinema deals with the subject—but his portraits and portrayals of murder and murderers certainly are.

Seen in *The Lodger, Blackmail, Murder!, Number Seventeen, The Man Who Knew Too Much* (1934), *The 39 Steps, Secret Agent, Sabotage, Young and Innocent, The Lady Vanishes, Jamaica Inn, Rebecca, Foreign Correspondent, Suspicion* (suspected), *Saboteur, Shadow of a Doubt, Lifeboat, Bon Voyage, Spellbound, Notorious* (attempted), *The Paradine Case, Rope, Under Capricorn, Stage Fright, Strangers on a Train, I Confess, Dial M for Murder* (attempted), *Rear Window, The Trouble with Harry, The Man Who Knew Too Much* (1956), *Vertigo, North by Northwest, Psycho, Marnie, Torn Curtain, Topaz, Frenzy*, and *Family Plot*.

MUSIC PLAYS A ROLE IN PLOT

Not one of the more common or important themes seen on this journey, it is still interesting to observe the number of pictures that rely on music as something that drives the plot forward. Who could forget the effects of the waltz on Uncle Charlie in *Shadow of a Doubt*, or the way in which music tells some of *Rear Window*'s side stories?

Seen in *The Man Who Knew Too Much* (1934), *The 39 Steps, Shadow of a Doubt, Stage Fright, Rear Window, The Man Who Knew Too Much* (1956), and *Vertigo*.

SPY SYNDICATE

A common story element particularly during Hitchcock's late British and early American periods, spies and spy syndicates play an important role in many of his more fascinating and entertaining thrillers. Again, this is a story element we see repeatedly, but because of Hitch's seemingly limitless creativity, his spy stories rarely seem like retreads. In conjunction with the MacGuffin, spies offered viewers intrigue, secrets, dire plots, and, most important of all, interesting characters in desperate situations.

Seen in *The Man Who Knew Too Much* (1934), *The 39 Steps, The Lady Vanishes, Sabotage, Foreign Correspondent, Saboteur, Bon Voyage, Aventure malgache, Notorious, The Man Who Knew Too Much* (1956), *North by Northwest, Torn Curtain,* and *Topaz.*

SUICIDE/ATTEMPTED SUICIDE

Suicide—or at least attempted suicide—appears in more Hitchcock films than one might guess. Often, as in *Lifeboat* or *Marnie,* the suicide isn't central to the plot, but serves as a means to an end (in each of these cases, to underscore the desperate situations the characters feel they're in). That suicide is seen in so many of Hitch's movies is further evidence that he was deeply concerned with examining the darker side of humankind.

Seen in *The Manxman, Murder!, The Skin Game, Lifeboat, Jamaica Inn, Rebecca, Lifeboat, Spellbound, Vertigo,* and *Marnie.*

TRAINS

Hitch loved to involve travel in his narratives, and what better way than on a train? One could set entire stories or fleeting moments on a train, from the chance encounter between a tennis star and a psychotic in *Strangers on a Train* to the unfolding mystery of *The Lady Vanishes.* As the action of his films raced across a landscape, trains acted as a great facilitator in moving the story forward, both figuratively and literally. When we see a train in a Hitchcock film, we know something important is about to happen.

Seen in *Number Seventeen, The 39 Steps, The Lady Vanishes, Blackmail, Suspicion, Saboteur, Shadow of a Doubt, Bon Voyage, Strangers on a Train, North by Northwest,* and *Marnie.*

UNWELCOME NEW WOMAN

Another theme of critical importance to more than a few Hitchcock films is that of a woman made to feel unwelcome in a new place. The second Mrs. de Winter in *Rebecca* is thoroughly unwelcome at Manderley, and therein lies the source of so much sorrow and her eventual breakdown. In

The Birds, Lydia Brenner's mistrust of Melanie Daniels is in many ways more important to the story than the ever-increasing magnitude of the bird attacks. And *Easy Virtue* revolves completely around a woman unwelcome in her new home.

Seen in *Easy Virtue, Jamaica Inn, Rebecca, Notorious, Under Capricorn, Psycho, The Birds*, and *Marnie*.

WOMAN SCREAMING
DIRECTLY AT CAMERA

Not so much a theme as a brief bit of cinematic technique, it is nevertheless interesting to see how often Hitchcock featured women not just screaming, but screaming directly at the camera. The terror and impact of these screams are certainly heightened by this technique.

Seen in *The Lodger, Young and Innocent, To Catch a Thief, Psycho*, and *Frenzy*.

WOMAN WITH COP BOYFRIEND

An unimportant theme, to be sure, but it is fascinating to note that the female lead in no fewer than four Hitchcock pictures becomes involved with a police officer. In each instance, the police officer is also directly involved in the investigation of the murder around which the film's plot revolves. Hitchcock never goes out on any limbs with these relationships (they are all safe in nature), but it is interesting to observe from a trivial perspective, if nothing else.

Seen in *The Lodger, Blackmail, Shadow of a Doubt*, and *Stage Fright*.

WRONGLY ACCUSED

Last alphabetically, but perhaps first in importance, the wrongly accused man is at the forefront of many a Hitchcock classic. So in love with the motif of the innocent man accused of a crime he did not commit, Hitch explored its many possibilities in films spanning six different decades. He even found time to make a film based on the true story of a wrongly accused man in the appropriately titled *The Wrong Man*. This works hand in hand with the broader theme of people who have lost control of their lives, forced to act or react thanks to outside forces. He was certainly compelled by the notion of the loss of free will; maybe this is why he was so controlling in his work. As a storyteller, what certainly appealed to Hitchcock about the "wrong man" theme was the infinite narrative possibilities it offered him in exploring the lengths to which good people will go when pushed to the edge.

Seen in *The Lodger*, *Murder!*, *The 39 Steps*, *Suspicion*, *Saboteur*, *Spellbound*, *Stage Fright*, *Strangers on a Train*, *I Confess*, *Dial M for Murder*, *To Catch a Thief*, *The Trouble with Harry*, *The Wrong Man*, *North by Northwest*, *Psycho*, *Topaz*, and *Frenzy*.

Appendix B
Filmography

FEATURE FILMS

The Pleasure Garden (A Gainsbororough-Emelka Picture); Produced 1925, Released 1927

PRODUCERS: Michael Balcon and Erich Pommer

WRITER: Eliot Stannard, based on the novel by Oliver Sandys

CAST:

Virginia Valli	Patsy Brand
Carmelita Geraghty	Jill Cheyne
Miles Mander	Levett
John Stuart	Hugh Fielding
Ferdinand Martini	Mr. Sidey
Florence Helminger	Mrs. Sidey
Georg H. Schnell	Oscar Hamilton
Karl Falkenberg	Prince Ivan

The Mountain Eagle (A Gainsborough-Emelka Picture); Produced 1925, Released 1927

PRODUCER: Michael Balcon

WRITERS: Max Ferner and Eliot Stannard, based on a story by Charles Lapworth

CAST:

Nita Naldi	Beatrice
Malcolm Keen	John Fulton
John F. Hamilton	Edward Pettigrew
Bernhard Goetzke	Mr. Pettigrew

The Lodger (A Gainsborough Picture); Produced 1926, Released 1927
PRODUCER: Michael Balcon
WRITER: Eliot Stannard, based on the novel by Marie Belloc Lowndes
CAST:

Marie Ault	The Landlady
Arthur Chesney	Her Husband
June	Daisy Bunting
Malcolm Keen	Joe
Ivor Novello	The Lodger

The Ring (A British International Picture); Produced and released 1927
PRODUCER: John Maxwell
WRITER: Alfred Hitchcock
CAST:

Carl Brisson	Jack Sander
Lillian Hall-Davis	The Girl
Ian Hunter	Bob Corby
Forrester Harvey	The Promoter
Harry Terry	The Showman
Gordon Harke	Jack's Trainer

Downhill (A Gainsborough Picture); Produced and released 1927
PRODUCERS: Michael Balcon and C. M. Woolf
WRITER: Eliot Stannard, based on a play by Constance Collier and Ivor Novello
CAST:

Ivor Novello	Roddy Berwick
Robin Irvine	Tim Wakely
Isabel Jeans	Julia
Ian Hunter	Archie
Norman McKinnel	Sir Thomas Berwick
Annette Benson	Mabel
Sybil Rhoda	Sybil Wakely
Lilian Braithwaite	Lady Berwick

Easy Virtue (A Gainsborough Picture); Produced and released 1927
PRODUCER: Michael Balcon
WRITER: Eliot Stannard, based on the novel by Noël Coward

CAST:

Isabel Jeans	Larita Filton
Franklin Dyall	Aubrey Filton
Eric Bransby Williams	Claude Robson
Ian Hunter	The Plaintiff's Counsel
Robin Irvine	John Whitaker
Violet Farebrother	Mrs. Whittaker
Frank Elliott	Colonel Whittaker
Dacia Deane	Marion Whittaker

Champagne (A British International Picture); Produced and released 1928
PRODUCER: John Maxwell
WRITERS: Alfred Hitchcock and Eliot Stannard, based on the novel by Walter C. Mycroft
CAST:

Betty Balfour	Betty
Gordon Harker	Mark, Betty's Father
Jean Bradin	The Boy
Ferdinand von Alten	The Man

The Farmer's Wife (A British International Picture); Produced 1927, Released 1928
PRODUCER: John Maxwell
WRITER: Eliot Stannard, based on a play by Eden Phillpotts
CAST:

Jameson Thomas	Samuel Sweetland
Lillian Hall-Davis	Araminta Dench
Gordon Harker	Churdles Ash
Gibb McLaughlin	Henry Coaker
Maud Gill	Thirza Tapper
Louie Pounds	Widow Windeatt

The Manxman (A British International Picture); Produced 1928, Released 1929
PRODUCER: John Maxwell
WRITER: Eliot Stannard, based on the novel by Hall Caine
CAST:

Carl Brisson	Pete Quilliam
Malcolm Keen	Philip Christian

Anny Ondra	Kate Cregeen
Randle Ayrton	Caesar Cregeen
Clare Greet	Mother

Blackmail (A British International Picture); Produced and released 1929
PRODUCER: John Maxwell
WRITERS: Benn Levy and Alfred Hitchcock, based on a play by Charles Bennett
CAST:

Anny Ondra	Alice White
Sara Allgood	Mrs. White
Charles Paton	Mr. White
John Longden	Det. Frank Webber
Donald Calthrop	Tracy
Cyril Ritchard	Mr. Crewe
Hannah Jones	Mrs. Humphries
Harvey Braban	The Chief Inspector

Juno and the Paycock (A British International Picture); Produced and released 1930
PRODUCER: John Maxwell
WRITERS: Alfred Hitchcock and Alma Reville, based on a play by Sean O'Casey
CAST:

Barry Fitzgerald	The Orator
Maire O'Neill	Mrs. Madigan
Edward Chapman	Captain Boyle
Sidney Morgan	"Joxer" Daly
Sara Allgood	Mrs. Boyle ("Juno")
John Laurie	Johnny Boyle
Dave Morris	Jerry Devine
Kathleen O'Regan	Mary Boyle

Murder! (A British International Picture); Produced and released 1930
PRODUCER: John Maxwell
WRITERS: Alfred Hitchcock and Walter C. Mycroft, based on the novel *Enter Sir John* by Clemence Dane and Helen Simpson
CAST:

Herbert Marshall	Sir John Menier
Norah Baring	Diana Baring

Phillis Konstam	Doucie Markham
Edward Chapman	Ted Markham
Miles Mander	Gordon Druce
Esme Percy	Handel Fane
Donald Calthrop	Ion Stewart

Mary (A British International Picture); Produced 1930, Released 1931
PRODUCER: John Maxwell
WRITERS: Alfred Hitchcock and Walter C. Mycroft, based on the novel
Enter Sir John by Clemence Dane and Helen Simpson
CAST:

Alfred Abel	Sir John Menier
Olga Tschechowa	Mary Baring
Paul Graetz	Bobby Brown
Lotte Stein	Bebe Brown
Ekkehard Arendt	Handel Fane
Jack Mylong-Münz	John Stuart
Louis Ralph	Bennet

The Skin Game (A British International Picture); Produced 1930–31,
Released 1931
PRODUCER: John Maxwell
WRITERS: Alfred Hitchcock and Alma Reville, based on a play by John
Galsworthy
CAST:

C. V. France	Mr. Hillcrist
Helen Haye	Mrs. Hillcrist
Jill Esmond	Jill
Edmund Gwenn	Mr. Hornblower
John Longden	Charles
Phyllis Konstam	Chloe
Frank Lawton	Rolf

Rich and Strange (A British International Picture); produced and released 1932
PRODUCER: John Maxwell
WRITERS: Alfred Hitchcock, Alma Reville, and Val Valentine, based on
the novel by Dale Collins
CAST:

| Henry Kendall | Fred Hill |
| Joan Barry | Emily Hill |

Percy Marmont	Commander Gordon
Betty Amann	The Princess
Elsie Randolph	The Old Maid

Number Seventeen (A British International Picture); Produced 1931, Released 1932

PRODUCERS: Leon M. Lion and John Maxwell

WRITERS: Alma Reville, Alfred Hitchcock, and Rodney Ackland, based on the play by Joseph Jefferson Farjeon

CAST:

Leon M. Lion	Ben
Ann Grey	Nora
John Stuart	Barton
Donald Calthrop	Brant
Barry Jones	Henry Doyle
Ann Casson	Rose Ackroyd
Henry Caine	Mr. Ackroyd
Garry Marsh	Sheldrake

Waltzes from Vienna (A Tom Arnold Production); Produced and released 1933

PRODUCER: Tom Arnold

WRITERS: Alma Reville and Guy Bolton, based on a play by Bolton

CAST:

Esmond Knight	Johann Strauss, the Younger
Jessie Matthews	Rasi
Edmund Gwenn	Johann Strauss, the Elder
Fay Compton	Countess Helga von Stahl
Frank Vosper	Prince Gustav
Robert Hale	Ebedezer

The Man Who Knew Too Much (A Gaumont-British Picture); Produced and released 1934

PRODUCER: Michael Balcon

WRITERS: Edwin Greenwood and A. R. Rawlinson, based on a story by Charles Bennett and D. B. Wyndham-Lewis

CAST:

Leslie Banks	Lawrence
Edna Best	Jill
Peter Lorre	Abbott

Frank Vosper	Ramon
Hugh Wakefield	Clive
Nova Pilbeam	Betty Lawrence
Pierre Fresnay	Louis
Cicely Oates	Nurse Agnes

The 39 Steps (A Gaumont-British Picture); Produced and released 1935
PRODUCER: Michael Balcon
WRITERS: Charles Bennett and Ian Hay, based on the novel *The Thirty-Nine Steps* by John Buchan
CAST:

Robert Donat	Richard Hannay
Madeleine Carroll	Pamela
Lucie Mannheim	Miss Annabella Smith
Godfrey Tearle	Professor Jordan
Peggy Ashcroft	Margaret
John Laurie	John
Helen Haye	Mrs. Louisa Jordan
Frank Cellier	Sheriff Watson
Wylie Watson	Mr. Memory

Secret Agent (A Gaumont-British Picture); Produced and released 1935
PRODUCERS: Michael Balcon and Ivor Montagu
WRITERS: Charles Bennett, Ian Hay, Jesse Lasky, and Alma Reville, from a play by Campbell Dixon, based on the novel *Ashenden* by W. Somerset Maugham
CAST:

John Gielgud	Edgar Brodie/Richard Ashenden
Peter Lorre	The General
Madeleine Carroll	Elsa Carrington
Robert Young	Robert Marvin
Percy Marmont	Caypor
Florence Kahn	Mrs. Caypor
Charles Carson	"R"
Lilli Palmer	Lilli

Sabotage (A Gaumont-British Picture); Produced and released 1936
PRODUCER: Michael Balcon
WRITERS: Charles Bennett, Ian Hay, and Helen Simpson, based on the novel *The Secret Agent* by Joseph Conrad

CAST:

Sylvia Sidney	Mrs. Verloc
Oskar Homolka	Her Husband
Desmond Tester	Her Young Brother
John Loder	Ted
Joyce Barbour	Renee
Matthew Boulton	Superintendent Talbot
S. J. Warmington	Hollingshead
William Dewhurst	The Professor

Young and Innocent (A Gaumont-British Picture); Produced 1937, Released 1938

PRODUCER: Edward Black

WRITERS: Charles Bennett, Edwin Greenwood, Anthony Armstrong, Gerald Savory, and Alma Reville, based on the novel *A Shilling for Candles* by Josephine Tey

CAST:

Nova Pilbeam	Erica Burgoyne
Derrick De Marney	Robert Tisdall
Percy Marmont	Col. Burgoyne
Edward Rigby	Old Will
Mary Clare	Erica's Aunt
John Longden	Det. Insp. Kent
George Curzon	Guy
Basil Radford	Erica's Uncle
Pamela Carme	Christine
George Merritt	Det. Sgt. Miller

The Lady Vanishes (A Gaumont-British Picture); Produced 1937, Released 1938

PRODUCER: Edward Black

WRITERS: Sidney Gilliat and Frank Launder, based on the novel *The Wheel Spins* by Ethel Lina White

CAST:

Margaret Lockwood	Iris Henderson
Michael Redgrave	Gilbert
Paul Lukas	Dr. Hartz
Dame May Whitty	Miss Froy

Cecil Parker	Mr. Todhunter
Linden Travers	Mrs. Todhunter
Naunton Wayne	Caldicott
Basil Radford	Charters
Mary Clare	Baroness
Emile Boreo	Boris
Googie Withers	Blanche

Jamaica Inn (An Erich Pommer Production); Produced 1938, Released 1939

PRODUCERS: Erich Pommer and Charles Laughton

WRITERS: Sidney Gilliat, Joan Harrison, and J. B. Priestley, based on the novel by Daphne Du Maurier

CAST:

Charles Laughton	Sir Humphrey Pengallan
Leslie Banks	Joss Merlyn
Marie Ney	Patience
Maureen O'Hara	Mary
Emlyn Williams	Harry
Wylie Watson	Salvation
Mervyn Johns	Thomas

Rebecca (A Selznick Studio Production); Produced 1939, Released 1939

PRODUCER: David O. Selznick

WRITERS: Philip MacDonald, Michael Hogan, Robert E. Sherwood, and Joan Harrison, based on the novel by Daphne Du Maurier

CAST:

Laurence Olivier	Maxim de Winter
Joan Fontaine	The Second Mrs. de Winter
George Sanders	Jack Favell
Judith Anderson	Mrs. Danvers
Nigel Bruce	Major Giles Lacy
Reginald Denny	Frank Crawley
C. Aubrey Smith	Colonel Julyan
Gladys Cooper	Beatrice Lacy
Florence Bates	Mrs. Edythe Van Hopper
Melville Cooper	Coroner
Leo G. Carroll	Dr. Baker

Foreign Correspondent (A Wanger Production); Produced and released 1940
PRODUCER: Walter Wanger
WRITERS: Charles Bennett, Joan Harrison, James Hilton, and Robert Benchley
CAST:

Joel McCrea	Johnny Jones
Laraine Day	Carol Fisher
Herbert Marshall	Stephen Fisher
George Sanders	Scott ffolliott
Albert Basserman	Van Meer
Robert Benchley	Stebbins
Edmund Gwenn	Rowley
Eduardo Ciannelli	Mr. Krug
Harry Davenport	Mr. Powers

Mr. & Mrs. Smith (An RKO Radio Picture); Produced 1940, Released 1941
PRODUCER: Harry E. Edington
WRITER: Norman Krasna
CAST:

Carole Lombard	Ann Krausheimer Smith
Robert Montgomery	David Smith
Gene Raymond	Jefferson "Jeff" Custer
Jack Carson	Chuck Benson
Philip Merivale	Ashley Custer
Lucile Watson	Mrs. Custer
William Tracy	Sammy
Charles Halton	Mr. Harry Deever

Suspicion (An RKO Radio Picture); Produced and released 1941
PRODUCER: Harry E. Edington
WRITERS: Samson Raphaelson, Joan Harrison, and Alma Reville, based on the novel *Before the Fact* by Francis Iles
CAST:

Cary Grant	Johnnie
Joan Fontaine	Lina
Cedric Hardwicke	General McLaidlaw
Nigel Bruce	Beaky
Dame May Whitty	Mrs. McLaidlaw

Isabel Jeans	Mrs. Newsham
Heather Angel	Ethel
Auriol Lee	Isobel Sedbusk
Reginald Sheffield	Reggie Wetherby
Leo G. Carroll	Captain Melbeck

Saboteur (A Frank Lloyd Production); Produced and released 1942
PRODUCER: Frank Lloyd
WRITERS: Joan Harrison, Dorothy Parker, and Peter Viertel
CAST:

Priscilla Lane	Pat
Robert Cummings	Barry
Otto Kruger	Tobin
Alan Baxter	Freeman
Clem Bevans	Neilson
Norman Lloyd	Fry

Shadow of a Doubt (A Jack H. Skirball Production); Produced 1942, Released 1943
PRODUCER: Jack H. Skirball
WRITERS: Thornton Wilder, Sally Benson, and Alma Reville, based on a story by Gordon McDonnell
CAST:

Teresa Wright	Young Charlie
Joseph Cotten	Uncle Charlie
Macdonald Carey	Jack Graham
Henry Travers	Joseph Newton
Patricia Collinge	Emma Newton
Hume Cronyn	Herbie Hawkins
Wallace Ford	Fred Saunders
Edna May Wonacott	Ann Newton
Charles Bates	Roger Newton

Lifeboat (A 20th Century-Fox Picture); Produced 1943, Released 1944
PRODUCER: Kenneth Macgowan
WRITER: Jo Swerling, based on a story by John Steinbeck
CAST:

| Tallulah Bankhead | Constance Porter |
| William Bendix | Gus Smith |

Walter Slezak	Willy
Mary Anderson	Alice MacKenzie
John Hodiak	John Kovac
Henry Hull	Charles D. Rittenhouse
Heather Angel	Mrs. Higley
Hume Cronyn	Stanley Garrett
Canada Lee	Joe Spencer

Bon Voyage (A Ministry of Information Production); Produced 1944, Released 1993
    WRITERS: Angus MacPhail and J. O. C. Orton
    CAST:

John Blythe	John Dougall

    (Rest of cast credited as The Molière Players)

Aventure malgache (A Ministry of Information Production); Produced 1944, Released 1993
    WRITER: Jules Francois Clermont
    CAST (all credited as The Molière Players):

Paul Bonifas	Michel
Paul Clarus	Paul Clarus
Jean Dattas	Man behind Michel
Andre Frere	Pierre
Guy Le Feuvre	General
Paulette Preney	Yvonne

Spellbound (A Selznick International Picture); Produced 1944, Released 1945
    PRODUCER: David O. Selznick
    WRITERS: Angus MacPhail and Ben Hecht, based on the novel *The House of Dr. Edwardes* by Francis Beeding
    CAST:

Ingrid Bergman	Dr. Constance Petersen
Gregory Peck	John Ballantine
Michael Chekhov	Dr. Alexander Brulov
Leo G. Carroll	Dr. Murchison
Rhonda Fleming	Mary Carmichael
John Emery	Dr. Fleurot
Norman Lloyd	Mr. Garmes
Bill Goodwin	House Detective
Steven Geray	Dr. Graff

Notorious (An RKO Radio Picture); Produced 1945, Released 1946
PRODUCER: Alfred Hitchcock
WRITER: Ben Hecht
CAST:

Cary Grant	T. R. Devlin
Ingrid Bergman	Alicia Huberman
Claude Rains	Alexander Sebastian
Louis Calhern	Captain Paul Prescott
Leopoldine Konstantin	Madame Anna Sebastian
Reinhold Schünzel	Dr. Anderson
Moroni Olsen	Walter Beardsley
Ivan Triesault	Eric Mathis
Alex Minotis	Joseph
Wally Brown	Mr. Hopkins
Charles Mendl	Commodore

The Paradine Case (A David O. Selznick/Vanguard Film); Produced 1946, Released 1947
PRODUCER: David O. Selznick
WRITERS: Alma Reville and David O. Selznick, based on the novel by Robert Hichens
CAST:

Gregory Peck	Anthony Keane
Ann Todd	Gay Keane
Charles Laughton	Judge Horfield
Charles Coburn	Sir Simon Flaquer
Ethel Barrymore	Lady Sophie Horfield
Louis Jordan	Andre Latour
Alida Valli	Mrs. Paradine
Leo G. Carroll	Sir Joseph
Joan Tetzel	Judy Flaquer
Isobel Elsom	Innkeeper

Rope (A Transatlantic Picture); Produced and released 1948
PRODUCERS: Sidney Bernstein and Alfred Hitchcock
WRITERS: Hume Cronyn and Arthur Laurents, based on the play *Rope's End* by Patrick Hamilton
CAST:

James Stewart	Rupert Cadell
John Dall	Brandon Shaw

Farley Granger	Phillip Morgan
Cedric Hardwicke	Mr. Kentley
Constance Collier	Mrs. Atwater
Douglas Dick	Kenneth Lawrence
Edith Evanson	Mrs. Wilson
Dick Hogan	David Kentley
Joan Chandler	Janet Walker

Under Capricorn (A Transatlantic Picture); Produced 1948, Released 1949
>PRODUCERS: Sidney Bernstein and Alfred Hitchcock
>WRITERS: Hume Cronyn and James Bridie, from the play by John
Colton and Margaret Linden, based on the novel by Helen Simpson
>CAST:

Ingrid Bergman	Lady Henrietta Flusky
Joseph Cotten	Sam Flusky
Michael Wilding	Hon. Charles Adare
Margaret Leighton	Milly
Cecil Parker	The Governor
Denis O'Dea	Mr. Corrigan
Jack Watling	Winter
Harcourt Williams	The Coachman

Stage Fright (A Warner Brothers-First National Picture); Produced 1949,
Released 1950
>PRODUCER: Alfred Hitchcock
>WRITERS: Alma Reville and Whitfield Cook, based on the novel *Man
Running* by Selwyn Jepson
>CAST:

Jane Wyman	Eve Gill
Marlene Dietrich	Charlotte Inwood
Michael Wilding	Det. Insp. Wilfred Smith
Richard Todd	Jonathan Cooper
Alastair Sim	Commodore Gill
Sybil Thorndike	Mrs. Gill
Kay Walsh	Nellie Goode
Miles Malleson	Mr. Fortesque
Patricia Hitchcock	Chubby Bannister

Strangers on a Train (A Warner Brothers–First National Picture); Produced 1950, Released 1951

PRODUCER: Alfred Hitchcock

WRITERS: Whitfield Cook, Raymond Chandler, and Czenzi Ormonde, based on the novel by Patricia Highsmith

CAST:

Farley Granger	Guy Haines
Ruth Roman	Anne Morton
Robert Walker	Bruno Anthony
Leo G. Carroll	Sen. Morton
Patricia Hitchcock	Barbara Morton
Laura Elliott	Miriam Joyce Haines
Marion Lorne	Mrs. Anthony
Jonathan Hale	Mr. Anthony

I Confess (A Warner Brothers-First National Picture); Produced 1952, Released 1953

PRODUCER: Alfred Hitchcock

WRITERS: George Tabori and William Archibald, based on a play by Paul Anthelme

CAST:

Montgomery Clift	Fr. Michael William Logan
Anne Baxter	Ruth Grandfort
Karl Malden	Inspector Larrue
Brian Aherne	Willy Robertson
Roger Dann	Pierre Grandfort
Dolly Haas	Alma Keller
Charles Andre	Fr. Millars
O. E. Hasse	Otto Keller

Dial M for Murder (A Warner Brothers–First National Picture); Produced 1953, Released 1954

PRODUCER: Alfred Hitchcock

WRITER: Frederick Knott, based on his play

CAST:

Ray Milland	Tony Wendice
Grace Kelly	Margot Mary Wendice
Robert Cummings	Mark Halliday

John Williams	Chief Insp. Hubbard
Anthony Dawson	Charles Alexander Swann
Leo Britt	The Storyteller
Patrick Allen	Det. Pearson
George Leigh	Det. Williams

Rear Window (A Paramount Picture); Produced 1953, Released 1954
PRODUCER: Alfred Hitchcock
WRITER: John Michael Hayes, based on the short story *It Had to be Murder* by Cornell Woolrich
CAST:

James Stewart	L. B. Jefferies
Grace Kelly	Lisa Carol Fremont
Wendell Corey	Det. Lt. Thomas J. Doyle
Thelma Ritter	Stella
Raymond Burr	Lars Thorwald
Judith Evelyn	Miss Lonelyheart
Ross Bagdasarian	Songwriter
Georgine Darcy	Miss Torso

To Catch a Thief (A Paramount Picture); Produced 1954, Released 1955
PRODUCER: Alfred Hitchcock
WRITER: John Michael Hayes, based on the novel by David Dodge
CAST:

Cary Grant	John Robie
Grace Kelly	Frances Stevens
Jessie Royce Landis	Jessie Stevens
John Williams	H. H. Hughson
Charles Vanel	Bertani
Brigitte Auber	Danielle Foussard
Jean Martinelli	Foussard
Georgette Anys	Germaine

The Trouble with Harry (A Paramount Picture); Produced 1954, Released 1955
PRODUCER: Alfred Hitchcock
WRITER: John Michael Hayes, based on the novel by Jack Trevor Story
CAST:

Edmund Gwenn	Capt. Albert Wiles
John Forsythe	Sam Marlowe

Mildred Natwick	Miss Ivy Gravely
Mildred Dunnock	Mrs. Wiggs
Jerry Mathers	Arnie Rogers
Royal Dano	Dep. Sheriff Calvin Wiggs
Parker Fennelly	Millionaire
Barry Macollum	Tramp
Dwight Marfield	Dr. Greenbow
Shirley MacLaine	Jennifer Rogers

The Man Who Knew Too Much (A Paramount Picture); Produced 1955, Released 1956
PRODUCER: Alfred Hitchcock
WRITER: John Michael Hayes, based on a story by Charles Bennett and D. B. Wyndham-Lewis
CAST:

James Stewart	Dr. Benjamin McKenna
Doris Day	Josephine Conway McKenna
Brenda De Banzie	Lucy Drayton
Bernard Miles	Edward Drayton
Ralph Truman	Inspector Buchanan
Daniel Gélin	Louis Bernard
Mogens Wieth	Ambassador
Alan Mowbray	Val Parnell
Hillary Brooke	Jan Peterson
Christopher Olsen	Henry McKenna

The Wrong Man (A Warner Brothers–First National Picture); Produced and released 1956
PRODUCER: Alfred Hitchcock
WRITERS: Angus MacPhail and Maxwell Anderson, based on the novel *The True Story of Christopher Emmanuel Balestrero* by Maxwell Anderson
CAST:

Henry Fonda	Christopher Emmanuel Balestrero
Vera Miles	Rose Balestrero
Anthony Quayle	Frank D. O'Connor
Harold J. Stone	Dt. Lt. Bowers
John Heldabrand	Tomasini
Doreen Lang	Ann James
Norma Connolly	Betty Todd
Lola D'Annunzio	Olga Conforti

Vertigo (A Paramount Release); Produced 1957, Released 1958
  PRODUCER: Alfred Hitchcock
  WRITERS: Alec Coppel and Samuel A. Taylor, based on the novel
d'Entre les Morts by Pierre Boileau and Thomas Narcejac
  CAST:

James Stewart	Det. John "Scottie" Ferguson
Kim Novak	Madeleine Elster/Judy Barton
Barbara Bel Geddes	Marjorie "Midge" Wood
Tom Helmore	Gavin Elster
Henry Jones	Coroner
Raymond Bailey	Scottie's Doctor
Ellen Corby	Manager of McKittrick Hotel
Konstantin Shayne	Pop Leibel
Lee Patrick	Car owner mistaken for Madeleine

North by Northwest (An MGM Picture); Produced 1958, Released 1959
  PRODUCER: Alfred Hitchcock
  WRITER: Ernest Lehman
  CAST:

Cary Grant	Roger O. Thornhill
Eva Marie Saint	Eve Kendall
James Mason	Phillip Vandamm
Jessie Royce Landis	Clara Thornhill
Leo G. Carroll	The Professor
Josephine Hutchinson	Mrs. Townsend
Philip Ober	Lester Townsend
Martin Landau	Leonard
Adam Williams	Valerian
Edward Platt	Victor Larrabee

Psycho (A Paramount Release); Produced 1959–60, Released 1960
  PRODUCER: Alfred Hitchcock
  WRITER: Joseph Stefano, based on the novel by Robert Bloch
  CAST:

Anthony Perkins	Norman Bates
Janet Leigh	Marion Crane
Vera Miles	Lila Crane
John Gavin	Sam Loomis
Martin Balsam	Milton Arbogast

John McIntire	Sheriff Al Chambers
Simon Oakland	Dr. Fred Richmond
Vaughn Taylor	George Lowery
Frank Albertson	Tom Cassidy
Lurene Tuttle	Eliza Chambers
Patricia Hitchcock	Caroline
John Anderson	Charlie
Mort Mills	Highway Patrol Officer

The Birds (A Universal Release); Produced 1962, Released 1963
PRODUCER: Alfred Hitchcock
WRITER: Evan Hunter, based on a story by Daphne Du Maurier
CAST:

Rod Taylor	Mitch Brenner
Jessica Tandy	Lydia Brenner
Suzanne Pleshette	Annie Hayworth
Tippi Hedren	Melanie Daniels
Veronica Cartwright	Cathy Brenner
Ethel Griffies	Mrs. Bundy
Charles McGraw	Sebastian Sholes
Ruth McDevitt	Mrs. MacGruder
Lonny Chapman	Deke Carter
Malcolm Atterbury	Deputy Al Malone

Marnie (A Universal Release); Produced 1963–64, Released 1964
PRODUCER: Alfred Hitchcock
WRITER: Jay Presson Allen, based on the novel by Winston Graham
CAST:

Tippi Hedren	Marnie Edgar
Martin Gabel	Sidney Strutt
Sean Connery	Mark Rutland
Louise Latham	Bernice Edgar
Dian Baker	Lil Mainwaring
Alan Napier	Mr. Rutland
Bob Sweeney	Cousin Bob
Milton Selzer	Man at Track
Mariette Hartley	Susan Clabon
Bruce Dern	Sailor

Torn Curtain (A Universal Release); Produced 1965–66, Released 1966
  PRODUCER Alfred Hitchcock
  WRITER: Brian Moore
  CAST:

Paul Newman	Professor Michael Armstrong
Julie Andrews	Sarah Sherman
Lila Kedrova	Countess Kuchinska
Hansjoerg Felmy	Heinrich Gerhard
Tamara Toumanova	Ballerina
Ludwig Donath	Professor Gustav Lindt
Wolfgang Kieling	Hermann Gromek
Günter Strack	Professor Karl Manfred
David Opatoshu	Mr. Jacobi
Gisela Fischer	Dr. Koska

Topaz (A Universal Release); Produced 1968–69, Released 1969
  PRODUCER: Alfred Hitchcock
  WRITER: Samuel A. Taylor, based on the novel by Leon Uris
  CAST:

Frederick Stafford	Andre Devereaux
Dany Robin	Nicole Devereaux
John Vernon	Rico Parra
Karin Dor	Juanita de Cordoba
Michel Piccoli	Jacques Granville
Philippe Noiret	Henri Jarre
Claude Jade	Michele Picard
Michel Subor	Francois Picard
Roscoe Lee Browne	Philippe Dubois
Per-Axel Arosenius	Boris Kusenov
John Forsythe	Michael Nordstrom

Frenzy (A Universal Release); Produced 1971, Released 1972
  PRODUCER: Alfred Hitchcock
  WRITER: Anthony Shaffer, based on the novel *Goodbye Piccadilly, Farewell Leicester Square* by Arthur La Bern
  CAST:

Jon Finch	Richard Ian "Dick" Blaney
Barry Foster	Robert "Bob" Rusk
Barbara Leigh-Hunt	Brenda Margaret Blaney

Anna Massey	Barbara Jane "Babs" Milligan
Alec McCowen	Chief Inspector Oxford
Vivien Merchant	Mrs. Oxford
Billie Whitelaw	Hetty Porter
Clive Swift	Johnny Porter
Bernard Cribbins	Felix Forsythe
Michael Bates	Sergeant Spearman

Family Plot (A Universal Release); Produced 1975, Released 1976
PRODUCER: Alfred Hitchcock
WRITER: Ernest Lehman, based on the novel *The Rainbird Pattern* by Victor Canning
CAST:

Karen Black	Fran
Bruce Dern	George
Barbara Harris	Blanche
William Devane	Adamson
Ed Lauter	Maloney
Cathleen Nesbitt	Julia Rainbird
Katherine Helmond	Mrs. Maloney
Warren J. Kemmerling	Grandison
Edith Atwater	Mrs. Clay
William Prince	Bishop

TELEVISION PROGRAMS

Alfred Hitchcock Presents (A Shamley Production)
PRODUCERS: Alfred Hitchcock and Joan Harrison

Episode Listing (17 episodes)

"Revenge" (originally aired October 2, 1955)
WRITER: Francis Cockrell, based on a story by Samuel Blas
CAST:

Ralph Meeker	Carl Spann
Vera Miles	Elsa Spann
Frances Bavier	Mrs. Fergusen
Ray Montgomery	Man in Grey Suit
John Gallaudet	Doctor

Ray Teal	Police Lieutenant
Norman Willis	Cop
John Day	Cop
Lillian O'Malley	Hotel Maid
Herbert Lytton	Police Lieutenant

"Breakdown" (Originally aired November 13, 1955)
WRITERS: Francis Cockrell and Louis Pollock, based on a story by Pollock
CAST:

Joseph Cotten	William Callew
Raymond Bailey	Ed Johnson
Forrest Stanley	Hubka
Harry Shannon	Dr. Harner
Lane Chandler	Sheriff
James Edwards	Convict
Marvin Press	Chessy
Murray Alper	Lloyd

"The Case of Mr. Pelham" (Originally aired December 4, 1955)
WRITER: Francis Cockrell, based on a story by Anthony Armstrong
CAST:

Tom Ewell	Albert Pelham
Raymond Bailey	Dr. Harley
Justice Watson	Henry Peterson
Kirby Smith	Tom Mason
Kay Stewart	Miss Clement
John Compton	Vincent
Jan Arvan	Harry
Norman Willis	Intern
Tim Graham	Lawyer
Richard Collier	Bartender
Diane Brewster	Secretary

"Back for Christmas" (Originally aired March 4, 1956)
WRITER: Francis Cockrell, based on a story by John Collier
CAST:

John Williams	Herbert Carpenter
Isabel Elsom	Hermione Carpenter
A. E. Gould-Porter	Major Sinclair

Lily Kemble-Cooper	Mrs. Sinclair
Gavin Muir	Mr. Wallingford
Katherine Warren	Mrs. Freda Wallingford
Gerald Hamer	Mr. Hewitt
Irene Tedrow	Mrs. Hewitt
Ross Ford	Butler
Theresa Harris	Servant
Mollie Glessing	Maid

"Wet Saturday" (Originally aired September 30, 1956)
WRITER: Marian B. Cockrell, based on a story by John Collier
CAST:

Cedric Hardwicke	Mr. Princey
John Williams	Capt. Smollet
Tita Purdom	Millicent "Millie" Princey
Kathryn Givney	Mrs. Princey
Jered Barclay	George Princey
Irene Lang	Jane

"Mr. Blanchard's Secret" (Originally aired December 23, 1956)
WRITER: Emily Neff, based on a story by Sarett Rudley
CAST:

Robert Horton	John Fenton
Meg Mundy	Mrs. Blanchard
Mary Scott	Babs Fenton
Dayton Lummis	Charles Blanchard
Eloise Hardt	Maid

"One More Mile to Go" (Originally aired April 7, 1957)
WRITER: James P. Cavanagh, based on a story by F. J. Smith
CAST:

David Wayne	Sam Jacoby
Steve Brodie	Motorcycle Cop
Louise Larabee	Mrs. Jacoby
Norman Leavitt	Ed

"The Perfect Crime" (Originally aired October 20, 1957)
WRITER: Stirling Silliphant, based on a story by Ben Ray Redman
CAST:

Vincent Price	Charles Courtney
James Gregory	John Gregory
Gavin Gordon	Ernest West
Marianne Stewart	Alice West
Mark Dana	Harrington
John Zaremba	Photographer
Therese Lyon	West's Housekeeper

"Lamb to the Slaughter" (Originally aired April 13, 1958)
WRITER: Roald Dahl, based on his own story
CAST:

Barbara Bel Geddes	Mary Maloney
Harold J. Stone	Lieutenant Jack Noonan
Allan Lane	Patrick Maloney
Ken Clark	Mike
William Keene	Print Man
Otto Waldis	Sam

"A Dip in the Pool" (Originally aired June 1, 1958)
WRITER: Robert C. Dennis, based on a story by Roald Dahl
CAST:

Keenan Wynn	William Botibol
Fay Wray	Mrs. Renshaw
Philip Bourneuf	Mr. Renshaw
Louise Platt	Ethel Botibol
Doreen Lang	Emily
Ralph Clanton	Ship's Purser
Doris Lloyd	Emily's Mother
Ashley Cowan	Captain

"Poison" (Originally aired October 5, 1958)
WRITER: Casey Robinson, based on a story by Roald Dahl
CAST:

Wendell Corey	Timber Woods
James Donald	Harry Pope
Arnold Moss	Dr. Ganderbay
Weaver Levy	Dr. Ganderbay's assistant

"Banquo's Chair" (Originally aired May 3, 1959)
WRITER: Francis M. Cockrell, based on a short story by Rupert Croft-Cooke
CAST:

John Williams	Inspector Brent
Hilda Plowright	Mae Thorpe/Miss Ferguson's ghost
Max Adrian	Robert Stone
Reginald Gardiner	Major Cock-Finch
Kenneth Haigh	John Bedford

"Arthur" (Originally aired September 27, 1959)
WRITER: James P. Cavanagh, based on a story by Arthur Williams
CAST:

Laurence Harvey	Arthur Williams
Hazel Court	Helen Brathwaite
Patrick Macnee	Sergeant Farrell
Robert Douglas	Inspector Ben Liebenberg
Barry Harvey	Constable Barry

"The Crystal Trench" (Originally aired October 4, 1959)
WRITER: Stirling Silliphant, based on a story by A. E. W. Mason
CAST:

James Donald	Mark Cavendidge
Patricia Owens	Stella Ballister
Werner Klemperer	Mr. Ranks
Patricia Macnee	Professor Kersley
Ben Astar	Swiss Innkeeper

"Mrs. Bixby and the Colonel's Coat" (Originally aired September 27, 1960)
WRITER: Halsted Welles, based on a story by Roald Dahl
CAST:

Audrey Meadows	Mrs. Bixby
Les Tremayne	Dr. Fred Bixby
Sally Hughes	Miss Putney
Alden 'Stephen' Chase	The Colonel
Howard Caine	Pawnbroker Employee
Maidie Norman	Eloise
Bernie Hamilton	Dawson the Butler

"The Horse Player" (Originally aired March 14, 1961)
WRITER: Henry Slesar
CAST:

Claude Rains	Father Amion
Ed Gardner	Sheridan
Percy Helton	Church Sexton
Kenneth MacKenna	Bishop Cannon
Mike Ragan	Mr. Cheever
William Newell	Second Bank Teller
David Carlile	First Bank Teller
Ada Murphy	Elderly Woman

"Bang! You're Dead" (Originally aired October 17, 1961)
WRITER: Margery Vosper, based on a story by Harold Swanton
CAST:

Mary Grace Canfield	Supermarket Customer
Craig Duncan	Clerk
Stephen Dunne	Rick Sheffield
Biff Elliot	Fred Chester
Kelly Flynn	Stephen
Marta Kristen	Jiffy Snack Girl
Karl Lukas	Mailman
Juanita Moore	Cleo
Billy Mumy	Jackie Chester
Lucy Prentis	Mrs. Chester
Olan Soule	Darlene's Father
John Zaremba	Supermarket Manager

Suspicion (A Shamley Production)
PRODUCER: Alfred Hitchcock

Episode Listing (1 episode)

"Four O'Clock" (Originally aired September 30, 1957)
WRITER: Francis M. Cockrell, based on a story by Cornell Woolrich
CAST:

David Armstrong	Policeman
Brian Corcoran	Boy

Juney Ellis	Mother
Jesslyn Fax	Wife
Nancy Kelly	Fran Steppe
Richard Long	Dave
E.G. Marshall	Paul Steppe
Dennis O'Keefe	Himself
Tom Pittman	Joe
Vernon Rich	Doctor
Charles Seel	Customer
Dean Stanton	Bill
Chuck Webster	Boy

Startime (A Shamley Production)
Episode Listing (1 episode)

"Incident at a Corner" (Originally aired April 5, 1960)
WRITER: Charlotte Armstrong
CAST:

Jack Albertson	Harry
Alice Backes	Aunt Pauline
Leslie Barrett	Batle
Barbara Beaird	Mary Jane
Warren Berlinger	Ron Tawley
Leora Dana	Mrs. Tawley
Joe Flynn	Sidney Sinden
Charity Grace	Elsa Medwick
Paul Hartman	James Medwick
Mary Alan Hokanson	Mrs. Parker
Wendell Holmes	Rigsby
Hollis Irving	Mrs. Sidney
Eve McVeagh	Georgia
Tyler McVey	Chief Taylor
Vera Miles	Jean Medwick
Philip Ober	Malcolm Tawley
Jerry Paris	Grimes
George Peppard	Pat Lawrence
Bob Sweeney	Uncle Jeffrey

The Alfred Hitchcock Hour (A Shamley Production)
PRODUCERS: Alfred Hitchcock and Joan Harrison

Episode Listing (1 episode)

"I Saw the Whole Thing" (Originally aired October 11, 1962)
WRITER: Henry Slesar, based on a story by Henry Cecil
CAST:

John Forsythe	Michael Barnes
Kent Smith	Jerry O'Hara
Evans Evans	Penny Sanford
John Fiedler	Malcolm Stuart
Philip Ober	Colonel John Hoey
John Zaremba	Richard Anderson
Barney Phillips	Lt. Sweet
William Newell	Sam Peterson
Willis Bouchey	Judge B. Neilson
Rusty Lane	Judge R. Martin

Notes

1. François Truffaut, *Hitchcock* (New York: Simon & Schuster, 1985), 43.
2. Donald Spoto, *The Dark Side of Genius: The Life of Alfred Hitchcock* (New York: Da Capo Press, 1999), 43.
3. Truffaut, *Hitchcock*, 57.
4. Truffaut, *Hitchcock*, 69.
5. Patrick McGilligan, *Alfred Hitchcock: A Life of Darkness and Light* (New York: HarperCollins, 2003), 141.
6. Spoto, *The Art of Alfred Hitchcock*, 30.
7. Truffaut, *Hitchcock*, 77.
8. McGilligan, *Alfred Hitchcock*, 148.
9. Truffaut, *Hitchcock*, 82.
10. Truffaut, *Hitchcock*, 109.
11. McGilligan, *Alfred Hitchcock*, 190–91.
12. *New Society* (London), May 10, 1984, as quoted in *The Encarta World Dictionary of Quotations* (London: Bloomsbury, 2000), 433.
13. Truffaut, *Hitchcock*, 122.
14. Truffaut, *Hitchcock*, 129.
15. Rui Nogueira and Nicoletta Zalaffi, "Entretien avec Alfred Hitchcock," *Écran* 7 (July–August 1972).
16. Truffaut, *Hitchcock*, 139–40.
17. Truffaut, *Hitchcock*, 139.
18. Spoto, *The Art of Alfred Hitchcock*, 101.
19. Truffaut, *Hitchcock*, 151.
20. Truffaut, *Hitchcock*, 159.
21. Truffaut, *Hitchcock*, 179.
22. Truffaut, *Hitchcock*, 186.
23. Truffaut, *Hitchcock*, 189.
24. Spoto, *The Art of Alfred Hitchcock*, 267.
25. Truffaut, *Hitchcock*, 283.
26. Laurent Bouzereau, *Plotting 'Family Plot'*, documentary featured on the DVD release of *Family Plot* (Universal Studios Home Video, 2000).

Selected Bibliography

Bouzereau, Laurent. *Plotting 'Family Plot.'* Documentary featured on the DVD release of *Family Plot.* Universal Studios Home Video, 2000.

Ebert, Roger. *The Great Movies.* New York: Broadway Books, 2002.

McGilligan, Patrick. *Alfred Hitchcock: A Life in Darkness and Light.* New York: HarperCollins, 2003.

Spoto, Donald. *The Art of Alfred Hitchcock: Fifty Years of His Motion Pictures.* New York: Anchor Books, 1992.

———. *The Dark Side of Genius: The Life of Alfred Hitchcock.* New York: Da Capo Press, 1983, 1999.

Truffaut, François. *Hitchcock.* New York: Simon & Schuster, 1985.

Index

About the Authors

Jim McDevitt, a banker and freelance writer, has written numerous articles and stories for a variety of paper and Internet publications, including the *Times* newspapers of New Jersey. He spent time as a newspaper sports editor, and he has contributed dozens of film reviews to pop culture website dvdinmypants.com. His areas of special interest are films of the 1930s, 1940s, and 1950s, along with a soft spot for teen comedies of the 1980s. Before he began writing about cinema, he viewed it, spending time as a projectionist. Visit jimmcdevitt.com, where he muses on such topics as baseball, movies, pop culture, and, occasionally, giraffes.

Eric San Juan is an editor for a family of seven weekly newspapers in New Jersey. He has written hundreds of pieces on a wealth of topics, ranging from history to politics to sports to science and the environment. His writings on film, entertainment, and pop culture have been featured on numerous websites, where he has contributed interviews with stars like Dave Foley (*NewsRadio, Kids in the Hall*), film reviews, essays on the work of Alfred Hitchcock and graphic novelist Alan Moore, irreverent commentary on the world of entertainment, and more. His work has appeared in magazines such as the legendary *Weird Tales* and music and technology hybrid *Oscillator 3*. He is the author of *Stuff Every Husband Should Know* and a contributing author on *Geek Wisdom: The Sacred Teachings of Nerd Culture*. Find out more at ericsanjuan.com.